SKETCHES

OF SOME OF THE

First Settlers of Upper Georgia,

OF THE

Cherokees, and the Author.

REVISED AND CORRECTED BY THE AUTHOR.

AMERICUS BOOK COMPANY
AMERICUS, GA.
1926

Notice

In many older books, foxing (or discoloration) occurs and, in some instances, print lightens with wear and age. Reprinted books, such as this, often duplicate these flaws, notwithstanding efforts to reduce or eliminate them. The pages of this reprint have been digitally enhanced and, where possible, the flaws eliminated in order to provide clarity of content and a pleasant reading experience.

Sketches of Some of the First Settlers of Upper Georgia, of the Cherokees, and the Author.

Revised and Corrected by the Author.

Copyright © 1926 George R. Gilmer

Originally published
New York
1855

Reprinted by:

Janaway Publishing, Inc.
732 Kelsey Ct.
Santa Maria, California 93454
(805) 925-1038
www.janawaygenealogy.com
2018

ISBN: 978-1-59641-395-5

Made in the United States of America

TO

THE VIRGINIANS, NORTH CAROLINIANS,

AND THEIR DESCENDANTS,

WHOSE INDUSTRY AND ECONOMY, HONESTY AND ENERGY,

HAVE MADE GEORGIA

THE MOST PROSPEROUS OF STATES,

THIS BOOK

IS RESPECTFULLY DEDICATED BY

THE AUTHOR.

FOREWORD

For a long time that most charming book, GILMER'S GEORGIANS, has been out of print. The original edition was soon exhausted, as it was said, because of the chatty style, unpleasant gossip, minutiae of descriptions, and the too candid truths therein about so many prominent people. The author's unvarnished story and lack of extenuation made his book distasteful to many who were aggrieved thereby. This history, however, written as it is in this most unusual style will always remain as an oasis in the moral desert of truculent and time serving literature.

Just before his death Governor Gilmer in his own handwriting revised and corrected his book. This emendated volume was purchased just as it left the hands of its distinguished author and the same is now given to the public without the slightest change in word or letter.

On the blank leaf preceding the title page of this revised version, Gov. Gilmer wrote the following:

"Old age and long continued ill-health have made the author's hand tremulous and his sight dim, so that he writes badly and cannot readily perceive mistakes. He employed copyists to transcribe his manuscript. They made many mistakes. The author could not supervise the printing. The printer added to the mistakes of the author and copyists." (The remainder of this page is torn and unintelligible).

Only 500 copies of this book is now reprinted as revised and offered to a generous public.   J. E. D. SHIPP.

Hill Crest Grange,
    Americus, Ga., April 20, 1926.

INTRODUCTION.

It may be proper to say a word or two about the contents of this book, and why it was written. The Author is an old man, who has passed his sixty-fourth year. Continued ill health rendered him unable for a long time to undergo labor, or bear much jostling from others. He has endeavored to pass quietly on, by getting into an untrodden track. Scribbling, when tired of reading, he found to be a pleasant relief from the tedium of unoccupied time. He wrote until he disliked to lose his labor. He publishes his scribblings with the hope that others may think that he did right in not throwing them away.

The first part of his book is an account of the settlement made by a number of Virginia families on Broad River, immediately after the revolutionary war. In tracing the causes of the present happy condition of the people of Georgia to the character of the settlers, the Author infers that low, impotent, beggarly men and women had not the strength, activity, enterprise, nor spirit, to separate themselves from their accustomed haunts, their kindred and country, to encounter untried and unknown difficulties in a new land beyond a vast ocean. And that the strong, the brave, the determined to be free, must have made up the migrating class from Europe to the Colonies. He shows how the descendants of these emigrants, operated upon by the desire of bettering their condition, left the old States to form settlements in the new. How the Harvies, Meriwethers, Taliaferros, Gilmers, Mathewses, Barnetts, Crawfords, Johnsons, Jordans, and McGehees removed, with their families, from Virginia to Broad River at different times from 1733 to 1790. How they were descended from the most vigorous and industrious class of the Irish, Scotch, English and Welsh. And how the Dutch, French and Italian blood added to the crossings which gave value to the stock. He describes how these settlers formed the most intimate friendly social union ever known among the same number of persons; how exceedingly active they were in business; economical in their expenditures; honest in their business dealings, and how they prospered beyond example. He hopes that though now scattered widely apart through the southern and southwestern States, his book may unite them together once more in the kind feelings of kinsfolk.

The second part describes the settlement made by the North Carolinians in that part of Georgia which is now included in the counties of Wilkes and Lincoln. The Author shows that some of them were prominent among the southern people in their struggle for independence, and that many have filled the highest offices of the State since that struggle ended successfully. He mentions as particularly distinguished Clarke, Dooly, Hart, Jack and Dabney.

The third part describes the Creek and Cherokee Indians; the relations between them, Georgia, and the United States; the causes and manner of their removal to the west of the Mississippi, and some incidents in the private and public life of the Author.

GEORGIANS

PART I.

The war of the Revolution left the people of Virginia penniless in purse and restless in spirit. They had made great exertions and sacrifices to secure their country's independence. Most of their luxuries, and many of their necessities, had before the Revolution been derived from abroad in exchange for their tobacco. The war cut off commerce. Virginia merchants owned but few trading vessels, and these their country could not protect from capture.

The hope that great blessings would be derived from the right of self-government, stimulated the people to make the exertions necessary to obtain it. When the Independence of the States was acknowledged by Great Britain, the advantages which the people had expected to follow were so deferred as to appear for a while delusive. The capital with which trade had been carried on was exhausted by the war, and it required time to create it anew. The means of making money were obstructed by Great Britain, through restrictions upon the trade of the States. The people, immediately after the acquisition of national freedom had fewer of the good things of life than when they paid the stamp-tax. How to improve their condition was the question which they most anxiously sought to solve. The restless and dissatisfied spirits of the old States found relief by emigrating to the new. Georgia held out to emigrants very seductive offers of land. The absence of all undergrowth in the woods, the large trees, and the luxuriant grass, caused the most favorable opinion to be formed of the productiveness of the land by the officers and soldiers who had passed over it.

General Mathews had served in Georgia during the war. He made preparations soon after for removing to a tract of land, then and yet known as the Goosepond, a disputed title to which he had purchased for a very small consideration. He was well known in Augusta and Albemarle Counties, in Virginia. Influenced by his judgment, Francis Meriwether, Benjamin Taliaferro, and one or two others, visited Georgia in 1784. They went to the neighborhood of the Goosepond, were pleased with the land, and purchased. They and many of their friends and relations removed to Georgia with their families immediately afterwards. They formed a society of the greatest intimacy—mutual wants making the surest foundation for the interchange of mutual kindness.

The sketches of the Broad River people, which follow were drawn chiefly from the author's intimate social intercourse with his kinsfolk and neighbors. He found but few written documents to aid him in his work. Some of the biographies are therefore very limited. Those that are most so, may yet describe what may be worth remembering, and which might otherwise be soon unknown or forgotten.

THE GILMERS.

GEORGE GILMER was born near Edinburgh, in Scotland. After acquiring the usual fund of medical knowledge for the commencement of practice, he went to London, as was the fashion then of young Scotch physicians who were eager for fame and fortune, where he connected himself in professional business with Dr. Ridgway. Not long afterwards, he was employed by the London Land Company to go to Virginia to manage the affairs of the firm. He and the daughter (the only child) of Dr. Ridgway had been previously interchanging tender looks and soft words. Their imagination so magnified the extent of the ocean which would separate them, and the unknown dangers of the distant land, that they could not part without being united for life. They were married privately in the presence of Mrs. Ridgway. When Dr. Gilmer returned to London he found his wife dead. He went back to Virginia, and settled in Williamsburg, the capital of the colony, where he practiced physic, and supplied the people of the colony with medicines. Dr. Gilmer's second wife, Mary Peachy Walker was the sister of Dr. Thomas Walker, a citizen of the colony, distinguished by the high offices which he filled, and the large estate which he acquired. After the death of his second wife, Dr. Gilmer married Miss Harrison Blair, the kinswoman of Dr. Blair, the principal founder and the first President of

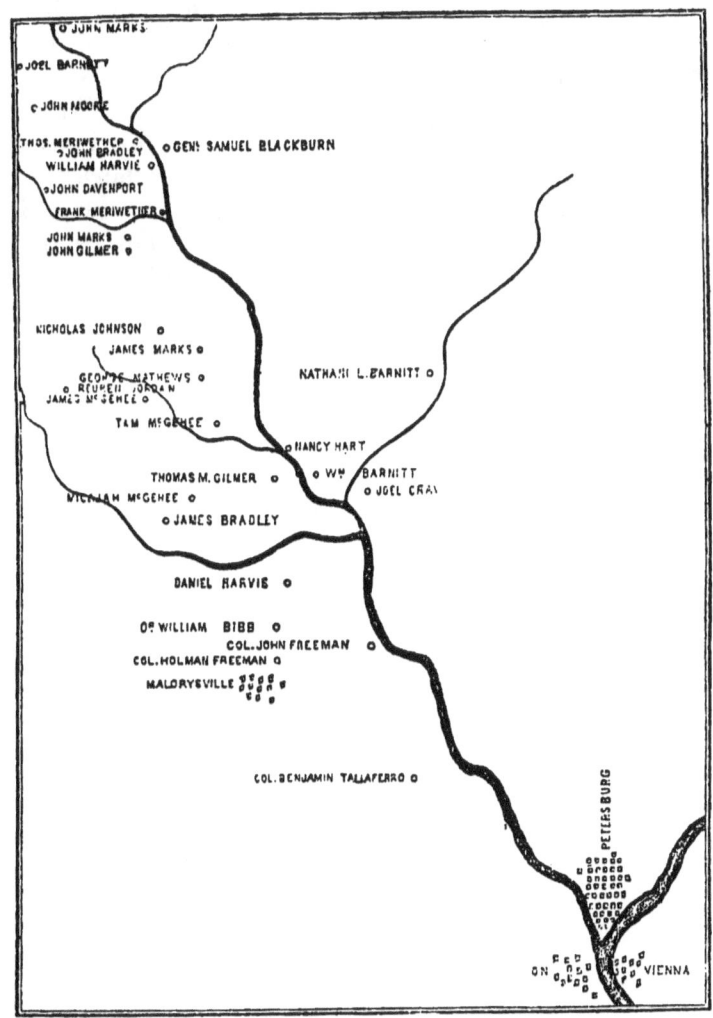

William and Mary College, the head of the Episcopal Church, and at one time acting Governor of the colony of Virginia, and the sister of the Honorable John Blair, President of the Council, whose son John was the intimate friend of Washington, and one of the first Judges of the Supreme Court of the United States. Grigsby says that John Blair belonged to a more distinguished family than any other member of the Virginia Convention of 1776. Dr. Gilmer lost his third wife, and was engaged to be married to Miss Ambler for his fourth, when he died.

Dr. Gilmer left London for Williamsburg in 1731. He died there in 1757. He left three sons, Peachy Ridgway, and George, by his second wife, and John by his third.

The copy of the coat-of-arms given below, was obtained by Mr. Frank Gilmer when he was in Europe. The gentleman upon whom it was conferred, was certainly not an ancestor of any of the Gilmers of Virginia who settled on Broad River.

Their relationship to him must therefore have been very distant, if any at all. It is inserted here to gratify those who may be curious to know something of heraldy, about which so much is written in modern times.

Extract from the Register of Armorial Bearings for Scotland.

"The right worshipful Sir Charles Gilmer, of Craig Miller, Baronet, bears azure, a chevron, between two fluer de lis in chief D'or; and in base, a writing pen, full feathered argent, with the badge of Nova Scotia as Baronet. Crest, a garland of laurel proper. Motto, 'Perseveranti dabitur.' Matriculated 18th Dec. 1735."

The following memoranda were copied from the family Bible of Dr. George Gilmer, my great-grandfather, now in my possession:

"Mary Peachy Walker, daughter of Thomas and Susan Walker, of King and Queen, was married by the Rev. Mr. Jno. Shaife, at his house, her Stepfather, to George Gilmer, May 13th 1732."

March 6th, 1737-8. A son born, christened the 20th by the Rev. Mr. Hith, by the name of Peachy Ridgway, Maj. Nicholas and William Prentis, Godfathers, and Miss Robertson, Godmother—now Mrs. Lidderdale."

"Jan. 19th, 1742-3. A son born, christened the 30th inst. by Mr. Thomas Dawson, George. Walter King (and Jms. Harmer by proxy) Godfathers, Miss Elizabeth Pratt, Godmother—afterwards Mrs. King."

"October 1st, 1745. Mary Peachy Gilmer, the mother of the above dear children, after a severe but short fit of sickness, departed this life to the great loss of her said children, but more immediately to her Husband, who had experienced her Christian life and fondness for him."

"Dec. 11th, 1745. George Gilmer was married to Miss Harrison Blair, at her Brother's, the Hon. Jno. Blair, by the Rev. Mr. Thomas Dawson, Rector of Bruton, in Williamsburg."

"April 26th, 1748. Mrs. Gilmer brought to bed of a son, between six and seven in the morning. 27th. Was christened by the Rev. Mr. Thomas Dawson, by the name of John. The Hon. Jno. Blair and Mr. John Blair, Godfathers, and Mrs. Blair, Godmother—God preserve him."

"May 22d, 1753. Mrs. Gilmer delivered of a Boy, about five o'clock in the morning; apprehending danger, had him christened in the afternoon by the name of William, my Father's name. Armstead Burwell and John Holt, Mayor, Godfathers; Miss Sally Blair, Godmother. This poor baby died the 30th, and was buried the 31st, by the Commissary, in a grave so close to my dear former wife that his coffin touched hers."

"Nov. 2d, 1755. Mrs. Gilmer, after a severe and long painful illness, departed this life, Sunday evening, between 8 and 9."
"Dr. George Gilmer departed this life, Jan. 15th, 1757."

Peachy Ridgway Gilmer, the oldest son of Dr. George Gilmer, of Williamsburg, was blunt, open-hearted, and careless about the accumulation of riches. He accompanied Frank Meriwether, his college crony, to Albemarle, when Braddock's expedition against the French and Indians suspended for a while. William and Mary College. Whilst at Frank Meriwether's home, he and Frank's sister, Mary, fancied each other, and married. The Meriwethers were then, as they are now, plain in manners and dress. Peachy Gilmer, from being the most dashing beau of the metropolis of the colony became as unpretending in his appearance and manners as any of his new relations. To make his home accord with this change, he settled in Rockingham county, in the midst of the Dutch, at a place still called Lethe, from the forgetfulness of care by its owner and his numerous Low Country visitors. He lived to old age without troubling himself about any thing. The Lethe tract of land was large and fertile. He had many negroes, kept fat horses and cattle, and lived bountifully upon the products of his farm, selling only what was sufficient to pay his taxes, and buy sugar and coffee in small quantities then used. His wife was a most notable housekeeper. She managed the children and servants, made their clothing, and provided furniture for the house. Peachy Gilmer's unruffled temper, frank manners, and unrestricted hospitality, made his house the collecting place of old and young, who were fond of frolic and fun. He was his father's executor, and so negligent in collecting the debts of the estate, that large sums were never collected at all.

Peachy R. Gilmer had two sons, Thomas Meriwether and George, and four daughters, Mary Peachy, Elizabeth Thornton, Lucy, and Frances Walker.

Thomas M. married Elizabeth Lewis before he was twenty-one. He removed to Georgia the year after, and settled on Broad River, at the place marked on the map as his. He had small hands and feet. His features were regular, his head large, his nose straight and well-formed, his eyes very gray, and his teeth good. He was somewhat under the common height. His frame of body was small, and his limbs of proper proportions and much muscular strength. He was very fat from childhood, weighing at the age of eighteen two hundred pounds. He floated on water without any effort, except straightening his legs. The school to which he went when a boy was up the Shenandoah River, a mile or two from his father's. During the summer months he went home by float- and swimming down the river, to save himself from walking. The current of the river was so continued and strong that he could easily outstrip the usual speed of his school companions. He was insensible to cold, but could not bear heat. The doors of his house were never closed day or night, summer or winter. He continued to grow more and more corpulent, until he weighed upwards of three hundred pounds. He was an excellent rider, sitting his horse so easily that few men could ride as far in the day. Though he never worked himself, he impressed the habit very strongly upon his children and negroes. He had governing manners and temper, so that his children never disobeyed him. He managed all his affairs with admirable judgment. He had eight negroes, a small tract of land, a considerable sum of money, a large amount in notes due him, besides having previously provided liberally for his children who were married. The estates which they have accumulated are equal at this time to more than a million dollars. They are all planters except one. The lawyer and politician is the poorest of them all. Thomas Gilmer was a man of good sense, aided but little by reading. He was punctual in the discharge of every requirement of law. He attended musters and juries, though at great inconvenience. He was a justice of the peace for some time, and was once elected a member of the legislature. He was truthful and upright. I have often heard him mention that he never but once loaned money at more than the legal interest. He was induced to do so then by the borrower being a negro trader. The mistake was corrected by the difficulty he met with in collecting any part of the loan. He never suffered his children to harass or hunt birds or beasts. I recollect a cousin, who was about my own age, instructing me during the idleness of Sunday how to prepare a chicken-cock for fighting by cutting off his comb. My father finding out our employment, took me between his knees, and pulled my own comb until I scarcely knew whether the crown of my head had hair left upon it.

He bought what he wanted, and sold what he wished to part with. He had a great dislike to chaffering and swapping, believing that the habit of such trading generally ended in the habit of lying. He expressed his thought and purposes without equivocation. He had great contempt for foppery of all sorts. When I first went abroad to school, I found most of the boys occasionally wearing fine clothes, and told him on my return home that I desired to do as they did. His answer was, that boys neither learned more nor were less wicked by being dressed finely, that when I grew up, it would be well enough to attend to dress, because it would influence many persons' opinion of me, and thereby increase my capacity for usefulness. After going through school without shoes in the summer, or a broadcloth coat at any time, I was immediately upon quitting, dressed in the very best which his merchant's store could supply.

During his youth my father performed a tour of militia duty under the Marquis La Fayette. He had previously gone out with a militia company to disperse or make prisoners of some Tories, who occasionally met in the North Mountain. The company caught a Tory, or, what was the same to the prisoner, one suspected by the Whigs. He was carried to a distillery, underwent examination, and was punished by being put headforemost into a large hogshead of water. He kicked his feet free from those who held him, and was about drowning in the confused and failing efforts to draw him out, when a half-witted fellow standing by, turned over the hogshead, letting out the Tory and the water.

My father was temperate in the use of all liquors except water. He was never even slightly intoxicated but once, and that was when he was a boy. Like most of the Gilmers, he loved good eating. He was subject to violent attacks of fever. At one time his physician thought it absolutely necessry to take blood from him. No vein could be found. The temple artery was cut. He had a violent cough, which, whenever he lay down, threw off the pressure from the artery, and covered the room with blood before the pressure could be reapplied. He was compelled to sit up in a chair for six or seven weeks, sleeping when he could by leaning his head upon a table before him. He died July, 1817, at his residence on Broad River. He was a member of the Methodist Church from 1809 until his death. He left a widow and nine children.

Elizabeth Lewis, the wife of Thomas M. Gilmer, was the daughter of Thomas Lewis and Jane Strother. She has now passed her 89th year, and been a widow more than thirty-five. Her ceaseless industry and untiring care have aided to make her children rich. She still enjoys the good things of life with a pleasant relish. She has endured its evils with unfailing patience. Malice and envy seem never to have found a resting-place with her for a moment. Cheerfulness constantly shines in her face, and is heard in her voice. Her gentle spirit never reproaches. Necessity alone limits the extent of her kindness. Charity covers the faults of others from her sight, whilst gratitude is ever filling her heart for the forgiveness of her own.

Peachy Ridgway, oldest son of Thomas Gilmer, is social, hospitable, and free-spoken, like his grandfather, after whom he was named, with the industrious habits which the necessities of a new country and his father's control forced upon him. He is the best rider, the best shot, and most successful hunter of the country. He married Mary Boutwell, daughter of Daniel Harvie, of Broad River—a guileless, pretty, modest woman, whom it was impossible to know and not to love. After her death, he married Mrs. Caroline Thomas, whose goodness made her a suitable successor to his first wife. He has lost all of his children, except his youngest daughter, the widow of Dr. Grattan. He is a capital planter, and has acquired great wealth. His present residence is in the State of Alabama, near the City of Montgomery.

Mary Meriwether, the oldest daughter, is a woman of good understanding. She married successively two very indolent, inefficient men, whom by her industry she saved from poverty. The first was Warren Taliaferro, brother of Col. Benjamin Taliaferro; the second, Nicholas Powers, a handsome Irishman. She is now a widow with ten children—four by her first husband, and six by her last.

Thomas Lewis, the second son, is a frugal, industrious planter. He was well educated, and had commenced the study of medicine, when he found Nancy Harvie more attractive than the doctor's shop. She was not very pretty in the eyes of others, but all agreed with her husband that she made a good wife. Since her death, he has recently married Mrs. Anne Harper. He has six children.

George Rockingham, the third son, married Eliza Frances Grattan. Though he has had no children he is as happy as any man ever was who had. His residence is within twenty miles of where he was born. He hopes to have the pleasure of giving in this book some further particulars of his wife and himself.

John, the fourth son, is clear-headed, sharp-witted, attentive to his interests, and thriving. He married Lucy Johnson, the daughter of Col. Nicholas Johnson, of Broad River. She was very pretty, and acted her part well as a wife. After her death, he married Mrs. Susan Gresham, the daughter of Mr. Joel Barnett, a sensible, economical woman. He is very wealthy. He resides in Mississippi, not far from the town of Columbus. He has three children by his first wife, and four by his second.

William Benjamin Strother, the fifth son, is a judicious planter, and a very kind, good man. He is very wealthy and gives his money freely to his kin, and those who need his assistance. He takes special delight in educating poor, clever young ladies, and giving them such other advantages as may add to their usefulness and success in life. He married Elizabeth Marks, the daughter of Meriwether Marks, and great granddaughter of Gov. Mathews. He resides in Alabama, near West Point, in Georgia.

Charles Lewis, the sixth son, is kind, truthful, and honest. He has been all his life devoted to books, but has not yet learned to be wise in the ways of the world. He never cheats, but has been very often cheated. He does not believe in the maxim, "fallitur fallentem non est fraus." Fortunately his brother William has always taken special concern in his moneyed affairs. When the receipts of the year are not equal to his expenditures, William usually squares them. He married Miss Nancy Marks and after her death, Mrs. Matilda Kyle. The first was modest and unpretending, and the last is yet acting her most difficult part in the most exemplary way. He has six sons and one daughter by his first wife, and two sons by his last. He resides in the City of Montgomery, Alabama.

Lucy Ann Sophia, the second daughter, is a most notable housekeeper, a very loving wife, fond mother, and efficient member of society. Her husband, B. S. Bibb, of Montgomery, Alabama, the present senator from that county, is a gentleman of wealth and great respectability. They have five children. One of their daughters married a descendant of the Indian Princess, Pocahontas.

James Jackson, the seventh son, was named after General Jackson, of Georgia, whom every body admitted to be a brave man and devoted patriot. This youngest son missed the training to work which his brothers received, and yet has escaped the spendthrift habits which usually follow idleness. He is a successful planter, and one of the wealthy men of Alabama. He married Elizabeth, daughter of Reuben Jordan, a descendant of the Indian Princess, Pocahontas. They have five children.

George, the second son of Peachy Ridgway Gilmer, had regular features, and an erect, perfectly-formed person. His father never sent him from home to school, or to mix in society. His modest diffidence was never worn off. He sought for a wife only among his cousins, because they were free in their intercourse with him. They happened always to be engaged. His understanding was capable of great things; but its exercise was confined to a very limited circle of observation. His discernment was quick and clear, and his judgment unequalled for correct conclusions upon all matters within his examination. His temper and feelings were as simple, sincere, and affectionate as a child's. He never bought or sold for profit. He inherited the valuable Lethe land, upon which he lived, spending its products in hospitality and kindness, without seeking or making any accumulation. His truthfulness and integrity were never doubted. His kindness to his negroes was without limit.

His man, "Great Billy," owned three horses through his master's means. After "Great Billy" lost his first wife, he courted a young girl at Lethe, and tempted her to marry him, by offering his gig for her to ride in. When he died, his master sold his horses, and paid the proceeds of the sale, amounting to between two and three hundred dollars, to Great Billy's children, the negroes of a neighbor. Sterne's description of Uncle Toby was realized in my uncle George's character. Not a fly ever perished by his thoughtlessness or cruelty. For the last twenty years of his life, he rode a noble horse of his own raising. Sorrel never was in harness. He carried his master wherever he went, especially once a week during the summer months across the Shenandoah River, to the top of the Blue Ridge Mountain, where he salted his cattle. Sorrel was never known to leave him, though often without confinement. When his master died, Sorrel was carried from Lethe to Major Grattan's, where he continued to be served by Major Grattan's children as if he were akin to them. Only the youngest was ever put upon his back. When he was, Sorrel would walk about with as much care as if he knew the preciousness of what he carried. Occasionally he would leave his pasture and go to Lethe, as if in search of something he had lost. He was always sent for as soon as missed lest he should suffer for the want of food. Sorrel lived to be twenty-seven years old. When he died, he was buried with the greatest affection by Major Grattan's children and grandchildren, as if he had been the last remnant of their good uncle.

George Gilmer continued to indulge his negroes as long as he lived. During the last years of his life he was unable to attend his farm. His negroes were so idle that he was obliged to buy corn and meat to feed them. He died a bachelor beyond seventy years, without having been once drunk, or done one act of stinginess.

Mary Peachy, the oldest daughter of Peachy R. Gilmer, was a round-faced, full-personed, black-eyed brunette. Her cheerfulness, and unaffected simplicity, kind manners, and affectionate temper, made her a universal favorite. Her want of guile was beyond the belief of the bad. She loved her father, mother, brothers, sisters, uncles, aunts, and cousins, so much that there was no spare place in her heart for suitors. She was more courted than any young lady of the country. Andrew Lewis loved her from her youth to his death. He lost an arm whilst he was an officer under General Wayne, in his campaigns against the western Indians, where he also confirmed his habit of drinking whiskey, which he had formed when young. He was intelligent, and would have been handsome but for his want of an arm. He had too much respect for Peachy Gilmer, when sober, to ask her to marry him. He never failed pressing her to do so if he saw her when drunk.

Peachy Gilmer had neither the taste nor capacity for investigating sectarian controversies. She was by inheritance an Episcopalian. When she died, she left part of her estate to build a church in Mississippi, for the special use of the Episcopalians.

Elizabeth Thornton, the second daughter of Peachy R. Gilmer, married Major Robert Grattan. She is described elsewhere.

Lucy, the third daughter of Peachy R. Gilmer, was clearminded, strong-willed, and high-principled. She was not handsome. She was seldom courted when young. When she was beyond thirty, she met Burton Taliaferro, a handsome, agreeable man, who pressed her with such an appearance of earnest love to marry him, that her heart yielded before her judgment was informed. He was known by her friends to be such a selfish, profligate fellow, that when she told her sister Peachy that she intended to marry him, she fell fainting at her feet. Upon being convinced of his unworthiness she rejected him. But the effort came near taking her life. When I went to Virginia three years after, I found my aunt but a shadow of what she had been. She ventured one day, when we were alone, to ask me what had become of Burton Taliaferro? I told her that immediately after his visit to Lethe, he had married an old maiden miser, that before their marriage, she had secured her property to her own use, permitting her husband to have only sufficient for good eating, drinking, and dressing, and that his appearance, when I had seen him a short time before, indicated that he would soon eat and drink himself to death. My aunt made no comments upon my information.

She gradually recovered her health from that time. It was long, however, before she ceased to remember unpleasantly those who opposed her will to marry Burton Taliaferro. Her affection for Major Grattan and his family had always been very great. It became more and more engrossing, until she almost ceased to care for any body else after the death of her brother George. She loved her niece, Lucy Grattan, as if she had been her own child—petting her, and doing whatever she could to please her as long as she lived.

The last years of Lucy Gilmer's life were passed in great bodily suffering. The consolations of religion, the devoted love of her niece, Lucy Grattan (now Mrs. Dr. Harris), the never-tiring patience and care of Robert Grattan and his admirable wife, and the affection of their children, made the last years of my aunt as tolerable as possible.

Frances Walker, fourth daughter of Peachy R. Gilmer, was ten years younger than the next youngest child. She was the petted and humored one of her family. She married Richard Taliaferro. They had seven children. Their daughter Elizabeth married Gov. Brown, of Mississippi, now Senator in Congress from that State. They are all dead but one, Mrs. Mary Adams, of Mississippi.

Richard Taliaferro was near six feet high, full and well-proportioned, with black curling hair, handsome features, easy, graceful manners, and an abundant supply of agreeable chit-chat. He belonged to an Italian family, who were famous for fighting in the time of chivalry. Richard Taliaferro was the relation of President Monroe, and connected by marriage with President Madison, and through Achille Murat, with the Emperor Napoleon Bonaparte.

George Gilmer the second son of Dr. George Gilmer, of Williamsburg, availed himself fully of the advantages afforded by William and Mary College, then the best classical school in the colonies. He studied medicine with his uncle, Dr. Thomas Walker, and afterwards attended the Medical College in Edinburgh. He married his first cousin, the daughter of Dr. Walker. He practiced his profession for some time in Charlottesville, and afterwards at Penpark, his residence in the country. His reputation as a physician was unsurpassed.

His habit was to devote himself exclusively to each case of doubtful issue until its termination. A father once left a child under his care so hopelessly ill, that upon meeting the doctor before he got home, he asked how long his child had lingered before its death, and was told to his astonishment that he had recovered. Dr. Gilmer's temper was ardent, his habits social, and his taste literary. He was occasionally called upon to speak during the revolutionary war, and the first formation of parties under the Constitution. The old people who remember these addresses, report them to have been unequalled in eloquence. He was the neighbor and intimate friend of Mr. Jefferson, and a decided republican in politics. He loved conversation and good eating, and died of paralysis. He left a numerous family of children.

Walker, the oldest son of Dr. George Gilmer, studied medicine with his father, and attended the medical college in Edinburgh. His extraordinary genius and acquirements were exciting in his friends the most flattering hopes of his future greatness when he died.

Peachy Ridgway, the second son, was a lawyer, and remarkable for agreeable conversation and social habits. He married the niece of Mrs. Trist, the friend and correspondent of Mr. Jefferson, whose grandson was lately United States Commissioner to Mexico. Peachy R. Gilmer loved good eating, like his father, and like him died of paralysis. His daughter, Emma, a very charming young lady, married a son of General Brackenridge. William, his oldest son, is unrivalled as a wit. His son George is one of the Judges of the Circuit Court of Virginia, and a man of very great wealth.

George Gilmer, the third son, was the only male member of Dr. Gilmer's family who was not distinguished for talents. He was a man of truth and probity, of unrivalled amenity of manners, and great kindness. He married Miss Hudson, whose taste, cultivation, superior intellect and piety, made her an admirable mother to fit sons for usefulness and greatness.

Thomas Walker, the oldest son of George Gilmer, entered upon the business of life without the advantages of wealth or thorough education. He labored however with his might after the best ends, by the best means he could command. His success proved that his talents were equal to his energy. His profession was the law. Whilst engaged in practice, he edited a newspaper. He assailed what was wrong with such hearty, vigorous blows, that he brought upon himself the violent enmity of the bad, and had to fight for his life. As soon as his merits became publicly known, the people of Albemarle (the county of his birth and residence) chose him for their representative in the State Legislature. His industry and eloquence soon made him the most prominently useful member of the house in which he served. He was elected its Speaker. Each ascent showed more and more obviously his fitness for elevated station. He was made Governor of the State. His duty required him to enforce the rights of the citizens of Virginia against violators of them in other States. He made a demand of the Governor of New York for the delivery up of a fugitive slave, who declined doing what the Constitution and his official oath required—cloaking his refusal under the mantle of conscience—a covering which the dishonest find but little difficulty in stretching to suit their wicked purposes. Walker Gilmer advised the Legislature to retaliate upon the citizens of New York, until justice should be done to the citizens of Virginia. The Legislature declined following the advice. He resigned. He was soon afterwards appointed by the President of the United States Secretary of the Navy. Whilst he was attending to his official duty, by endeavoring to increase the efficiency of the navy, he lost his life by the bursting of a cannon.

He was eminently suited for public station, and still more for the walks of private life. He was the staff of his father, and the joy of his mother. He sought a wife who could think, feel and act with him and for him. He found her without fortune, but above all price. He died in the prime of life. What his indomitable energy would have done, strengthened and directed as it was by purity of purpose, and clear, strong, vigorous intellect, none can say. Judging by what he did, he would have been the first man of his country, as he was of his name.

A gentleman walking on the banks of the Potomac River, early on a Sunday morning, whilst Walker Gilmer was Secretary of the Navy, saw a crowd standing with their hats off, listening most attentively. Approaching, he found Walker Gilmer on his knees, praying with the fishermen.

John, the fourth son of Dr. Gilmer, was silent and reserved in manners, of good understanding, and excellent character. He was a physician. He married Miss Minor. His daughter Lucy, his only child now living, is married to Mr. Frank Minor, her first cousin.

James and Harmer, the fifth and sixth sons of Dr. Gilmer, were clever and talented. Both died young and unmarried.

Frank, the youngest son, was the most talented of this talented family. His genius, extraordinary capacity, great industry, sober habits, and ambition, would have made him one of the most distinguished of his countrymen, if his life had been spared long enough. He wrote one or two numbers of "The Old Bachelor," several articles in the Virginia Evangelical Magazine, and published a volume of essays whilst he was yet a youth. He was an enthusiastic admirer of John Randolph's eloquence. He used to leave his school in Georgetown, when a boy to listen to Mr. Randolph whenever he knew that he was about to speak. The peculiar thoughts, and emphatic manner of expressing them by the orator, made so ineffaceable an impression upon him, that he could repeat whatever he heard from him in his own words. He studied law with Mr. Wirt, his brother-in-law, and continued through life upon the most intimate terms with him. His love of science was as great as his devotion to literature. He travelled through the Western and Southern States in company with Abbe Couric, when a young man, that he might be assisted in his investigations by the learning of that great naturalist. When the University of Virginia was about going into operation, he was employed by Mr. Jefferson and its Board of Trustees, to go to Europe and select professors of it. As he returned home, after executing his commission very satisfactorily, he suffered so much from a violent storm, to which the vessel in which he sailed was exposed, that his health was wrecked though the vessel was saved. He was appointed Law Professor of the University, but died before he commenced the discharge of his duties.

Dr. Gilmer's daughter Mildred, was a cheerful, frank, sensible woman. She married William Wirt, whose glossy curling hair, fine person, and expressive features, made him one of the handsomest of men;—whose clear, strong, melodious voice, extraordinary taste, and admirable execution in music, ready wit, humor, and hilarity, made him the most charming companion;—whose talents, learning, and graceful address, made him the equal of the most celebrated American orators.

Lucy, Dr. Gilmer's second daughter, was a most excellent lady. She married Peter Minor, of Albemarle, a planter of wealth and respectability. Their son Frank has the industry, mental capacity and learning of his grandfather, Dr. Gilmer, with equable temper and firm physical constitution. Although he is a gentleman of wealth, he devotes his time and talents to training the promising youth of his country for future usefulness—conduct worthy of the highest honor, and will not be forgotten when his country counts its jewels.

John Gilmer, the third son of Dr. George Gilmer, of Williamsburg, was a very handsome, gay, gallant man, whose person and purse were at the service of every pretty woman who would command them. He went to Scotland to receive the fortune left him by his grandfather Blair. He indulged in the pleasures of European society until he spent more than his Scotch inheritance. Soon after his return to Virginia, he married Mildred Meriwether, whose industry and economy prevented her husband's generous wastefulness making his children destitute. He was an officer under the Marquis La Fayette at the siege of York, and performed his duty well. Soon after the termination of the war, he removed to Georgia, and settled on Broad River. He had a large family of children. Sober reflection, and the hard realities of frontier life, made an altered man of him. He became pious, and died at the place marked on the map as his in 1790.

John Thornton, the oldest son of John Gilmer, married Martha Harvie. He was a very handsome, honorable, upright man, well educated for the practice of physic, and devoted to it. He did not succeed, however, as most of the Broad River people did, in acquiring riches. He was like a musical instrument strung too high for the room in which it is played. His lofty, gentlemanly bearing did not move in unison with those upon whom he depended for practice. He removed to Kentucky, and afterwards to Illinois, where he still lives very much respected.

Nicholas, the second son, married Amelia Clark, the daughter of Micajah Clark. He is a kind-hearted, truthful, honest man, with uncommon capacity for mechanism. He removed to Kentucky more than thirty years ago, where he still resides. His wife became deranged as her mother had been. His trials have been the hardest to which good people are ever subjected. His patience in bearing them has been most exemplary.

Francis Meriwether, the third son, married Martha Barnett, daughter of William Barnett, of Broad River. He removed to Montgomery, Alabama, where he still resides. He is very industrious, and has acquired great wealth. His wife is a sensible, energetic woman. They have five children.

George Oglethorpe, fourth son, was a man of decision, enterprise, and good understanding. He removed to Kentucky, then to Alabama, and afterwards to Louisiana, where he died. He married Martha Johnson, daughter of Nicholas Johnson, of Broad River. He acquired great wealth. His oldest son, James Blair Gilmer, married Eliza Gilmer, daughter of Peachy R. Gilmer, and after her death, the Widow Picket, of Red River, the daughter of W. D. Graftenreid, of South Carolina. He is enterprising to recklessness, and very determined in his purposes. He is possessed of one of the largest planting estates in the United States. His crop of cotton the year 1850 exceeded three thousand bags.

David, fifth son of John Gilmer, married a daughter of Micajah Clark. She became deranged like her mother and sister. He now resides in Arkansas.

Harrison Blair, oldest daughter of John Gilmer, married Gabriel Christian, a Methodist preacher, whom scarcely any one ever heard from inclination the second time. Though he was wanting in the powers to persuade others to become Christians, he followed faithfully the straight and narrow path himself. Mrs. Christian was a mild, amiable woman. They had children.

Betsey, the second daughter, married Tom McGehee, the oldest son of Micajah McGehee. They resided on Goosepond

Creek, at the place marked as his on the map of the Broad River Settlement. Tom was a rough, truthful, hard-working man. His wife, though pretty, was very attentive to her domestic affairs.

Sally, the third daughter, married Burton Taliaferro, the brother of Col. Benjamin Taliaferro. She died within the year afterwards, leaving a daughter, who died whilst a child.

Jane, the fourth daughter, married Tom Johnson, the nephew of Nicholas Johnson, of Broad River, and after his death, Abner McGehee, now of Montgomery, Alabama. She was a stirring, bustling woman, and made herself very acceptable to both her husbands.

THE GRATTANS.

JOHN GRATTAN was a native of Ireland, and remarkable for those qualities which make the best class of the Irish the cleverest of European people. He and Henry Grattan, the most eloquent man of modern times, belonged to the same family stock.

The first act which tradition makes known of John Grattan, was his going into Scotland, and, Irishman-like, falling desperately in love with a beautiful young lady, whom he accidentally met with at a boarding-school, asking her father to let him marry her, and upon his consenting only upon condition that his daughter should first finish her education, courting her until she married him without the required delay. The bold, ardent spirit with which he commenced life, led John Grattan to emigrate to America. He remained in Philadelphia a few years, and then settled where the great road from the west to the north crosses the Shenandoah River. He was a merchant, and continued for most of his after life to supply that part of the valley with foreign goods. In the contest between liberty and power, he, like most of his countrymen, took the side of the weak and the oppressed. He was an actor in the meeting at Staunton, in 1775, when the people declared their determination to "devote themselves to the support of the measures for the preservation of American liberty." Though he was too old for soldiering when the fight for Independence commenced, he did the work of a good Whig, by encouraging others to do so. He built the first good manufacturing flour-mill in the Shenandoah Valley, and contributed from it a portion of the two hundred barrels which were sent by the people of Augusta County to the relief of the inhabitants of Boston when besieged by the British army.

When John Grattan settled in Western Virginia, but little coin circulated there. Trade was managed in the old way of barter. The goods bought of the merchant were paid for in cattle, ginseng, pink-root, bear and deer skins. These articles were disposed of in Philadelphia. This part of John Grattan's business was usually transacted by his wife. She went to Philadelphia on horseback, directed the drovers, sold the roots, cattle and pelfries, and bought the goods for her husband's stores. She was frequently accompanied by one of her daughters, usually Catharine, who was afterwards Mrs. Gamble, of Richmond. Her Irish friends in the city enabled her and her daughter to pass what time they had to spare for pleasure very agreeably in the best society. The old lady, smart as she was, made one trade still remembered freshly by the family. She was in Philadelphia during the revolutionary war, selling her stock of cattle for a stock of goods, when some trader offered her scrip, or continental paper money, for cattle, at the rate of two dollars for one of coin. When she left home, the depreciation was but fifty per cent. The apparent profits were too large to be resisted. Paper was bought instead of goods. The lady speculator set off for home, exulting in her financial shrewdness. Each day's travel lowered her anticipations of profit, until she reached home, when three dollars in scrip were worth only one in specie. But an Irishman's heart is ever fuller of love for woman than money. John Grattan removed the depression from his wife's feelings by impressing his love upon her lips.

John Grattan was a Scotch-Irish Presbyterian, of the old Covenanters' faith and practice. He sung David's Psalms in long metre. Nothing gave him more the temper to swear, than to hear in church, upon a sacramental occasion, a Methodist spiritual song sung in short measure. According to the fashion of his people, he prayed long prayers with his family before they went to bed, especially on Sabbath evenings. On one occasion he was unusually prolix. When he got up from his knees, one of the boys remained in his praying posture. The old lady went to him, patted him softly on the head, saying, Johnny, Johnny! I thought Father Grattan was long enough!" Though John Grattan's residence was on the frontiers, he retained the manners and dress of the old-time gentleman, wearing always a full suit of black, and powdered wig, when he went into company. Mrs. Grattan was one of the most beautiful women of the country. She retained until old age the charms which so captivated her husband when he first saw her. She was a warm patriot in the time of the Stamp Act and duty upon tea. The anti-tea resolutions of the patriot ladies of the Colonies disturbed her very much. She had acquired such a strong love for it, that she could not dispense with its use. So she discarded the tea-pot from the table, drew her tea in a pitcher, and drank it as usual, letting it pass for a decoction of medicinal herbs, then very much in use for various complaints.

Mr. and Mrs. Grattan had seven children. They desired to marry their daughter Catharine to a rich old Philadelphia merchant, who, seeing her in company with her mother in one of her trading expeditions, fancied and followed her in a fine carriage to Virginia. The Scotch-Irish rule of obedience to parents was too implicit in those times to permit a daughter to say nay. So Catharine ran away, and concealed herself in the house of a friend, until the man of money lost his patience and returned home. Her will was strengthened by the entreaties of Robert Gamble, a neighbor, and her devoted admirer, whose merits she discovered before her father and mother. Their consent was at last given, and the young lovers married. Robert Gamble was an officer in the Revolutionary Army, very early in the war for Independence, and continued to serve to its close. He was always with the main army, and under the immediate command of General Washington. Once in every two years he visited his wife on furlough. At each succeeding visit he found a prattling babe to add to the pleasures of his renewed visit. Immediately after the war ended, Col. Gamble removed from his residence in the country near the old stone church, to Staunton, where he commenced his continued vocation afterwards of buying and selling goods. His sound sense, constant application to his employment, integrity and aptness at securing the confidence of those with whom he dealt, soon rendered him so prosperous, that he removed to Richmond, as a theatre more suitable for his enlarged capacity. He became one of the principal traders to Europe in that city. Whilst he was yet hale in health, active in his pursuit, and becoming more and more respected and confided in by his countrymen, he was killed by being thrown from his horse. Mrs. Gamble survived her husband many years. She is still remembered as one of the most sensible, pious, efficient women who has ever influenced the society of the City of Richmond. Their son John, was educated at the best schools in the country, and graduated at Princeton with the first honor of his class. He was Chief Justice Marshall's Secretary, when he was United States Minister at the Court of France. He married Miss Duncan, the daughter of a wealthy English gentleman; and after her death, Miss Greenup, the daughter of Governor Greenup, of Kentucky. He and his brother Robert continued the mercantile business of their father, until they lost most of their inherited wealth from embarrassments created by the restrictive policy of Mr. Jefferson's administration, and the war that followed.

Robert, their second son, married the daughter of Gen. Brackenridge, of Virginia. The brothers have removed to Florida, where they are distinguished for their generous hospitality.

Nancy, their oldest daughter, is a most excellent lady. She married William H. Cabell, who was Governor of Virginia at an age when other aspiring men are mounting the first round of ambition's ladder. He was Judge of the Court of Appeals for forty years, and its President when he died. Conjugal affection was never seen in a more pleasing aspect, than when the eyes of the old President of the Court of Appeals met his aged wife's.

Elizabeth, the second daughter of Col. and Mrs. Gamble, married William Wirt, who was Attorney-General of the United States—a beautiful writer, talented lawyer, and eloquent public speaker. She is one of the most accomplished and intellectual ladies who has ever figured in the cabinet coteries of Washington City.

John Grattan's daughter Elizabeth married Col. Samuel Brown, of Greenbrier. Samuel Brown and his brother John were, when boys (in 1764) made prisoners by the northwestern Indians, and carried by them to their wigwams, near the lakes. Samuel was restored to his family in Virginia after five years captivity. His brother John married an Indian woman, and became a great chief. He acted quite a conspicuous part in the last war with Great Britain.

Samuel Brown was a quiet, good man, who thought every thing his wife said and did, right.

John Grattan's daughter Agnes married Col. Elijah Page. They removed to Kentucky, and settled within a mile or two of Lexington. Two of their sons volunteered to serve against the Indians and British in 1812, when the oldest was too young to be drafted. At Winchester's defeat, they stood by the gallant Major Madison, fighting until all other resistance ceased. They were made prisoners. Having been greatly heated in the fight, when the battle was over they became very cold. The old chief to whom they surrendered, seeing their sufferings, took the blanket from his own shoulders, and threw it over the youngest. When they arrived at the wigwam of their captor, they were ordered to cut wood and make a fire. Whilst they were obeying, they observed the young squaws laughing at them for doing squaws' work. They threw down their axes, and refused to cut any more. The Indian to which they belonged was delighted at their spirit. After remaining prisoners for several months, they made their escape, through many wonderful adventures, to Detroit, from whence they were sent home. Mrs. Page was one of the most beautiful women of our country, and as sensitive and affectionate as she was good-looking. Her brother, Major Grattan, visited the western country, and went into her house without her expecting him. The sight of her beloved brother, whom she had not seen for years, so overcame her, that she fell to the floor senseless. Alexander Herring, who knew her well when in her youthful beauty, said, after a visit she made to her friends in Virginia when she was old, that "she had lost more beauty than any other woman ever had." And when thus old and deprived of her beauty, Dr. Speee said that her countenance was one of the most interesting he had ever looked at.

John Grattan's daughter Margaret married Samuel Miller, of Miller's Iron Works—a powerful, cheerful, sensible man whom most men feared in anger, and all loved who met him in kindness. Mrs. Miller was an open-hearted, free-spoken, fearless woman. When her husband was about fighting a pitched battle, soon after their marriage, according to the custom among neighbors at that time, she advised him not to strike too high, saying that a blow in the face might disfigure, but one about the short ribs would shorten the combat.

John Grattan's son John was a promising young officer in one of the Virginia regiments in the Revolutionary Army. He died in service, near Sunbury, Georgia.

Robert Grattan, the youngest child of John Grattan, was the pet and indulged one of his old age. Every one did some work in former times. When Robert was a boy, and employed in minding the gap whilst the grain was hauled from the field, his mother had a counterpane stretched over him to keep off the sun, whilst he scratched on the fiddle in the shade. He commenced business with a good estate, in partnership with his frugal brother-in-law, Col. Gamble. His open-handed liberality and generous hospitality lessened it more than it was increased by the profits of trade. He commanded a splendid company of cavalry against the whiskey insurgents of Pennsylvania. His intercourse with General Washington during the time, made the strongest impression upon his excitable nature. One of the incidents of this service which he used to tell, was of a bet made by Harry Lee, the most impudent of men, that he could tap General Washington on the shoulder, look him in the face, and ask him an impertinent question. How when General Lee went up to the side of General Washington, then standing on the parade ground directing the movements of the army, and placed his hand familiarly on the general's arm, the great chief turned upon him his stern commanding look, until Lee shrunk away, and paid his debt—the only kind of debt he ever paid.

Major Grattan's health failed from the unsuitableness of storekeeping to his quick, active spirit. He returned to his farm on North River, where he resided until his death. He had all the admirable qualities of the Irish race, to which he belonged. His house was open to every one. His kindness was ever pressing upon his means. He resided near the public road from Staunton to Winchester. For twenty years the stage never passed his gate without some kind of refreshments being sent to the passengers, and to Bogget, the old crippled soldier of the Revolution, who owned and usually accompanied it.

The cordial affection and unlimited confidence between Major Grattan and George Gilmer was scarcely ever equalled. Their entire trust in each other used to renew the impressions made by my early reading how Damon stood composedly at the place of execution, expecting his friend, yet more than willing to die for him, how, soon after, a shout away beyond the crowd was heard, and Pythias was seen with arm uplifted, pressing with might and main on towards the place of execution, to save his friend from death by dying himself.

No one ever doubted Major Grattan's word who looked at him, or listened to him. His face, voice, and every thing about him, declared his sincerity. He had a fine commanding person, six feet high, gray hair when young, and dark bright eyes. His spirit of command was so natural and easy, that his children never thought of disobedience. All his household reverenced and loved him without measure. He was devoted to his wife, and as kind a father as ever lived.

I was often at Major Grattan's during a visit I made to Virginia, in 1813, for the recovery of my health. He invited me to become a citizen of Virginia, proffering, if I would settle in Rockingham, to do his best to send me to Congress, Democrat as I was. And yet, when I tried to ask him for his daughter nine years after, I found it one of the most difficult matters I had ever undertaken to do. When I was able to say, by his assistance, what I desired, he answered that he preferred me for his daughter's husband to any one in the world. His only distress in our after intercourse was, that he could not do enough for me.

Mrs. Grattan was the daughter of Peachy R. Gilmer, of Rockingham. She survived her husband many years. Her temper was firm, and her understanding vigorous. Her clear perception of right, and sensitive conscientiousness of duty made her entire life a pattern of excellence for all who knew her. Her precepts and example are exciting her children to do for themselves, their families and society, what riches could not do for them. Her sons are making their way to fortune and fame along the road opened to them by the constant labor and perseverance of their mother. Her daughters, acting from the impulse of early impressions, are diffusing happiness around them, so that they may truly call their mother blessed. The devotion and purity of their mother have placed a talisman in the bosom of her children to charm away evil, and a bright star of hope to lead them on to a common home in heaven.

Robert and Elizabeth Grattan left at their death five children—three sons and two daughters.

Eliza Frances, the oldest, is written about so much hereafter, that it would be out of place to say anything of her here.

Robert, their oldest son, was educated for the bar, and had commenced practice, when his father's health failed so entirely, that his presence become necessary to take care of him and his affairs. He quitted his law-office, and devoted himself to the discharge of the duties of a son. After his father's death, he continued his services to his aged mother and an infirm blind aunt. When he took charge of his father's plantation, it was overrun with briers and yielded but little profit. It is now covered with clover and stock, and is one of the most beautiful and productive farms in the valley. In all his efforts to improve his condition, he has been aided by his cheerful, industrious, sensible wife. They have a house full of promising children, whose future success is provided for in the best way, by constant employment on the farm, in the school-room, and at whatever else may tend to the formation of habits of industry and usefulness.

Peachy Ridgway, the second son, is a lawyer, and has been constantly from his youth devoted to his profession. His capital understanding and untiring industry have placed him upon an equality with the most distinguished men of the Richmond bar. His truthfulness, integrity, love of wife, children, friends, country, and sincere piety, make him a friend worth having, and a kinsman to be proud of. He married at twenty-one, Elvira Furgerson, a descendant of the Bollings, of the Pocahontas stock. She is well informed, neat, and agreeable. They have so many sons and daughters, as to impose upon their father the necessity of most incessant and laborious exertions to educate and provide for them. His fate looks hard; but the young Grattans are so pretty and promising, that what would otherwise be very heavy, loses its weight in the buoyancy of hope for their future success and happiness.

Lucy Gilmer, Major Grattan's second daughter, is said to be very much like her beautiful grandmother, Elizabeth Brown. She married Dr. George W. Harris, of Goochland, Virginia, who is as good a husband as any woman ever was blessed with. She devotes herself to flowers, home affairs, visiting the sick, and doing whatever she can to add to the happiness of others. She is indeed too good to be described truthfully to those who do not know her as I do.

John, the youngest son of Dr. Grattan, studied medicine, and upon being prepared for practice, settled in Morgan County, Georgia. He afterwards removed to Columbus, Mississippi, where he died when the prospect was opening of profitable practice, and of great professional reputation. He had the gay, cheerful spirit of his father, and the clear perceptions of his mother,—was truthful and upright. He married Martha, the daughter of Peachy R. Gilmer. She now lives with her three children near her father, in Montgomery, Alabama. She is a fond mother, an affectionate daughter, and a kind kinswoman.

THE LEWISES.

JOHN LEWIS was a native of the County of Dublin, in Ireland. His grandfather, or some still more remote ancestor, removed from Wales to Ireland during the civil wars of the time of Charles the First. Several accounts of the Lewises have been written of late years, in which they are said to have been descended from a family of French Huguenots, who were driven to England by the Edict of Nantz. My mother is in her eighty-ninth year. I read aloud to her when a small boy Hume's History. When listening to the account of the conquest of Wales, by Edward the First, I recollect her saying that she had heard from her father that the Lewellens were his kinspeople, and that his ancestors had emigrated to Ireland from Wales. She remembers Cromwell's picture hanging in his office-room, and his regarding it as a precious relic of former times. The red hair and irascible temper, which still continue to distinguish the Lewises, indicate Welsh rather than French or English origin.

John Lewis married Margaret Linn. The biographers of the Lewises say that Margaret Linn was of the Linns of Lock Linn, in Scotland. This sounds very well, and may be so, But some circumstances, very slight indeed, incline me to the opinion that the Linns emigrated to Ireland from Wales, with the Lewises.

In 1720, the Irish lord of whom John Lewis held land, attempted to enforce some unjust demands upon his tenant. An affray ensued, in which, according to the account told of the affair by the Lewises, their ancestor performed wonderful feats of strength and courage. It is certain that the attacking lord lost his life. John Lewis took refuge in Portugal, with his brother-in-law, Linn, a resident merchant there. Finding that the power and influence of his enemies made his continuance in Lisbon unsafe, he crossed the Atlantic. On being joined by his wife, he pushed into the interior of Pennsylvania, and up the valley between the first mountain ranges, until having passed beyond the white settlements, he located near where the town of Staunton now is, giving strong proof by his movements that he dreaded Irish vengeance more than Indian massacre. The remains of an old stone house on Lewis's Creek, a mile east of Staunton, still points out the place where the white man first planted himself in Western Virginia.

John Lewis was brave and enterprising. He surveyed many tracts of valuable land, when fear of the Indians deterred others from venturing into the backwoods, and thus acquired sufficient territory in his adopted country to have formed a principality in the country from which he had fled in consequence of a contest for a few acres. The Warm Springs, Sweet Springs, and many other places of great value belonged to him. His accounts to his friends and kinsmen in Ireland of the advantages of New Virginia, attracted to it the Alexanders, McDowels, Prestons, Pattons, Matthewses and others.

The frontier men of that part of the Colony of Virginia were but little restrained by law or the fear of punishment. The Indian trail, which led from the north to the south, and along which the warriors of the northwestern Indians, the Cherokees, and Creeks, wended their way in attacks upon each other, passed near John Lewis's house. They never failed in going by to partake of his frontier fare, and give him some token of their friendship.

In June, 1754, a party of twelve Northwestern Indian warriors stopped at John Lewis's on their return from the South, where they had been satisfying their revenge upon the Cherokees for some injury received. Some of his neighbors happened to be there whose families or friends had suffered from attacks of the Indians. They insisted upon the party remaining until night, and exhibiting their dances. Upon their consenting, they left and employed the time until dark collecting the neighbors who had suffered from Indian murders. A beef was killed, and a large log fire made, around which the Indians assembled, cooking and eating to their stomach's content. They danced and drank whiskey until their lookers-on were satisfied with the display of their antics, and then went on their way homeward as far as the Middle River, where they lodged in Anderson's barn. As soon as they were sound asleep, the whites were upon them with their axes, knives and guns. Only one escaped. For that night's doings many Virginia wives were made widows, and mothers childless. The government of Virginia endeavored to punish the perpetrators. All fled to some distant part of the extended frontier of the Colonies, except one by the name of King, who lived a skulking life for a long time, always keeping his gun near him. He sometimes would go to the old Augusta Church, the great assembling place for worship of the Scotch-Irish of that part of the country, where, seated upon the sill of the door with his inseparable companion the rifle in his hand, he listened to the words of the preacher, so necessary to the comfort of the Irish spirit, whether Protestant or Catholic. He was suffered to work out his own punishment, avoiding all men and avoided by all.

During the war which followed this outrage, John Lewis provided for the defence of his family by fortifying his house. An attack was once made upon it by a party of Indians, when his sons and men-servants were absent. Though old and infirm, he stationed himself at a port-hole and kept up a constant shooting at the Indians by his wife reloading the guns. His sons and servants, hearing the repeated report of guns, returned home and drove the Indians off.

John Lewis's person was tall and muscular. He had great strength, a fearless spirit, hardy habits, and was the best backswoodman of his day. Being at some public place, after the country about Staunton was settled, he laid down his shillalah for a moment. A Tuckahoe, who was present, took it up to examine its curious workmanship. John Lewis told him that the custom in his country was, that he who took up another's cudgel must fight or treat. The people of the old countries acquired by coming to the colonies, the spirit of doing, without restraint, what they pleased. The Tuckahoe announced that he would not treat through a threat. He prepared for the cudgelling by going into the woods close by and cutting a long hickory stick, which he flailed in the middle until the two ends could be brought together. He went back to the company and announced himself ready to receive the cudgelling. The Cohee and Tuckahoe stood up near by, facing each other, with the ends of their sticks touching, as was the fashion in cudgel-playing. When the word "ready" was pronounced by the judges of the contest, the Tuckahoe drew back his hickory cudgel and struck a blow with both hands and all his might across the Cohee's shillalah, then at the scientific guard. The flailed part gave way, so that the upper end came down with great force upon John Lewis's head and finished the fight.

John Lewis had four sons, Thomas, Andrew, Charles and William.

Thomas, the oldest, was the Colonial Surveyor of Augusta County, which then included within its limits most of Western Virginia. A part of Gen. Washington's great wealth was acquired by surveys of land under his authority, or in common with him. After the revolutionary war, Gen. Washington passed several days at his house, arranging their land claims; a visit as well remembered as King Charles's to Tillietudlum. My father, then a youth of nineteen, returning from my grandfather Lewis's, where he had been visiting my mother, met Gen. Washington fording the Shenandoah River, in the dusk of the evening. Gen. Washington asked him how he should go to Mr. Lewis's. My father, taking him for some big Dutchman of the neighborhood who was poking fun at him for his frequent visitings there, answered, "Follow your nose."

The people of Augusta County met in Staunton the 22d of February, 1775, to take into consideration the proceedings of the General Congress of the Colonies in opposition to the unjust measures of Great Britain, and to appoint delegates to a Colonial Convention, to be held in Richmond. They chose Thomas Lewis and Samuel McDowell. In their instructions to their delegates, they say, "Our rights we are fully resolved, with our lives and fortunes, inviolably to preserve." Thomas Lewis and Samuel McDowell addressed a letter to Peyton Randolph, Richard Henry Lee, George Washington, Patrick Henry, Richard Bland, Benjamin Harrison, and Edward Pendleton, members from Virginia to the General Congress, in which they thank them for their maintenance of the cause of liberty, and say, "May our hearts be open to receive, and our arms strong to defend that liberty." The Congressmen reply: "The assurance from the grave and spirited people of Augusta, that their hearts and hands shall be devoted to the support of the measures for the preservation of American liberty, gives us the highest satisfaction, and must afford pleasure to every friend of the just rights of mankind."

Thomas Lewis was Commissioner of the Confederation, in 1777, to treat with the Indian tribes who had been defeated at the battle of Point Pleasant. He concluded a peace by which the best soldiers of the Colony of Virginia were left at liberty to join the army under Gen. Washington, to fight for the independence of their country, instead of remaining at home to defend the frontiers from Indian massacres.

Thomas Lewis was a member of the Virginia Legislature, when its proceedings gave tone to the public voice throughout the Colonies. He was a member of the Virginia Convention which ratified the Constitution of the United States, by a vote so nearly divided, that the patriot yet rejoices at his country's escape from the anarchy which would have been the consequence of a different result. He voted for ratification.

Thomas Lewis's habits were studious, and his taste literary. His library was large, and made up of classical books, when learning was a singular distinction in Western Virginia. He married Jane Strother. They had thirteen children.

Thomas Lewis's three oldest sons, John, Andrew, and Thomas, were officers in the revolutionary army. John and Andrew were with Gen. Washington at Valley Forge, and throughout the Jersey campaign. John and Thomas were at the surrender of Cornwallis. Andrew was an officer under General Wayne, in his expedition against the Western Indians, in 1795, and lost an arm.

Thomas Lewis bequeathed most of his large estate to his youngest sons, Charles and Benjamin. They lived near each other in Rockingham County, on the Shenandoah River. They were very social, well informed, respectable gentlemen. They were excluded from office by their being federalists, when almost all others in Rockingham were republicans.

Margaret Lewis, the oldest daughter of Thomas Lewis, was a very sensible, well-informed woman. She married Capt. McClannahan, who was afterwards killed at the battle of the Point. Her second husband was Col. Bowyer.

Agatha, the second daughter of Thomas Lewis, married when quite young, Capt. John Frog, her first cousin.

About mid-day on the 10th of October, 1774, in the town of Staunton, a little girl, the daughter of John and Agatha Frog, and grand-daughter of Thomas and Jane Lewis, was sleeping near her mother, when suddenly she waked, screaming that the Indians were killing her father. She was quieted by her mother, and again went to sleep. She again waked, screaming that the Indians were killing her father. She was again quieted and went to sleep, and was waked up by the same horrid vision, and continued screaming beyond being hushed. The child's mother was very much alarmed at the first dream. But when the same horrid sight was seen the third time, her Irish imagination, quickened by inherited superstition, presented to her the spectacle of her husband scalped by the Indians. Her cries drew together her neighbors, who, upon being informed of what had happened, joined their lamentations to her's, until all Staunton was in a state of commotion.

It so happened that the great battle of the Point, between the Western Indians and the Virginians, was fought on the very day when all Staunton was thus agitated. And what was still more wonderful, John Frog, the father of the child who saw in her dream the Indians killing her father, was actually killed by the Indians on that day.

Mrs. Frog's second husband was Capt. John Stuart.

When, in 1752, Robert Dinwiddie came over as Governor of Virginia, he was accompanied by John Stuart, his intimate friend. John Paul, son of Hugh, Bishop of Nottingham, a partisan of the house of Stuart, was killed at the siege of Dalrymple Castle, in 1745. He left a widow and three children; —John, who became a Roman Catholic priest, and died on the eastern shore of Maryland; Audley, who was for ten years an officer in the British colonial forces in Virginia; and Ann, who married George Mathews, afterwards Governor of Georgia. Mrs. Paul, formerly Margaret Linn, of the Linns of Lock Linn, a niece of Mrs. John Lewis, married John Stuart. They had two children; John, who married Mrs. Frog, and known as Col. Stuart of Greenbrier; and Betsey, who became the wife of Col. Richard Woods, of Albemarle County, Virginia.

Capt. John Stuart did great service for his country, and acquired distinguished reputation by his courage and skill at the battle of the Point. His fame and the fame of the incident which connected the widow Frog with the battle of the Point, created such a sympathy between them that when they met they married.

Col. Stuart's estate was estimated, when he died, at $200,-

000. His son Lewis was for a long time clerk of Greenbrier County, then one of the most lucrative offices of Western Virginia.

His son Charles graduated at Yale College. He was a very sensible, respectable gentleman, and for some time President of the Board of Public Works of Virginia.

Felder, the son of a poor German Switzer, who settled and died in Richland District, South Carolina, had industrious habits, and a strong desire to improve his condition in life. Upon his acquiring sufficient knowledge of the classics for admittance into college, he travelled on foot and on the top of wagons to Charleston, and in the most economical way to New Haven. When he arrived there he strolled into the yard of Yale College, knowing nobody, and without letters to any one. As he was walking about, at a loss what to do, stared at and laughed at by the passing college boys, his distress was noticed by Charles Stuart, then belonging to the senior class. He accosted Felder in a friendly way, and upon being informed that he wished to be admitted into college, aided him in his purpose, and kept him with him until his rawness was overcome. I served in Congress with Felder in 1827-8-9. We met at the White Sulphur Springs in the summer of 1845, and went together to Lewisburg, the seat of justice of Greenbrier County, where we found Charles Stuart presiding in the County Court. I witnessed their meeting, and sympathized with Felder's great pleasure from the grateful recollection of kindness received when needed, and Charles Stuart's for the success of his uncultivated protege.

Col. Stuart's only daughter married Col. Crocket, of Wythe County, Virginia, a wealthy and highly respectable gentleman. Miss Frog, Mrs. Stuart's daughter by her first husband, married Mr. Estill. Their daughter married Mr. Erskine, of Lewisburg.

In 1848, whilst I was at the White Sulphur Springs, I saw my kinswoman, Mrs. Erskine, very frequently. She was then very much chagrined at a strange freak of her kind and affectionate husband. He had gone to Mexico in search of fame. His imagination had become so excited by the recollection of the impressions which the adventures of the Lewises and Erskines, in the Indian wars of former times, had made upon him when young, that he could not be restrained from trying to perform some great exploit himself. I heard soon after I left the Springs that my kinswoman was in great distress. Her husband's Quixotism had terminated in his death.

In 1777, Cornstalk, the great chief of the Shawnees, visited the fort at Point Pleasant to inform Capt. Stuart, then stationed there, that the Shawnees intended to take part with the British against Virginia. The officers detained him as a hostage. Ellenipsco, the son of Cornstalk, hearing of his father's confinement, left his nation to remain with him. The day after his arrival at the fort, two men crossed the Kenhawa to hunt. A party of Indians killed and scalped one of them, and pursued the other to the river. The company to which the man who was killed belonged, became so enraged that they marched in a body to the fort, crying out, "let us kill the Indians." Capt. Stuart endeavored in vain to prevent the execution of their murderous purpose. The interpreter's wife, who had been a captive among the Shawnees, and had great affection for Cornstalk, ran to him and informed him that the men of the fort were about to put him to death. Ellenipsco was at first very much alarmed. But Cornstalk urged him to meet death fearlessly, telling him that the Great Spirit had sent his son to him that they might die together. Immediately after, seven bullets passed through the body of Cornstalk. Ellenipsco, seeing his father die, met his own death with composure.

In 1778, Donnell's fort was attacked by the Indians. A white man and a negro held the door whilst the Indians were endeavoring to push it open. They let the door suddenly fly open, got an Indian into their clutches, shut the door, and killed him. Whilst the white man was holding the door shut with all his might, the negro seized a gun and fired at the Indians, which waked the men, women, and children who were sleeping in another part of the fort in time to secure all the entrances. Capt. Stuart, Capt. Arbuckle, and Col. Samuel Lewis collected in great haste, a body of men and drove the Indians off. Virginia purchased the freedom of the negro in reward for his services.

Jane, the third daughter of Thomas Lewis, married Capt.

Hughs, of the continental army. They removed to Kentucky, where Mrs. Hughs died, leaving only one child, an infant son. The last request she made of her husband was, that when her son was old enough, he should be sent to my mother, to be brought up with her children. He came to Georgia and remained some time with Patrick Hughs, his uncle, a frolicking, card-playing Irishman, who lived in Burke County. Young Hughs soon acquired the habit of his kinsman. He came as far as Washington, on his way to visit my mother, where he fell in with a party of gamblers, and accompanied them to the western country. As he and his companions were riding through a dense forest, he fell behind. Those before, hearing the report of a pistol, looked back and saw young Hughs falling from his horse, covered with his blood and brains.

Mary, the fourth daughter, married Capt. McElhany, of the continental army.

Elizabeth, my mother, the fifth daughter, married Thomas M. Gilmer.

Ann, the sixth daughter, married ——— Doutha, fresh from Ireland, where he had learned in the River Shannon, to catch trout with unsurpassed skill. His proficiency in fishing was too great to admit of excellency in any other art. After his death, his widow married Mr. French. They removed to Kentucky.

Fanny, the seventh daughter of Thomas Lewis, was very pretty and amiable. She married Col. Layton Yancey, who was an officer in the American army during the revolutionary war, and was afterwards a member of the County Court of Rockingham so long that he enjoyed the perquisites of the sheriffalty twice before his death.

Sophia, the youngest daughter of Thomas Lewis, was one of the most agreeable of all the kin, and as good and kind as she was witty. She married John Carthae, a very handsome, wealthy young man, who kept so busy trading all through his life that he died centless. Their daughter Mary married Col. Bankhead, whose first wife was the daughter of Col. Tom Man Randolph, and grand-daughter of Mr. Jefferson.

Andrew Lewis, second son of John Lewis, became familiar with danger and accustomed to hardship in early life. He was Major of the regiment commanded by George Washington, whose special service was the defence of the frontiers of Virginia from Indian incursions.

The great events of the war for independence, and their glorious results, so overshadowed the incidents of the immediately preceding Indian war, that the hair-breadth escapes, daning exploits, and fierce encounters of the officers and men of that regiment,—the scalpings, burnings, and horrid massacres of the Indians, have been scarcely noticed in history.

For ten years previous to actual hostilities, Great Britain had been passing laws to control her American colonies. Lord Dunmore, a thorough Scotch tory, and subtle agent of its will, was made Governor of Virginia. To force the colonies to acquiesce in its measures, or suppress opposition, Lord Dunmore contrived to unite the western Indians in a combined attack upon the frontier Irish people, who being the readiest to resist any violation of the liberties of the colony, were therefore the first to feel the weight of British domination. When troops were raised by the colonial legislature to war with the Indians, he put himself in command, and ordered two regiments, composed chiefly of Western Virginians, to the most exposed part of the frontiers, whilst he marched the disciplined forces in another direction. These two regiments were under the command of Gen. Andrew Lewis. They reached the Ohio at Point Pleasant the 1st of October, 1774, where they encamped, waiting for reinforcments. On the morning of the 10th they were attacked by the Western Indians, under the command of Logan, Cornstalk and other distinguished chiefs. The battle lasted all day, the officers and soldiers, the chiefs and warriors, fighting hand to hand, with tomahawk and scalping-knife, and from tree to tree, with rifles. In the evening, whilst the contest was going on doubtfully, Gen. Lewis ordered Capt. Stuart, Capt. Mathews, and Capt. Shelby to proceed with their companies up the Ohio under cover of the thick undergrowth near its banks, to Crooked Creek, and up it until they got into the rear of the Indians, and then to attack them. This order was executed so successfully that the Indians were driven across the Ohio. Seventy-five of the Virginians were killed, and one hundred and forty wounded. The Indians threw their killed into the river, so that their numbers were never known. Gen. Lewis's army numbered eleven hundred; the Indians were probably more numerous.

Gen. Lewis was appointed Brigadier General by the Continental Congress in the war for independence. Capt. Isaac Shelby was made Governor of Kentucky and Secretary of War of the United States. Capt. Evans Shelby, Governor of Tennessee, Capt. William Campbell, and John Campbell, became famous as the heroes of Long Island and King's Mountain. Andrew Moore was made Senator in Congress, and Col. William Fleming Governor of Virginia. Capts. Stuart, Cameron, Tate, McKee, and others, were also honored for their meritorious services on that day.

Andrew Lewis commanded the Virginia troops at the commencement of the revolutionary war. His first important service was to drive the Scotch Governor Dunmore and his tory adherents from the State. His military service was afterwards confined to the defence of the country bordering on the Chesapeake Bay. His mountain constitution gave way from the unhealthiness of the climate. He resigned, set out for his home, but died before he reached it.

John Lewis, the son of Gen. Andrew, was an officer under his father at Grant's defeat. He was made prisoner, and carried to Quebec, and from thence to France. Upon his liberation, he went to London. His very tall, erect, handsome person, his colonial commission, and suffering as a prisoner, attracted the attention of royalty sufficiently to procure for him a commission in the British army. He belonged to a corps stationed near London, either the King's or Queen's Guards. After some years spent in acquiring the idle, dissipated habits of the corps to which he belongd, he resigned and returned to Virginia. Upon his arrival in Alexandria, he was greeted with a splendid ball. Very few Virginians had been honored with a commission in the regular army of Great Britain, and still fewer had been permitted to serve in the troops which immediately surrounded royalty. His fine, manly person, aided by courtly manners, and gallant spirit, captivated Miss Love, the most dashing belle of the town. He married, and carried her to the home of his family in the valley of Virginia. His residence abroad had not deprived him of his inclination for enterprise. He settled a farm upon the extreme of the Virginia frontier. The negroes whom he carried with him, found no associates in that western wilderness, and were constantly frightened lest they should be massacred by the Indians, or eaten up by the bears, panthers, or wolves. Whilst at work with their master in the woods, they killed him, with the belief that their mistress would return with them to the part of the country from whence they had come. The body was not discovered for some days. The neighbors who were scattered distantly around assembled to search for it. They noticed that his dog absented himself for a day or two before he returned home for food. They followed his lead and found the body where it had been covered with leaves, and guarded from the wild beasts by his dog.

Charles Lewis, the third son of John Lewis, was a noble fellow; generous, gallant, and fearless. He was the readiest and most skillful of all the frontier Indian fighters. Once he was captured by the Indians whilst on a hunting excursion. After some days' march, and much suffering from their barbarous treatment, he effected his escape. He was pursued and put to his utmost speed in running. Leaping a prostrate tree, which lay in his course, he fell. Finding himself concealed by the tree, the grass, and weeds, and being very much exhausted, he determined to remain still, as he was just then out of sight of the Indians. His pursuers passed by and on. When he ventured to look about, he saw a large rattlesnake in his coil, within striking distance of his ear. He scarcely breathed lest the movement might bring the fatal stroke. His suspended breath got relief after a while by the rattlesnake slowly uncoiling himself and moving away.

Charles Lewis commanded a regiment at the battle of the Point. He led in the onset upon the Indians. To encourage his men to deeds of daring in the fight, he showed them his own indifference to danger by putting on a red waistcoat and exposing himself every where. His heroism cost him his life. Virginia perpetuated its remembrance by naming a county after him. His daughter wrote a song descriptive of the battle, which was sung as long as Indians and their warfare continued subjects of interest.

Many Charles Lewises are still to be found among the descendants of the Western Virginians, named in memory of the brave man who died in defence of their mothers.

William Lewis, the fourth son of John Lewis, though as powerful in person and brave in spirit as either of his brothers, was less disposed to seek fame by the sacrifice of human life. He served in the army only when required. He was an officer under Braddock, and was wounded at his defeat. He was an elder in the Presbyterian Church, of the old covenanting sort. His son Tom was an officer in Wayne's army, of high reputation for soldierly conduct. Soon after his return home from service, he saw, on a Sunday morning, wild ducks in the Sweet Spring Creek, which ran near his father's house. Taking a loaded gun in his hand, he crept along a zigzag fence until he got within shooting distance, and was about to fire, when he felt the forcible application of a large brush to his shoulders. Turning suddenly round to return the blow, he saw descending a second stroke, and heard from his father, "I will teach you, sir, that you shall not profane the Sabbath day here!"

William Lewis' wife was Ann Montgomery.

Among the stories told for a long time after the dispersion of the Virginia Legislature, at Charlottesville, by Col. Tarleton and his dragoons, was one, that Mr. Jefferson concealed himself in Carters mountain, and another, that Patrick Henry, flying in the greatest trepidation, met Mrs. William Lewis in the streets of Staunton, who, upon hearing him tell of the breaking up of the Legislature, said to him, without knowing who he was, that if the great Patrick Henry had been there, the British never would have crossed the Rivannah river. William Lewis was sick in bed at the time. His wife immediately called her three sons, the oldest of whom was under one and twenty, ordered them to take their rifles, be off immediately to Rockfish Gap, and see to it, that the valley was not polluted by the foot of a British soldier. Tradition still tells many stories of the stern, pure life of William Lewis, and the admirable qualities of his wife. Their union, commencing in love, continued to grow closer and closer, as they drew nearer and nearer to the end of life. They lived to be old people. Mrs. William Lewis died first. From his wife's death until his own approached nigh, he went every day to her grave, where, seated by its side, he read the Bible.

Their oldest son, John, was an officer in the revolutionary war, and commanded a company at the battle of Monmouth. He was reputed to be the most athletic man in Virginia. He threw down and out-jumped Andrew Jackson until the future hero had the greatest admiration for him.

He once visited his son-in-law Mr. Thompson, who lived in the low country of South Carolina, where bullfrogs abound. He mentioned jocularly in a company of aristocratic gentlemen, that he had seen a frog six feet long in the mountains of Virginia, alluding to John Frog, who married his cousin. He was insulted by a very rude remark, for which his fighting Irish spirit required ample amends. He married Mary Preston, sister of Gov. Preston and aunt of Gov. McDowell and of Gov. Floyd. One of his daughters married Dr. Trent, of Cumberland, whose daughter married Judge Robertson, of Richmond, a descendant of the Princess Pocahontas.

William Lewis's son, William T. Lewis, married Miss Cabell, was a member of Congress, and only wanted a vote or two of being elected Governor of Virginia.

THE STROTHERS.

THE STROTHERS emigrated from England to Virginia in the early times of the colony. One of them, who died thirty years ago, and was near a hundred years old, used to say, that she could trace her descent through five Virginia grandmothers in a direct line. They were connected by blood and marriage, with many of the most respectable families of Virginia, were distinguished for courage and talents, members of the State Legislatures, officers of the army and members of Congress. The first whig who died in the cause of liberty in Georgia was a Strother. William Strother, of Stafford, and his wife Margaret Watts, had thirteen children, all daughters.

Jane, their oldest daughter, married Thomas Lewis, my grandfather.

Margaret married Mr. Morton, a gentleman of fortune, who dying soon after, left her a young wealthy widow, unincumbered with children. Her second husband was Gabriel Jones, a well educted Welshman, the friend, kinsman, and executor of Lord Fairfax. His residence was in the valley of Virginia, on the Shenandoah River, in view of mountains in every direction, upon a farm of great fertility and extent, adjoining the farms of his three brothers-in-law, Thomas Lewis, John Madison and John Frog, and his friend Peachy R. Gilmer. He was the most distinguished lawyer of New Virginia. He was a member of the Convention which ratified the Constitution of the United States. He left a large estate to his descendants. Mrs. Jones lived to the extended age of ninety-seven years, and passed that long time in the uniform and exemplary discharge of all the duties of her elevated position in society. Her daughter Margaret married Col. John Harvie.

The political contests, in the time of James the First, Charles, Cromwell, and their immediate successors, induced a great many of the gentry of Great Britain and Ireland, to make the colony of Virginia their permanent abode. They formed many of the institutions of the colony, modelled its laws, and fashioned its society. The fees upon the grants of the rich alluvial lands on the rivers, were made so high, that only those who had property could acquire them; and were, as intended, monopolized by the rich. The introduction of African slaves, increased the separation between the wealthy, who owned them, and the poor, who had none, and thus added to the aristocratic state and temper of the highest class. British policy placed the control of the colonial government in the same class. With the selfishness which has ever distinguished it, the aristocracy of the colony made all the offices which gentlemen would accept, very lucrative, and retained the disposition of them in their own hands.

Whilst Mr. Jefferson was Governor of Virginia, he used his influence to have Bob John Harvie of Albemarle, his neighbor and friend, appointed Register of the land office, one of the most lucrative offices of the State.

The high salaries attached to the most important offices of the government of Virginia, and the wealth and cultivation of the incumbents, made clerkships under them the most improving school for the young gentlemen of the country; the best introduction to fashionable society; and the most desirable means of acquiring knowledge of business. Indeed, with the exception of William and Mary College, there were no others suited for that purpose.

Col. Harvie received into the Register's office a young gentleman by the name of Marshall, who proved so acceptable, that he very soon became domesticated in his family.

Gabriella Harvie, Col. Harvie's oldest daughter, was too young when Marshall became a member of her father's family, to be distrustful in her association with gentlemen. She charmed him by her sprightliness, while he engaged her regard by many little flattering attentions and kindnesses, and especially by talking to her about what she read; her vivid imagination making realizations of the heroes and heroines of romance. The intimacy between Marshall and Gabriella Harvie remained unrestrained until the young miss became a captivating woman. Before she or Marshall were aware of it, the cords of love had bound their hearts together so strong, that old time himself found the tie hard to loosen. Soon afterwards Gabriella Harvie's quick grey eyes, *en bon point* person, and sprightly elastic step, attracted the admiration of Col. Tom Man Randolph, of Tuckahoe, and so revived in the old gentleman the feelings of youth, that though then a widower, with children and grandchildren, he asked Col. Harvie for his daughter in marriage. Col. Randolph was a descendant of the Princess Pocahontas, the head of one of the most aristocratic families in Virginia, and as distinguished for wealth as nobility. Col. Harvie was a gentleman of high character, proud bearing, and otherwise distinguished among his countrymen. Mrs. Harvie inherited from her Welsh father a high appreciation of rank and fortune. Both Col. and Mrs. Harvie were exceedingly gratified by Col. Randolph's proposal, and accepted it unhesitatingly for their daughter. When Gabriella was informed by them that they had provided a husband for her, whose greatness would make her the first lady of the land, she surprised and offended them beyond measure by her prompt refusal of the proffered honor. Marshall had not proposed marriage to Gabriella Harvie when Col. Randolph made the offer of his hand. He had not even declared in words how much he loved her. Indeed, neither were perhaps aware until the trial came of the state of their feelings. When Gabriella reported to him what had passed between her parents and herself upon the subject of Col. Randolph's suit, they found themselves in each other's arms, plighting their love for life. Gabriella's ingenuous noble nature prompted her at once to inform her father and mother of what had passed between Marshall and herself. The prospect of the marriage of their daughter with Col. Randolph was too gratifying to yield up its indulgence willingly. They insisted that the marriage should take place. People of the present day know but little of the strong rule which parents exercised over their children in the Old Dominion of former times. It is yet strong. But it was then as strong as it had ever been in Old England. Gabriella and Marshall were at once hopeless. Marshall was under so many obligations to Col. and Mrs. Harvie that he would not attempt to marry their daughter against their will. Believing that his duty to them demanded that his engagement to their daughter should cease, and that his and Gabriella's happiness required that they should not continue to see each other, he left Virginia for a foreign land. The young lady's high spirit would have prompted to a different course. But it was not for her to act or direct on such an occasion. Her self-esteem was offended at the tame submission of her lover. She felt that in justice to herself she ought to forget him who had deserted her and his country. Anger and pride made her desire to show that she was above repining. So, after sighing and crying had taken the color from her cheeks, and the usual cheerful smile from her countenance, she ended by doing as she was bid, by going through the ceremony of marriage with Col. Randolph. Col. Harvie, though prompt in accepting Col. Randolph's proposals, and firm in insisting upon his daughter's compliance with his wishes, took care that she was well provided for by a marriage contract. Col. Randolph settled most of his large estate upon his affianced bride and her issue, to the exclusion of his children by his previous marriage. The old fancy-stricken widower became the husband of the high-spirited, gay, beautiful young lady of eighteen. Marriage is a capital alembic for testing the nature and value of the materials of which the parties are made. Col. Randolph was soon the same proud, irritable old man which he had been before his excited imagination made him feel young and courteous. Mrs. Randolph underwent a metamorphis, greater if possible, than her husband. The haughty pride which she inherited from her lordly-descended Welsh grandfather, and her old Virginia aristocratic grandmother, which had been suppressed before by her laughing, joyous temper, and her kind, social affections, now became conspicuous in her intercourse with her husband, and his own special associates. Love and its kindred feelings had their place supplied by ostentation and fashionable employments. Her husband, having married her without seeking her regard, obtained what usually follows marriage without love between parties of unsuitable age. The pleaures of society soon engrossed all her time. Her house, furniture, carriage, horses, servants, dress, and other paraphernalia were the most splendid in Virginia. They were put into constant requisition. Her vivacity and intelligence attracted around her at home, and wherever she appeared, a coterie of the choicest wits and most agreeable gentlemen of the country. Those who knew but little of her character, and envied her rank and fortune, sometimes vented their malice in slanderous tittle-tattle. Her pride and conscious purity made her despise all aspersions. The great orator, John Randolph, was the special admirer of his kinsman's wife. He knew too well the extent of the sacrifice which she had made in marriage to condemn her for not feigning love for her husband. Whilst Mrs. Randolph was entertaining company by her pleasantry, wit, and literary taste, her husband was often heard complaining of his want of enjoyment. The agreeable social qualities of the wife added but little to his happiness. He fretted and fumed until he exhausted the little of life that was in him.

The luxuries supplied by great wealth, the habits of fashionable life, and the constant intercourse with the most intelligent and refined society, created other tastes and desires in Mrs. Randolph than those which she enjoyed when Gabriella Harvie. When Marshall heard that Mrs. Randolph was a widow, and at liberty to follow her own inclination in marriage, he hastened to see her. He addressed her at once upon the subject which had been so mutually interesting to them when they parted. He was mortified beyond measure at the apparent indifference with which he was listened to. When he pressed Mrs. Randolph to be his wife, he received an evasive answer. The widow had yet fresh in memory the miseries she had suffered from wedlock. She was not then tired of being freed from them. She wanted to lose sight of the phantasmagoria which she had been seeing before she tried the state a second time. Her acquired waywardness added to her disposition to delay indulging in what her heart panted after. Marshall, overcome by the apparent indifference of her whom he had loved so long and so devotedly, and misunderstanding the influences which controlled her conduct, quitted her for ever. When Mrs. Randolph next heard of him he was married. She had suffered the deepest mortification from his abrupt departure. She was conscious that she had trifled with his constancy and her own hopes of happiness. But when she heard of his marrige, though she suffered intensely for a short time, she was soon herself again.

Mrs. Randolph was yet young and charming when she acquired the right to dispose of herself according to her own will. Her wealth and rare accomplishments soon attracted suitors. Her experience enabled her to know the folly of making rank and fortune the sole inducements in selecting a husband. She had convinced herself that fashionable gayeties afford but transient amusement. She determined to marry the man of her choice, and to choose him for qualities which would command her respect. From among her many admirers she suited herself by accepting Dr. Brokenbough, whose sound sense, high reputation, excellent character, and social qualities, answered the description she had made of him who was to be her second husband. His proper appreciation of her character and worth pleased her self-esteem, and his merits secured her regard.

Dr. Brokenbough, after acting for a long time as president of one of the banks of Virginia, and living with his wife in a style fitting their fortune, found himself ruined by the indebtedness which he had incurred for his social and political friends. He expected to feel the disgrace of being unable to pay his debts. He would not ask his wife to sacrifice her property and accustomed enjoyments. He had not then learned to understand fully her noble nature. She required no asking. She parted with her fine house, furniture, plate, carriage and horses, and as much of her other property as saved his honor. Dr. Brokenbough kept the Warm Springs and the lands about it. Mrs. Brokenbough would not part with her family negroes. With the profits arising from this most delightful bathing-place in the United States, they passed their old age in easy competence and social enjoyments. The Doctor was a kind and considerate husband, and Mrs. Brokenbough the most cheerful and agreeable wife.

How short-sighted are the most knowing, when they see objects through their selfishness! How greatly mistaken the old, when they disregard the wishes and judgment of their children to acquire for them and themselves distinction by marriage! Riches and rank often take wings and fly away. Reciprocal love, founded upon congeniality of temper, taste, and character, never does.

Among the inducements which Col. Harvie had for inattention to his daughter's attachment for Marshall, by marrying her to Col. Randolph, was the greatness of Col. Randolph's family. His son, Thomas Man Randolph, was married to Mr. Jefferson's daughter. Mr. Jefferson had been Governor of Virginia, Minister of the Confederation at the Court of France, and was then Secretary of State under Gen. Washington. Peyton Randolph had been president of the Congress of the Confederation, and Edmund Randolph was then one of the distinguished men of Virginia, and had been President Washington's Attorney-general. Mrs. Brokenbough lived to know that Mr. Jefferson died insolvent, after obtaining from Virginia the authority of law to acquire money to pay his debts, by a lottery or gaming machine. Col. Thomas Man Randolph, Mr. Jefferson's son-in-law, and the son of Mrs. Brokenbough's first husband, after being a distinguished Member of Congress, became so penniless as to propose to eke out his little means of support in his last days by the translation of a book in French on the cultivation of the vine. Mrs. Randolph, Mr. Jefferson's daughter, had her wants supplied by the liberality of the State of South Carolina and of Congress. Edmund Randolph was reduced to the necessity in his old age, of practicing law for whatever fees he could get.

The following extract of a letter received from Dr. Brokenbough, on the subject of this sketch, may add value to it:—

"Col. Harvie, in early life, became a successful lawyer in the County of Albemarle; then a delegate in the Virginia House of Burgesses; and was appointed, jointly with Mr. John Walker, a commissioner to treat with the Indians at Fort Pitt. On his return, he was chosen a member of the old Congress, and remained in that place until he was elected Register of the Land Office of the Commonwealth—then a very laborious, but very lucrative office—which he held several years; and, after his resignation, was elected by the City of Richmond a member of the House of Delegates, but only served one or two years, when he retired to private life, and died at his seat, Belvidere, near Richmond, in the year 1807, leaving a family of seven children, of whom none remain but Gen. Jaqueline Harvie and Mrs. Brokenbough, now in the 78th year of her age.

"Mr. Jones, as you know, was a very distinguished and influentiel lawyer in Western Virginia. Mrs. Jones, who survived her husband many years, was a most exemplary woman in all the relations of life. She possessed a fine mind, was well informed, benevolent, charitable and pious. All who knew her loved and respected her.

"Col. Harvie's son Lewis died young, after exciting in his friends the strongest hopes of his success.

"Col. Harvie's son John married his cousin Miss Hawkins. He was a man of education and accomplished manners.

"His son General Jaqueline Harvie married the only daughter of Chief Justice Marshall.

"His son Edwin married Miss Hardaway. He died from injuries received from the burning of the Richmond theatre. He left two sons, who are gentlemen of merit and distinction.

"Mrs. John Harvie survived her husband many years. Her family were among the principal sufferers from the burning of the Richmond theatre in 1811

"Mrs Jones's daughter ———— married John Lewis, a distinguished lawyer of Fredericksburg, whose brother married Betty, the sister of General Washington.

"Another daughter of Mrs. Jones married ———— Hawkins. They removed to Kentucky.

"Strother Jones, the only son of Mrs. Jones, was an officer in the revolutionary war. He died young, leaving one son, who married Miss Marshall, a niece of Chief Justice Marshall, a most charming young woman."

Agatha Strother, sister of my grandmother, Mrs. Thomas Lewis, and of Mrs. Gabriel Jones, married John Madison, who held the clerkship of Augusta County, then one of the most profitable offices of Virginia. He was distinguished among other qualities for his love of practical jokes. An Irish showman, by the name of Curry, once obtained his permission to exhibit his performances in the Court House in Staunton. Whilst Curry was taking his supper, and before the company assembled to witness his exploits, John Madison placed a pile of powder under the table upon which Curry was to stand, and laid a train from it to his office. Just as he was exhibiting the Devil—his phiz, tail, claws, and cloven foot—the train was fired. It blowed the poor devil Curry sky high, and made the lookers on imagine that Old Nick was actually present in propria persona. John Curry's descendants still acknowledge their obligations to John Madison for making a good citizen of their mountebank ancestor. Col. Frog was well known for his swelling agricultural pretensions. John Madison, who was his brother-in-law, procured from his Low Country friends a large quantity of the seed of the Jamestown weed, which he presented to Col. Frog for clover. He sowed them upon his richest Shenandoah bottom-land, and, for some days after they came up, exultingly exhibited the product of his field as the broadest-leafed clover that had ever been seen.

John Madison's son James was a churchman of accomplished education, and for a long time President of William and Mary College. He was appointed Bishop of Virginia. He went to England to receive the investiture of that dignity. Upon being presented to the King, then George the Third, as a Virginian who had crossed the Atlantic to receive the Bishop's ring, he cried out in wonder, "What! what! what!" as humorously described by Peter Pindar.

Mrs. Madison's son George removed to the State of Kentucky. He commanded a battalion in the campaign against the British and Indians in 1812-13. When Winchesster was defeated, he and his battalion stood their ground, and continued fighting after all others of the army had surrendered or been dispersed. He was afterwards Governor of Kentucky.

One of John Madison's sons married the daughter of the great orator, Patrick Henry; another Miss Preston, the kinswoman of William C. Preston, the eloquent senator of South Carolina, and lately President of Columbia College. Roland, another son, married the daughter of Gen. Andrew Lewis, and was the father of Captain Madison, of the United States Army.

Miss Madison, granddaughter of Mrs. John Madison, married Howe Peyton, a distinguished lawyer of Western Virginia.

The Lewises, Strothers and Madisons, are gone hither and thither, and most of their large landed estates into other hands. General Samuel Lewis and his sons still own and occupy a part of the large tract which belonged to Thomas Lewis, our common grandfather. He has removed from the house in which his father, Col. Charles Lewis, my mother, and himself were born, to a handsome brick edifice, which he has built about half a mile distant, on the first elevation from the Shenandoah towards the Blue Ridge Mountains. He has surrounded it with orchards and meadows. The view from the front portico takes in the course of the river, numerous fertile fields, and extended elevated mountains. When the painter's art does justice to the beautiful and sublime scenery of the romantic valley of the Shenandoah, this place will become celebrated as one of the most desirable in our country.

General Lewis married, when a youth, his cousin, a daughter of John Lewis, of Bath. His wife's mother had so many children, that she counted them at night when she put them to bed, to be certain that none of them had been eaten by the bears during the day. They numbered fifteen.

After the death of his first wife, General Lewis married Miss Lomax, the daughter of Judge Lomax. He has filled his house with children. One of his sons by his first wife has married a daughter of Daniel Sheffey, the great genius of Western Virginia.

General Lewis is a man of talent, education, and general information. He has represented Rockingham County in the Legislature, been for a long time a member of the County Court, and is now its President.

His tall person, marked features, florid complexion, ardent temper, and fearless spirit, prove him to be a true scion of the old Irish Lewis stock.

THE MATHEWS.

JOHN MATHEWS with many others of his countrymen, emigrated from Ireland to Western Virginia, about the year 1737, in pursuance of the advice of John Lewis, who had located himself some year before, in the neighborhood of Staunton. His son George was yet a youth, when he became familiar with danger, from constant contact with the wild beasts, and savage men of the forest. The Indians west of the Ohio River, the most warlike of all the aborigines of America, carried on a predatory and scalping warfare against the British colonies from 1754 to 1763. George Mathews was ever ready for any foray, in resisting, attacking, and pursuing them.

In 1761, a family not far from his father's residence was massacred. He and two or three youths, supposing from the firing that there was a shooting match at the place, went to join in the sport. Upon riding up, they saw dead bodies lying in the yard. Perceiving at once their mistake, they turned their horses and fled. The Indians rose from their concealment, and fired their rifles at them, as they passed in full speed. A ball grazed the head of George Mathews, so as to cut off his cue. Stimulated by the danger he had escaped, and the murder of his neighbors, he collected a party, put himself at their head, pursued the Indians, overtook them, and killed nine. At the great battle of the Point, he commanded a company, and contributed much by his bravery and military skill to the victory gained by the Virginians over the Indians. The fighting commenced at sunrise, and had continued until evening without any decided advantage; when Capt. Mathews, Capt. Shelby and Capt. Stuart, withdrew their companies from the fighting, out of sight of the combatants, got into the bed of Crooked Creek, then very low in water, and concealed by the banks, obtained a position in the rear of the Indians, from whence they attacked them so unexpectedly, that they succeeded in driving them across the Ohio.

Soon after the commencement of the Revolutionary war, George Mathews received substantial proofs of the high estimation in which he was held by his countrymen, for the efficient services he had rendered the frontier people. He was, in 1775, appointed Lieut. Colonel of the Ninth regiment of the Virginia troops; and was soon after, with his regiment, placed by Congress on the continental establishment. For near two years, he and his regiment were stationed on the Chesapeake Bay, under the command of Gen. Andrew Lewis. The malaria proved more destructive of the mountain men and their officers, than the rifles of the enemy.

Gen. Washington knew well the value of Col. Mathews as an officer; his own knowledge of war, having been principally acquired on the frontiers of Virginia, fighting Indians. When the contest with the mother country became a war for life and liberty, he ordered Col. Mathews to join the main army. Col. Mathews did good service at the battle of Brandywine. At the battle of Germantown, he attacked with his regiment, the British troops immediately opposed to him, pushed them triumphantly back, and had just captured them, when he and his command became so embarrassed by the density of the fog which enveloped the place, that in the confusion which followed, he was attacked, knocked down, and a bayonet driven through his body. He was made prisoner, sent to the British prison ship in the harbor of New York, where he was confined for a long time, and suffered cruelties and deprivations, which British officers never impose, except upon offending rebels. He appealed to his government for relief.

Mr. Jefferson, then governor of Virginia, wrote to him: "We know that the ardent spirit and hatred of tyranny which brought you into your present situation, will enable you to bear up against it, with the firmness which has distinguished you as a soldier, and to look forward with pleasure to the day, when events shall take place, against which the wounded spirits of your enemies will find no comfort, even from reflections on the most refined of the cruelties with which they have glutted themselves."

Col. Mathews was not exchanged, until near the termination of the war; when he joined the army under Gen. Greene as commander of the Third Virginia regiment. Whilst in the south, he purchased the Goosepond tract of land on Broad River. He removed to it with his family in 1784.

The high reputation acquired by Col. Mathews during the war, and the readiness with which he ever claimed what he was entitled to, made him at once the principal man in Georgia. He was elected Governor in 1786. He was the first representative of the people of Georgia, in the Congress of the United States, under the present Constitution. He was again Governor of Georgia in 1794-5. The policy adopted by the State, during and immediately after the revolutionary war, of encouraging emigration to it by grants of land gratis, excited among its people the greatest greediness for the acquisition of that kind of property. The State came to be considered but the agent for the distribution among them of what the people claimed to be theirs. Many schemes were devised, and attempted to be executed, for transferring the public domain to individuals, at a mere nominal price. Each defeat showed the gathering strength of the people's advocates. In 1795, a majority of the members of the Legislature were found favorable to the parting with its territory by the State in some way. The speculators of the day had been looking on, preparing means for seizing upon what they considered their proper prey. An act was passed by the Legislature, usually called the Yazoo fraud, for selling for five hundred thousand dollars to several companies, upwards of forty millions of acres in that part of the territory of Georgia, which now makes the States of Alabama and Mississippi. All the members of the Legislature who voted for the act, secured shares, or money, in the companies except one. The Governor had been opposed to all the previous schemes for disposing of the public land. It was with great difficulty that his consent was obtained to put his signature to the act for its sale. The morning after it was rumored that his scruples had been overcome, his secretary, Urquhart, endeavored to arrest his intended signature through his inherited Irish superstition. He dipped the pen which was used by the Governor into oil. Though startled by his pen obstinately refusing to make a mark, he was not thus to be deterred from his purpose. He directed his secretary to make another pen, with which he signed his approval. The bribery was noised abroad by rumor's hundred tongues. The disappointed in getting a share of the public land for little or nothing, united with the honest and patriotic in raising such a clamor of indignation as had never been heard before. Stout as the Governor's spirit was, he had to yield to the storm. He quitted Georgia, never afterwards to make it his home long at a time.

In 1811, runaway rogues and all sorts of lawless men got the upper hand of the old Spanish inhabitants in Florida. They called themselves patriots. Some one described them as having so strong a habit of appropriating what did not belong to them, that a patriot could scarcely turn his back, but his blanket was taken possession of by a brother in arms. They threw off the Spanish rule, declared themselves free, and put themselves under their own government. They petitioned the United States to make Florida one of its territories. Gen. Mathews was appointed by Mr. Madison, then President, Agent, to negotiate with the constituted authorities of Florida for the annexation of the country to the United States. The military leader of the patriots, who had shortly before disappeared from the upper part of Georgia without leave or license, and their civil head, Col. McIntosh, made a contract with Gen. Mathews, that Florida should be annexed to the United States. Gen. Mathews's treaty was strongly remonstrated against by the Spanish government, and finally disavowed by the President, as not having been made with the constituted authorities, according to the terms of Gen.

Mathews's instructions. This quibble upon the words, constituted authorities, was so unintelligible to Gen. Mathews's unbookish mind, and so entirely different from what he supposed to be the intention of the government from his conversations with its officers, that he became enraged beyond measure, and set off for Washington City to subject the President to personal chastisement; swearing that it was Mr. Madison's cowardly democratic fear of Spain and Great Britain, and not his Agent's doings, that occasioned his disavowal of what had been done; that he would expose to the world the whole affair. This high state of excitement, added to the fatigue and exposure which he had undergone in Florida, brought on a fever, whilst on his way to Washington City to thrash the President, of which he died in Augusta, Georgia, March, 1812.

General Mathews was a short, thick man, with stout legs, on which he stood very straight. He carried his head rather thrown back. His features were full and bluff; his hair, light red; and his complexion, fair and florid. His looks spoke out that he would not fear the devil, should he meet him face to face. He admitted no superior but Gen. Washington. He spoke of his services to the country as unsurpassed but by those of his great chief. He loved to talk of himself, and spoke as freely and encomiastically as enthusiastic youths do of Alexander and Caesar. His dress was in unison with his look and conversation. He wore a three-cornered cocked hat, fair top boots, a full ruffled shirt at the bosom and wrists, and occasionally a long sword at his side. Qualities were united in him which are never found in one person, except an Irishman. To listen to his talk about himself, his children, and his affairs, one might have thought he was but a puff of wind; trade with him, he was found to be one of the shrewdest of men; fight him, and he never failed to act the hero. He was unlearned. When he read it was always aloud, and with the confidence which accompanies the consciousness of doing a thing well. He pronounced fully the *l* in "would," "should," &c., &c., and *ed* at the termination of compound words with a long drawling accent. He spelled "coffee" Kaughphy. He wrote "congress" with a k. When

Governor, he dictated his messages to his secretary, and then sent them to James Mason Simmons, the Irish schoolmaster, to put them into grammar. His memory was unequalled. Whilst he was a Member of Congress, an important document, which had been read during the session, was lost. He was able to repeat its contents verbatim. Previous to the Revolutionary War, he was Sheriff of Augusta County, and had to collect the taxes from the inhabitants. He recollected for a long time the name of every taxpayer. His memory, and sharpness in trade, enabled him to make lucrative speculations in the most unusual way. He used to go from Philadelphia to Ohio with three or four horses for his capital in trade. He knew all the officers of the Revolutionary Army entitled to land in Ohio. He found that men would take a horse for an uncertain claim who would refuse to sell at all if money were offered, from the opinion that money, which was very scarce, would not be given but for what was known to be very valuable. He acquired a large estate in lands, principally by this kind of traffic. Mr. Adams, when President, nominated him to the Senate for Governor of the Mississippi Territory, and afterwards withdrew the nomination upon finding the opposition to his appointment very great. Mr. Adams's conduct coming to Gen. Mathews's knowledge, he immediately set off for Philadelphia, where Congress then assembled, to chastise the President. Upon his arrival in Philadelphia, he rode directly to Mr. Adams's house, hitched his horse, and went to the door, his revolutionary sword at his thigh, his three-cornered cocked hat on his head, and gave a thundering knock. Upon a servant opening it, he demanded to see the President. He was told that he was engaged. He said to the servant: "I presume your business is to carry messages to the President. Now, if you do not immediately inform him that a gentleman wishes to spake to him, your head shall answer the consequences." The servant bowed, retired, and informed the President that a very strange old fellow, who called himself General Mathews, wished to see him, and would take no denial. Mr. Adams directed that he should be admitted. Upon entering the room where the President was, he said: "I presume you are Mr. Adams, President of these United

States. My name is Mathews, sometimes called Gov. Mathews; well known at the battle of Garmantown as Col. Mathews, of the Virginia line. Now, Sar, I understand that you nominated me to the Senate of these United States to be Governor of the Massassappa Tarràtory, and that afterwards you took back the nomination. Sar, if you had known me, you would not have taken the nomination back. If you did not know me, you should not have nominated me to so important an office. Now, Sar, unless you can satisfy me, your station of President of these United States shall not screen you from my vangance." Mr. Adams accordingly set about satisfying him, which he did with the more good will on account of the General being a stanch federalist. Upon inquiring after Gen. Mathews's sons, and receiving a most laudatory description of them, he promised to appoint John supervisor of the public revenue in Georgia. Upon which the General expressed himself content, saying: "My son John is a man of about my inches, with the advantage of a labral education, and for his intagrity I pledge my head."

The first business before the Legislature of 1785-6, after its organization, was to determine whether Governor Mathews was to be considered in office. Whilst engaged in the discussion, the Clerk of the House went into the Executive office. The Governor accosted him, saying: "What are those fellows about that they do not let me know that they are organized and ready to receive my message?" The Clerk told him that the members were discussing the question whether he was constitutionally Governor. "By the Atarnal," he exclaimed, "if they don't, I will cut an avanue from this office through them."

General Mathews married Miss Woods, of Albemarle County, the half-sister of Col. John Stuart, of Greenbrier.

After her death, he married Mrs. Reed, of Staunton. A year or two afterwards Mrs. Matthews, accompanied by two of her husband's daughters by his first wife, visited his and her relations and friends in Virginia. When the time had passed allowed for her visit, she wrote to her husband to come or send for her. He answered that she had gone without him, and might return in the same way. She replied that she would not again travel so far without his protection. The case was referred to the legislature. A divorce was granted, though he and his wife had never quarrelled, had parted in kindness, and had no intention at the time of continuing to live apart. He married for his third wife Mrs. Flowers of Mississippi. Though he married three wives, he cared too much for himself to be very devoted to either of them. Most of his time was passed from home, in the service of the public or in busy speculation.

General Mathews' residence on Broad River was in a cabin of small logs, with the sides scalped off, the openings between them chinked with puncheons, and daubed with red mud. It had one room and an entry, through which there was a way upstairs, where the young ladies slept. His sons occupied round log, upscalped, clapboard cabins in the yard. These cabins were made to accommodate the family until the Governor left Georgia, his son George went to Mississippi, and Col. Charles was about to marry Miss Lucy Early, the sister of Gov. Early, when they gave place to a fine house.

"At Brandywine and Germantown,
　His flowing blood from many a wound,
　　His country's freedom seal'd;
He's gone—but left his glorious name
　Engraved on the rolls of fame,
　　In council and in field."

John Mathews, the oldest son of Gen. Mathews, whilst employed in learning Latin and Greek at an academy in Western Virginia, fell in love with a pretty cousin and married her. He returned to Georgia, and was authorized by an Act of the Legislature, to practice law. There was some peculiarity in the Mathewes which prevented their success at the bar. Many tried; not one ever succeeded. They were either too proud, too passionate, or too much devoted to other pursuits, to secure the confidence of those who wanted the aid of lawyers. John Mathews, getting along rather badly at the bar, procured, through his father, from President Adams, the office of supervisor of the revenue. The cousin whom he married, though a very pretty woman, did not prove a very good helpmate. They had a large family of children.

They, as the children of cousins are apt to do, showed that those who are so near akin ought not to marry if they can do otherwise; that crossing the breed is as important for man as other animals.

William Mathews, second son of Gen. Mathews, married Elizabeth Meriwether, daughter of Mr. Frank Meriwether, an exceedingly clever woman, as she proved in her after life by the admirable manner in which she discharged all the duties of wife, mother, friend, and relative. William Mathews never studied Latin or Greek, was a planter and succeeded very well. He never held any office higher than captain of the militia of his district, and that was forced upon him, rather than sought for. Militia musters were great bores to many of the Broad River people. It was a subject of long contest in the company, which included most of them, whether much mustering or no mustering should be done. Upon vacancy occurring in the captaincy, the musterers and anti-musterers had a trial of strength. The musterers put up William Mathews for their candidate, supposing that his father's great fame in war would enable him to put down opposition. The anti-musterers showed their thorough contempt of the practice of taking men from their useful employments, to be made to stand in the sun, run about the old fields, and get drunk, by putting up in opposition a mulatto free negro. The most active and noisy electioneering was carried on by the parties. The result is not recollected. I am inclined to think that the negro got the most votes, but that the Governor commissioned William Mathews, upon a decision that a negro could not hold a commission from the State. William Mathews survived the contest but a short time.

I was the innocent cause of the final triumph of the anti-musterers. A poor young fellow, by the name of Mar, of the Goolsby gang, performed a tour of militia duty during the war with Great Britain. He got to be sergeant, and acquired a great spirit of parade. Soon after the close of the war, he was rewarded for what he had done by being elected Captain. I was at my father's at the time, in very bad health. Captain Mar applied to me for the use of my sword. I gave him my coat and epaulettes. Mar had never been fine before. He showed off to the company by mustering the men to death. Once on a hot summer day, being a little lame, he mounted a horse, and carried the company through all Steuben and Duane's evolutions. An insurrection broke out the next muster day. The company resolved that Captain Mar was a nuisance, and militia mustering all humbuggery. Mar's command ceased. From that time until now, the Broad River people have refused to elect any one captain who would have made them muster.

William Mathews lived at the Goosepond until his death. His family soon after removed to the plantation which had been owned by General Blackburn, in Elbert County.

George Mathews, third son of General Mathews, was a man of talent and literary taste. He was a lawyer, but loved his ease better than practice, and so got none. He resided for many years with his brother William, and afterwards with his brother Charles, at the Goosepond. He was appointed by the President Judge of the Mississippi Territory. He married soon after Miss Flowers, the daughter of his father's last wife. He afterwards removed to Louisiana, and became one of the Judges of the Supreme Court of that State. He loved good eating and drinking, became fat, and died long before he arrived at his threescore years and ten. He was very moderate in his expenditures, and died very wealthy. His daughter is married to Major Chase, of the United States Army. During the summer of 1823, my wife and myself were seated for several days at dinner opposite to Major Chase, his wife and little daughter, in the Astor House, New York. I had never seen either of them, and yet there was something about Mrs. Chase and her child that constantly drew my eyes to them. I met with Major Chase and his family afterwards in Washington City. I made their acquaintance, and found out that the attraction was the resemblance of Mrs. Chase and her little daughter to Judge Mathews, whose appearance continued impressed upon my memory, though I had not seen him for fifty years.

Charles Lewis Mathews, youngest son of General Mathews, was a man of good understanding, well improved. His temper was sociable, and his character honorable. I was but a boy when he returned to Georgia from Virginia, where he had been at school and college. There was a large party of neighbors enjoying a Christmas frolic at my father's, given upon his removing into a new frame-house from the old log structure. The young people were all excitement, dancing in one room, and the old drinking and playing whist in another. Politics was then a very exciting subject of conversation. The contest between Mr. Jefferson and Mr. Adams had set the whole country into a blaze. The Yazoo affair still added fuel to the flames. Charles Mathews, William Barnett, and two others were playing. William Barnett, who was a very active politician of the Democratic party, said something disparaging of the Federalists and Yazooites. The Irish blood of Charles Mathews was immediately in full gallop. He swore an oath, and made at Barnett. Their partners kept them apart. Every one present became agitated, and most talked as fast as they would have fought. Dancing and whist stopped, and all was hubbub. Charles Mathews was my mother's kin, and William Barnett my father's. Charles Mathews found himself without backers. No one thought with him, or felt with him, except my mother. The McGehees wanted, as they said, to thrash Federalism out of him. The next day brought talks about challenges. The quarrel gradually subsided into a fixed dislike between the Mathewes and McGehees.

Charles Mathews married Lucy Early, the sister of Gov. Peter Early. He owned and lived at the Goosepond until his wife's death. Some years after he removed to Alabama, and settled near Cahaba, where he died in 184(—), one of the wealthiest planters in the United States.

Anne Mathews, oldest daughter of Gen. Mathews, married Samuel Blackburn, who was of Irish descent, if not an Irishman. He was a classical scholar, and for some time after his removal to Georgia, principal teacher of the academy in Washington, Wilks county. Whilst thus employed he prepared himself for the practice of the law. After his marriage, he settled in Elbert County, on Broad River, where he commenced the life of a lawyer. He was advancing successfully in his profession and political influence, when the Legislature met in 1795. He was a member. His conduct in relation to the Yazoo Act, was such as to excite suspicion that he held with the hare whilst he ran with the dogs. Though he voted against the act, it was alleged that he spoke for it, and would have voted the same way if it could not have otherwise passed, and that his voting against it was done by consent of the speculators, to save the Governor, his father-in-law, from suspicion of being concerned in the purchase. The allegations against the integrity of General Blackburn were founded upon the most trivial circumstances. They were, however, so noised abroad among his constituents, that he quitted Georgia, and settled in Staunton, Virginia, and afterwards upon his plantation, called the Wilderness, in Bath County. He several times represented Bath County in the Virginia Legislature. His fine voice, expressive features, noble person, perfect self-possession, keen wit, and forcible language, directed by a well-cultivated and powerful intellect, made him one of the most eloquent men of his time. He was a Federalist in politics. His abusive denunciations of the Republicans, when he was a member of the Virginia Legislature, made him long remembered by the parties of the State.

In 1812, I met with him at the Warm Springs, where he was attending the session of the County Court at Bath. I left the Springs in his company, to pass a few days at his house, where Mrs. Charles Mathews, my neighbor in Georgia, then was. He was excited by drinking, and poured forth as we travelled along the most violent philippic against my friends and relations on Broad River, for their suspicions of his integrity. We did not reach his house the evening that we left the Springs. The next day he was sober and sufficiently respectful in his conduct to enable me to make the visit to his family with great pleasure.

I afterwards met with him at Rockingham Court, and heard him defend with great power a criminal, eighty years old, who had, when in the poor-house of the county, killed a beggar like himself, of about the same age, in a fight about a cucumber. The witness to prove the facts was ninety. Such a trial, of such a criminal, for such an offence, proved by such a witness, and advocated by such a lawyer, made a strong impression upon my memory. He and my oldest brother met at Major Grattan's, as he was going to Rockingham Court. They both drank very freely. The presence of Georgians made General Blackburn feel the old sore. He charged Col. Taliaferro with setting afloat the rumor which had driven him from Georgia, and began to abuse him. My brother's wife was Col. Taliaferro's niece. Naturally waspish, the whiskey which he and the general had been taking together, made his temper ungovernable. They fell to fighting.

THE MERIWETHERS.

DURING the persecution of the people of Wales in the time of Charles the Second, three brothers, Nicholas, William, and David Meriwether, all young unmarried men, avoided the oppression of the government by emigrating to the colony of Virginia. The Meriwethers were too frank and sincere to be formalists, and too sensible to be bigoted, and were, therefore, neither Roman Catholics nor Episcopalians in Wales, nor conformists to the government church in the colony of Virginia. As long as religion was forced upon them, they seemed to be infidels. When the revolution permitted every one to worship God according to the dictates of his own conscience, many of them became distinguished for piety. They brought more wealth with them to Virginia than was usual for emigrants in the seventeenth century. Most of them were peculiar in manners and habits; low and stout in stature, with round heads, dark complexion, and bright hazel eyes. They were very industrious and economical, and yet ever ready to serve the sick, and those who needed their assistance. They were too proud to be vain. They looked to their own thoughts and conduct rather than to what others might be thinking of them. The stock must have come from some singular union. Their long intermixture with other families has not yet deprived them of their uniqueness. No one ever looked at, or talked with one of them, but he heard or saw something which made him listen, or look again. They were slow in forming opinions, and obstinate in adhering to them. They were very knowing. But their investigations were minute and accurate rather than speculative and profound. Mr. Jefferson said of Col. Nicholas Meriwether, that he was the most sensible man he ever knew; and William H. Crawford made the same remark of Mr. Frank Meriwether.

David Meriwether, the Welshman, had one child, who married, and died without descendants.

William Meriwether, David's brother, had one daughter, who married ——— Skelton. From them descended Meriwether Jones, of Richmond, celebrated as a political writer fifty years ago; Gen. Walter Jones, the distinguished lawyer, of Washington City; Gen. Roger Jones, of the regular army; and Commodore Catesby Jones, of the navy, whose son was lately wounded by the cannonade upon the people in the streets of Paris, devilishly ordered by Louis Napoleon Bonaparte.

Nicholas, the Welshman, married Elizabeth, the daughter of David Crawford, of New Kent County. Most, if not all, in the United States who are called Meriwether are descended from them. They had two sons, William and David, and several daughters.

William's children were John, Thomas, Richard, Jane, Sarah and Mary.

David's children were Nicholas, Francis, James and William.

Jane, daughter of Nicholas the elder, married Robert Lewis. From them descended most of the Lewises of Virginia, Georgia, and Kentucky, who are not descended from the Irishman, John Lewis, my great-grandfather. Another daughter of Nicholas married ——— Johnson, whose descendant, Chapman Johnson, was the most eminent of the lawyers of Virginia. Another daughter married ——— Littlepage, of a highly respectable family.

Nicholas Meriwether died at a very advanced age, in 1774, having outlived all his children. He acquired very great wealth, which he distributed among his grandchildren and great-grandchildren. He owned many fine horses, some plate, a great many negroes, and several tracts of land, one of which contained 17,952 acres.

One of Nicholas Meriwether's great-granddaughters married Col. Syme, a travelled gentleman of rank and fortune, whose name is still freshly remembered from the delicious, tender, white-rinded, red-pulped watermelon which he brought to this country from the islands of the Mediterranean. Col. Syme's widow married Dr. Thomas Walker, the grandfather of Mrs. W. C. Rives. Another of Nicholas Meriwether's great-granddaughters married Maj. Hughs of the neighborhood of Louisville, Kentucky. She had twenty-six children, fourteen of whom arrived at maturity, who have stocked the western country with Meriwether descendants by doing as their progenitress did.

Nicholas Meriwether's grandson, Col. James Meriwether, the son of David, married Judith Burnly. From them descended Gen. David Meriwether of Georgia, who married Miss Wingfield, the sister of Mrs. Hope Hull. He was distinguished for plain dress, probity, and sound sense. He was a meritorious officer in the army of the revolution. After the close of the war he removed from Virginia to Georgia. He was often a member of the Legislature, several times a member of Congress, and performed important public service by the skill and success with which he treated with the Creeks and Cherokees for the relinquishment of their occupant right to the territory of the State.

John, his oldest son, married young and removed to Alabama.

James, his second son, was a graduate of Franklin College; one of its trustees; captain of a company under Gen. Floyd in the expedition against the Creeks in 1813-14; a Commissioner to hold treaties with the Creeks and Cherokees, and a member of Congress. He removed to Tennessee, and settled near Memphis, where he died.

Dr. William, Gen. Meriwether's third son, was a graduate of Franklin College. Finding himself, after trial, unable, from feeble health, to undergo the fatigue of medical practice, he studied law, and was admitted to the bar. His consumptive constitution alone prevented great success in his new profession. He married Miss Sarah Molloy, and died in the prime of life, leaving his excellent wife a widow, and two promising children. His daughter, a very clever young lady, died young and unmarried. His son has married Bishop Andrews' daughter.

Gen. Meriwether's only daughter married the Rev. Mr. Henning, a Methodist preacher, and very successful planter.

His sons Frank, George, and David removed to Alabama and Tennessee before they were old enough to have performed any distinguished public service in Georgia.

Nicholas Meriwether's grandson Francis, the son of David, married the sister of John Lewis, the son-in-law of Gabriel Jones, the great lawyer of the valley of Virginia. He removed to South Carolina, where he left a large family.

David, another son of David, married Miss Weaver in England. His brother James volunteered at the commencement of the revolution, when a youth of seventeen. He continued to serve to the end of the war with great distinction, first as a militiaman, in what was called the silk-stocking company of Richmond, and afterwards as captain in the Virginia Continental line. Whilst serving in the Southern States, he was associated with the gallant Col. William Washington, and formed an intimate friendship with him. At the close of the war, he settled in Georgia, where he married Miss Susan Hatcher. He was Secretary of the Executive Department, Comptroller General, and held other offices of high trust continuously for twenty years. He had two sons, Alexander, now "Ordinary" of Dooly County, and James, who was a man of education, talent, and integrity; Judge of the Superior Court, a member of Congress, frequently a member of the Legislature, and more than once Speaker of the House of Representatives. One of his daughters married Col. Thomas M. Berrien, brother of Senator John M. Berrien; one Dr. Robins, and another Mr. Patterson, who had two daughters;; one married Eleazer Early, the brother of Gov. Peter Early; and the other Daniel Sturges, Surveyor General of Georgia.

Thomas Meriwether, the grandson of Nicholas, the Welshman, and son of William, was a man of excellent character, and great wealth. He married Elizabeth Thornton, who belonged to one of the most respectable of the untitled families of England. Her sister, Mildred married Samuel Washington, brother of Gen. George Washington. Thomas Meriwether had ten children. His rank in society may be estimated by his intimate friends, the executors of his will. They were Col. Joshua Fry, Peter Jefferson, Dr. Thomas Walker, and Col. John Thornton. Col. Fry was the brother-in-law of Dr. George Gilmer. He was Colonel Commandant of the first Virginia troops raised to act against the French and Indians in the war of 1756-63, usually known in Virginia as Braddock's. George Washington was his Lieutenant-Colonel, and succeeded, upon his death, to his command. Peter Jefferson, was the father of President Jefferson. Dr. Thomas Walker was the brother-in-law of Dr. George Gilmer, and grandfather of Mrs. Rives, wife of the American Minister at Paris; Commissioner with Thomas Lewis to hold treaties with the western Indians, after their defeat at the Point, and Commissioner to run the line between Virginia and North Carolina. He performed other public services, and was distinguished for his wealth and virtues. Col. Thornton was a brother of Mrs. Meriwether.

Nicholas, the oldest son of Thomas Meriwether, was brave in danger and self-possessed in the most difficult situations. He was one of the four Americans who bore the wounded Braddock from the field of battle at his disastrous defeat. A gold-laced, embroidered coat sent him from Ireland, by Gen. Braddock's sister, remained for a long time a curiosity in his plain household. He once descended a nearly perpendicular precipice of the Humpback Mountain by the use of his fingers and toes, and drank water which issued from its side, whilst his brother Frank tremblingly looked on, expecting him to be dashed to pieces on the rocks below, imagining that nobody would believe him when he told what his sensible brother had done. His wife, Margaret Douglas, was the sister of Parson Douglas, a learned Scotchman, and distinguished in the annals of Albemarle County as one of its most remarkable men. Mrs. Meriwether never lost the consciousness that she was descended from the most chivalrous of the gallant men of the old world. Their son Charles was a very handsome, accomplished man. He perfected his medical education by attending the College of

Physicians at Edinburgh. He removed to Tennessee, where he married and left a family of children. William Douglas, another son, continued to live at Meriwether's place until he died, upwards of eighty years old. He had the characteristics of the Meriwethers; simplicity of manners and dress, truth and honesty.

Frank Meriwether, the second son of Thomas Meriwether, attended William and Mary College. He studied medicine for some time afterwards. The war between France and England prevented his going to Edinburgh. He therefore declined practising professionally. He married Martha Jamieson, the sister of Colonel Jamieson, of the Virginia Continental line. He removed to Georgia in 1784-5. Within the circle of his acquaintances, he was thought the best man in the world. The first settlers of upper Georgia suffered very much from sickness. He laid out a portion of the proceeds of his crop every year in medicines, and devoted as much of his time as was called for in attending upon the sick without charge. The equanimity of his temper, kindness of heart, and clearness of understanding, enabled him to do in the best manner all that duty and benevolence required of him. He had no pride or vanity. His house was the collecting-place for the poor and ignorant, the rich and learned. He made himself equally acceptable to every one. His truth and integrity were so obvious in his countenance, and in all that he said and did, that no one ever questioned either. He once sold a horse he had to spare to a neighbor who wanted one. His son, Thomas, coming up after the sale was completed, by the payment of the price, asked his father what he had received for the horse. He answered, seventy dollars. "Why," says Tom, "I do not think, father, that the horse is worth more than sixty." "Well, son, if you think so, I am not willing to take more"—and returned ten to the purchaser. This was a sample of the conduct of his whole life. His wife seemed to think that if there was not more stir in the family than her husband made, all would go to the dogs. She was constantly in a state of restless anxiety. Her face was drawn to a pucker by the smallpox, which she caught when the British Army scattered it through Virginia. She was constantly afraid that the boys would be shot when hunting, or drowned when fishing. A stranger riding up to the house one day, and hearing her crying, Where is Val? Where is Nick? was greatly distressed, imagining that the Indians might have carried off some of the children, and was amusingly relieved upon finding that her alarm was about two grown sons, who had not returned to the house at the usual time.

The intermixture of the inherited qualities of the children of Frank Meriwether and his wife was very striking. Tom, the oldest, had his father's aptitude for knowledge, truthfulness, and integrity, and his mother's restless, uneasy disposition. He was very industrious and economical. He built his own house and chimneys, and made and mended his farming tools. He was a militia soldier in the revolutionary war. When he was old, he loved to tell how he served under the Marquis La Fayette;—how that great general and good man selected him from all his army, as its best rifleman, to fire upon Cornwallis's lookout at an important place of observation; and how, after his fire, the soldier disappeared: and then a twinge could be seen in his face, as if he felt that a human being might have died by his hand. Though brave, he was near fainting in the ranks, upon seeing a wounded soldier pass by on a white horse, showing very plainly the trickling blood as it flowed from a mortal wound. He was once in a skirmish, when the detachment to which he belonged was obliged by superior force to fly. He refused to run until he got into woods close by, where he could run without being seen by the British. The only fear he seemed sensible of, was the fear of doing wrong. His scrupulousness subjected him to many difficulties. He would not administer upon estates, nor perform the duties of a justice of the peace, lest he might not do exactly what the official oath required.

He was so modest and diffident when young, that he found it difficult to address any young lady upon the subject of marriage. Yet he was constantly in love. Rebekah Mathews, the daughter of Governor Mathews, had the shrewdness to divine his wishes, when she became the object of his devotion, and said yes, whilst the question was sticking in his throat. His worth was not set off by fine clothes, nor very polished manners. He put on a cloth coat when he married the Governor's daughter. It was the first and the last time that he ever wore any thing which looked like finery. He worked with his own hands very industriously from early youth to his death. He commenced life with two or three negroes and a small tract of land. He died worth sixty thousand dollars. He never speculated, was exceedingly social and kind in temper, and ardent in feelings. He talked with enthusiasm about all things in which he took an interest, and especially of politics. He was a Federalist, and idolized General Washington as the ancients used to do their deceased great men, whom they made gods of. He hated Mr. Jefferson with a perfect hatred. His Fourth of July toast was, Jefferson, Madison, and the Devil, a trio of similar character and common purposes. He and his brother-in-law, William Barnett, the member of Congress, attended the sale of James Olive's property, their brother-in-law. Among other things, they bought a bed for Olive's wife. William Barnett, the leading democrat of the country, sent for a negro to carry the bed to Olive's dwelling. Tom Meriwether took the bed upon his own shoulders, and carried it, to show how much of pretence there was in the assertions of the Democrats that pride was monopolized by the Federalists.

He valued knowledge very much, but was too constantly employed in labor, and the performance of social and domestic duties, to become very learned. What he read he understood well and relished greatly. He was familiar with the rudiments of geography, history, mathematics, and astronomy. His kindness was only limited by the extent of his capacity to relieve those who stood in need of his services. He never knew any one in sickness or difficulty whom he did not assist if he could.

Iin old times, when the Georgia settlements were new, tobacco was the staple production of the State. The roads were very bad. It was difficult for the planters to get their crops to market. Tom Meriwether was usually delayed with his, by the time which he gave to others, in aiding them to get their wagons and rolling hogsheads out of the mud and up the hills. He had the greatest reverence for truth, and never violated its spirit, knowingly, in the least. A man who never prevaricated, was always dressed in the oddest fashion, wore a long cue, and talked enthusiastically, was an oddity in society, and could not mingle freely with it. He was therefore almost unknown, except to his kin and neighbors. No one ever followed with more constancy the golden rule of doing unto others as you would they should do unto you. He was an affectionate father, obliging neighbor, and kind master. He took great pleasure in giving delight to children, shooting and hunting with them when they desired him. His love for his wife was without intermission, and extended to the extent of his loving nature. His gallantry equalled his love. When she tired of sleeping on one side, and turned on the other, he alway crossed over, if awake, that they might be ever face to face. Only one time in his life did he put any constraint upon her. They were attending preaching at a camp-meeting, where there was great religious excitement. It was Sunday, and the altar before the stand for the preachers became filled with shouting converts and devoted believers. Mrs. Meriwether looked upon their glowing, happy faces, until she began to sympathize with them. Tom Meriwether became alarmed, lest his wife's love might be drawn away from him, and placed upon what he took no interest in. He seized her arm, and led her forcibly away. His matter-of-fact, demonstrative mind, was unable to arrive at truth through the imagination.

Col. Fleming Jordan, Dr. David Reese, Dr. George Meriwether, and David Meriwether, Tom Meriwether's sons and sons-in-law, settled in Jasper County. Tom Meriwether's affectionate temper could not bear the separation from his children. He and his wife left their happy home to follow after them. When Mrs. Meriwether died, he distributed his property among his descendants, reserving for himself only a small tract of land, and two old faithful negroes; where and with whom he labored day by day, never forgetting for a moment the absence of her who had been by his side for more than forty years.

Ann, Tom Meriwether's oldest child, married Col. Fleming Jordan, now of Jasper. She was the most industrious of housekeepers, and yet found time to visit all the sick and suffering about her, and to do for them whatever her kindness and medical skill suggested.

Frank, Tom Meriwether's oldest son, married Miss Butler.

Dr. George, his second son, married, first, Miss Jordan, a sister of Col. F. Jordan, and after her death, Miss Watkins, a niece of Governor Early.

Mary, his second daughter, married Dr. Reese, who has been for a long time a trustee of Franklin College, frequently a member of the Legislature, and is now a member of Congress. He is a man of kind temper, good sense, and excellent character.

David, the youngest son of Tom Meriwether, was one of the electors of President and Vice-President in 1840, has married his fourth wife, and is one of the wealthy planters of Georgia. He is a man of industry, truth and probity.

Valentine, the second son of Frank Meriwether, married Barbara Cosby. He has been at all times exceedingly industrious and economical, and is as remarkable for his skill and success in planting, as his father and brother Nick for doctoring diseases. He is so careful in selecting seed, tending, picking, and ginning his crops, that a sample of his cotton has been kept for many years in New York, as the test by which to determine the quality of other cotton. His, and his son Frank's crops of the year 1851 sold, in the Augusta market, the best up-country market in the United States, half a cent for the pound higher than any other crops. Valentine Meriwether has his mother's anxious temper. He is often alarmed lest his family should starve, though his corn cribs are always the fullest in his neighborhood.

Nick, the third son of Frank Meriwether, has his father's kindness and constitutional aptness for understanding and curing diseases. He devoted his time, day and night for several years, attending the sick without pay, until his friends prevailed upon him to take a doctor's degree, and practice as a professional physician.

Mary, Frank Meriwether's oldest daughter, married William Barnett. She was so devotedly attached to her husband, that upon being informed that his recovery from the sickness then afflicting him was hopeless, became frantic and died.

Mildred, the second daughter of Frank Meriwether, married Joel Barnett, the brother of William.

Elizabeth, the third daughter, married William Mathews, son of Governor Mathews.

Lucy married Groves Howard.

Margaret, Dr. John Bradley.

Nancy, William Glenn; and

Sarah, James Olive. James Olive was very apt at acquiring knowledge. He used to say that much more credit was given to General Washington than he was entitled to, and that he could himself have done much greater things if he had had the same advantages, though he never did anything of the least value with those which he had.

David Meriwether, the third son of Thomas, and brother of Frank, was a very quiet, upright man. He sold his plantation in Amherst, Virginia, now worth forty or fifty thousand dollars, to follow his kinsfolk to Georgia, where he bought land worth now less than one thousand dollars. He married Mary Harvie, a very sensible, good woman, and one of the best of wives. She was so fat when old, that she seldom left the house. Her husband was usually found by her side. She weighed between three and four hundred and was tall in proportion. He was low in stature and weighed about one hundred and twenty. Her seat was a broad split-bottom chair. When she rose, she put each hand upon the opposite knobs and ascended so gradually, and for so long time, that she looked as if she would never stop. They had but one child, a daughter, who was beautiful, sprightly and intelligent. She married Col. Benjamin Taliaferro.

Thomas Meriwether's daughter, Mildred, married John Gilmer.

Mary married Peachy Ridgway Gilmer.

Elizabeth married Thomas Johnson, of Louisa, Virginia, called Sheriff Tom. They had a large family of children. Nicholas, the oldest, moved to Georgia. David, Frank and Tom, married and continued to live in Virginia until their deaths. Each of them had a family of children. They were social and respectable men. I knew them so slightly that I am unable to give any particulars of their lives.

Mr. and Mrs. Johnson's daughter, Lucy, married William Quarles. They were exceedingly industrious and economical. Having no children, they worked, saved and accumulated, until they were worth two hundred thousand dollars.

Mrs. Quarles had such an abhorrence of dirt, that the little left by the feet of their few visitors annoyed her very much. She kept the fences about her house, and to the far gate in front, whitewashed. The little negroes were usually employed in picking up straws, twigs and feathers. William Quarles was devoted to his wife. He died first, and left her all his estate, except some small legacies to his own relations at her request. Fifty thousand dollars of his estate was in United States Bank stock, and prized so highly by her that she continued to hold on to it until it became valueless.

Mary Johnson married Harry Winston, and Rebekah, Joseph Winston. No particulars are known of them, except that one had a large family of very pretty daughters. I passed a day with them when I was nineteen.

Elizabeth married the Rev. John Poindexter. Their nephew, George Poindexter, Governor of the State of Mississippi and its Senator in Congress, was nurtured and educated by them.

Sally married Richard Overton. They lived on the side of Monticello, and high enough to command a beautiful view of the country about Charlottesville. Mrs. Overton was a cheerful, chatty, stirring woman, as she was entitled to be by inheritance from her Meriwether mother. Mr. Overton lolled about the house more than he attended to business. They moved to Tennessee.

Mr. and Mrs. Johnson's daughter, Nancy, married Charles Barret.

Sally Meriwether, daughter of Thomas and sister of Frank, married Michael Anderson. Their children were Thomas, Reuben, Pouncey, Richard and Nancy, who married Edmund Thompson.

Nancy Meriwether, another daughter of Thomas, married Richard Anderson. Their children were Jasper, Nicholas (who moved to Kentucky), David, Elizabeth (who married Waddy Thompson), Sarah, who married William Clark (who moved to Kentucky), Cicely, who married, first Mr. Watson, and afterwards Dr. Lewis Carr, and removed to Kentucky.

Many of the descendants of Sally and Nancy Meriwether have been distinguished for wealth and worth, but the knowledge of them is too indistinct to be written about.

Lucy Meriwether, another daughter of Thomas, married William Lewis, and after his death, John Marks, each a distinguished officer in the revolutionary army. Her person was perfect and her activity beyond her sex. She was sincere, truthful, industrious, and kind without limit. She removed from Virginia to Georgia with her second husband, along with her brother Frank and other relatives. Soon after her husband's death she returned to Virginia, and resided at the place where she had lived with her first husband about seven miles west of Charlottesville, on an elevation of the southwest mountains. There she continued to reside to a very old age, serving every body whom she could, who stood in need of her assistance.

Meriwether Lewis, Mrs. Marks's oldest son by her first husband, inherited the energy, courage, activity, and good understanding of his admirable mother. He acquired in youth hardy habits and a firm constitution. He possessed in the highest degree self-possession in danger, the great quality of great generals.

From 1790 to 1795, the Cherokee Indians were very troublesome to the frontier people of upper Georgia; stealing their negroes and horses; occasionally killing defenceless women and children, and exciting alarm lest more extensive mischief might be perpetrated. During the restless, uneasy state of the people, created by the constant apprehension of attack, a report reached the Virginia settlement on Broad River, that the Cherokees were on the war path for Georgia. Men, women and children collected together. It was agreed that the house where they were could not be defended, and might easily be burnt. They, therefore, sought safety in a deep secluded forest. Whilst they were assembled round a fire at night, preparing something to eat, the report of a gun was heard. Indians! Indians! was heard from every tongue. Mothers clasped their infants in their arms, whilst the older children hung around them. The men seized their guns—all were in commotion and dismay. There belonged to the company a boy, who alone retained self-possession. When every one was hesitating what to do, the light of the fire was suddenly extinguished by his throwing a vessel of water upon it. When all was dark, the sense of safety came upon every one. That boy was Meriwether Lewis. When he arrived at maturity his love of action and enterprising spirit led him into the regular army. He was the private secretary of President Jefferson, when the government determined to have the territory of Louisiana explored, which had shortly before been purchased of France. His known intrepidity and habit of perseverance in the execution of his determinations, pointed him out as the fittest person to head an expedition for that purpose. By the permission of Mr. Jefferson he selected for his aid and companion his friend Capt. Clark of the army. He passed from St. Louis, through difficulties which few men would have undertaken, and still fewer could have overcome; and acquired for his country by the possession which he took of the Pacific coast, the title which was acknowledged to be the best to the Oregon Territory in the late controversy with Great Britain. In his expedition to the Pacific he discovered a gold mine. The fact was not made public, nor the place pointed out at the time, lest it might become known to the Indians and Spaniards, and thereby be a public injury instead of a public benefit. He informed his friends, upon his return home, of the discovery which he had made, and his intention of making out such a description of the place that it might be found if he should die before the information could be made useful to the country. As he was travelling from St. Louis, the seat of government of the Missouri Territory, of which he was then Governor, to Washington City, he stopped for the night at a little inn on the roadside, somewhere in Tennessee. In the morning his throat was found cut, and he dead; whether by his own hand, or others in search of his account of the place where gold was to be found, is not certainly known.

Reuben Lewis, the second son of Mrs. Marks, was too irritable and impatient tempered to be very successful in seeking public distinction. He was Indian Agent in the far West for a while. He married his first cousin, Mildred Dabney, a very estimable woman. They had no children.

Jane, Mrs. Mark's only daughter by her first husband, was a very worthy woman. She married her first cousin, Edmund Anderson, whose drunken, spendthrift habits brought his family to poverty.

Mrs. Marks had two children by her second husband.

Her son, Dr. John Marks, was very intellectual, but so defectively organized that he went deranged, and died in a lunatic asylum. Her daughter Mary married William Moore, a man of fortune, the son of Mr. and Mrs. William Moore, of Broad River, and adopted son of Mrs. Davenport, his aunt.

Jane, the youngest daughter of Thomas Meriwether, was very pretty, very rich, and very much courted. Going through a forest, searching for a stick, it is so difficult to find one perfectly straight and free from knots, that a crooked one is taken from necessity as the outskirts are left. Jane married Samuel Dabney. The cleverness of their mother has been shown in the talents and success of her children. They were William, Samuel, Thomas, Frank, Elizabeth, George, Charles, Richard, Edmund, John, and Mildred. Richard was the most intellectual poet of Virginia. He was so severely burnt in the Richmond theatre, in the winter of 1811-12, that he never recovered. Frank was a captain in the regular army in the last war with Great Britain. Charles married Elizabeth Price, of Hanover. Mildred married her cousin, Reuben Lewis. Edmund and John married Ann and Eliza Blount, the near kinswomen of Governor Blount of Tennessee.

THE BIBBS.

Miss Sally Wyatt was a native of Charlotte County, Virginia. Her brother, Joseph Wyatt, represented, in the Senate of Virginia, for more than twenty years, a part of Mr.

John Randolph's congressional district. Sally Wyatt, and a cousin of the same name, married, at the same time, two cousins by the name of Bibb. Both the ladies were talented and aspiring. The first-born of each was a son. Mrs. Sally Bibb and her husband moved to Georgia. Her cousin and her husband to Kentucky. In their after-correspondence each of the ladies dwelt with great delight on the beauty and promising genius of her son, predicting that he would, before he died, be President of the United States.

Mrs. Sally Bibb's son was afterwards well known as Dr. William Wyatt Bibb, of Georgia; her cousin's as Mr. George Bibb of Kentucky. Each for a long time showed by his rapid strides ahead of others, that he might be the foremost man of his country in the race for office. William Wyatt Bibb acquired his professional education at the Medical School in Philadelphia, then decidedly the best in the United States, where he graduated with distinguished reputation. He located himself in the town of Petersburg, and practiced physic until the demands of the people required him to devote his talents to the public service. He married Miss Mary Freeman, the only daughter of Col. Holman Freeman, then the beauty of Broad River. My first knowledge of Dr. Bibb was his rescuing me and several other boys, scholars of Dr. Waddell, from an old tumbling down warehouse in Petersburg, into which we had retreated upon the approach of a terrible hurricane. Shortly after his marriage, Dr. Bibb removed to a plantation in Wilks County, a mile or two from Broad River, and a few miles from the residence of Col. Taliaferro.

Dr. Bibb was a member of the Georgia Legislature at a very early age for entrance into public life. William H. Crawford and John Forsyth had, perhaps, more of the confidence of the authorities of the State than Dr. Bibb. George M. Troup alone rivalled him in the love of the people. He was elected a member of the House of Representatives in 1806, and, some years after, Senator in Congress. He was a very influential member during the restrictive commercial policy of Mr. Jefferson's administration, and afterwards one of Mr. Madison's most confidential advisers. The passage of the compensation law excited the indignation of the people to such fury that all the members of Congress from Georgia, except one, were turned out of office, though the measure was not voted for by some of them; because, as the people said, they talked at all times upon every subject, but objected not a word against getting increased pay per day. Mr. Madison soothed Dr. Bibb's mortification for this withdrawal of their confidence by his constituents, by appointing him Governor of Alabama Territory. He accepted the appointment, and removed to Huntsville. Two years after the people of Alabama organized a State Government. Dr. Bibb was their first governor. During the summer of 1820, whilst riding rapidly to escape from a shower of rain, his horse stumbled, and injured him so that he died.

Dr. Bibb was a tall spare man, with head and features admirably expressive of his mild, benevolent temper, his sincere upright character, and good understanding. He was in the prime of life at the time of his death. Had he lived on without accident he might have realized his mother's hopes and won her bet. He was the intimate friend and political associate of Wm. H. Crawford. He had two children, a son and a daughter. George Baily, his son, acquired the elements of his education at the Pestilozzian school, which was established and sustained for some years in Georgia through the influence and patronage of Wm. H. Crawford and his father. He resides in Alabama, and is one of the richest men of the South. Dr. Bibb's daughter married Mr. Alfred Scott, of Montgomery, a gentleman of talents, education, and great wealth. Mrs. Bibb, who was so charming when young, still lives, a good-looking widow. Dr. Bibb, though not of the blood of the Broad River people, resided among them, and was related to them by the marriage of his mother, after his father's death, to Mr. Wm. Barnett, and the marriage of his youngest brother, B. S. Bibb, to my youngest sister.

Dr. Bibb had five brothers: Thomas, Peyton, John, Dandridge, Joseph and Benajah Smith; and two sisters, Dolly and Martha. Thomas was a man of talents, energy, and possessed great wealth. He married a daughter of Capt.

Thompson of Petersburg, and soon after removed, along with his father-in-law and several other family connections, to the Valley of the Tennessee River, in Upper Alabama. He was a member of the Legislature, President of the Senate, and, for a while, Governor of the State.

Peyton was an honest, warm-hearted, enthusiastic man. He occasionally became so devoted to aiding others on in what he believed, without doubting, to be the straight way to heaven, as to give himself up to preaching. He married a great niece of Old Tom Cobb, who lived, according to some accounts, one hundred and twenty years, according to others, only one hundred and eleven, and married, when one hundred and ten, a young woman of eighteen. Mrs. Bibb inherited by way of legacy, a part of his estate.

John Dandridge married a daughter of Mr. John Oliver, of Petersburg, whose wealth enabled him to quit the profession of law for planting. He removed to Alabama, and died before he arrived at middle age.

Joseph was a very worthy man. He was educated for a physician, but became so deaf that he declined to practice. He married Miss DuBose, a sister of Mrs. Robert Toombs, and, after her death, Miss ―――――.

Benajah Smith married L. A. Sophia Gilmer, and soon after moved to Alabama. He is an industrious, intelligent, wealthy planter. He has been frequently a member of the Legislature, and is now Senator from Montgomery County. Though he is not a lawyer by profession, the Legislature showed its great confidence in his integrity and capacity by making him Judge of the County Court of Montgomery.

Dr. Bibb's oldest sister married Alexander Pope, a gentleman of taste and intelligence. He moved from Georgia to Alabama, where he held, for many years, some office under the Government of the United States.

Martha married Fleming Freeman, son of Col. Holman Freeman, who was one of the first settlers on Broad River, and a Whig leader under Gen. Elijah Clark.

NANCY HART.

A HIGH hill at the northwest corner of my father's plantation jutted into and overlooked a long stretch of Broad River. The strong current of the river, when swelled by heavy rains, formed a passage at its base. That pass-way was called, in former times, Kennedy's gate, from the last Broad River beaver-trapper, whose hut remained standing close by when I was a small boy. I have often seen from the top of that hill the wreck of a cabin lodged against the trees on the opposite side of the river, by the great freshet of 1795. It originally stood a mile or more up the river, and nearly opposite the residence of Governor Mathews. It was built and first occupied by Nancy Hart and her husband. The cabin was called Nancy Hart's, because her husband was nobody when she was by. Nancy Hart was one of the North Carolina emigrants. She was a tall, muscular, red-headed, cross-eyed woman. In the contest between the Whigs and Tories, in the revolutionary war, she proved herself every inch a Whig. One of the mistakes of the Mother Country, in her measures for exercising absolute dominion over her American Colonies, was taxing tea, the use of which was considered by the women a mark of gentility. The patience with which they bore the burdens of the war, and their determined spirit in urging the men to perseverance in its struggle, contributed greatly to its final success. Nancy Hart's confident courage stirred into patriotic action many vascillating, British-fearing men of the times. When Whigs of upper Georgia were flying from the murdering and plundering of the Tories and their superiors, she stood her ground, ever disposed and ready to defend herself and hers from her country's foes.

One of the stories told about her after she left the country, was, that the human bones said to have been found under her cabin, when it was washed away by the freshet, had belonged to Tories, whom she had killed. The tale was not true, and did great injustice to Nancy Hart, but its belief by many of her neighbors showed their opinion of her slaying capacity. All agreed that she knew no fear, and that she was untiring in attacking the Tories.

One of my father's negroes, when dying with the consumption, imagined that apples, such as he used to eat at Lethe, his old master's place in Virginia, would cool his fever. The only place where apples could be had in the neighborhood was Nancy Hart's. My mother, supposing that she could procure them more certainly than anyone else, went to Nancy Hart's cabin for that purpose. Soon after she was seated, two men rode up, and asked for apples for their longing wives. Nancy cursed them and their wives—swearing that every woman in the country got into the family-way when her apples got ripe. Though apples were given to the men, my mother was deterred by Nancy's rudeness from asking for any. But she was as kind as she was rude. She took my mother into the orchard, and filled her pockets, which, according to the custom of the times, were two little bags attached to a belt around the body, for holding every thing she had use for in keeping house.

Nancy Wilder, another of the North Carolina emigrants, was a lone woman, who lived in the slashes of Long Creek, did the weaving of the neighborhood, and other things appropriate for lone single women to do. Nancy Wilder had a web of cloth to weave for Nancy Hart, which she had more than once promised to finish. Nancy Hart, going for her cloth when she was assured she should have it, went into Nancy Wilder's cabin, found her absent, and the web still in the loom. She commenced cutting from the loom what was woven, intending to leave the unfinished part for Nancy Wilder's toll. Whilst thus employed, Nancy Wilder returned, and, seeing what she was doing, made at her. Solomon Jennings just then rode up with the warp and filling for a web of cloth, and, hearing a great noise in the cabin, jumped off his horse, and ran in. He found the hands of each of the women clenched in the other's hair, and they butting, biting and swearing with all their might.

The restless temper and fearless spirit which had urged Nancy Hart to fight for liberty, made her the best backwoods woman after the war ended. She traced the bee to its tree, and the deer to its lair, among snakes and wild beasts, with unequalled success.

When civilization began to extend its gentling influences

over the frontier people of upper Georgia, Nancy Hart left her accustomed haunts for the West. She settled for a while on the Tombigbee. A great rain flooded the river, destroyed her crop, and inclosed her house within its overflowing. She had no love for the Spaniards, nor for the ways of the French, her neighbors. She returned to Georgia, and finding her old residence occupied by others, settled in Edgefield, South Carolina.

When the preached word was heard instead of the drum, and the people's thoughts began to be occupied about the result of their final account, instead of sending others to the judgment-seat unprepared, Nancy Hart's conscience became troubled about her future. A Methodist Society was formed in her neighborhood. She went to the house of worship in search of relief. She found the good people assembled in class-meeting, and the door closed against intruders. She took out her knife, cut the fastening, and stalked in. She heard how the wicked might work out their salvation—became a shouting Christian, fought the Devil as manfully as she had fought the Tories, and died in good fellowship with the saints on earth, with bright hopes of being admitted into communion with the saints in heaven.

I was a member of Congress in 1828-9. General Jackson's successful election to the Presidency put the ambitious members all agog to attract his favorable notice. One of the means used, was proposing to fill the vacant nitches in the Rotunda with paintings descriptive of the Battle of New Orleans, and other great victories. I prepared a resolution, as an addition or substitute, to fill one nitch with a painting of Nancy Hart wading Broad River, her clothes tucked up under one arm, a musket under the other, and three Tories ahead, on her way to the camp of the Whigs, to deliver them up to the tender mercies of Col. Elijah Clark.

THE JOHNSONS.

NICHOLAS JOHNSON was the son of Thomas Johnson, of Louisa County, Virginia, and Ann Meriwether, the daughter of Thomas Meriwether, of Albemarle County. Whilst acting as deputy sheriff he rendered himself liable to arrest for some act of violence. To escape the danger, he left Virginia for the Broad River settlement, where he appeared in more dashing style than had ever been seen in that hard-working, economical, simple-habited frontier community. He was attended by a well-dressed servant, rode a fine blooded horse, his servant another, and a third followed for the relief of the other two. His dress was a blue coat, red waistcoat, and buff pantloons. He used to say that when a young man went into a crowd so dressed, every body made way for him, and he heard, as he passed along, Who is that? Who is he? His person was stout, his features full and round, his complexion fair and florid, his voice well modulated, and his address exceedingly civil. He was a constant and very plausible talker. He united grand scheming with successful doing in a very unusual and often amusing way. When he went to any public place, a crowd might generally be seen gathered about him, listening to his fervent account of some danger which threatened the nation, or some new fashion of planting corn, tobacco or cotton. His land was very poor, and his plantation very large, with granite rocks scattered about over it. He described to some acquaintances in Augusta the beauty of the native flowers and shrubs, and the wild scenery of the rocky hills about him in such glowing terms, that they planned a special visit to enjoy the pleasure of the sight.

He once told his neighbor, Dr. Bradly, a very bookish planter, in such seemingly earnest terms, how to make a fortune by raising hogs, that the Doctor was nigh losing the entire profits of a year's labor by following the plan.

He married Mary Marks, daughter of James Marks, of Broad River. He lived in log cabins for twenty years after his marriage, in the plainest style. The public road passed through his land, and not far from his residence. He fell in one day with a pompous fellow, travelling along his lane; who inquired where he could get his breakfast, and descanted largely upon the unfitness of the accommodations on the road for a gentleman. Col. Johnson told him that he could be served at his house. The fellow said that he would turn in and see if he could get any thing to suit his taste. Col. Johnson accompanied him, held his stirrup whilst he alighted, ordered the best to be got for his breakfast, waited upon him at table, and never ceased pressing him to eat until he could eat no more. When the fellow asked for his bill he was made to pay a dollar. When Mr. Pomposity opened his eyes in astonishment, Col. Johnson advised him to be more modest in future when he went among strangers.

It was difficult to keep good fences around his large fields of poor land. He comforted himself for the many inconveniences which he suffered from bad inclosures, by the advantages he enjoyed in the great number of rabbits which he caught by the rails sinking down so close to each other other, that they could not slip through and escape from the dogs. When he discovered a hog in a cornfield, he found the place of entry, and stopped it so that the hog could not get out, and show the whole stock the way in. Every traveller called at his house who chose, and partook of his wife's good fare without charge, if found worthy of hospitality. A peddling merchant once stopped, sold many of his tin things, and finding plentiful food for his horses, and good eating for himself, staid during the remainder of the day, and all night. Col. Johnson saw him go to his wagon after dining with his family, and eat apples, which were at the time a great rarity, without giving his children any. He made him pay twenty times the value of his apples for what he would otherwise have had for nothing.

Whenever a monkey or other show passed by his house, he sent into his fields for his negroes and treated them to the exhibition. His oldest children were daughters. He was so pleased when his first son was born that he planted in the fence corners of his extensive fields, a hundred thousand walnuts. According to his count, by the time the infant arrived at manhood, each of the walnuts would be grown into a tree, and be worth a dollar, which would make a fortune worth talking about.

Col. Johnson's plantation and Col. Mathew's rich Goosepond tract, adjoined. Col. Johnson was once riding along the public road, which passed through both, when he fell in with a traveller, who, after inquiring the names of the owners of the two places, said that he had heard that Col. Mathews was very rich, but that Col. Johnson was richer; that he owned five hundred sheep. Now he would say, see what a man of genius can do with small means. But little supplies our wants. We work for reputation. I, who do not own the fourth part of the wealth of Col. Mathews, have the credit of being the richest of the two. Men judge by comparison. If a man worth fifty thousand dollars usually keeps fifty sheep, how much must he be worth who keeps ten times that number?

He used to shirtee his fields along the public road with cow pens, so as to make the corn which was seen in passing by exhibit a very luxuriant appearance, and so create the opinion in the lookers-on that his land was very productive. His orders to the cowboys were, that the cattle must never leave the pen in the morning until they added to its fertility. A neighbor passing by found a boy running a cow, and crying as if his heart would break. Being a very kind man, he stopped to inquire what was the matter, and received for answer that Brownee would not do what master ordered.

When a daughter married, he gave to her husband five hundred dollars, in addition to what he would otherwise have given, if he removed to a new country, where fertile lands were to be had; saying, that it would mortify him to see his children laboring hard for a pittance, or coming about the old people to carry home on Sunday evenings a wallet of little family necessities.

Col. Charles Mathews, Col. Johnson's friend and neighbor, was very ambitious of being a member of the Legislature, offered several times, but was not elected. Col. Johnson accounted for his want of success, by saying that Col. Mathews on public days rode his big horse to the court-house, stood stiff in his stirrups, alighted at the tavern, and ordered with authority that his horse be taken, seated himself in the parlor, talked sensibly upon public affairs with the select few, instead of calling upon Mrs. Crossroads Smith, inquiring about the price of eggs and chickens, taking a drink of cider, and kissing the children.

Col. Johnson was a man of truth, in the liberal sense of the word. He never invented any thing, nor intended to deceive. But his fertile imagination and strong excitable temperament, led him constantly to exaggertion in his descriptions of things that were in any way remarkable.

Returning home from his harvest field one day, he found a partridge nest very full of eggs. Upon meeting his wife, he told her that he had found a partridge nest with a bushel of eggs in it. His wife, who saw things very clearly and as they were, exclaimed, It is not possible, husband, for a partridge nest to hold a bushel of eggs. Pshaw, wife, I only intended to give you an idea.

He was for a long time addicted to strong drink, was often drunk, and was always very violent when he was. On one occasion he alarmed his family by some threatened violence. His wife sent for the overseer and negroes, and directed them to confine him. Upon their coming into the room where he was, he put on an air of sorrow and submission, telling his negroes, in a plaintive voice, that he supposed that they had come to tie their master, who had always been very kind to them. He continued to address them in the sweetest and most insinuating way, until, finding them worked up to his purpose, he suddenly stamped his foot, and cried out, "The rascal shall die who attempts to tie me!" ordered the negroes to seize the overseer, and made at him himself. His house stood on the brow of a hill. There was a long, wide passage through it, inclosed on one side by a high railing, to prevent the children from breaking their necks by falling over. The overseer, comprehending fully his danger, leaped over the railing. As he descended, Col. Johnson grabbed his shirt at the back of his neck, the collar flew open, the overseer threw up his arms and slipped through. He darted, shirtless, for Col. Mathews's. Col. Johnson raised his highest hallo, and ordered the negroes to catch him. The whole posse of thirty or forty gave chase. It was a run for life. The foremost negro was about to seize hold of the overseer's breeches, when, breathless and exhausted, he stood before Mrs. Mathews, and implored her protection. In another drunken spree, Col. Johnson threw one of his daughters on the floor, and made such a plausible feint that he intended to take her life, by sticking his knife into the floor near her head, that his wife interfered to save her child. He immediately let go his daughter, and attempted to seize his wife. She fled from the house to Broad River, about half a mile distant. Whilst seated over the water, considering the question whether it were better to be or not to be, she was suddenly precipitated into the river, and turning her head, saw that her husband's hand had done the deed. As soon as he perceived that his wife's life was in imminent peril, his whole nature underwent a sudden revulsion. He was sober in a moment. Unable to swim, to have jumped into the water would have been certain destruction to both. He looked around with the quickness of thought for means to save her. He found nothing at hand, but a long weed. Extending it at once towards her, he spoke gently, and begged her to take hold. The voice of love never fails to find a vibrating chord in a woman's heart. Her clothes had held her up for a moment. She saw the change in her husband's feelings, and did as she was implored to do. He drew her slowly to him, reached down, pulled her into his arms, carried her upon the bank, set her down, threw himself on his knees before her, and called upon God with the utmost solemnity to witness his promise never to be drunk again. That promise was never violated.

Mrs. Johnson inherited her father's wit and her mother's clear understanding. Though she read but little, and her intercourse with general society was limited, her conversation was very agreeable and her knowledge accurate. She and her husband were both great talkers, and very excitable. Their animated controversies went sometimes beyond what was pleasant to listeners, especially when Col. Johnson was drinking.

Mrs. Johnson's table was the most loaded with home productions of any ever sat down to. Two hams of bacon, a large piece of beef, vast dishes of fowls and vegetables, were frequently seen at a family dinner. She had seven houses for her chickens. A bushel of corn was usually strewed around the yard every morning. Col. Johnson kept forty cows, five hundred sheep, and countless hogs, to supply his wife's table with butter, milk, fat beeves, mutton, pigs, &c., &c.

O. H. Prince and A. G. Clayton, the rival wits of the Georgia bar, expressed the opinion, in a social assemblage of lawyers, when Scott's poetry was first spouted by every body, that the rhyme was but doggerel, and could be written by any versifier. The conversation excited interest, and the assertion of the wits opposition. To prove the correctness of their criticism, Mr. Prince wrote off at once a string of lines ending in words of similar sound, to which Judge Clayton added a note after Scott's fashion. The subject was Brownee and the little negro cowboy. The rhyme and note appeared soon after in a paper published by Mr. David Hillhouse, in Columbia, South Carolina. Col. Johnson, when he heard of the pasquinade, only laughed, when he understood why it was written. Not so Mrs. Johnson. She asked a kinsman, who was a lawyer, to induce Mr. Prince to call in passing by to the court, that she might teach him a lesson in good behavior.

After Mrs. Johnson's death, which occurred in 1814-15, Col. Johnson removed with his unmarried children to Lauderdale County, Alabama, where he married again. When all his children left him, he indulged in love for dogs and cats, keeping about seventy of each.

Nancy, Col. Johnson's oldest daughter, married Reuben Jordan.

Betsy, his second daughter, Louis Bourbon Taliaferro.

Martha, George Oglethorpe Gilmer.

Lucy, John Gilmer.

Barbara, ———— Fraser.

Rebekah, Charles Jordan

Sarah, Morgan Smith.

His sons, Frank and James, died young and unmarried.

Edward, the youngest, was a youth of fine promise. Whilst on a visit to his brother-in-law, George O. Gilmer, in Montgomery, Alabama, he joined a party who were going deer hunting. All passed through a gate on their way to the forest; Edward was the last. The gate was heard to shut, and a gun to go off. Those who were before looked round and saw Edward falling from his horse. He was dead when they got to him. He had pushed the gate to its place with the butt end of his gun. It had gone off, and its load into some vital part.

WILLIAM H. CRAWFORD.

WILLIAM H. CRAWFORD, was born 24th of Feb. 1772, in Amherst County, a part of Virginia unsurpassed for good water, pure atmosphere, and the healthiness and heartiness of its inhabitants. Spencer of that county was reputed to be the largest man in the world. The nine Martins were as remarkable for height as Spencer was for weight. The Crawfords were both stout and tall. William H. was six feet three inches high, his brothers Charles and Joel about as tall, and Bennet, Robert and David, but little lower. The elevated, rough, productive mountains of his nativity seemed to have impressed their characteristics upon his constitution. His family were Scotch, and claimed kindred with the lairds of that name. He was a lad at the close of the revolutionary war, and grew up with the hardy habits of those scuffling times. He carried with him to his highest station a little of the rudeness of his mountain raising. Soon after peace his father removed to Columbia County, Georgia. William H. labored on the plantation with his brothers until Dr. Moses Waddell commenced his school in the neighborhood. He attended it, and soon learned to appreciate his extraordinary capacity. He had arrived at manhood before his education extended beyond the rudiments of learning. His quick apprehension and retentive memory enabled him to master the Latin and Greek languages in the shortest possible time, and to comprehend and enjoy with peculiar zest the beauties of the best ancient writers. He never lost his relish for Virgil, Horace, Cicero, Xenophon and Homer. He continued to attend the examinations of academies and colleges, to enjoy the pleasure of renewed acquaintance with these old favorites. And yet he was above the vanity of display, and entirely free from pedantry. His father lost most of his property by some singular casualty before Williahm H. derived any advantage from it. He knew when he commenced life's struggle that his success would be unaided by fortune, and made his exertions correspond with his necessities. As soon as he was qualified, he accepted the place of assistant to Charles, afterwards Judge Tait, then principal of the Augusta Academy, a connection which led to some of the most important events of his future career. Whilst engaged in teaching and studying law, he and Miss Gerdine became attached to each other and agreed to marry. The contract was consummated as soon afterwards as a competency was provided for housekeeping, which was so long that one less honorable and steadfast than Mr. Crawford might have forgotten the obligation, unattended as it was by the inducements of wealth and rank. Mrs. Crawford was an excellent wife. She still lives to keep fresh in the memories of her children the admirable qualities of their fond and indulgent father.

Mr. Crawford was in 1799 appointed, in conjunction with H. Marbury, to digest the laws of Georgia. He settled about the same time in Lexington, Oglethorpe County, to pursue his profession. Whilst he was compiling the laws, being then unmarried, he passed most of his time at William Barnett's his kinsman, who lived in Elbert County, on Broad River, immediately opposite my father's residence. His plain dress, frank manners and decided straightforward way of speaking and acting, rendered him very acceptable to all the Broad River people. My father specially admired and confided in him. He obtained his promise that as soon as I was old enough he would make a lawyer of me. When I was about to commence preparation for the profession, he acknowledged the obligation; but advised me to go into Mr. Upson's office, on account of his long absence from home attending Congress.

When Mr. Crawford commenced the life of a lawyer, many of the profession were engaged in the land speculations which at the time disgraced the State. An effort was made to induce him to act in unison with them. His refusal brought upon him the united opposition of the unprincipled clique. Finding his talents and integrity very much in the way of their success, a conspiracy was entered into to kill, or drive him away. Van Allen, an impudent fellow from New York, a first cousin of President Van Buren, was chosen to play the bully. He challenged Mr. Crawford and was killed. Gen. Clark having fought with fame at the battle of Jack's Creek, and distinguished himself by the active part which he took in the brawls, common in those days, thought his effort might be attended with better success. A challenge was sent to Mr. Crawford and accepted. On the day of the meeting, Clark and his second harassed him with quibbles and controversies until he was out of temper and off his guard. When he took his position his disengaged arm was forgotten, and suffered to hang outside of his body, so that Gen. Clark's ball struck his wrist, which would otherwise have passed harmlessly by. Clark's hatred was increased, instead of being appeased by his accidental success. He renewed his challenge without any renewed offence, and continued as long as he lived in Georgia, to obstruct by all the means which he could command, the way of Mr. Crawford's political advancement.

Mr. Crawford was elected a member of the Legislature by the people of Oglethorpe, for several successive years. His vigorous intellect and active industry entitled him to the first place among the members, a position which he was not slow in assuming.

He was elected to the United States Senate in 1807, and was soon considered one of the great men of the most select of the legislative bodies of the world. He had the confidence of Mr. Jefferson, and was one of Mr. Madison's most influential advisers. He showed his fearlessness in the discharge of public duty, by attacking Mr. Madison's Delphic-like recommendations, when decisive measures were required by the state of the country. He was rewarded for his independence by being sent Minister to France. His tall commanding person figured conspicuously among the diminutive Frenchmen, whilst his noble features and gallant temper rendered him a great favorite in Paris society. When he returned home, polished by intimate association with the highest class of the politest nation, his appearance and manners made him the most imposing gentleman who had ever been seen in Georgia. He indeed surpassed in personal appearance Mr. Clay, Mr. Calhoun, Mr. Lowndes, and General Jackson, his rivals for the Presidency, though each one of them would have attracted attention among a million.

I was a member of Congress, whilst Mr. Crawford was Secretary of the Treasury, and had frequent opportunities of observing his singular capacity for business; his contempt for pretences; his excellent memory, and the sagacity which enabled him to bring into the service of his department the best assistants which could be had for the performance of what was to be done. Rascals received no countenance from him. He employed none knowingly, and when he was deceived, told them so, and dismissed them.

The improper use of lobelia by Mr. Crawford for an attack of erysipelas through the advice of an unskilful physician, whilst temporarily absent from Washington City, brought on paralysis, from which he never entirely recovered. The electioneering for the Presidency was then going on very actively. He was never sensible of the injurious effects of the disease upon his mind, and refused to withdraw from the canvass. The ambitious men of his party had committed themselves to his support, and opposition to his rivals, before his enfeebled condition was known, so that their hopes of distinction through the favor of the President, rested upon him. There was no getting at the true state of his case during the pendency of the election. His chance for success was considered best of all the candidates, until the votes which determined the election were counted out. Complaining long afterwards to Mr. Crawford's most intimate friend, who was one of the ablest and most honorable citizens of our country, of this concealment of Mr. Crawford's condition from the country, he replied, that such was his confidence in the integrity of Mr. Crawford, and his thorough knowledge of men and measures that he believed that he would, though paralyzed, have made a better President than either of his rivals.

Mr. Crawford quitted office in 1825, poorer than when he went Minister to France. He had no love of money for its own sake. When his children grew up, married, and stood in need of more property than he could give them, he would sometimes express regret that he had not followed his profession and acquired wealth, as Mr. Cobb and Mr. Upson had done, who succeeded to his practice.

He was appointed Judge of the Superior Court by Governor Troup, in 1827, to fill the vacancy occasioned by the death of Judge Dooly, and was elected to the same office by the Legislature, in 1828. He made a better judge than seemed possible to those who were familiar with his paralyzed state. His clear and conscientious sense of right, and extraordinary recollection of what he had known in early life, kept him in the straight course.

He was violently opposed to the nullification movement, considering it but an ebullition excited by Mr. Calhoun's overleaping ambition.

Every one drank whiskey whilst Mr. Crawford was growing up. His mind and body were but little affected by this habit until he was paralyzed. He continued to use the accustomed quantity, often lost his self-control, and would talk of the rascality of the men of former times in mixed companies, to the great annoyance of some, and amusement of others. He retained his social temper and admirable conversational talents to the end of his life. He loved to tell anecdotes, and told them well. He saw the knob, and made others feel it. He was a capital laugher, and cared not a fig, when at his greatest elevation, for artificial dignity. He was as affectionate to his children as a father could be, loving them heartily, and learning them to treat him familiarly and confidingly. To his children, friends, and neighbors, he was what they liked best and admired most. With but limited learning and unpolished manners, he was found upon trial equal to any demands which his country could make upon him. He retained through life his love for his Broad River friends. He died among them, at the house of Mr. Valentine Meriwether, on his way to Elbert Court, of a disease of the heart.

Joel Crawford was tall and stout, like his distinguished brother, William H. The resemblance extended no further. He married his first cousin, Nancy, the daughter of old Nat. Barnett. The only public office which Joel Crawford ever held was tobacco inspector for the little town of Petersburg. His wife, never having associated with society before her marriage, when she went into company afterwards was as restless as if she was on thorns. They had only one child, a daughter, who married a man by the name of McDaniel.

Joel Crawford lived in a small hewed log-house, near Falling Creek, about two miles north of Broad River, in Elbert County, and near his brother-in-law, William Barnett.

THE BARNETTS.

NAT BARNETT must have been of English descent, being brave, obstinate, and perverse, without the calculating temper of the Scotch, or wit of the Irish. He was a native of Amherst County, Virginia. He married Miss Crawford, a neighbor's daughter, and aunt of William H. Crawford. The match was very suitable in many respects. Both were perfectly content with their clothes if they covered their nakedness, and their house if it sheltered them from the weather. Fancy was not a quality of their natures, and mental taste not known to them at all. And yet they were not altogether alike. Nat was active and supple of body, and not very strong of understanding; his wife was firm and sensible. Nat accompanied his relations, the Crawfords, in their removal from Amherst county, Virginia, to Columbia County, Georgia, about the beginning of the revolutionary war. The British troops, and their friends the Tories, drove, by their murderous warfare, most of the Whigs from upper Georgia. Nat, his two sons, William and Joel, and two of the young Crawfords, their kinsmen, determined to remain and war to the knife with them. Nat was made prisoner, and confined in Augusta jail. When the Whigs, under Clark, attacked Augusta, and drove out the Tories, Nat was liberated. Having been whilst confined in constant expectation of being put to death, when he felt himself free he leaped into the air, struck his feet three times together, threw his wool hat aloft, and cried out at the top of his voice. "Liberty for ever! liberty for ever!" &c.

William and Joel Barnett, and the two Crawfords, to avoid being burnt in the houses of their fathers, or captured and hung, took possession of a thicket of cedars, which grew near the centre of a great extent of otherwise bare rocks, some miles above Augusta. From this place they could see the approach of enemies, prepare for flight or fight, and choose the most favorble times for breaking up lodgments of the Tories.

Joel Barnett, the youngest of the four, especially distinguished himself by his daring adventures. He once crossed Savannah River, into Edgefield district, South Carolina, where the Tories had the upper hand at the time, and burnt the tippling house in which they were accustomed to assemble before going forth to plunder and murder. He was tarrying to see the fire under way, when he heard a party of Tories making for the place in the greatest haste. He mounted his horse and fled. There was no fort or friends near to give him protection. The British and their allies were in possession of Augusta, the only place where a boat could be had for crossing the Savannah River. It was a run for life on the part of Barnett. With might and main the pursuers and the pursued urged on their horses. When Barnett reached the river he plunged in. Lying on the water, he struck manfully into it with eager love of life. He had got just beyond gunshot when the Tories arrived at the bank. They vented their rage by firing their guns at him.

Joel Barnett's health gave way from constant exposure. Reduced to feebleness by fever and ague, he sought relief by taking shelter in the cabin of a poor Whig woman near by, who, in accordance with the spirit of her sex, loved her country and her countrymen who fought to defend it. One morning whilst Joel Barnett was at breakfast with his hostess, he saw, through the opening between the logs of her cabin, a party of Tories rapidly approaching. Having no ability or means to fly, he passed out of the cabin on the opposite side, climbed over a fence which inclosed a field near by, and dropped into some weeds and grass, which his quick eye saw would conceal him. He heard the curses of his enemies, and their threats of vengeance upon the woman, when they found that he had escaped, and their whoops of encouragement to each other, as they parted to meet on the opposite side of the little field. As soon as they were out of sight, going on in the direction which they supposed he had fled, Barnett eased his held-in breath, reclimbed the fence, passed through the cabin, shook the hand of the kind woman, and was off in the opposite direction.

The two Barnetts and two Crawfords, after a while, were obliged to leave Georgia. The two Barnetts went to Virginia, where the Marquis La Fayette and Cornwallis were exercising their military skill in efforts to get the advantage of each other. They joined the militia company from Amherst County, were in the conquering army at the siege of York, saw the British commander-in-chief yield his sword to an inferior American officer, and joined in the general exultation of their countrymen, when they knew that the struggle for freedom had ended successfully.

Joel Barnett returned to Georgia soon after, and married his first cousin, Miss Crawford. After her death he married Mildred Meriwether, the daughter of Mr. Frank Meriwether, and settled in Oglethorpe County, a little off from Broad River. Joel Barnett was firm to obstinacy. He never did favors for the sake of gaining favors, nor palavered any body. He did not talk much. Whatever he said he believed to be strictly true. He joined the Baptist Church upon his conscience becoming impressed with the force of religious truths; but found it impossible to conform himself to its rules, and withdrew, or was turned out. He was upright, and retained the confidence of the people of Oglethorpe County as long as he lived among them. He represented them frequently in the Legislature. He was industrious and economical. He removed to the State of Mississippi, where he died some years after, worth $200,000. He had one child by his first wife and eight by his last.

Joel was like the children of first cousins are apt to be.

Susan married John Gresham; secondly, John Gilmer.

Charles married Eliza Gresham.

Frank married Eliza Goolsby.

Nathaniel married William H. Smith.

———— married ———— Crawford.

Emily married Craven W. Totten; secondly, ———— Stewart.

Ann married ———— Burke.

Rebekah married Michael Johnson.

William Barnett married Mary Meriwether, the daughter of Mr. Frank Meriwether. He lived for a short time in Columbia County, and then settled on Broad River, in Elbert County. He was kind, plausible and agreeable. Though his education and reading were very limited, his observation was close, and perceptions clear. New settlements are necessarily very sickly in warm climates. William Barnett's kind disposition, and singular capacity for profiting by experience and observation, made him a good physician. His skill was exerted freely for the benefit of those who could not procure a doctor, or were without the means to employ one. He became the most popular man of his county. The first office which he held was the sheriffalty. His efficiency was soon put to a very severe trial.

Beverly Allen carried on the business of merchandise in the County of Elbert in 1794-5. His storehouse and residence were on the hill rising from Beaverdam Creek, on the side of the road leading from the Fishdam ford on Broad River to the Cherokee ford on the Savannah. He was young and handsome, with a fine voice, and ardent temperament. He came to Georgia an enthusiastic Methodist preacher. Without any of the learning of Whitfield, he had much of his inspiring eloquence. Episcopalianism had passed away from the country with the loss of titles. It was long before its place was supplied by the faith of the Baptist and the devotion of the Methodist. Preaching was a rarity when Beverly Allen settled in Georgia. Men's souls were stirred within them when they heard vivid descriptions of the punishment in the lower world for sin, and the happiness in heaven for those who died in the faith, and left their good works to follow them. When Beverly Allen held forth upon these subjects, the whole population crowded together to hear him. Some time during the year 1795, he went to Augusta to buy goods with the money he had, and the credit which he could obtain. Whilst there, the foreign merchant of whom he had purchased his first stock, found him buying goods of others, instead of discharging the debt due to himself. He caused a *ca. sa.* writ to be issued for Allen's arrest, returnable to the United States District Court. Being informed of his liability to arrest, he armed himself, took possession of a room in a public house, and fastened the door. The marshal, who was the father of the celebrated John Forsyth, pursued him, broke open the door, and was, upon his entrance, shot dead. Allen was arrested upon a charge of murder, escaped, and fled to his home in Elbert. William Barnett, upon receiving the warrant, assembled a guard and went in search of him. He ascertained that Allen was concealed in his house. After many fruitless attempts to get him out, the house was set on fire and kept burning until he delivered himself up. He was confined in the jail of the county. The news spread among the people with electric quickness, that their favorite preacher was in jail for resisting the process of the United States Court, the object of which had been to take from him his liberty, and separate him from his home, friends, and flock. The process of the Circuit Court of the United States was then very unpopular on account of the violent political contest between the democrats and federalists, in which the power of the United States Courts made one of the subjects of party disagreement. In those days the people were a law unto themselves. The restraints of government had been very slight during the dominion of Great Britain. They were scarcely felt at all on the frontiers of Georgia at the time of the arrest of Allen. Voluntary associations, called Lynch men, afforded some protection against thieves. Personal rights were defended by the fist. Liberty, and especially liberty of person, was, from the habits of speaking, acting, and feeling of the times of the revolution and immediately after, considered by many the chief good. In such times, among such people, operated upon by such causes, it was not wonderful that the imprisonment of Allen produced popular commotion. The sheriff, finding that the rescue of his prisoner would be attempted, set off with him for Washington, Wilks County. He was headed on the road and compelled to return. He increased his guard to sixteen men. One or more of them proved to be friends of the prisoner. On the night after William Barnett's return from this attempt to secure the criminal in Wilks jail, the jail of Elbert was attacked by two hundred men, the doors forced open, and Allen permitted to escape. The friends of the prisoner, had, previous to the attack, taken the powder from the locks of the guns of all the guard from whom any danger was apprehended, except one, and he was held so that he could not fire. Beverly Allen fled to the most distant frontier of the United States.

William Barnett was a member of the Legislature for a long time, and for several years President of the Senate. He and Mr. Forsyth were candidates for Congress, each for the first time, to fill a vacancy. Wm. Barnett's popularity was proven by his success over the most talented man of the time. He continued a member of Congress for some years. He received many other proofs of his countrymen's confidence. He and his first wife were devoted to each other. They had a large family of children. Mrs. Barnett's love was subjected to a test which proved too much for her capability of endurance. He was so dangerously ill of fever that his life was despaired of. His wife became frantic, and died. He recovered, and years after married Mrs. Bibb, the mother of Dr. William W. Bibb. Though Mrs. Barnett was very sensible and agreeable, it was not possible for her to make herself agreeable to a man who had lived most lovingly from his youth to advanced age with a wife who was altogether devoted to him, and had died for love of him. Each of them had children, most of whom were married. They had no common property. They began to separate in visiting their children, until they finally ceased to live together. He removed to Alabama, and died shortly after. He had six children by his first wife; none by his last.

Thomas Meriwether Barnett, the oldest child of William Barnett, inherited his mother's temper. He was instinctively industrious, frugal, truthful, and honest. He had none of the plausibility nor agreeableness of his father. He never electioneered, palavered, nor asked favors of any body, sought for nor held any office. He had no time to spare from his home employments to listen to the idle chat of others, and never took time to talk himself. For many years after he was a man he attended to both his father's plantation and his own, though they were several miles apart, walking daily from one to the other, and over each. He seldom visited, never sung, danced, nor attended frolics of any sort. He showed, when he was dressed in his best, that he did not expect to please by the cut of his coat nor the tie of his cravat. How he got married no one knows, except his wife. He had lived to be a bachelor of some standing, and never courted even a cousin, when a lady, who was herself considerably beyond her teens, became a frequent visitor at her sister's, who lived near by Tom Barnett's. She was social, and often very much in want of company. Some accident brought the maiden and bachelor together. The backwardness of the unpolished bachelor was overcome by the free and easy manners of the low country Virginia lady. Where there is a will there is a way. They married. Providing for children increased the motives which had made Tom Barnett exceedingly industrious and frugal. Though he never bartered nor trafficked he had clear perceptions of the value of money, and understood very well the best means of making it. He left his post oak, black-jack lands, near Broad River, in Elbert County, for the rich prairie lands of Montgomery, Alabama. He has gone on, working continually, and adding to his property, until he is now one of the wealthiest planters of the Southern States, probably the very richest whose patrimony was only five negroes and a tract of land of a few hundred acres of common quailty. He is the owner of upwards of sixty thousand acres of rich land, many negroes, and much other valuable property. He is near seventy years old, and is as industrious, frugal, honest, truthful, shabby in dress, and abstemious in talk, as he was in early life.

Martha, the next oldest of the living children of Wm. Barnett, married Francis M. Gilmer, originally of Broad River, now of Montgomery, Alabama. Her industry, smartness, and economy, has made her husband rich.

Mary, the second daughter, married David Taliaferro, son of Col. Ben. Taliaferro. She was left a widow with several young children. She has proved herself a match for any man in the management of property, and, indeed, superior to most in most other matters.

Nat, the second son, married Miss Hudson, and moved to the far Southwest.

Lucy, the third daughter, married George Mathews, grandson of Gov. Mathews. She was a clever woman, and her husband one of the best of all the Broad River kin.

———, fourth daughter, married ——— Ross.

Peter Barnett, the youngest son of Old Nat., never made the effort or failed to overcome the unrestrained rudeness of his youth. He married Miss Saffold, of Wilks County, whose peculiarities were found to agree so badly with his own that he left her to live among the Creek Indians with a squaw.

THE HARVIES AND ANDREWS.

THE HARVIES were the most numerous family of the original settlers on Broad River. They were of Scotch descent. Their name is distinguished from the English and Irish of the same sound by its being spelled Harvie instead of Harvey.

John Harvie, their last European ancestor, was born at Gargunnock, in the shire of Stirling, North Britain. He removed from Scotland to Virginia, and settled in Albemarle County, about forty years before the revolutionary war. His wife's maiden name was Gaines, a name which her relative, Edmund Pendleton, has rendered quite famous. Her husband being dead, she accompanied her children in their move from Virginia to Broad River, where she died when in her eighty- ——— year.

Mr. and Mrs. Harvie had nine children, four sons and five daughters. When Mr. Jefferson was in France, Ambassador for the Confederation, he found the opinion prevalent there and elsewhere in Europe that animal nature deteriorated in America. One of his purposes in writing Notes on Virginia was to correct this mistake. Whilst engaged in the work, he applied to Col. John Harvie for the weight of himself, his brothers and sisters. Col. Harvie so indignantly refused giving him the information asked for, that Mr. Jefferson made no reference in his book to their great weight. The nine weighed about twenty-seven hundred pounds; the four brothers, a little less than twelve hundred, and the five sisters, somewhat more than fifteen hundred. Daniel Harvie reached near four hundred, and exceeded other men as much in strength as he did in size. It was said that he righted the corner of a millhouse, which had been put out of its place by a freshet; that he raised a heavy hogshead of tobacco over the ground-sill through the door of the tobacco house; and that he could hold up for some time two men of ordinary size, one on each hand, with his arms extended their full length from his body. He was stronger than Francisco. Indeed he had the reputation among his acquaintances, of being the strongest man in the world. Daniel Harvie's muscle was better fitted for the exertion of strength than conveying the materials for thought to the brain. Fortunately for society, Providence usually orders that men of great strength shall be very good tempered. Daniel Harvie was never angry. He married Sally Tailaferro, of Amherst County, Virginia, sister of Col. Benjamin Taliaferro, whose capital good sense supplied what her husband was most deficient in. They removed to Georgia along with their kin, and settled on the eastern side of Long Creek, two miles from Broad River. Daniel Harvie, in displaying his great strength to his neighbors, in hauling a drag for fish in Long Creek, became so much heated by over-exertion that he took cold and died. Mrs. Harvie was left a widow in the prime of life, with five children, four daughters and a son. She devoted herself to them in the spirit of self-sacrifice, which men admire but seldom imitate. Though her estate was small, by great industry and economy, she sent them to the best schools in the country, and, when they arrived at the proper age, introduced them into its most polished society.

Martha Harvie, Daniel Harvie's oldest daughter, was very pretty, amiable, and clever. She married Dr. Thornton Gilmer, the handsomest of all the Broad River men.

Daniel Harvie's second daughter, Mary Boutwell, married Peachy Ridgway Gilmer.

His third daughter, Nancy, married Thomas Lewis Gilmer.

His fourth, Frances, had more strength of intellect than either of her sisters. She married in Kentucky, whilst on a visit at Dr. Gilmer's, a rough specimen of humanity by the name of Bostwick, and never afterwards lived on Broad River.

Daniel Harvie's son Daniel inherited some of the strength and much of the kindness and good temper of his father. The great care of his mother could not entirely prevent his showing the disposition to improvisation which he inherited from his Italian ancestors. He removed to Mississippi, where he died a bachelor.

William Harvie was social, kind-tempered, well read, and

conversable. His schemes were not always very practical, but were sustained with never-failing plausibility. His federal politics excluded him from holding office, except that of the Inferior Court, which having no pay attached to it, and yet requiring intelligence and integrity for the proper discharge of its duties, was filled by the patriotic, whose services could be obtained without any investigation about their opinions of Jay's treaty or the French revolution. He married Judith Cosby, the sister of the celebrated Judge Cosby, of Kentucky, and of James Cosby of Elbert County, Georgia, gentlemen of great worth and intelligence. Mrs. Harvie was a most amiable woman. Her pure and blameless life left an impression upon her children which may yet be seen in their intercourse with the world. Mr. and Mrs. Harvie joined the Methodist Church during the great revival of religion among the Broad River people in 1809, and gave ample evidence through their after lives of their sincere piety.

William Harvie had no son. His daughter Lucy was his darling pet child, who read to him, and talked to him of what she read. He loved flowers, and cultivated them successfully when all others on Broad River, considered such labor lost. A rose bush in one corner, and a hollyhock in another, was about as much as was allowed room for in the Broad River gardens of the things which could not be eaten. There is no training of the affections in the social state like the impressions made upon a daughter by the devoted love and care of a fond father. William Harvie's daughter Lucy continues to love and cultivate flowers, as if the pleasure derived from their fragrance and beauty is increased by the knowledge of the enjoyment which her father derived from the same sources. Lucy Harvie married Asbury Hull, whom every body has trusted from his youth with increasing confidence. They have six sons. Their oldest are men of genius and of the greatest social worth; their younger sons promise to equal in merit their older brothers.

William Harvie's daughter Martha married West Harris, a Methodist preacher.

His daughter Genette married Mr. Van Lenard, a gentleman of fortune and respectability.

His daughter Margaret married Mr. Littelbury Watts, who

has been a member of the Legislature, and received other evidences of the confidence of his fellow-citizens.

His youngest daughter, Mary, married John T. Groves, a graduate of Franklin College, who has devoted his life to the useful employment of educating the youth of his country.

Richard Harvie, the elder brother of Willim Harvie, never married. He was the only gentleman of the Broad River people, who enjoyed otium cum dignitatie. His taste was literary, and his time devoted to reading. His library was large and made up of the best books He, his mother, and brother William, were one family until William's marriage. They lived at a beautiful place on Broad River, between Mr. Frank Meriwether's and Mr. Tom Meriwether's.

Martha, the oldest daughter of Mr. and Mrs. Harvie, was a worthy woman, and much beloved by her family. She married, when very young, John Moore, a handsome, light, fantastic man, who loved fiddling, dancing and drinking, better than work, and so passed days, with few of the comforts of life, and a very meagre share of its pleasures. John Moore wrote a fair hand, and from the scarcity of that qualification for business among the early settlers, was, upon the first organization of Oglethorpe County, made Clerk of the Superior Court. The confidence of the people had ceased long before the expiration of the term of his office. The unsuitableness of Mr. and Mrs. Moore for sustaining the relation of husband and wife, was shown in the unfortunate peculiarities of their children.

Harvie, the oldest, was but little removed from idiocy. His memory was the only faculty which performed its functions well. That was developed so admirably, as to prove that one branch of the stock from which he was descended had intellect. He could repeat any sermon which he heard, word for word, though he had no judgment to understand or appreciate its merits. Mrs. Moore's son William was adopted by his aunt, Mrs. Devenport. He married Mary Marks, the half sister of Meriwether Lewis. He inherited a large estate from Mr. and Mrs. Devenport, which he reduced to a pittance by his out of the way efforts to increase it.

Mary Harvie married David Meriwether. Something has

already been written, descripitive of her and her only child, Martha, who married Col. Benjamin Taliaferro.

Margaret Harvie married John Devenport, who belonged to a numerous family, most of whom were in the habit of fuddling their very good intellects by drinking whiskey. John was, to his credit, a sober, industrious man, who made a good estate. His chief merit was to be found in his success in marrying a wife of the most admirable qualities.

Genette Harvie married Reuben Jordan, one of the descendants of the Indian Princess Pocahontas. She was the largest of the Harvie sisters. When Mrs. Jordan's size became too great to visit, or go to preaching in a carriage, she travelled in a wagon. She had great conversational talents, loved to talk, had an inexhaustible fund of anecdotes, and was not less remarkable for her wit, than for her weight.

Reuben Jordan's black eyes, dark hair and complexion, erect, active person, made him very handsome when young. A rich old maid fancied him. Being without fortune himself, he married her. After having one child, she died, leaving him at liberty to choose his second wife, according to his inclination.

Reuben Jordan's taste followed his Indian blood. When he could not hunt, he sought excitement from cards or whiskey; when neither hunting, cards, nor whiskey, were accessible, he employed himself in preparing himself to enjoy them when they were, by busying himself often for days together, in fixing his guns.

Martha, the oldest daughter of Mrs. Jordan, was a very pleasant, pretty girl. It was the rule of the Broad River people, that their children should begin to improve their condition at the earliest possible time. As soon as girls began to advance in their teens, a lookout was kept for a suitable husband. When Martha Jordan arrived at sixteen, there was no Broad River youth unmarried, who was in a fix, or old enough to marry, so Martha was married to Dr. Bradley, who was more than double her age, because marry she must. Old Bradley, the father of the doctor, lived on Savannah River, below Augusta, during the revolution. He was an active whig, was made prisoner by the British and tories, took the small-pox from an infected soldier, and died in the camp of the enemy.

He left two sons. His widow married a Dutch doctor by the name of De Yembert. James, the oldest of the two, was educated at Mr. Wilson's classical school, in the Wax-Haw settlement, in South Carolina, and afterwards studied medicine with his stepfather. He was the first regular bred physician who settled among the Broad River people. Previous to his time they relied on the voluntary services of Mr. Frank Meriwether, or the practical knowledge of the head of each family. The sufferings of the inhabitants from bilious fever and other diseases, created by extensive clearings, a warm climate, Broad River, and its low grounds, were very great. Dr. Bradley practiced for a long time very acceptably. He was one-eyed, pot-bellied, clumsy, and otherwise odd enough looking to give the people confidence in his skill at discovering the hidden causes of diseases. His perceptions were quick, his temper well disposed, and his character truthful and honest. His frugal habits enabled him to acquire a competency, and to quit practice, before he was very old. He willed the liberation of his slaves, about forty in number, at the death of his wife, provided they chose to go to Liberia, and furnished them with the means of going. All went, except a youth, who could not leave the girl he loved behind. Poor fellow, his fate was hard. He preferred the expected bliss from love, to the enjoyment of liberty. He served for life, without obtaining his wished for wife.

Mrs. Bradley and the Doctor joined the Methodist Church during the great revival of religion among the Broad River people in 1809, and were devout until death.

Dr. Bradley's residence was about two miles south from Broad River, adjoining the plantation of old Micajah McGehee.

Reuben, the oldest son of Mrs. Jordan, is a talking, sensible man, who, by constant and vigilant attention to the main chance, has become wealthy. He has been several times a member of the Legislature, and held other public offices. His first wife was Nancy, the oldest daughter of Col. Nicholas Johnson, a mild-tempered and excellent woman. After her death, he married a very beautiful young lady, the daughter of Col. Williamson, and a niece of the wife of Gen. John Clark.

Fleming, the second son of Mrs. Jordan, married Anna, the oldest daughter of Mr. Thomas Meriwether, of Broad River. He lives in Jasper County, which he has frequently represented in the Legislature. He is a man of intelligence and wealth. His wife, now dead, was, when living a pattern of excellence.

Margaret, the second daughter of Mrs. Jordan, became a cripple when a child. With the usual fate of such females, her lot in marriage was a husband much below her in fortune, and quality. She was so kind, patient, and good tempered, that she made her husband love her. Her fortune and economy, aided by his skill in planting, made them rich.

Betsey, the third daughter of Mrs. Jordan, married Dr. George Meriwether, and died soon after.

Mortimer, the third son of Mrs. Jordan, married the daughter of Hezekiah Grey, of Broad River, the niece of Gen. John Scott. His Broad River habits have made him wealthy.

Charles the fourth son of Mrs. Jordan, married Rebekah, daughter of Col. Nick Johnson. He resides in Jasper County. He is cheerful and happy, and like most lazy men, not very successful in acquiring riches, or distinguished station. He has lost his first wife, and married another.

Elizabeth Harvie, another of the nine, was very large, weighing over three hundred. She was one of the most cheerful, sensible, agreeable women in any country, at any time, and as good and kind as she was agreeable. She married James Marks. He was a little, low man, who weighed about one hundred and twenty. He was so tough and lean, as to be insensible to heat or cold. When the weather became hot, it was the custom of his wife, who could not bear heat, to double over upon him the blankets which covered the bed in winter. He was shrewd, and sharp-witted. The good things which he said, would, if they could be collected, add to the merits of Comus. He was very plain in dress, and economical in his expenditures. A year or two after he settled on Broad River, he bought, for the first time, a small quantity of coffee, to luxuriate upon at breakfast on Sunday mornings. One of the grains was dropt on the floor by accident, and swept into the yard. A little negro found it, and supposing it to be a young terrapin, put it upon a chip, and carried it with great wonderment to her mistress. James Marks was devotedly attached to his wife. His desire to please her, made him often do what no other motive could have done. Mrs. Marks enjoyed pretty things, and loved comfort. Her husband overcame his indisposition to spend money, so far as to build for her the finest house on Broad River.

Mr. and Mrs. Marks were the first of the Broad River people to who quitted the forms of the Episcopal Church for the devotion of the Methodist. They were special friends of Bishop Asbury, who made their house his home when he visited Georgia. The first organized Methodist congregation on Broad River was formed in their neighborhood and through their influence.

Their beautiful daughter Martha married, by their entreaties, a Methodist preacher, named Guerry. The sorry fellow had no love for his wife. He imagined that he would, by the marriage, become rich. Upon finding himself mistaken, he treated her like a brute, and, a year or two after their marriage, abandoned her. Standing at the window of her father's fine new house, looking out at the flashes of lightning during a thunderstorm, wondering at the mystery of God's ways, the electric fluid passed through the window into her heart, and ended her unhappy life.

The Markses were constitutionally perverse. James Marks used to say in his old age, that he had been in some respects the most unfortunate of men. That he was a most devoted Methodist, and decided Democrat; and that all of his children, except his ill-fated daughter, who had the least cause to love him, were Infidels and Federalists.

James Marks's residence was on Broad River between Governor Mathews's and Colonel Johnson's plantations.

John Marks, the oldest son of James and Elizabeth Marks, was thick and clumsy in person, with a superb head, set off by speaking gray eyes. When quite a youth, he fell in love with Mary Tomkins, a very pretty girl, the daughter of a rude, ill-tempered old fellow of the neighborhood, who had nothing in common, in character, taste or feelings, with the Broad River people. Jack's father and mother did and said whatever they could to prevent the match; but Jack had a large share of the quality mules are most remarkable for. He would go his own way. His marriage did not make his family like his wife. He loved her but the more. Though he continued for a long time to belong to the Broad River settlement, he got a little off from the kin. He had in a moment of excitement, when a youth, joined the Methodist church, of which his father and mother were members. His sharp intellect saw, or made him imagine he saw, so much that was unworthy of religion in its professors, that he quit his connection with them, to indulge in jesting through life against cant and hypocrisy. He grew up in the political faith of the Democrats. His father was a most enthusiastic admirer and follower of Mr. Jefferson. Jack found so much palaver and pretence of patriotism among those in power, that his satire exercised itself against them until he was ranked with the most confirmed Federalists.

There were no schools in the country when Jack Marks was a youth. He could read, but it had to be done slowly, and was accompanied with such defective pronunciation, that a boy of six years old would now be punished if he did not read better. But he understood what he read as perfectly as any one. His humor was constantly hunting materials for enjoyment. He was once building a log cabin in his yard for some domestic purpose. He and several negroes were upon the frame, when his wife came to the place, and began objecting to the manner in which he was fashioning what he was doing. He listened to her for some time, and reasoned the matter with her; but she still insisted upon having the house made according to her own notions. He pulled off his breeches, and threw them down to her, telling her to put them on and wear them.

As Tam O'Shanter made his way home from the tippling-house on his mare Maggy, late on a dark night, he saw lights streaming from the old church on the road side. Being a brave fellow in his cups, he ventured up, and, looking in, saw the Old Boy seated on a three-legged stool, playing the bagpipes to the witches of the neighborhood. Recognizing one who was younger than the rest, as she jigged a great whirl about, he cried out in ecstacies at what he saw, "Well done, Cutty Sark!" If Tam had been passing by when Jack's dumpy person was standing aloft breechless, and had heard his speech to his wife, how he would have hallooed out, "Well said, Short Shirt!"

Jack Marks's father showed by his will that he had not forgotten his son's disobedience in his marriage—his sarcasms at the Methodist people and their ways—the Democrats and their policy. He left him a thousand dollars only, giving the principal part of his estate to his daughter, Mrs. Johnson, and his son Meriwether. Jack was as stout as his father was unforgiving. Though he was not rich, he made a donation of the thousand dollars to Franklin College.

Jack Marks was capable of the greatest intellectual efforts, and the highest attainments in science, philosophy, and politics. Though he was without education, his quick repartee, keen sarcasm, close extensive observation, made him one of the most sensible, agreeable talkers of his day.

He removed from Broad River, in Madison County, to Jasper, where he found a larger field for fun and satire, better lands for cultivation, and more improved society for his children. One of his daughters married Judge Kenan, and another David Meriwether.

He was very industrious and economical, and acquired a very good estate.

Meriwether Marks, the second son of Mrs. Marks was, like his brother Jack, remarkable for quick, clear mental perceptions, and successful disputation. He married Ann Mathews, the daughter of William, and granddaughter of Governor Mathews. He removed from Broad River, shortly after his marriage, to Montgomery, Alabama, where he acquired a great extent of the most productive lands, and died very wealthy. His son William is now probably the richest man in the United States of his age whose occupation has been confined to planting. His daughter Elizabeth married William B. S. Gilmer. His daughter Ann married Thomas Scott, son of General Scott. His daughter Martha married

James Watkins, the son of Thomson Watkins. His daughter Rebekah married George Mathews, son of Charles, and grandson of Governor Mathews. Samuel, his youngest son, married Miss Crane, and is very rich.

Mary, Mr. and Mrs. Marks's oldest daughter, married Col. Nick Johnson. They are described elsewhere.

Mary Cosby, the sister of Mrs. William Harvie, married John Andrew, a Methodist preacher. He quit the circuit for his locality, which was on the Elbert side of Broad River, opposite to Mr. William Harvie's, where he commenced the trade of merchandise with the property which he got with his wife, and the very little which he had himself. The spirit of trade and the spirit of preaching never agree together. One or the other will get the upper hand, if the unnatural union is continued. It is certain that John Andrew failed in trade, and found many stumbling blocks in the way of preaching. After all his property was taken to pay his mercantile liabilities, and he and his wife left to labor without assistance for their own and their children's support, he took to school keeping. The little ones are pretty sure to have a sore time who learn their A B C from a harassed, broken trader. Many had knowledge forced upon them by the switching looks of John Andrew. Being very hard visaged, he appeared as if he was always ready to cut the truant scholar in two. The pay for school keeping was in early times, in upper Georgia, the poorest pittance. The people wanted their children for work and kept them at it, except at leisure times, and when schooling could be had cheap. John Andrew, his wife and children, had to scuffle and pinch to provide food, and oftentimes, with all their exertions, found it scarce. It was then that the spirit of devotion strengthened the spirit of the wife and mother in her cares, and comforted her in her troubles.

Mrs. Andrew had loved her husband, homely as he was, with increased affection, because of the holy purposes of his life. It is in sore trials and great suffering that woman's love shows its true value. Mrs. Andrew made herself more precious than gold when her husband's purse became empty. With the strong faith of the true Christian, she labored without ceasing during her life, to perform all the duties of wife and mother. The blessing of heaven never fails to follow the prayers and industry of such a wife and mother. Her oldest son James, excited by her spirit and example, worked hard in the field during the day, collected light-wood knots on his return home, and toiled by their light after knowledge during the night. Nobody works in vain who works aright. The light which enlightens the world shined into the heart of James Andrew so brightly, that he could not restrain his desire to be the medium of communicating it to others. He was licensed to preach. The brotherhood by whom the license was granted, when they heard his first sermon regretted what they had done, so hesitating and unsatisfactory was the young enthusiast's effort. But the right spirit was in him, though the knowledge and aptness to communicate had not been acquired. James Andrew found the assistance, which in his devotion he asked for, to aid his efforts to overcome the deficiencies of ignorance and inexperience. He soon made himself greatly superior in learning and the art of public speaking to those who were most opposed to his being licensed. And now the Methodist Church has no member of greater usefulness, nor one more efficiently devoted to the great purpose of its organization—the making known, with power in simplicity, the truths of the Gospel—than Bishop Andrew.

Herbert Andrew, the second son of Mrs. Andrew, had his dependence as a child increased by disease, which made him a cripple for life. His feet and legs became so contracted as to rest on his body instead of the ground. When other children were running about, he was confined to his mother's side. Whilst thus seated, receiving her instruction how to read, he heard from that fond, devoted, pious mother, how the best and holiest of all had suffered without repining, because it was the will of his Heavenly Father, until there came upon the spirit of the deformed boy the strongest desire to imitate his example. Herbert Andrew struggled to do whatever was possible in aid of his mother, in her hard effort to support her family, and effected more than most imagined possible. When he had learned what his mother could teach him, he went to school, moving upon his hands instead of his feet. By his mother's assistance, some little schooling, and his own untiring exertions, he qualified himself for teaching others. He has now been teaching near twenty years. His energy and ceaseless industry have secured him the greatest success. Whilst keeping school, he has acquired by his unassisted exertions such knowledge of the various departments of learning, that his scholars are admirably qualified for entrance into college. His pure life, the strength of his determination in overcoming difficulties, and the energy of his efforts in doing good, made such an impression upon the people among whom he lived, that they gave him some assistanse by electing him to a public office, the duties of which he could discharge without interfering with the attention due to his school.

Mrs. Andrew's burdens were increased by her care for her husband's deaf, blind, dumb brother, whose filthy habits and irascible disposition added to the unbearableness of his idiocy. He put him into a hut in the yard of the family cabin. Every morning the unfortunate came out by light, walked round the hut twenty times; then went to each of three trees close by, and round them twenty times; then to the cabin-door, stepped on the sill with his left foot foremost, and down twenty times; then with his right foot foremost, and down twenty times; then went into the cabin, put his hand on the facing of the door and thumped the upper part twenty times; then thumped below twenty times; and then ate voraciously of what was prepared for breakfast. This unvaried round was continued for near twenty years, and until his death. When the idiot became outrageous, as he often did, Mrs. Andrew would lay her hand upon his arm. It quieted him, as if he felt the force of sympathy coming from her kind heart. He regarded nobody else. Cut off from society by constant confinement at home—seeing there at all times the most painful object which is ever looked upon—her children harassed—the scanty food and clothing which she provided for them by her own hard labor, divided with one who had no good quality, and without hope, and incapable of being made better—Mrs. Andrew never forgot to care for the idiot, and to do for him all possible good—thus giving to the world an example of love and charity, which the world for its own sake should keep in perpetual remembrance. Sir Philip Sidney, when dying of wounds on the field of battle, took the cup of water from his own parched lips, to cool the burning thirst of the soldier, then struggling for life by his side. The divinity which sometimes stirs man's, abides in woman's heart.

THE TALIAFERROS.

SIRNAMES, which now belong to every body, were origininally acquired by our European ancestors through remarkable traits of character, great feats at fighting, or some personal peculiarity. The name Taliaferro was derived from the Latin words talis and ferrum, or, as Mr. John Taliaferro says, from the Italian words Tagliari and ferro; both the Latin and Italian signifying to cut with iron. The name indicates for what virtue, as a Roman would say, the original stock of Taliaferros got their cognomen.

Two brothers emigrated from Italy to Virginia in the early colonial times, and settled in the neighborhood of Williamsburg. Only one of them left male descendants. They have increased and scattered, until the name of Taliaferro is now known in most of the States south of the Potomac, their Italian blood not suiting the climate of the north, nor their taste the phlegm of the northern people. Individuals here and there still show their origin by the practice of improvisation. Mr. Jefferson describes the family in Virginia as wealthy and respectable. Chancellor Wythe, who signed the Declaration of Independence, and was a great Virginian, married one of them.

Zack Taliaferro removed from the neighborhood of Williamsburg to Amherst County, where he settled and married. From the crossings of his immediate ancestors he lost the beauty and effeminacy of the original stock. He was as rough in looks and temper as the face of the country of his new home. At the time when he located in Amherst County, and for some time after, disputes among the mountain men were usually settled by the law of arms, in which fist fights were the weapons of war. When champion pugilists were about to fight, a ring was formed, with the combatants inside, and the crowd out. The contest frequently ended with the loss of an eye, or an ear; scarcely ever without blacking or bluing the face and ribs. Zack was a capital hand at such affairs, and never backed out, however overmatched. He was one of the justices of Amherst County when the senior justice was entitled to be sheriff of the county; the perquisites of that office being the only pay which the justice received for even a life-time of service. Old Zack had much higher qualifications for acting sheriff than judge. A little after the commencement of the year when he became senior justice, and his sheriffalty was to begin, but before he was sworn in, he met with a notorious outlaw, who had been able previously to avoid punishment for his misdeeds by avoiding arrest. The outlaw took to his heels, and old Zack after him. The pursued, finding that he was about to be overtaken, plunged into a mill-pond near by, though the January cold was then pinching severely, taking it for granted that he would not be followed. He reckoned without his host. Old Zack deliberately walked in after him, took the scamp by the collar, drew him out of the water, and then turned him loose, telling him that he might know by what he had done what he would have to do when he was sheriff.

Benjamin Taliaferro was the oldest son of Zack. He had just begun to mix with men, when he was challenged by a bully before a crowd in the court-yard to a contest at fisty-cuffs. He was too proud to accept, and was threatened with disinheritance by his father for his supposed want of courage. That he was not afraid to fight, when fighting was right, he proved in many of the hardest fought battles of the Revolution. He was appointed at the beginning of the war a lieutenant in one of the Virginia regiments, which was afterwards placed upon the Continental establishment. He commanded a company under Gen. Washington during the severe service in the Jerseys, in 1777-78. At the battle of Princeton he captured, with his company, a British captain and his command. When the British officer stepped forward in his dashing regimentals to deliver up his sword, the proud barefooted captain ordered his lieutenant to receive it. At the call of Gen. Washington he volunteered to join the southern army, then under command of Gen. Lincoln. He served under Gen. Lee, and took part in many of the successful exploits of that dashing officer.

He was made prisoner at the capture of Charleston, and permitted to return home on parole. He was in the full vigor of young manhood when he left the British quarters to mix again with his neighbors in Amherst. His person was six feet high, his features handsome, and his understanding good. Army intercourse had refined his manners and made his conversation agreeable.

Martha Meriwether, the only child of David Meriwether, a neighbor of old Zack, was a blooming, charming young woman, when Capt. Taliaferro returned to Amherst. They soon met, admired, and loved. Martha Meriwether had previously been engaged to marry Zack Taliaferro, a brother of Capt. Taliaferro. The struggle was hard on the part of the army man of honor to resist the temptation to supersede his brother. But love conquers all. The red-coat got the better of the gown. The brothers quarrelled and parted, never again to meet in friendship. The disappointed lover quit the country for a residence in Pendleton, South Carolina, where he remained a bachelor until the bright hopes inspired by youthful beauty were dissipated by the loose habits of frontier society and the struggles of a lawyer's life.

Capt. Taliaferro moved to Georgia in 1784. He became one of the leading men of the State; was President of the Senate, a member of Congress, and filled many other high offices. He was a member of the Legislature which passed the Yazoo Act, and resisted all the efforts of the speculators to induce him to vote for it. When the people of Georgia rescinded that Act, and discarded from office those concerned in its passage, Col. Taliaferro was made Judge of the Superior Court, though he was no lawyer. The members of the bar who had the law learning necessary for the office, and were willing to accept it, had been concerned in some way or other in that disgraceful contract. It became very important to the fraudulent land jobbers, who were interested in land causes depending in the courts of the circuit in which Col. Taliaferro presided, to drive him from the bench. By agreement among them, he was challenged by Col. Willis, upon some frivolous pretence, to fight a duel, upon the supposition that his army opinions would compel him to fight, and therefore to resign his judgeship. They were mistaken. He accepted the challenge without resigning. The speculators tried a novel expedient to effect their purpose. Judge Taliaferro's attachment to his wife was well known. Col. Willis and his friends, to overcome the Judge's determination to fight, made their preparations for the duel by practising within sight and hearing of Mrs. Taliaferro, intending thereby so to frighten her as to make it impossible for her husband to meet the challengers. They were again mistaken. Whilst they were practising, Mrs. Taliaferro was aiding the Judge to put in order the horseman's pistols which he had used when he belonged to Lee's Legion. The Judge and his opponent met. The pistol, which had been oiled by the wife, sent its ball so near the speculator's vitals that he declined receiving a second shot.

Col. Taliaferro's residence was on the south side, and about half mile from Broad River, and ten miles from its junction with the Savannah. His house was of the order called framed, in contradistinction to the round and hewed log buildings in general use. It was a story and a half high, with dormer windows, structures which projected from the sides of the roof of the house, and were in fashion in that part of the Old Dominion, where Col. Taliaferro's ancestors had lived before his father moved to Amherst County. They were designed to give air at night to the crowds who assembled to frolic, and whose homes were too distant to be reached for sleep after they left off dancing. A few such windows are yet to be seen from the steamboats which ply between Richmond and Norfolk in the antiquated houses which stand on the first hills above the low grounds of James River, and about the last remnants of the times when social enjoyments were more eagerly sought after than money. This story and a half house, with its dormer windows, was considered for a long time the head-quarters of Broad River gentility.

Colonel Taliaferro had nine children by his first wife. After her death, he outraged the romance of their strong attachment by marrying a dependent young woman of the neighborhood, of the name of Cox, about whom any romance would have been ridiculous. She had one child, a son.

Colonel Taliaferro's Children.

Emily married Isham Watkins.

Louis Bourbon (after Louis, the King of France) married Betsy Johnson.

Betsy died unmarried.

Benjamin married Martha Watkins.

Martha married William McGehee.

David married Mary Barnett.

Thornton married Miss Green; second wife, Mrs. Lamar.

Margaret married Joseph Green.

Nicholas married Melinda Hill.

Zack married ———.

Sally, the oldest sister of Col. Taliaferro, married Daniel Harvie. She was one of the most sensible, exemplary women on Broad River. Her residence and children are described in the account of the Harvies.

Richard Taliaferro was deformed—his legs and thighs being only a span or two long, whilst his body was of ordinary length and size, and his head unusually large. His mind was of good capacity, but his deformity so soured his temper, and mortified his pride, as to drive him from society. He never married, became very penurious, and died without ever having enjoyed the love or commiseration of any but his nearest kin. His residence was near his brother-in-law, Thompson Watkins.

Warren Taliaferro was tall, muscular, good-tempered, very indolent and inefficient. He constantly reminded those who listened to his conversation of his Italian descent. He married Mary M. Gilmer, daughter of Thomas M. Gilmer. He was a fond husband and father. His residence was south of Broad river, and between the dwellings of his brother-in-law, Thompson Watkins, and his brother, Col. Taliaferro.

Burton, the youngest of the Taliaferros, was very handsome—had the manners, and wore the dress, of a well-bred gentleman. He read and enjoyed novels and plays, and fashioned his habits accordingly. He married Sally Gilmer, daughter of John Gilmer. He resided, during the year that his wife lived, near Broad River, on the land, and close by Thomas M. Gilmer. He loved good eating, drinking and fine clothes. His property was not sufficient for free indulgence. After the death of his first wife, he went to Virginia, and married the miser, Miss Carter, who counted her gold by stockings full, upon condition that she would allow him enough of her gold to enable him to feast his animal appetites.

Nancy Taliaferro married Thompson Watkins. She was a very industrious, economical woman. By her exertions she made her husband a citizen of property. They lived a mile or two from Broad River, and near Mrs. Sally Harvie's, Mrs. Watkins's sister. They had but two children. Zachariah, the oldest, married Edna Bibb, the daughter of Mr. Peyton Bibb. James married Martha Marks, daughter of Mr. Meriwether Marks.

Frances Taliaferro married Moses Penn. They removed from Virginia many years after the first settlement was made on Broad River by their relations, and fixed their abode between the north and south rivers, whose confluence make Broad River, where Mr. Penn died soon after. Mrs. Penn was a good woman, a kind and affectionate mother, and most enthusiastic Methodist. One of her daughters married the Rev. Dabney Jones, whose long continued efforts to lessen the evils of drunkenness—the disgrace of our glorious country entitle him to be called one of its great benefactors.

Another of Mrs. Penn's daughters married Mr. Edward Ware, who proved himself a good husband and kind father.

Mrs. Penn's son Richard was a very respectable citizen.

THE McGEHEES.

MICAJAH McGEHEE was a native of Virginia, and descended, as his name indicates, from a Scotch family. He was broad-shouldered, short-necked, and showed by his looks and ways that he was a tobacco planter of the right sort. He knew nothing about books, and spoke out what he thought directly, and in the plainest way. Soon after he became his own man, he was employed by Mr. Scott, a wealthy gentleman, of the family to which Gen. Winfield Scott belongs, to do some plantation business for him. According to Virginia fashion, intercourse between employers and employed was without restraint. Nancy Scott soon saw in the looks of young McGehee that she suited his fancy. It is not in woman's heart to be unmoved by admiration. She looked in return at the hearty, hale, strong-built, rosy-cheeked youth, until his image became so impressed upon her imagination that she saw others very indifferently. When two such people have wills under such influences, they are very apt to find a way to do as they desire. The gentility of the Scotts disposed them to look down upon the working Micajah, and to oppose the union. The young people, nevertheless, got married. Not choosing to belong to the society of those who thought themselves above them, they removed to Georgia, and settled on Broad River. Though Micajah was wanting in polish, his father-in-law understood his worth, as a man of industry, economy and honesty. He gave him liberally of his property. Micajah made good use of it, by purchasing a large body of the best land in Georgia, particularly suited for the production of tobacco, then the staple of the State. He was an adept at cultivating and packing it up in the best way. Though he was without book-learning, he had the instinctive capacity of the Scotch people and their descendants for making and keeping money. He was the first of the settlers who planted a peach-orchard on the waters of Broad River, turned its fruit into brandy, and then into dollars. The habit of drinking what makes drunkenness was, in early times among the frontier folks, almost universal. Brandy making and selling was the most profitable of all employments. Micajah McGehee made from his orchard sixteen hundred dollars a year, when that sum purchased as much as five thousand dollars does now. He had twelve children, upon each of whom he enforced the habit of hard work. He became rich through the labor of his negroes, his children's industry, and his own economy. He built the first comfortable frame-house on Broad River. It had four rooms below stairs, several above, was covered with shingles, and painted red. It was a great place for the old Virginia amusement of dancing.

Micajah McGehee's constitution was so strong, that he battled with death, taking brandy until he was upwards of eighty years old. When he was young, it took drinking all day to make him drunk. When he was old, he got drunk twice a day. He became a member of the Methodist Church during the great religious excitement of 1809-10-11. He still continued to get drunk. When he was spoken to about it, he said that the habit was so confirmed that he could not live without the free use of brandy. He was requested to say what quantity was necessary for his health. He agreed to try to limit himself to a quart a day, but the allowance failed to keep him alive.

Mrs. McGehee was exceedingly kind and hospitable. It belonged to her Scott temper to be so. After her marriage, she added to the genteel habits of her own family the industry of her husband's. She never stopped or tired of working for her husband and children. Her house was a place of hard work and of good eating. She had a very pressing way of urging her friends to partake of what she set before them. During the early pinching times, when tempting food was reserved for Sundays and friends, Mr. Thomas Meriwether called one day when very hungry—the family meal over—and was set down to what he liked very much. Mrs. McGehee very politely urged him to eat, saying that he was taking so little that he could not relish what she had provided for him. His own candid temper and way of talking made him suppose that Mrs. McGehee might be hurt if he did not consume more than he was disposed to do. He eat on until suffering stopped him.

Mrs. McGehee once performed a feat of industry which was hard to beat. She spun, wove, cut out, and made up a petticoat in one day, and wore it the next.

Industrious as she was, she continued to have the quality of taste of her family for display. She induced her husband to buy a carriage, when nobody else on Broad River had one. It was a stick-backed gig. Sunday was their visiting day. The next after the purchase, the old gentleman and his wife came in it to my father's to dinner. The road had just been cut around a new-ground fence, and was very full of stumps. The old man turned the gig over. When they arrived at my father's, the old lady complained of great pain. The old man insisted that she ought not to moan so, for that, when he found the gig going over, he had spread himself, and caught her upon his back, to prevent her being hurt.

Tom McGehee, the oldest son of Micajah, was a very stout, coarse, strong man. He was industrious, economical, straightforward, truthful, and honest. His plantation was on Broad River, between the Goosepond creek and the Goosepond plantation. It was very fertile, and Tom grew rich upon it. He and his neighbor, Col. Charles Mathews, never agreed after his threat to thrash federalism out of him, when he and William Barnett quarrelled at my father's. They met one day in the public road, where they had an altercation about some hogs getting into corn fields. Tom McGehee made some offensive speech, to which Col. Mathews replied by a cutting sarcasm, which so enraged Tom, that he swore he could whip three such as he was, and made at him. Col. Mathews drew out his penknife, and presented it in a threatening aspect. Cold steel kept off Tom's big fist.

When Tom McGehee acquired more negroes than he had land to cultivate, he was obliged to sell because nobody else would whose land adjoined his. He removed to Upper Alabama, where he died. His wife was Betsey Gilmer, the daughter of my father's uncle, John Gilmer. Their children have all gone to Texas, in search of what all the McGehees have peculiar genius for finding.

James, the second son of Micajah McGehee, was said by the old people to have been very smart when a boy. A horse threw his head against a tree, which so confused his brain that he was never smart again. He once got the better of Gov. Mathews in a horse trade, though the Governor was acknowledged by every body to be the best judge of a horse in the whole country. The feat was more prized by Jemmy than if he had got the first honor at college.

He married a busy, bustling little woman, whose name I do not recollect. He lived on the south of his brother Tom, a mile and a half from Broad River. He removed to Putnam County. My wife was with me on my return home from serving in the Legislature of 1824. When we arrived at Garner's Ferry, the Oconee was so high, from the great quantity of rain which had fallen, that the ferryman would not put us across. We had been so long from home that we were very anxious to get there; so we went below a mile or two, with a large party, to a ferry kept by James McGehee. In consideration of large pay he agreed to ferry us over. The river was out of its banks on the Green County side. It was sweeping, booming, and dashing through the trees on the side where we were, carrying off with its current great quantities of floating timber. James McGehee, assisted by his sons and several negroes, towed the boat up the river, along the bank, by ropes, hooks, and the limbs of the trees. My wife standing near by the workers, at the head of the boat, quietly looked on. After going up some distance, the head of the boat was turned, and being worked manfully with oars, landed us in an open field on the other side. James McGehee was afterwards often heard to tell of what a wonderful woman his neighbor's son had married.

Frank, the third son, was very clever. He died just after he reached manhood.

Abner, the fourth son, is social, polite, courteous and affable, kind and hospitable. He settled on a high hill, not far from Broad River, on the Elbert side, opposite his brother Tom. He turned his hand to any thing to make money. He was a planter, tanner, and general trader. The Legislature, in the year ———, incorporated a company to improve the navigation of Broad River. The company contracted with Abner to do the necessary work. He went on for a week or two, and quit upon finding that he had made a losing bargain. The company sued him, and recovered the full amount of his bond.

He removed from Broad River to Montgomery, Alabama, where his untiring industry, money, and credit, has contributed most essentially to the building of the railroad to West Point. Though his losses have been very great, from his liberal expenditures upon that important railroad, he has overcome them, and is now possessed of a large estate.

His first wife was Miss Spencer, his first cousin. His second, Mrs. Jane Johnson, the daughter of John Gilmer. His third, Mrs. Graves.

William, the fifth son, contrary to the cautious habits of

his family, entered upon the great ocean of trade, and was stranded. He was a quiet, gentlemanly man; married first a daughter of Col. Taliaferro, and after her death, a daughter of James Watkins. He built and occupied the white house on the Augusta Road, between his father's and the Goosepond. He afterwards removed to Mississippi.

Edmund, the sixth son, was an active, finely proportioned man, very courteous and affable, very industrious. His desire for mental improvement was such, that he agreed to pay his father, out of the property which he should receive from him when he came of age, twelve dollars per month for the time he went to school more than his brothers had gone. Though he was very industrious, and desirous of acquiring riches, he was liberal, kind-hearted, and hospitable. He fell in love with, and married Miss Cosby, an exceedingly clever young lady, but without fortune. He removed to Louisiana. The last time I saw him was in Washington City, on his way to place his daughter at Mr. Willard's school in Troy. He is now reputed to be worth near a million of dollars. He has given as much as five thousand dollars at a time to benevolent purposes. President Taylor was his near neighbor, and had so great confidence in his financial capacity and honesty that he made him his executor.

Jack, the seventh son, was not in the least bookish. When at school he made such slow progress in arithmetic that he seemed incapable of abstraction. But he proved himself a perfect adept at calculation when it was with sensible objects. He did addition and multiplication with acres of land, negroes, and bags of cotton, with as much certainty, and extending to as large a quotient, as the most learned.

Jack married Melinda Hill, daughter of Miles Hill, and settled in Wilks County, near Mallorysville, a few miles south from Broad River. He afterwards moved to Upper Mississippi, where he still resides. He told me the other day that his oldest son, Miles, made last year eleven hundred bags of cotton. Few German princes have incomes equal to the value of eleven hundred bags of cotton. All the Broad River settlers together did not make as much money for many years after their arrival in Georgia.

Abram, the eighth son, was about my age. At our first common school we had a contest, which I mention here, because it shows the habits of the times. The school-boys determined to turn out William P. Culbertson, the schoolmaster, for a day's holiday. They assembled early in the morning, and barred the entry into the school-house by filling the door with the benches and other heavy things. The school-master was then boarding with Abram's father. He and all his brothers took part with him against the boys. They got to the school-house before Culbertson, and commenced threatening the boys inside with the master's hickory. They dared any boy inside to come out. Those inside shoved me through the opening cut in a log for lighting the writing bench, to accept Abram's banter. At it we went. I made a missing blow, slipped, or somehow else got down on the ground, and Abram on me. His brothers surrounded us, urging Abram to give it to me well. This was too much for the boys inside to bear. They tore away the fastenings from the door, and rescued me from my perilous position, put me upon my feet, and secured a fair fight. Let any one set out when young, and go straight forward, yielding to no obstruction, and resisting all temptations to turn aside, he will have gone no inconsiderable distance by the time he arrives at sixty. Abram, when a little boy, commenced buying fish hooks and pins, and selling them for profit. He has gone on unceasingly, buying and selling at a profit, until he is reputed to be worth four hundred thousand dollars.

Hugh, the ninth and youngest son, was mild and amiable. He married the daughter of Shelton White, and settled on the Elbert side of Broad River, a little below Webb's Ferry, where his uncle Gray had lived. He has removed to the upper part of the State of Mississippi, where he has become very rich, and is regarded by every body as a very good man.

Betsey, the oldest daughter of Micajah McGehee married Abram Hill. My brother Peachy and Abram Hill, lived upon equal parts of a tract of land which had belonged to my father and Micajah McGehee, and which they divided between the son of the one and the son-in-law of the other. The entire tract contained 2100 acres. It had been bought at a

Sheriff sale. Old Bob Lumpkin, his sons and daughters, got possession in a way that they could not be removed but by a possessory writ. Old Bob was sued, and a recovery had of him. He still refused to leave the land. The Sheriff required the services of the posse comitatus to aid him in giving possession to the successful litigants. Upon the appearance of the Sheriff and his command in great force, Old Bob, and his sons were forced to quit the house. His daughters declared that they would themselves hold on. So, the men bore them away on their backs.

My brother and his family, and Mr. Hill and his, having known each other familiarly, their neighborly intercourse went on for some time in a very friendly way. Mrs. Hill was on exceedingly nice woman, considering a speck of dirt upon her floor or furniture, a great stigma upon her character. My brother was a voracious tobacco chewer. He found Mrs. Hill so much annoyed by the stains he put upon her floor, hearth, and very clean steps, that he was compelled to go out of the house to spit. His visits became short and far between, though he and his liked their nice neighbor and her husband very much.

Mrs. Hill was exceedingly prim and formal. She had no children for sixteen years. Afterwards she had two, now Dr. Abram Hill and Mrs. Blanton Hill, of Athens.

Sally, the second daughter of Micajah McGehee, was the prettiest woman on the frontiers of Georgia, according to frontier taste. Her eyes were large, liquidly bright, with long dark eyelashes shading them so as to add to their fascination. Her features were regular, and her cheeks rosy. Her person was straight and all the roundings of her limbs and chest beautifully perfect. She had just begun to run all the young men crazy who saw her, when she and Tom Hill fancied each other, and married. After the death of Tom Hill, she married her brother-in-law, Dionysius Oliver. They moved west, whither all her children by her first marriage are gone. She had none by her last.

Lucinda, the youngest child of Micajah McGehee, married Dionysius Oliver, and died a few years after.

The likenesses of the Broad River kin which I have been

sketching, would be incomplete, without the one which I am about to draw. Some may not be pleased, at hanging side by side with a poor body, entirely unknown to fame. But, as he was kind, truthful, and honest, and these qualities make up the largest portion of human excellence, I cannot refuse him a place among the Broad River people. I had an affection for him which he returned heartily. But to satisfy the squeamishness of others he shall be nameless, though his name and probably his family, were identical with one of the Presidents of the United States.

He was a soldier from the beginning to the end of the revolutionary war. He fought without fear, in many of its hardest battles; but was so unambitious, that he never rose above the rank and file of the army. During his long citizen's life, he did whatever was required of him faithfully, but was so poke-easy, that he never held any office as high as constable.

Soon after the peace permitted every body to attend to their own affairs, the soldier came across a young woman in the Ragged Mountains of Amherst County, Virginia, who considering him a good match, married him. He found out when inquiry was useless that she was as lazy and thriftless as himself. The soldier and his wife followed his commanding officers, Gen. Mathews and Col. Taliaferro, to Georgia, and settled in their neighborhood, near Broad River. He had only money enough to locate a warrant of survey, and pay for the grant of a small piece of poor land. He built upon it a round log cabin of one room, in which he and his wife lived, until it was too small to hold them and their children. The range and the forest supplied them with milk and meat. The soldier, his wife and children, never had abundance of any thing else, and of these, only for part of the year. What they had, was, however, always freely shared with wanting neighbors, and needy new comers. Neither husband nor wife ever loved to work, though they filled their cabin to overflowing with their progeny. Next after idleness, the soldier's greatest pleasure was in reading. He had no books. Mr. Richard Harvie, who knew his taste and integrity, supplied him with them. I used, when a boy, to visit him frequently. I loved to hear him talk of his campaigning under General

Washington. He described the battles in which he fought, and the stirring incidents of war, with such earnest, simple truthfulness, that I often felt the desire to have been by his side.

The first change for the better in the old soldier's poor way of living was effected by his lazy wife. By some happy hit of good fortune, or peculiar adaptedness to the employment, she got the reputation of skill in midwifery. Her services were so often called for by the prolific frontier women, that money was made by the handfull. After some years of successful practice, the old soldier's wife died. His oldest son, when he became of age to act for himself, married a wife who belonged to the meanest family who ever left the Old World for the New; a host of whom had removed from Virginia to Georgia, and settled upon every poor vacant piece of land in the Broad River neighborhood. As many as ten of them lived within the limits of the tract owned afterwards by Col. Nick Johnson. Most of them would cheat for six and a quarter cents, and sue each other for a quarter of a dollar. Horse swapping was their favorite trade. There was but one of them who rose to greatness even in rascality. He was called Gentleman Will. One of his sons was a professional gambler; another was hung for negro or horse stealing.

I once heard one of the sorry scamps of the clan begging a Justice of the Peace of the district in which they lived, for a warrant to arrest a kinsman, who had given him a kick, or a cuff. The fellow was called Coony, from his climbing a tree after a coon, going out on the limb upon which the animal was, cutting it off between himself and the body of the tree, falling among the dogs, and being bitten for the beast.

The old soldier's married son was soon no better than his wife's kin. To save his younger sons from the influence of their bad brother and his near relations, the old soldier removed to a distant part of the country. They profited by the change. One of them is now a Methodist preacher of some celebrity.

The old soldier passed the remainder of his life in comparative comfort, beloved and respected by every one who knew him.

I desired to conclude the biographies of the Broad River settlers by showing the great amount of riches which has been accumulated by their extraordinary industry, economy, and honesty, and the honors conferred upon them on account of their patriotism and integrity, so that my book might do good, by stimulating others to follow their example. It is not known that any so small community of planting people, ever created so much wealth, and filled so many offices in so short a time. I endeavored for a year or two, to ascertain the facts which would enable me to give an exact account of what each one was worth. I have failed, because those whom I asked for information, thought it would look like bragging to answer my questions. Others, that it might degrade them to let it be known how little property their Broad River ancestors brought with them to Virginia. I have written, urged, and labored, with such slight success, that I am obliged to be contented with making the following general statement.

The descendants of George Mathews are now worth several millions of dollars, so are the descendants of Frank Meriwether, Nat Barnett, Micajah McGehee and Mrs. Harvie. The descendants of Nicholas Johnson are supposed to be worth two millions, those of John Gilmer about the same amount, and those of Thomas Gilmer one million.

Not a descendant of any one of the Broad River people is now known to be so poor, as to be dependent on others for support. Not one has been lost to society by continued gambling, drinking, or other violations of morals and law. One of them has been a prominent candidate for the Presidency. Three have been Governors of States. Three have been Judges of the highest courts. Two have been Presidents of the Senate of Georgia; many of them have been members of the Legislature of Georgia and other Southern States; and many have been members of the Congress of the United States, and two of them have been electors of President and Vice-President of the United States.

PART II

In the part of Wilkes County below Long Creek, and extending southwardly from Savannah River, a settlement was made before and during the revolutionary war by the Clarks, Dooleys, Murrays, Waltons, and others. They were from Bertie and the adjoining counties of North Carolina, and were all connected together by blood or intermarriages. Gen. Jackson was their countryman, and Col. Benton their kinsman.

These North Carolina settlers lived upon game and the milk of the cattle which they carried with them in their emigration. Hogs, sheep, and poultry, were not to be had, except in the fewest numbers. A sufficient supply of these indispensables for a new country could only be obtained from South Carolina, whither the settlers went for that purpose when they had sufficient money to purchase. Many years passed before they owned hogs and sheep enough for bacon and clothing. Those were hard times, when the breakfast of the family depended upon catching an opossum the over night or a rabbit in the morning. The range was so unrestricted that the cows often wandered away beyond returning or finding, so that the children had no milk to wash down their otherwise dry bread. The horses which did the ploughing had to be turned on the wild grass to get their food. They strayed beyond finding, if their legs were not fastened together, so that the art of hobbling was as important as the blacksmith's. Bells were put upon them, for the purpose of indicating their whereabouts; and then the Indians, if on the frontiers, carried them off. It was difficult to clear of its timber enough of land for corn and tobacco. The term patch was for a long time used for the land sown in wheat, because only a small quantity was allotted for that grain. Even these patches were not seen for years after the settlement began, so that flour could not be had at times for love or money. It was a long time before the children had more than a biscuit a-piece on Sunday mornings. Traps, snares, pens, and other contrivances, were resorted to for catching birds and turkeys. The end of a switch was twisted in the hair of a rabbit, to draw him from his refuge up in a hollow tree. Food was eaten then with the greatest relish, which the lady descendants of the settlers would be horrified to see on their tables now. An opossum, with its full dish of gravy, occupied the place of the sucking pig at present. There were no tanneries then to prepare leather for shoes, nor well-instructed shoemakers to manufacture them. Skins, taken from the cattle killed for beef, and those that died with the hollowhorn, were hung in running streams until the hair could be slipped off, and then put into troughs with bark until they became what was called fit for manufacture. Even this hard material could only be had in sufficient quantities to allow shoes to the children when the frost and snow made the cold too severe for their bare feet to bear. Most went without shoes the greater part of the year.

The first houses were log cabins, with dirt floors and clapboard coverings. Vile toads and venomous serpents were often found crawling over them, and occasionally on the beds. Snakes abounded, until the increase of hogs lessened their number. The rattle of the rattlesnake and the cry of a panther often sent the children home in a hurry from the woods when hunting the cows. The sheep had to be kept in inclosures about the cabins, or there was no wool for winter use. No school gave to the children an hour's play time. After working all day, they sat around the hearth at night, picking the lint from the cotton seed, to supply the material for their clothing. There was no fruit in the country to gratify their eager appetites, except wild grapes, haws, and whortleberries. The boys had no marbles nor tops, until their own labor added to their fathers' means to buy them. All work, little play, no fruit, poor eating, thin clothing, open houses, hard beds, and few blankets, made children hardy or killed them. No novels, pianos, or idleness filled the heads of the girls with vain imaginings. The singing at the meeting-houses of the primitive Baptists tempted but few to attend for the sake of the melody.

The great pleasure indulged in by the young people was dancing at night. The married women sought recreation from their six days' work by visiting their neighbors on Sunday. The men went to musters, shooting matches, and horse races, on Saturdays. Housekeepers treated their friends and their own families to a pudding for dinner when company came, and the man of the house drew forth his bottle of whiskey. Many a little fellow had a hearty cry when the last piece of pudding disappeared before he got to the table. The pretty girls, dressed in striped and checked cotton cloth, spun and wove with their own hands, and their sweethearts in the sumach and walnut dyed stuff, made by their mothers. Courting was done when riding to meetings on Sunday, and walking to the spring when there. Newly-married couples went to see the old folks on Saturday, and carried home on Sunday evenings what could be spared them. There was no ennui among the women for want of something to do. If there had been leisure to read, there were but few books for the indulgence. Hollow trees supplied cradles for babies. The fine voices which are now heard in the pulpit and at the bar from the first native Georgians began their practice by crying, when infants, for the want of good nursing.

The preacher and the schoolmaster, the first to commence the onward march of civilization, were slow in reaching outskirt settlements. Most who did were drunken Irishmen or dissolute Virginians, who found the restraints of society in the old countries too binding for their comfort, and therefore moved to the new. Newspapers were confined to the select few. It appears from the record of the Court of Ordinary of Wilks County, that five out of sixteen wills had the makers' mark put to them, instead of their signatures. The proportion of those who could not write must have been still greater among those who died intestate. In the inventories of estates from 1777 to 1783, the first five had only four books, and they valued at five shillings. In the next three there is an entry of one parcel of old books, valued at five shillings. In the next eight no mention is made of books. In the next five there is an entry of a prayer book. Then there are three, in which there is one entry of an old bible and hymn book. The next has an entry of a parcel of old books, valued at seven shillings and sixpence. The next thirteen have no entry of books. The succeeding one has an entry of a tomahawk, prayer-book and testament; the next, of a bible; the next six, one bible; and the next fourteen are without any entry of books at all.

The following inventories, given verbatim ad literatim, of the property of deceased persons, show the kind and value owned by the first settlers of Wilks:

An Inventory of the Estate of Capt. John Stwart, dec'd., late of the States of Georgia, Wilks County

1 Negro boy Pompey	£50	0	0
1 Bead without Furniture	0	7	0
1 Pail, 1 Pigin do	0	4	0
1 Washing tub, 2 Keelers	0	4	0
1 Sifter, 1 horse	24	0	0
1 Bay Mare, Proved away since	1	15	0
1 Saddle	0	0	0
1 Rasor, 2000 acres of land in Richmond County	50	0	0
1 Old Grey horse	0	5	0

True Inventory of Goods and Chattles of Andrew Canndy, late dec'd:

To 2 feather Beads	7	0	0
To 2 flax wheels	1	10	0
To 2 Pails and Churn	0	8	0
To 3 Keelons and Pigan	0	4	12
To 1 Pot, to two howes and Culter Plow	0	15	0
To 1 Desk and five Plates, to one horse colt	2	9	0
To 1 Gray Mare, to one Cow	13	0	0
To 2 Year old heepher	1	10	0

Appraisment of the Goods and Chattles of the Estate of John Mackeney, dec'd, by Ruth Mackeney, administrator:

To Cash and Purse	£0	5	0
To a Person Bit	0	1	0
To a Rasor	0	1	0
To one pare of Stockens	0	5	0
To one Close Bolted Shirt	0	3	0
To one old Coat	0	1	0
To one wastcoat	0	1	0
To one Blanket	0	5	0
To one year old	0	5	0

Goods and Chattles of David McCullone, dec'd:

One Sorril mar Praised to	£6	0	0
One mare to	1	0	0
One horse to	3	0	0
One horse Colt to	4	0	0
Six head of Cattle to	6	0	0
One Negro Boy to	20	0	0
One Negro Girl to	30	0	0
One ax, Friang Pan and Pothooks	0	5	0
One Linen wheel to	0	5	0
One spice morter to	0	5	0
Books and Sleis to	0	5	0
Cury Comb, drawing knife, and auger	0	5	0
Old Puter	0	15	0
One buter tub	0	2	0
fore old Feather Beads to	5	0	0
One Pot	0	10	0

When the contest for independence commenced, the North Carolina settlers in Wilks were so far removed from the scene of action, and so ignorant of the cause of the quarrel, that they took no part until the British troops extended their operations into Georgia. They were then very much divided in opinion as to which side they should take. Following the course of their friends in North Carolina, some were for the country and some for the king. The united British and Tory forces obliged the Whigs to retreat into the adjoining States. The Tories thus obtaining the ascendency in Wilks, plundered the property, burned the houses, and put to death the women, children, and old infirm men, who had been left behind. The battle of King's Mountain permitted the Whigs to return home and take ample vengeance upon the Tories for the injuries which they had done. The cruelty of the Tories, and retaliation by the Whigs, may be imagined from the following facts. Whilst the Tories were in the ascendency they went to the house of Col. Dooly, the father of Judge Dooly, found him concealed, and put him to death without trial or resistance. When the Whigs got the upper hand, they made nine Tories prisoners. The son of the murdered Dooly, then but a youth, sacrificed the nine without hindrance from his officers.

The records of the Superior Courts of Wilks show what

acts were considered most criminal, and how imperfectly and in what strange ways justice was administered in both civil and criminal cases.

Until 1785 there was no court-house or jail in Wilks County. The court consisted of the Chief Justice of the State and five Assistant Justices of the County. They held court at some private dwelling, or in some out-house. The jurors, when trying causes, left the house in which the court was held for some log on the neighboring ground; where all seated in a row, or squatted around when earnest debate broke up the row on the log, they consulted each other in making up their verdicts. Whilst a jury was once thus seated on a log deliberating upon a case, a man who was known to be a Tory came riding by. One cried out, "There goes a d—— Tory, let's have him," and gave chase, which was joined in by most of his fellows.

Prisoners who were in the custody of the sheriff were confined as means could be found, with hickory withs, cords, and chains, occasionally by putting their heads between the rails of a fence, and sometimes by putting them into pens. Prisoners who were treated kindly escaped, so that most were roughly handled, whether guilty or not.

The Tories had little chance for fair trials, if permitted to be tried at all. Summary justice was usually administered to them. They found the end of the law, when they came within its control, at the end of a rope. In 1779 the grand jury of Wilks presented as a grievance twenty-six Tories (naming them) for being permitted to run at large, and directed that they should be apprehended and brought to trial.

At a court, in 1779, seven men were tried at the same time for high treason against the State, found guilty, and hung.

About the same time, a man was indicted in the same bill for treason, horse stealing, hog stealing and other misdemeanors.

An acquittal by a jury did not secure the accused from another trial for the same offence upon the discovery of other and better testimony. Men did not then feel the force of forms. They thought that if it were ascertained with certainty that a man was guilty of a crime he ought to be punished, notwithstanding that the verdict of a jury found him not guilty, for want of testimony kept away, or which could not be had at the time of trial.

Horse stealing, next after Toryism, was the offensive crime of the times. It was easily committed, the temptation was great, and escape easy. Death followed conviction for it with more certainty than conviction for murder. Men had no money to be murdered for. Ill-will usually vented itself by fighting, so that if death was the consequence, the crime was manslaughter or excusable homicide.

A few years after the revolutionary war a horse was stolen from Gen. Elijah Clark. He arrested some trifling fellow in the neighborhood as the guilty person, and had him charged with the offence before the grand jury at the next Superior Court. The testimony was insufficient for finding a true bill, and the prisoner was discharged. Gen. Clark, not doubting his guilt, took the discharged man into his own custody, marched him to a convenient place, followed by the posse comitatus, judge and jury, and was about hanging him to some limb, when Judge Pendleton (the father of the members of Congress of that name from Virginia and Ohio) made so eloquent an address in favor of law and order that he succeeded in doing by words what he could not through the officers of the court.

The following copy of a part of the record of the proceedings of the County Court of Wilks gives some details which may be both novel and amusing to the people of the present day:

April 1 1783
The Court met agreeable to Constitution

Present

William Downs S. A. J.

Zachariah Lamar
Benjamin Catching
Absolum Bedell
Benj. Thomson
} Assistant Judges.

The following order was sent by the Assistant Justices to the Chief Justice.

Ordered that the Sherriff wate on his honor the Chief Justice to know whether he intends to take his seat as Chief Justice this Court.

The Honourable Chief Justice answered as follows:

To the Honourable the Assistant Justices of the County of Wilks.
The under written having been appointed Chief Justice by the Honourable the Legislature of this State intended to have rode the circuit but his honour the Governor and the honourable the council have seen cause to suspend him during the present sessions he does not think himself enabled to act at present.
GEORGE WALTON.

1784
The Honourable Chief Justice delivered the following charge to the Grand Jury.
Gentlemen of the Grand Jury.
Fourteen or fifteen years ago I several times rode over this Country when it was Wilderness and nothing to be seen but the Savage and his Game of the Woods, The Indian line being soon after mooved further out it began to settle, and altho it has been Interrupted by a seven or eight years war in which the first settlers greatly distinglished themselves, it has increased in number strength and cultivation to an astonishing degree this rapidity of settlement is an Incontrovertable proof of the Goodness of the climate the soil and Navigation as it has been in the face of almost insuperable difficulties. &c. &c.

Friday April the first 1785
The following charge was delivered by his Honour the Chief Justice to the Grand Jury at the opening of the Session.

Barred by unusual floods it was Impossible to execute my Intention of a punctual meating, but there is yet sufficient time I hope to administer private and publick Justice the object of the circuite, it is not in my power to dispence with the duty of going to Liberty court, and which being at the distance of two hundred and twenty miles, will compell me to Leave this on satterday afternoon the Interval on my part shall be filled with a pointed and patient attention and I trust that I shall experience a General disposition to expedite the business. &c. &c.

The following presentments of the Grand Jury of Wilks County, describe the habits and manners of the people in 1785:

We also present Hezekiah Wheat for profain swearing Also Stephen Brooks for profain swearing also John Boggs for profain swearing also William Vardiman for profain swearing also Robert Jackson also Andrew Frazer also Joseph Purham also Thomas Morris also William Osborn also Moses Harris also Peter Carnes also C. Z. William Moor also Jefrey Early also William Thornton also Grant Taylor also Richard Powell also Samuel Criswell also Daniel Young also Peter Stubblefield also Joseph Cook also James Stwert also B. Smith also Joseph Spradling also John Bragg for fighting and Gambling Joseph Parham for Gambling also Grant Taylor and William Osborne for fighting also Joseph Ryan for profane swearing Richard Powell for Gambling also James Williams for profane swearing Daniel Young for Gambling and suffering it to be done in his house Peter Stubblefield for Gambling Daniel Terondit for suffering Gambling in his house also Owin Shannon for swearing and Gambling also Thomas Shannon Jr. for Gambling also Frederick Lipham for suffering Gambling in his house also the Magestrates knowingly suffer the saboth to be Broke by Merchants dealing and negroes and others playing five and other vices, in particular the Majistrates about town who see it frequently C. Z. Micajah Williamson William Moore and Henry Mounger Esquires also that the Militia officers in diferant districts do not keep up a Patrole from which the Inhabitance suffer Great damage by negroes riding horses at night and many other Mischievous acts also that people are suffered to Galop and run horses through the town of Washington also that there is never a fine inflicted upon officers and privates for not obeying their orders and for omiting their duties in the town of Washington also in all other parts of the county and also that the constitution as it stands debars us from some priviledge easements.

If you speak of a libel in a crowd of old Georgia people they suppose that you are using a dandy phrase for lye bill. Libel instead of being a writing abusive of another, was in old times a writing acknowledging that the writer had told a lye, and was given to him whose character was slandered, and then put upon the records of the court the more certainly to do justice to the slandered.

The following is a copy of a recorded lye bill:

GEORGIA, Wilks County

Whereas on the seventh day of December one thousand seven hundred and eighty-five in the Town of Washington ther happened a Difference between myself and Micajah Williamson of the said Town in the cource of said difference By Good Authority I made use of language or words very prejudicial to the Reputation of said Williamson By calling him Rogue and several other unguarded Expressions which I am certain I should not have done had I not been much

Intoxicated both in Excess of Drinking, and spirit or heat of passion and I do further acknowledge that I do not of my own knowledge nor know that any Other person knows any dishonest action of said Williamson, which would authorize or induce me to make use of such Expressions and so do agree to pay the cost of a suit the said Williamson Entered against me on the Occasion, and to dismiss and drop the Suit commenced against him for assault and Battery Given under my hand this 20th November 1786.

ANDREW FRAZER.

It is agreed by the within Andrew Frazer and Micajah Williamson that the within Instrument of writing should be recorded in court. ANDREW FRAZER.

The North Carolina settlers had been so stinted in grants of land, whilst under the government of Great Britain, that, when they became undisputed rulers to do with the land as they pleased, they made amends, by granting very largely to every body who wanted and would use the means to get it. To increase the value of what they secured to themselves, they held out inducements, by their legislative enactments, to the people of other States to settle among them.

The spirit of speculation became the ruling spirit of the times. Soon after the adoption of the Constitution of the United States, most of the States which had unsettled territory conveyed their title to the soil to the General Government, for the purpose of paying the debts contracted in carrying on the war for Independence. The State of Georgia, which had the largest unsettled territory of any of the States, refused to part with what had become an object of desire to each one of her people. Various plans were formed for giving every body a share of this great fund of public wealth. It was found difficult to devise any measure which would satisfy the highly excited cravings of the people. The King of Great Britain had claimed all the ungranted land in Georgia to be his. Many of the people, when he was conquered by their fighting, thought that the land which was his became rightfully theirs. When they took the government of the State into their own hands, they seemed to consider that the chief purpose of legislation was to distribute the public lands among themselves. They had but slight comprehension of government, and but little use for that which they had, but as the instrument for satisfying their desire for more land. All the territory which had been acquired from the Indians by treaty was soon granted away. Schemes were then devised for getting title to the remainder.

In 1794, General Clark and his special friends, urged on by this spirit, took possession of the fertile country between the Oconee and Ocmulgee Rivers, before the possessory title of the Indians had been ceded to the State, and without any authority from the Legislature. They established a government, and built forts for their defence. It required the authority of General Washington, then President of the United States, and the energy of General Mathews, then Governor of the State, to convince General Clark and his adherents that they could not thus appropriate what did not belong to them.

The following extracts from the Public Documents of the United States, upon the subject of this attempt of the North Carolina Wilks settlers to appropriate the public lands occupied by the Indians, and establish an independent republic within the territory of Georgia, are thought interesting enough to be given here at the expense of some repetition:—

State House, Augusta, 19th August, 1794.

Sir,—I had the pleasure to receive your communication of the 28th ultimo this day, and it is with real regret that I inform you, that the information therein contained is, in a great part, too true. Some time in May, I learnt that settlements were making on the southwest side of the Oconee. The supposition then was, that the adventurers were part of those who had embarked in the French interest, and that in a short time they would of themselves disperse; but finding that not to be the case and fearing lest they might contemplate a serious settlement, I, on the 20th of May, ordered General Irwin to direct the settlers immediately to remove. Soon after I was informed the removal had taken place. On the 14th of July I received a letter from Lieutenant Colonel Gaither, stating that Elijah Clark, late Major General in the Militia of this State, with a party of men, had encamped on the southwest side of the Oconee, opposite to Fort Fidius. On the 24th, General Irwin sent a couple of officers to Clark, with orders for him to move off immediately, which he positively refused; and on the 28th I issued a proclamation, forbidding such unlawful proceedings. I also wrote to one of our Judges to issue his warrant, and have Clark apprehended. At the Supreme Court, in Wilks County, I am informed, he surrendered himself to the Judge, who, on consulting with the Attorney General, referred him to some of the justices of the county. A copy of their decision is herewith inclosed, and from which, there is reason to conclude, there are too many who think favorably of the settlement; but I still flatter myself a large majority of the citizens are opposed to such lawless acts. &c., &c.

GEORGE MATHEWS.

State of Georgia, Wilks County:—
Whereas a proclamation was issued on the 28th day of July last, by his Excellency George Mathews, Esquire, Governor of this State, stating that Elijah Clark, Esquire, late Maj. General of the Militia of this State, has gone over the Oconee River, with an intent to establish a separate and independent government on the lands allotted for the Indians for their hunting ground, and commanded, in the said proclamation, all judges, justices, sheriffs, and other officers, and all the other citizens of this State, to be diligent in aiding and assisting in apprehending the said Elijah Clark, and his adherents, in order that they might severally be brought to justice. And whereas the said Elijah Clark, who is the object of the said proclamation, hath this day personally appeared before us, the undersigned, Justices of the Peace for the County of Wilks, and surrendered himself into custody, and it being our duty to do speedy justice to the said State, as well as the party charged, we proceeded to the most mature consideration of the cause, and, after an examination of the laws of the State, and the treaties made, and the laws passed by the United States, do give it as our decided and unanimous opinion, that said Elijah Clark be, and is hereby, discharged.

R. WOOSHAM, J. P.
R. CHRISTMAS, J. P.
G. WOOLDRIDGE, J. P.
WILLIAM BELL, J. P.

Fort Advance, 5th Sept., 1794.

Gentlemen,—Your favor of the 3d instant is now before me. Accept my thanks for your information and attention to what may, if ever neglected so materially, injure our enterprise. I consider myself honored by the unanimous voice of all the officers belonging to the different garrisons. I shall always endeavor to acquit myself worthy of the command committed to my charge. The information you have received agrees with mine from Augusta. The artillery of Augusta are ordered to be in readiness to march in eight or ten days, and one third of the militia are ordered to be draughted. It has been tried in Burk and Richmond Counties, but quite unsuccessful; the troops declare that they will not fight against us. I am happy to find the disposition of the people with you so exactly agrees with my own friends here; I believe it to be the general disposition of every garrison. I am determinately fixed to risk every thing with my life upon the issue, and for the success of the enterprise. You will apply to the inclosed orders how to conduct yourselves with inimical individuals. In case of a body appearing, you will give me the earliest information. If you are summoned to surrender in the garrison, you must refuse with a firmness ever accompanying the brave. Inform those who apply, that if you have done wrong, and the grand jury of the county have cognizance of your crime, you will cheerfully submit to be tried by a jury of your fellow-citizens. But you will consider any orders from the Secretary of War as unconstitutional. The Governor's proclamation, as determined in Wilks, illegal, &c., &c. Yours &c.

E. CLARK.

Sir,—I have the pleasure to inform you, that the post opposite to us, on the south side of the Oconee, has been taken and destroyed by the militia, and that Clark and his adherents have been removed.

Soon after the Governor's proclamation was issued against General Clark, he delivered himself up to the Superior Court of the County of Wilks, who dismissed him, because it was their opinion that he had not violated the laws of the State. This decision greatly encouraged his party, and the settlements were pushed with vigor. The measure had also become very popular, and it was believed by him and his adherents that the militia would never march against him. Under these flattering circumstances, his works were completed, houses were erected within his forts, a town was laid off at Fort Advance (the post opposite to us), Gen. Clark was chosen Major General, and placed at the head of the enterprise; the members were elected for the general committee, or committee of safety, and every thing bore the appearance of a permanent settlement, &c., &c. I have the honor to be, &c., &c.

CONSTANT FREEMAN.

Extract from Judge Walton's charge to the Grand Jury of Richmond County:—

Should the spirit which generated the plan of this new settlement still urge its pursuit, what mischief may it not produce to the community. A young country, scarcely recovered from former ravages, but with means of progressive amplification and aggrandizement, to be involved in a civil war, with all the evils incident to it, will have the effect of arresting its progress and putting it back of any present calculation.

It is already known that the President of the United States has directed, in the event of other means failing, that the settlement should be suppressed by military coercion. And shall the blood of citizens be spilled to support the pretensions of a small part of the people,—pretensions without law, and resting not on the foundations of justice? But it is said, they have expatriated themselves. This is neither fact, nor capable of being made so. The district, the object of their contemplation, is still Georgia; and they must be either citizens or insurgents. Would that these new settlers might attend to the voice of reason, of benevolence, and moderation, before they plunge themselves and their country in distress and trouble. A little time will extend our limits and we shall then be all upon a footing.

But suppose that the State, from the recollection of the past services of the principal in this adventure and a tender regard to his adherents (the United States out of view for the moment), should be disposed to wink at the establishment of this intended settlement, is the extent of the precedent perceived? The richest jewel the State of Georgia possesses, and the real basis of her future wealth and rank in the Union, is her western territory; and if one set of men should be permitted to take possession, and keep a part of it, without the consent of her government, will it not be an example of right for any other set of men to do the same with any other part or with the whole of it?

Hence, I conclude, that, if General Clark has the same regard for the State he has heretofore given so many proofs of, he will desist from an enterprise so pregnant with evils to her. It is not to be wished that the Federal Government should have occasion to exert its power upon such occasion. It might one day give color to pretensions not consonant with the interest of the State. There ought to exist no fears at present; but who can keep pace with the progress of time and revolution.

The failure of General Clark and the North Carolina Wilks settlers, did not put an end to enterprises of others having similar objects in view. An extensive secret association was soon after formed, called the Combined Society, whose members took an oath to elect, if they could, a Governor and members of the Legislature, who would dispose of the public land for their special benefit. One of its most active members was detected in his operations for success, stripped, tied to a tree, and whipped without mercy. The existence and objects of the society becoming thus noised abroad, the people succeeded in electing a Governor and a majority of the members of the Legislature pledged to oppose them. They relied with confidence upon the interposition of the Governor's veto, should the speculators succeed in influencing a majority of the Legislature.

The Governor elected had been in office before, and vetoed an act passed by the Legislature for disposing of the public lands for the following reasons:—

1st. I doubt whether the proper time has arrived for disposing of the territory in question.

2d. If it was the proper time, the sum offered is inadequate to the value of the land.

3d. The quantity reserved for the citizens is too small in proportion to the extent of the purchase.

4th. That greater advantages are secured to the purchasers than the citizens.

5th. That so large an extent of territory being disposed of to companies of individuals will operate as monopolies, which will prevent or retard settlements, population, and agriculture.

6th. That if public notice was given that the land was for sale, the rivalship in purchasers would most probably have increased the sums offered.

7th. The power given to the Executive by the constitution, the duty I owe the community, and the sacredness of my oath of office, will, I flatter myself, justify this dissent in the minds of the members of the Legislature, and of my fellow-citizens.

The speculators made many members of the Legislature and two of the Governor's sons members of their companies. The corrupt act passed, and was signed by the Governor.

Whilst the bill was on its passage, the bribery employed was made known to the people. Companies of men were embodying, and some on their way to the seat of government to disperse the members of the Legislature when they adjourned.

The constituents of one who was bribed, were excited to so great ferment that he became alarmed and fled into South Carolina. He was followed by an outraged county man, found sitting alone in a cabin at night, and shot dead. The sight of his death struggles arrested the strong current of indignant feelings which had led to the act. The avenger became the miserable sinner. He returned home, shut himself up in a dark room from intercourse with the world for eighteen years, begging as if for his own life, that God would pardon him for taking the life of another.

On the morning of the day of the first general meeting of the people of Oglethorpe after the passage of the Yazoo Act, a citizen who lived on the other side of the Crabtree, stopped at the gate whilst Miles Jinnings made ready to accompany him to town. Old Jinnings put a rope in his pocket. Upon being asked by his companion what he intended to do with the rope, he replied, "Hang Musgrove!" When they arrived at the court-house from their distant part of the county all the people had assembled. Miles Jinnings hitched his horse, went into the crowd, pulled from his pocket the rope, and holding it up at arm's length, cried out, "Neighbors, this rope is to hang Musgrove, who sold the people's land for a bribe." The lashing of the surge upon the shore when the ocean is driven by the most furious storm, was not louder than the noise of the people excited into tumult by old Jinnings's words and the sight of the elevated rope. No human power could have saved Musgrove from hanging if old Jinnings's neighbor had not given him notice to make his escape.

The Governor, after the expiration of his term of office, was never again trusted by the State. His son-in-law, who voted against the act, was so suspected of favoring its passage, that he was unable to stand up against the popular clamor, and left the State never to return to it.

At the session of the Legislature subsequent to the Yazoo fraud, (as the act of sale to the speculators was called), the people's party was in power without opposition. The Legislature made the following declaration in the form of law:

Be it therefore enacted, That the said Act, passed on the seventh day of January, in the year one thousand seven hundred and ninety-five be, and the same is hereby declared, null and void, and the grant or grants, right or rights, claim or claims, issuing or deduced, or derived therefrom, or from any clause, letter, or spirit of the same, is hereby also annulled, rendered void, and of no effect; and as the same was made without constitutional authority, and fraudulently obtained, it is hereby declared of no binding force or effect on this State or people hereafter, but is, and are to be considered, both law and grants, as they ought to be ipso facto of themselves, void, and the territory therein mentioned is also hereby declared to be the sole property of the State, subject only to the right of treaty of the United States to enable the State to purchase under its pre-emption right, the Indian title to the same.

And be it further enacted, That within three days after the passage of this Act, the different branches of the Legislature shall assemble together, at which meeting the officers shall attend with the several records and documents, and deeds in the Secretary's, Surveyor-General's, and other public offices, and which records and documents shall then and there be expunged from the face and indexes of the books of record of the State, and the enrolled law, or usurped Act, shall then be publicly burnt, in order that no trace of so unconstitutional, vile, and fraudulent a transaction other than the infamy attached to it by this law, shall remain in the public offices thereof.

All the documentary evidences of the act of sale were accordingly burnt. The consuming flames were kindled by drawing fire from the sun, so as to make heaven aid in the purifying sacrifice.

ELIJAH CLARK.

THE struggle between liberty and loyalty had gone on for some time, and the States declared their independence of Great Britain before much more was understood about the cause of the contest by the North Carolina settlers in Wilks than what was learned from passing rumor. When the British troops marched into Upper Georgia and required the people to submit to the power that would tax them, Elijah Clark felt that his forte was fighting. His bold, fearless spirit made him at once the chief of those who felt like him.

When Col. Boyd, the leader of the North Carolina tories retreated into Georgia, Elijah Clark, at the head of the Georgia whigs, and Col. Pickens, with the whigs of South Carolina, pursued and overtook him at Kettle Creek, in Wilks, where they drubbed him and many of his followers to death, and dispersed most of the remainder.

Shortly after the British troops and tories united in such strength that Elijah Clark could not meet them in the field. With the tact of the successful partisan, he got out of the way, that he might fight more advantageously another day. He fled to the mountains, taking with him most of the whig old men, women, and children, to secure them from the cruelties of the poor tory scamps, who thought that the best way of serving their king was to put to death those who refused to swear allegiance to him. Placing his non-combatants in security, he marched at the head of his fighters wherever the enemy were to be found. He had no pretensions to be the great general who, standing aloof from danger, directs and conquers by the skill of his manoeuvres. He led in the fight, and ordered his men to follow him. He was present, if he could be, wherever fighting was to be done, until liberty was won.

When the independence of the States was acknowledged, and the people of the other States enjoyed peace, there was no peace for the people of Georgia. The tories fled among the neighboring Indian tribes, and excited their warriors to plunder and murder the frontier people, until Elijah Clark, aided by his son, frightened them away by the great victory which he obtained over them at Jack's Creek.

Elijah Clark had but little scholastic learning, nor had he been very accurately taught in early youth the distinction between right and wrong, or the lessons afterwards slipped from his memory. He was very poor when he took to soldiering. He was better off when the war ended. He thought, as many great men have done, that those who fight against their country forfeit both life and property. He showed his faith in his doctrine by letting tory prisoners live by their letting him have what they had. He reversed the law of kings, that the people and their property are theirs, by his verdict, that what was claimed by the king should belong to the people. King George, whilst Georgia was a colony, granted his lands so stintingly to his subjects, that when they became freemen and the State under their government, they made amends to themselves by granting to every one land for little or nothing. The appetite for riches grows upon what it feeds on. Elijah Clark, and the other North Carolina settlers in Wilks, failing to get enough to satisfy their voracity, took possession of the fertile territory between the Oconee and Ocmulgee Rivers, without regard to the occupant rights of the Indians, established a republic, made Elijah Clark their chief ruler, and were preparing to parcel out the lands, when the militia, ordered into service by Governor Mathews, and the regular troops by President Washington, drove them off.

Elijah Clark had three sons; John, the general, and Elijah and Gibson, the lawyers; and three daughters, Mrs. ——— Thomson, Mrs. Josiah Walton, and Mrs. Benajah Smith. One of the daughters of Mrs. Smith married Eldrid Simpkins, a respectable lawyer of South Carolina. Miss Simpkins married the Hon. Francis Pickens, the grandson of Gen. Pickens, Elijah Clark's old associate in arms.

Elijah Clark's residence was several miles northwest of Washington, between the roads leading from Broad River and the Cherokee Corner to Augusta.

JOHN CLARK.

JOHN CLARK, the oldest son of Elijah Clark, was a lad when his father removed with his family from North Carolina to Wilks, Georgia. There were no high schools, academies, or colleges in Wilks during John's youth, and if there had been, it is not probable that he would have received much advantage from them. All the learning which he ever acquired was reading, writing, and ciphering in a small way. His early youth was passed in his father's camp, during the plundering, murdering warfare between the whigs and tories. Though but a boy he did the service of the best soldier at the battle of Kettle Creek. When fighting ceased, his camp habits received but little improvement from the association with the riotous North Carolina settlers. He acquired no profession, followed no trade, and never labored in the field. His time was passed in rowdying. He knew no fear, and never learned from his fighting with the tories to give quarter to his enemies. In his brawls he used knives and guns without regard to consequences. He once shot so carelessly at some one in the streets of Washington, with whom he was quarrelling, that the load took effect upon a poor woman, and wounded her so badly that she was for a long time disabled from clothing her children. His drunken, restless ways kept him perpetually in mischief. As long as the Indians continued to make inroads into the frontiers, he was ever ready for the foray. At the battle of Jack's Creek between the frontier Georgians, and the Creek Indians, he was the conquering officer, though not the chief in command. The reputation which he acquired by the battles of Kettle

Creek and Jack's Creek, made him feel that he was the cock of the walk wherever he stalked, and he was sure to show it if any crowing was done in his presence. Most persons yielded without resistance to what he demanded authoritatively or claimed petinaciously. Every associate was obliged to be for or against him. He suffered no one of any consequence to occupy middle ground. He had the temper of the clansman. He defended his friends, right or wrong, and expected the same fidelity to himself. He patted every young man on the back whom he wished to make his adherent. If he showed himself offish, he proved himself his enemy. Whatever his hands found to do he did with his might, and would have been the best of men if his evil inclinations had not got the better of his good: He and his father took part in the Yazoo sale, from some vague notion that the conquerors were entitled to share among them what had belonged to the conquerer. The State became divided into factions called the Yazoo and anti-Yazoo parties. John Clark was then too young and too little interested in these speculations to be the leader of his party. He was, however, one of its most efficient members. He backed Col. Willis when he challenged Judge Taliaferro to fight a duel. He belonged to the clique who put forward Van Allen to drive William H. Crawford from the bar. He waylaid Judge Tait whilst he was travelling his circuit in the discharge of his official duties, horsewhipped him, and whipped his horse at the same time, so that he could not jump from his carriage and defend himself, having a wooden leg. He committed this outrageous act of war upon society because an offidavit had been taken before Judge Tait charging him with some offence. He challenged Mr. Crawford because he was a friend of Judge Tait. In the fight which followed he shot Mr. Crawford through the wrist. Not satisfied because he had not killed him, he sent another challenge, though they had had no quarrel. When Mr. Crawford's prospects for the presidency began to look like success, he attempted to mar them by publishing a defamatory pamphlet, which he circulated far and wide. He felt that Mr. Crawford and his friends had thwarted his ambitious designs, and never ceased struggling for revenge. He was always in want of money; ever spending, and but seldom making. Upon the pleas of his public services, the Legislature relinquished five thousand dollars due from him to the State for public lands bought by him at much less than their real value. He was jealous of the influence of Franklin College. He felt the want of learning, and knew that the trustees were beyond his control. Mr. Crawford was a very influential trustee, and never failed attending the board when he could. Athens was for a long time, during the college commencements, the great assembling place of the ambitious politicians of the State. Gen. Clark could not therefore keep away, though very few of the literari were of his party. In 1822 both he and William H. Crawford attended. He was then Governor, and Mr. Crawford Secretary of the Treasury. Dr. Waddell, the president of the college, had been Mr. Crawford's preceptor, and was very proud of his scholar. In the procession of the college officers, trustees, and students, through the campus to their places in the chapel, Mr. Crawford, at the request of the president, walked on his right hand and Governor Clark on his left. This appearance before the great crowd assembled to witness the college exercises in an inferior position to Mr. Crawford, made Clark, harassed as he then was from other causes, feel as if he would burst with rage. A vile practice was just then in vogue of sending slanderous anonymous letters, called buckets, to those whom the writers wished to annoy. Soon after Gen. Clark arrived in Athens, his known hostility to the college induced some of the mischief-makers of the place to send him a number of these buckets. Enraged at their contents, and suspecting that their authors were college students, he laid them before the Board of Trustees, with the request that the delinquents be ferretted out and punished. Mr. Crawford was present when the letters were received, and called for their reading. He enjoyed their satire greatly, and continued for a long time after to repeat the expression which were most irritating to Clark.

Soon after I went to Lexington to reside, General Clark and his daughter Nancy stopped at a public house in the village. Miss Nancy was a charming young lady. She and my youngest sister had been a short time before at school together in Raleigh, where I had met her. Being then a bachelor, I went to see her. Upon asking for Miss Clark, her father made his appearance. After a few moments' conversation, he directed a servant to carry a candle to his room, and asked me to follow him. Upon being seated, he commenced talking about the introduction of negroes from Africa into the State in violation of the laws, an instance of which was then exciting public attention. He charged Gen. Mitchel, the Creek Agent at Fort Hawkins, with being concerned in the traffic. I told him unhesitatingly that I had no doubt about the impropriety of Mitchel's conduct. Pleased that my answer accorded so well with his wishes, he went on to say that a man high in office at Washington City was also implicated in the guilt, alluding very plainly to Mr. Crawford. I answered that I did not believe it. This prompt reply caused silence for a moment. Perceiving that I had offended, I rose, bowed, and left the room. It was the only tete-a-tete I ever had with Gen. Clark. He could never forget it, nor to do me whatever injury he could.

General John Scott was the special friend of Gen. Clark. He found him one day in Milledgeville, preparing himself by getting drunk, for abusing or doing some violence to his enemy, Gen. Mitchel, who was then Governor of the State. To prevent the execution of his purpose, Gen. Scott endeavored to draw him away by inviting him to dinner. Gen. Scott lived two or three miles out of town. Clark insisted that he should go on home, promising that he would follow soon. Scott, knowing that it would be useless to attempt to control him, and that he would only incur his displeasure by offering to do so, went home. He delayed dinner until night. Apprehending that Clark might have become so drunk as to have lost his way, or suffered some other mishap, he went in search of him, accompanied by many of his negroes, with torches. He found him asleep upon a log which projected over a precipice, where a turn the wrong way would have precipitated him below, and probably killed him—the recklessness of his temper and his desire to fight Mitchel having put him into the humor to hunt for danger.

In the war of 1812 with Great Britain, Gen. Clark was appointed by Gov. Early to command the Georgia militia.

After long seeking for high political distinction, he was at last gratified by being elected Governor. The people thought that the man who had fought for the country in youth and in manhood, and whose father had done capital service in securing the independence of the States, was entitled to this evidence of their gratitude. They would have been undoubtedly right if Gen. Clark had given sufficient proofs that he would be the Governor of the State instead of the head of a party. After being elected Governor twice, he was defeated at the third election by Governor Troup. It was the hardest and hottest battle ever fought by the Georgia factions in their long war of words. Gen. Clark was then an old man. Feeling that his connection with public affairs was ended, there came over his temper the most pleasant change ever experienced by any one who had passed a long life in hot-headed violence and evil-hearted hatred. With the exception of William H. Crawford, he became friendly with all the world. He was in want of means to support the elevation at which he had arrived. He and Gen. Jackson were born not far apart, had fought for their country in youth in the same way, had belonged afterwards to the same kind of rude frontier society, and were alike fearless in fight and unrelenting in hostility. Gen. Jackson, when President, showed his sympathy for Gen. Clark by appointing him keeper of the public forests in Florida. The pay given by the Government for his services afforded him a comfortable support in his old age. He was hospitable and kind to every body who went to his neighborhood in that new country until his death.

General Clark's faults proceeded from the vices of the society to which he belonged in early life. His virtues were his own. He was brave, firm and patriotic. He married the only daughter of Col. Micajah Williamson. Their only son died from the smallpox at the house of their devoted friend, Dr. Fort. Their only daughter married Col. John Campbell. Mrs. Clark was a worthy woman. One of her sisters married John Griffin, a Virginia gentleman, a lawyer, and, for a short time, a Judge of the Superior Courts. After his death, his widow and Judge Tait indulged their old age in a freak of fancy, to show the world what they could do in reconciling the violence of the Clark and Crawford factions by marrying.

Another of Mrs. Clark's sisters married Peterson Thweat; one of whose daughters married Mr. Thacker Howard formerly Comptroller General of the State, a most upright man and faithful public officer. Another married Homer Howard, Secretary of the Executive Department when Mr. Forsyth was Governor. Mr. Peterson Thweat, of Columbus is their brother.

Another sister of Mrs. Clark married Mr. Fitch, a Yankee lawyer of some reputation.

Mrs. Clark's youngest sister married Col. Duncan G. Campbell.

DUNCAN G. CAMPBELL.

DUNCAN G. CAMPBELL was born in North Carolina, and educated at Chapel Hill. His countrymen, the Clarks, Dooleys, Waltons, and Murrays, were not his kin. His father was a well-descended, respectable Scotchman, who, contrary to the habits of his countrymen contrived to throw away a large estate. His descendants, though poor, contrived to show that they were of gentle blood and quality raising. Duncan G. Campbell, soon after his college graduation, removed to Georgia, and settled in Washington, Wilks County. His first employment was to teach the young ladies of the town the elements of learning. Whilst thus occupied, he devoted his spare time to the study of the law under the direction of Judge Griffin. After some years' attentive practice, he was elected Solicitor-General of his circuit. He represented Wilks County several times in the Legislature. He married Miss Williamson, the sister of Mrs. John Clark, and was the most influential of all the followers of his chief, the most talented excepting Judge Dooly, and would have succeeded to John Clark's party position had he lived a few years longer.

Colonel Campbell and Major Meriwether were, in 1824, appointed to treat with the Indians of Georgia for cession of their occupant rights. In 1825 they made the treaty with the Creek Indians, which became the subject of so much altercation in Congress and violent opposition on the part of the Northern people. The pretence for sympathizing with the Indians was, that the Commissioners had done great wrong to them by making presents to their chiefs. Its true object, was to prevent the acquisition of territory and increase of the population of the Southern States. Presents had always been given to the Indians by the authorities of Great Britain, the Colonies, and the States, when treaties were made with them. Col. Campbell lived long enough to feel most painfully the slanderous abuse with which he was assailed, and died before he reaped the rewards of public favor for the great services which he rendered the State. He was a member of the Board of Trustees of Franklin College for many years, and took great interest in its advancement, and the success of every measure designed to promote the cause of education throughout the State. He died in 1828, in the prime of life.

Col. Campbell had none of the rowdy habits of the North Carolina Wilks settlers. He avoided violence, and was courteous and kind to every body. Though his talents were not of the highest order, nor his public speaking what could be called eloquent, he was among the most successful lawyers at the bar, and useful members of the Legislature. He was very industrious, and ever ready to do the part of a good citizen. The amenity of his temper was constantly shown, in the delight which he derived from pleasing the young. His house continued, as long as he lived, to be one of their favorite resorts.

Col. Campbell's son, John, gave early proofs of the extraordinary acumen, which has since made him the great lawyer of the South. Whilst he was a student of Franklin College, his father visited Athens, and was invited to attend a meeting of the Demosthenian Society, of which both father and son were members. Col. Campbell held forth by request, upon the topic of debate. When he was done speaking, John asked leave to answer the gentleman, and so knocked all his father's conclusions into non sequiturs, that it was difficult to tell which had the uppermost in the father's feelings, mortified vanity, or gratified pride. John Campbell has lately been appointed an Associate Judge of the Supreme Court of the

United States, the highest honor, except that of Chief Justice, which can be conferred by the government upon a lawyer. All who know him concur in the opinion that the office will be well filled.

Col. Campbell's daughter, Sarah, was remarkable in early childhood for precocity, and in womanhood for superior attainments. She married Daniel Chandler, one of the handsomest and very cleverest young men of Georgia. He removed to Alabama, where he has long practiced law with distinguished success.

JUDGE DOOLY.

John Murry Dooly was the intellectual superior of the North Carolina whig settlers. His capacity was sufficient for any attainment, if it had been properly directed, and actively employed. Unfortunately for himself, and for society, he was, when young, under the constant influence of idle, drunken, gambling associates. Though his estate was large, his education was neglected. His scholastic knowledge was limited to what he learned from the common schoolmasters of his time. His person was erect, and of proper proportions. His features were of the finest cast. His large protruding black eyes indicated to every one who looked into them his extraordinary genius. He was a lawyer, and would have been the most successful at the Georgia bar, if his habits had corresponded with his talents. He was born, continued to live, and died within the limits of Lincoln County. Its people were always gratified when they could make him their representative. He was a member of the Legislature during the embargo and restrictive measures of the General Government, and the war with Great Britain, and successfully advocated the alleviating, thirding, and stop laws then passed. His wit, keen satire; quick perception, and extraordinary speaking capacity, were never surpassed by any one in Georgia. Mr. Forsyth was his only countryman who equalled him in polemic party debate. They were never pitted against each other, so that their debating powers could be compared.

Judge Dooly was the neighbor and political follower of

John Clark. Being destitute of the quality which the Romans called virtue, he could not avoid doing as his leader directed. John Clark ruled him to his purposes, as long as they belonged to the same community, through his determined will. His party, when in power, made him judge. He had only occasionally looked into the laws, as an advocate, in preparing cases for trial; and yet, when causes came before him, and were discussed by able counsel, his clear perception and discriminating judgment enabled him to comprehend the merits of the most intricate, and to decide accordingly. His deficiency in the discharge of his duty as a judge, proceeded from the control which his early habits of drinking and gambling continued to have over him. More than once after delivering a strong charge against gambling to the Grand Jury at the opening of the court, he went to the faro table at night, and by his bold, hazardous playing, sent the gamblers off for the want of money, who had continued to play in defiance of his judicial authority. He never went upon the bench drunk, but his red eyes and trembling hands sometimes showed that he had been in his cups the night before. Dissipation and degrading practices prevented his seeking the society of ladies. His taste was never so refined as to reform his low indulgences. He was advanced in life when he married a young woman, who knew him well, and was satisfied with him as he was. He was kind, and would have been good-tempered, but for the perpetual excitement of whiskey. His agreeable social qualities would have made him the delight of the best society, if his vicious inclinations had not carried him elsewhere. Nobody ever conversed with him or heard him speak, who did not admire him, and regret that his unfortunate fate had subjected him to temptations too strong to overcome. He had the organization and endowments of the greatest man of his age and country. As he was, he only played second part to one of the most ignorant and lawless.

AUSTIN DABNEY.

MANY years before the revolutionary war, a Virginia gentleman of the old school resided upon his plantation not many miles from Richmond. He was a bachelor of long standing, who indulged in card-playing, drinking, horse-racing, and other dissolute practices. His wealth consisted in a large landed estate, and many negroes. No white person lived with him, except a little girl, whose parentage was unknown. When the bachelor gentleman left home upon his frolics, this little girl remained under the care of a negro mammy. She grew up until she ceased to be a child, knowing scarcely any one except the bachelor, and the negroes of the household. Suddenly and secretly the old gentleman left his plantation, taking her with him. He went to North Carolina, where he remained some time with a man by the name of Aycock. Aycock afterwards removed to Georgia, along with the emigrants from North Carolin, who first settled Wilks County, carrying with him a mulatto boy.

When the contest between the whigs and tories became a struggle for the lives and liberty of all who favored the cause of freedom, Aycock was called upon to do his part in defending his fireside. From the time when he was required to fight, he saw a terrible tory constantly pointing a loaded gun at him. Fearing to face the danger, he offered as a substitute his mulatto boy, then transformed into a stout lad, who had previously passed as his slave. He acknowledged that he was not, when he found that he would not otherwise be received as a soldier. The mulatto was accordingly enrolled in a captain's company, by the name of Austin Dabney. No soldier under Clark was braver, or did better service during the revolutionary struggle. In the battle of Kettle Creek, the hardest ever fought in Georgia between the whigs and tories, Austin Dabney was shot down, and left on the battle ground very dangerously wounded. He was found, carried home, and cared for by a man of the name of Harris. It was long before Austin Dabney recovered. Gratitude for the kindness which he had received became the ruling feeling of his heart. He worked for Harris and his children, and served them more faithfully and efficiently than any slave ever served a master. He moved with them from Wilks County to Madison, soon after the latter county was organized. He sent his benefactor's oldest son to school, and afterwards to college, by the hard earnings of his own hands. He lived upon the poorest food, and wore old patched clothes, that he might make young Harris a gentleman. When his protege left Franklin College, Austin Dabney, placed him in the office of Stephen Upson, then at the head of the legal profession in Upper Georgia. When he was examined for admission to the bar, and received the fraternal shake of the hand from the members of the profession, Austin Dabney was standing outside, leaning on the railing which inclosed the court, two currents of tears trickling down his mulatto face, from remembrance of the kindness which he had received and thankfulness for the power which had been given him to do something in return.

Stephen Upson was a member of the Legislature when the surveys of public land, which were too small to be drawn for in the lottery of 1819, were disposed of by law. Austin Dabney had not been permitted to have a chance in the lottery with the other soldiers of the revolutionary war. Stephen Upson used his controlling influence in the Legislature to procure the passage of a law giving to Austin Dabney a valuable fraction. One of the members from Madison County voted for the law. At the next election, his constituents were excited into the hottest party contest by this conduct of their representative. They said that it was an indignity to white men, for a mulatto to be put upon an equality with them in the distribution of the public land, though not one had done such long and useful public service.

The United States Government allowed Austin Dabney a pension, on account of his thigh, which was broken at the battle of Kettle Creek. He went once a year to Savannah to draw what was due him. On one occasion he travelled thither with Col. Wiley Pope. They were very intimate and social on the road, and until they entered the streets of Savannah. As they were passing along through the city, Colonel Pope observed to Austin Dabney, that he was a sensible man, and knew the prejudices which forbade his associating with him in city society. Austin Dabney checked his horse, and fell in the rear, after the fashion of mulatto servants following their masters. They passed the house of Gen. James Jackson, then Governor of the State. He was standing in his door at the time. Col. Pope passed on without notice. Recognizing Austin Dabney, he ran into the street, seized him by the hand, drew him from his horse and carried him into his house, where he continued his guest whilst business kept him in Savannah.

It was very strange that Austin Dabney, who never knew his grandfather, should have inherited the taste of the Virginia gentlemen for horse-racing. He owned fine horses, attended the race-course, entered the list for the stake, and betted with all the eagerness of a professional sportsman.

It was Austin Dabney's custom to be at the tavern when Judge Dooly arrived at Danielsville to hold Madison court. He held the judge's horse until he got from his carriage, and then held his hand most affectionately. The judge's father had died in the whig cause. Austin was always an adherent of the son, without regard to party politics. In the evening after the adjournment of court, he usually went into the room occupied by the judge and the lawyers, where, taking a low seat, he listened to what was said, or himself told of the stirring incidents of the struggle between the whigs and tories in Upper Georgia and South Carolina. His memory was retentive, his understanding good, and he described what he knew well.

Harris, Austin Dabney's protege, moved away from Madison County. Austin Dabney went with him, and continued to give him his devoted personal services and his property as long as he lived.

FELIX GILBERT.

FELIX GILBERT was a Scotchman, and, like most of his countrymen who emigrated to the colonies, followed trading in preference to agriculture. He married Miss Grant, the daughter of Peter Grant, whose second wife was my great grandmother Strother. He lived among the Strothers in Spotsylvania, for some time, and then removed into the Shenandoah Valley, and settled at the foot of the Peaked Mountain. His trade was in a very small way until he went to London, and returned with a large stock of goods. A story got into circulation, accounting for this favorable change in the fortune of

Felix Gilbert, which is still occasionally heard about the Peaked Mountain. The Dutch and Irish of the valley have so great love for the wonderful, that it is impossible now to ascertain what foundation in truth there was for it. They say that Felix Gilbert saw, of a dark night, high upon the Peaked Mountain, soon after he settled near by, a bright sparkling object. His Scotch inquisitiveness forced him to try and find out what it was. His superstitious dread of what was mysterious induced him to take a companion with him when he went in search. He found a diamond, or some other precious stone, embedded in a rock so large that the two could not carry it away. They turned it over to conceal it. When the two afterwards hunted for the rock, there were such vast numbers on the mountain side like it, that they did not discover it. The sum derived from the sale to the King of England, or some nobleman in London, of what was found in the rock which was so bright at night, made, according to gossip, the great change for the better in the mercantile business of Felix Gilbert.

The Peaked Mountain is a few miles from where my grandfathers, Peachy R. Gilmer and Thomas Lewis, resided. The young Gilberts, Lewises, and Gilmers, called each other cousin, and the old people uncle and aunt. They lived in the most intimate social way—meeting together very often—dancing and frolicking with the unrestrained freedom of the days before quality airs superseded simple doings, and money-making idle jollity.

When the revolutionary war was over, and the people became restless for want of excitement, many of the Virginians sought to better their condition by emigrating to Georgia. Felix Gilbert followed the movement, and settled in Wilks, a few miles northeast of Washington. Though my father and mother loved Mr. and Mrs. Gilbert and their children as kinspeople, the distance from Broad River to their residence was too great to admit of much intercourse in those hard-working times. The oldest daughter of Mr. Gilbert married Henry Gibson. She and my mother were very intimate friends when young. They did not meet for twenty years. I was present when they did, and saw the exciting embrace which hastened

Mrs. Gibson's death, then fast approaching from pulmonary consumption.

Ann Gilbert, the second daughter, married John Taylor, of the family of President Taylor. He showed the relationship by his bluntness and obdurate obstinacy. He was a democrat, and called every one a fool who did not believe in Mr. Jefferson. He told the truth so roughly, that many would have preferred a little palaver to his way of talking. My father and his brother George were democrats, and early friends of John Taylor. He never failed to visit them when he went near enough. Mrs. Taylor was as agreeable and conciliatory as her husband was short and huffy. Their last residence was on the side of the southwest mountains in the County of Orange, Virginia, and immediately opposite to the eminence on the side of which Mr. Richard Taliaferro lived, who married my father's youngest sister.

John, the oldest son of Mr. and Mrs. Taylor, married Miss Foote, of the family of the interminable talking member of Congress. He removed from Virginia to Western Alabama.

Gilbert, their second son, was a Methodist preacher, and resided somewhere in Tennessee.

William, the third son, married Miss Booker, of Wilks County, and moved to the Far West.

Elizabeth, Mrs. Gilbert's third daughter, married Gilbert Hay, a physician of reputation, who resided in the town of Washington, Wilks County, and practiced his profession there most of his life, and until his death. He belonged to the Clark faction, and was second to General Clark in his duel with William H. Crawford. Mrs. Hay was a very worthy, sensible woman. Mr. and Mrs. Hay had two sons and two daughters. Their sons were gentlemen of talents and respectability. Nancy, their oldest daughter, married Richard Long, Esq., the oldest son of Col. Nicholas Long. She was a very amiable woman. Her patience and fortitude under suffering was put to the severest test, by years of suffering from a cancer, which killed her. Maria, the youngest daughter, married Joseph Worsham, a relative of Mrs. Hope Hull and Mrs. David Meriwether.

Mr. and Mrs. Gilbert's daughter Maria married Mr. Christmas, and after his death, Andrew Shepherd, of Wilks, a very respectable and wealthy Virginia planter. They had one daughter, a beautiful young lady, who passed a winter in Washington City with Dr. Laurie, her uncle, mixed freely with the gay throng there, and forced the conviction on many bachelors and widowers, that Southern beauties are very attractive. She married the son of General Winder, of Maryland.

Andrew Shepherd, after the death of his first wife, married Miss Hillhouse, the sister of Mrs. Felix Gilbert. They had several children. Their three daughters, Mrs. Weems, Mrs. Baker, and Mrs. Hansel, are our special friends.

Andrew Shepherd showed the feelings of clanship which united our families, by making me executor of his will when he died, though I was then unmarried, and did not live near him.

Mr. and Mrs. Gilbert had two sons. William, the oldest by many years, was gay, good-looking, and thoughtless. He was a merchant. The goods and the money went in every way but accumulation, until he became the copartner of his brother Felix. After the death of his brother, his easy yielding temper induced him to lend the use of his credit to two or three speculating nephews, by whom he lost most of his great estate. What was left, depended for its value upon the uncertain issue of a lawsuit in Elbert Superior Court. Col. Campbell and myself were his lawyers; the cause came on for trial, and the parties announced themselves ready. Immediately after, Col. Campbell was sent for to see a dying child, so that the management of the case depended entirely upon me. Both the law and the facts, which controlled the decision, were so doubtful, that the result depended upon the manner in which the jury might be influenced by the argument and showing of the advocate. When Col. Campbell left, Mr. Gilbert became pale and trembling, and willing to compromise his rights for half the amount which he claimed. I had great regard for him, and knew that the loss of the suit would leave him dependent upon others for his support in after life. My excitement became intense. As I went on in the investigation and pleadings, my confidence increased. I stood firm upon my feet. My voice became strong and clear; and my mind without doubt as to the law and the facts. I had been familiar with the Elbert people from my youth, and addressed them with the freedom of friends. I succeeded.

Felix Gilbert, the youngest brother, was one of the cleverest men of Georgia. To great energy, industry and perfect integrity, he united vigorous intellect, enlarged patriotism, benevolent temper, and high social qualities. He was unrivalled in reputation among the merchants of the upper country. He was a member of the Legislature, and showed by the influence which he exercised that his talents for politics were equal to his knowledge of commerce. He died in the prime of life with the constitutional disease of his family.

Felix Gilbert married Miss Hillhouse, the daughter of David Hillhouse, and niece of James Hillhouse, the great Senator of Connecticut. When Felix Gilbert courted Miss Hillhouse, her father was dead. She referred him to Mr. James Hillhouse. He visited the stern old puritan, in New Haven, and was questioned very minutely and authoritatively about his ability to take care of a wife, before the consent was given. Mrs. Gilbert lived only a few years.

I was Mr. Gilbert's nurse one night, a few weeks before his death. Whilst I was sitting by his bedside, his daughter Sarah, his only child, then a little girl, seven or eight years old, came into his chamber. When she left the room, he told me that it would be a great relief to his anxiety about her future fate, if he could know that I was to be her husband. When I left him the next morning, he called Sarah to him, told her that he wished her when she was old enough to marry me. Sarah supposing that she was obliged to do what her father enjoined upon her, cried herself to sleep the night after because the man whom she was to marry was so ugly.

Sarah Gilbert was intrusted by her father's will to her grandmother, Mrs. David Hillhouse, a very sensible, well-informed, precise old lady, who had been left a widow without property, and by her own exertions sustained and educated a family of children in the very best way. She had showed her independent spirit, and strength of understanding, by the manner in which she had edited the first newspaper published in the section of the State in which she lived. The trust confided to her by her son-in-law she discharged in the most faithful and useful way. When Sarah became Miss Gilbert, she travelled with her for her pleasure and information to many cities and through several States. They visited the Peaked Mountain, in Rockingham, Virginia, the birth-place of Sarah's father, and Major Grattan's residence, whose wife was a particular friend of his family. Their son Peachy, a youth of sixteen, was reduced to the poetical state by his love for the young lady. Miss Gilbert's education was perfected by passing some time with her intellectual and highly cultivated relations in New Haven, and the neighborhood. Mr. Adam Alexander was then going through college. He was the handsomest youth of his class, intelligent and courteous, and like Miss Gilbert, a native Georgian. The young gentleman had not in the three years he had been in Yale, seen any one so beautiful and accomplished as his countrywoman. He made their admiration mutual, by the pleasing manner in which he pressed his admiration upon her. They became more and more attached to each other, until they felt that life would be a lifeless life unless spent together.

I saw Miss Gilbert for the first time after girlhood at the Madison Springs, with her uncle, Mr. William Gilbert, and Mr. Alexander. I was then most happily married, and very much gratified that the trust which her father wished might be mine, was about to be placed upon one so worthy of it. They were soon after married. Mr. Alexander is now as distinguished for his good understanding, cultivated taste, and excellent character, as he was when a collegiate for his fine person and regular features. He has done what few Southern men possessed of great riches in early life ever done before, devote his time constantly and industriously to laborious and useful employment. He was for a long time cashier of the branch of the State bank at Washington. He has directed very attentively the management of the large plantation on which he resides. He has constantly either instructed or superintended the education of his numerous family of children. He founded, and has been the principal patron and director of one of the best literary institutions of the State. Mr. and Mrs. Alexander, their sons and daughters, are among our best friends. They visit us, and treat us as their near kinsfolk. Distant as the relationship is between Mrs. Alexander and my wife, they are in some particulars singularly alike. Mrs. Alexander is many years younger than my wife. Mr. Alexander appreciates her beauty very highly, and was a little slow in acknowledging the remembrance. It was forced upon him in the most convincing way. We visited him when Mrs. Alexander happened to be from home. The nurse brought the youngest child to my wife. The little one with joy put its arms around her neck, and kissed her for its mother.

Their three oldest daughters are very happily married to gentlemen of great respectability. The prettiest and wittiest is still unmarried.

William Felix, Mr. and Mrs. Alexander's oldest son, was educated at Yale College. He has succeeded his father in the cashiership of the bank at Washington. He is married to the oldest daughter of the Honorable Robert Toombs, whom he has loved and claimed for his wife from early boyhood. It is a delightful sight to see two young people after marriage making it their controlling purpose to make each other happy. That pleasure is enjoyed by the friends of Felix and Louisa Alexander.

The Saxon Scotch emigrated in such numbers to the fine country in the north of Ireland, during the sixteenth and seventeenth centuries, as to form a distinct race from the native Celts. Their women were the prettiest in person, and purest in character, of European ladies; and their men were equally distinguished for enterprise, intellectual capacity, and love of liberty. The inferior station assigned by the British government to Irishmen in the public service, induced most of those who could to emigrate to the American Colonies. In the early part of the eighteenth century, several Scotch-Irish Presbyterian congregations settled the fertile territory in North Carolina, between the Catawba and Yadkin Rivers. The arbitrary dominion of Great Britain followed the emigrants to their new homes. They were forbid to take the evidence of any existing debt in the form of a promissory note, or buy a pound of tea without first paying the government for the privilege. A large British army crossed the Atlantic to compel them, and others like them, to do what they would not voluntarily. The colonists were obliged to choose between submission and resistance. The rumors about the battles of Lexington and Bunker Hill so excited the Scotch-Irish of Mecklenburg, that on the 10th of May, 1775, they assembled in the little village of Charlotte, to agree what they would do. They made the following declaration of their opinions and purposes:—

THE MECKLENBURG DECLARATION.

"Resolved 1st. That whosoever directly or indirectly abetted or in any way, form, or manner, countenanced the unchartered and dangerous invasion of our rights, as claimed by Great Britain, is an enemy to this country, to America, and to the inherent and unalienable rights of man.

"Resolved 2d. That we, the citizens of Mecklenburg County, do hereby dissolve the political bonds which have connected us with the Mother Country, and hereby absolve ourselves from all allegiance to the British Crown, and abjure all political connection, contract, or association with that nation, who have wantonly trampled on our rights and liberties, and inhumanly shed the blood of American Patriots at Lexington.

Resolved 3d. That we do hereby declare ourselves a free and independent people; are, and of right ought to be, a sovereign and self-governing association, under the control of no power other than that of our God, and the General Government of the Congress; to the maintenance of which independence, we solemnly pledge to each other our mutual co-operation, our lives, our fortunes, and our most sacred honor.

Resolved 4th. That, as we acknowledge the existence and control of no law, nor legal office, civil or military, within this county, we do hereby ordain and adopt as a rule of life, all, each, and every of our former laws; wherein, nevertheless, the Crown of Great Britain never can be considered as holding rights, privileges, immunities, or authority therein.

"Resolved 5th. That it is further decreed, that all, each and every military officer in this county is hereby retained in his former command and authority, he acting conformably to these regulations. And that every member present of this delegation shall henceforth be a civil officer, viz.: a justice of the peace, in the character of committee-man, to issue process, hear and determine all matters of controversy, according to said adopted laws; and to preserve peace, union, and harmony in said county; and to use every exertion to spread the love of country and fire of freedom throughout America, until a general organized government be established in this province."

A voice from the crowd called out for "three cheers," and the whole company shouted three times, and threw their hats in the air.

The resolutions were read again and again during the day to different companies, desirous of retaining in their memories sentiments so congenial to their feelings. There are still living some whose parents were in that assembly, and heard and read the resolutions; and from whose lips they heard the circumstances and sentiments of this remarkable declaration..

When the chairman of the meeting put the question, "Who will carry our resolves to the Congress of the Confederation," James Jack, a bold, enthusiastic man, answered, "I will." Immediately after, a lone horseman might have been seen, with intent look, pressing his horse on through the country towards the north. When James Jack arrived in Philadelphia, he attended the Congress, and delivered his message to some of its members. That body took no notice of it in its proceedings. The majority were not then prepared to jeopard their lives and property by doing what was treasonable. Whilst the Declaration of Independence, made by the Congress of the Confederation, on the 4th of July, 1776, has been upon the lips of every American, upon every return of its anniversary, the Declaration of Independence, made more than a year before by the Mecklenburg people, remained for a long time unknown to fame. The fact that such a declaration had been made, was unnoticed in history, unknown to the public, and denied when asserted, until placed beyond dispute by the production of two copies, which had continued in the possession of the descendants of persons present when it was made; and by the finding of a copy, which was sent to his government by some British officer in the Southern Colonies, and deposited in the colonial office in London.

When liberty triumphed, James Jack removed from North Carolina to Georgia, and after a while to Wilks, and from thence to Elbert County, near Broad River.

When James Jack offered to be the bearer to Congress of the Mecklenburg Declaration of Independence, Francis Cummings, his neighbor and friend, was standing by, full of the spirit which prompted Jack to act. He was the finest specimen of manly person, noble head and impressive features, in the crowd of fine-looking Scotch-Irishmen there. For fifty years afterwards, Francis Cummings might have been seen on the walls of Zion, and his clarion voice heard proclaiming liberty to the children of Adam enchained in sin, who would fight the good fight of faith in the form prescribed by the Presbyterian Church.

Francis Cummings followed his friend Jack to Wilks County. His last residence and preaching-place was Greensborough.

William Jack, the son of the ever-to-be-remembered James Jack, married the oldest daughter of Dr. Francis Cummings. He was a long time a merchant in Augusta, of the firm of Jack & Ennis. No trader of that town was ever so confided in by the Broad River people as William Jack. When he quit business, he settled among them, on the Elbert side of Broad River.

Patrick Jack, the second son of James Jack, was a small, active, well-formed man, of good temper, sweet, insinuating voice, and full of frolic and fun. When he married Miss Spencer, the niece of Mrs. Micajah McGehee, he quitted idle, dissipated ways, settled on the Elbert side of Broad River, and joined the Methodists during the great religious excitement of 1809-10. He was appointed Colonel of the 8th Regiment during the war of 1812. His addictedness to prayer, and the saving of his pay, did not prove the best qualities for enforcing discipline. The 8th Infantry was remarkable for the dissolute habits of its officers, and the disorderly conduct of the soldiers.

Leroy M. Wiley, of New York, reputed to be one of the richest men in the world, is a nephew of James Jack.

Alexander Bowie, formerly Chancellor of Alabama, married James Jack's niece.

As James Jack was a North Carolinian by birth, and one of the emigrants to Wilks, he is placed among the North

Carolina settlers, though his residence and death were among the Broad River Virginia people.

COLONEL NICHOLAS LONG.

THOUGH Nicholas Long was too young to render any very important service to the cause of liberty during the revolutionary war, he was old enough to show by his whig enthusiasm, what he would have done had be been older. When he arrived at manhood, his tall, well-formed person, expressive features, polished, courteous manners, kind temper, cultivated taste, and good understanding, made him the most admired gentleman of his day. It is indeed singular that the most accomplished man of the southern country should have been born and educated in North Carolina, and have chosen for his residence in after-life the frontiers of Georgia. He married a fine lady in that part of North Carolina which is near enough to the border for the people to call themselves Virginians. He settled immediately afterwards in Wilks County, Georgia. The professions of the law, medicine, and the pulpit, monopolized, in early times, in Georgia, the very small number of the educated. It is not now known why Nicholas Long, having as he did, an unusual share of learning, and capacity for influencing others, was not a lawyer. It is probable that his temper urged him to action in preference to the lawyer's office. He planted, surveyed, and speculated in land, and acquired more wealth than those who sought success by professional practice. He resided in sight and within a short walk of the town of Washington. His house, and the grounds about it, were in better style than those elsewhere in any part of the upper country. His employments led him into connection with the companies who purchased millions of acres of the State of Georgia in 1795. The conduct of some of the agents of those companies made every body who belonged to them so unpopular, that Col. Long never held any high public office dependent upon the voice of the people. His known gallantry and intelligence induced the Government of the United States to appoint him Colonel of the 43d Regiment of Infantry in the war of 1812. When the law passed for raising and organizing that regiment, the materials out of which the regular army was formed had been already so used up, that soldiers could only be found for a few companies, squads and detachments. These were never in the field, nor Col. Long in full command.

Mrs. Long died of pulmonary consumption. Col. Long's tall, spare person and narrow chest, could not resist the destructive tendency of the feverish influence of the wife whom he loved. Some time after her death, his own health began to decline. I had been a first lieutenant of one of the companies of the 43d, and greatly indebted to Col. Long for his constant courtesy and kindness. My own health was then very bad. He invited me to be his companion in a visit to some of the southern Atlantic islands. Circumstances which I could not control prevented my going with him. Consumption had too strong hold upon his lungs to be loosened by climate or place. He died soon after his return home.

Margaret, Col. Long's oldest daughter, was educated at Bethlehem, in Pennsylvania, then considered by the people of the South, the highest quality school for young ladies. When Miss Long returned to Washington, her finished education and family distinction made acquaintance with her the most certain means of favorable admittance into fashionable society. Two young gentlemen, whose aspirations were most ardent to head the beau monde, sought that distinction, by going through the forms of a challenge to fight a duel, upon the pretence of some exceptionable incident in the attentions of one or the other to Miss Long. She married Mr. Thomas Telfair, the son of Governor Telfair, who was afterwards a member of Congress. Mr. Telfair is now dead. Mrs. Telfair is a most amiable, benevolent lady. She continues to live in Savannah, the place of her husband's birth, residence and death.

Richard, Col. Long's oldest son, had all the advantages which education at the best literary institutions could give him. He married Miss Hay, a most estimable young lady, the daughter of Dr. Hay, and niece of Mr. Felix Gilbert. He practiced law for a while, and represented at one time the people of the County of Wilks in the Legislature. He moved to Florida, where his wife died soon after.

Sarah Rebekah, Col. Long's second daughter, was a sensible, well educated young lady. She married Mr. James Rembert, a respectable gentleman, who was more than once a member of the Georgia Legislature. He moved to the West. He is now dead. Mrs. Rembert resides in or near the City of Memphis.

Eliza, Col. Long's third daughter, married Mr. ——— Dubose. She is dead.

Eugenia, the fourth daughter, married Mr. Lock Weems. Both are dead.

John, Col. Long's youngest son, is a wealthy, hospitable gentleman. His residence is in Washington County.

PART III.

GEORGE R. GILMER.

CHAPTER I.

I WAS born the 11th of April, 1790, on the south side of Broad River, about a mile and a half above the Fish Dam Ford, in that part of Wilks which is now Oglethorpe County. I have often been a candidate for public office during great party excitement, without obtaining any favor for being a native Georgian. I was believed to be a Virginian, as all my immediate ancestors had been.

The first distinct recollection which I have of myself, was my confinement in bed, by an attack of bilious fever, and slow recovery. I was occasionally allowed a grown negro woman for my nurse, who was very kindly disposed. She amused me with handfuls of buckeye seed. I was pleased with their variegated colors, and first learned to count with them. Grown people were usually too busy then providing subsistence, or otherwise bettering their condition, to attend to children. My knowledge of numbers extended, and my counting abilities made quite a noise in the family circle. When company came to my father's, I was called up, to add and multiply.

When I was a child, puddings, pies, and sweetmeats were great rarities, and only seen at the tables of our people when visited by select company. I can recollect my great impatience, when a small boy, because the company at my father's remained sitting at table chatting, after they had finished their meal, and my asking Governor Mathews to get up.

From my childhood, I have suffered greatly from headache and toothache. There was some defect in the organization of my nervous system, from which I have suffered pain, more or less, every day of my life.

My father's children would have had good constitutions, if health and strength had resulted from fresh air and daily labor. We rose by light in the morning and busied ourselves at some employment or other. Until I was ten years old, my father lived in a house made of hewed logs. I slept with a crack at my back, large enough for my body to pass through. I went bare-footed every winter, until after frost, and suffered from it more than my father thought possible.

My first schoolmaster was a deserter from the British navy. He wrote a good hand, and I suppose could read. During the time he kept school, he secretly entered the desks of several of his employers in search of money. The school-house had no chimney. The weather was occasionally cold. He warmed his scholars by making them join hands, and run round, whilst he hastened their speed by the free use of the switch. At other times the boys were paired off, and set to wrestling. In the evening, he amused himself by threatening to fasten them up in the school-house until the next day, unless they would give some sufficient reason why they should go home. Asking a little boy, the son of the ferryman on Broad River, where he got the mutton he was eating for his twelve o'clock meal, he answered that his daddy had caught one of Mr. Gilmer's sheep in the brier patch, and killed it. The deserter was driven away upon the discovery of his habit of thieving, and his skill in detecting the like propensity in others.

My next schoolmaster was William P. Culberson, a very handsome, gay young man, from North Carolina. The neighborhood lost his services at the end of the year, by his marriage. I liked him very much, and learned from him how to read with pleasure.

My next teacher was an Irishman by the name of Nolan. Wandering, drunken Irishmen, were the only class of the frontier people who had the leisure and requisite knowledge for teaching. Nolan knocked, kicked, cuffed, and whipped at a great rate. My brother John, and George Mathews, two very smart boys, were sometimes punished ten times a day. John, when he saw Nolan coming towards him, expecting to get a pommelling, would set as lightly as possible on his seat, so that the first knock brought him to the floor; whilst George

Mathews would drop his book, seize hold of the bench with both hands, and was consequently cuffed most unmercifully before he was brought to the same position.

I happened once to be in Jasper Court, when Judge Strong was on the bench, and the lawyers arguing a certiorari. Nolan had sued a widow woman for a year's schooling of her daughter, who had been taken from school before the term was out. A jury had given a verdict for the widow, and Nolan had appealed to his honor to correct the verdict. The jury had found against Nolan, because he had knocked the widow's daughter down with his fist. I addressed Judge Strong in favor of our old schoolmaster, urging as a reason why he should be paid, that every body who sent to his school knew when they did so his way of correction; that his honor's head could prove, that knocking down had been long Nolan's mode of punishment.

My next teacher was Col. Hobson, an old Virginia gentleman, who had emigrated to Georgia, because his drunken habits had lost him most of his property, and otherwise disqualified him for the society of his class. He wrote a good hand, and could cipher. There was a distillery for making brandy not very far from the school-house. During play time he would sometimes go over to it, and then teaching ended for that day.

My next schoolmaster was John Rogers, who got drunk every Saturday when he had the money, and could get where whiskey was sold. My next was Charles Goss, a native of Elbert County, a sober, industrious, well-informed man, and very well qualified in every way for his employment. From that time, the teachers of country school have been usually native young men. Drunken Irishmen, instead of occupying the best situations, are now from necessity obliged to seek a pittance among those who will not pay common wages.

Many years afterwards, an old man trudged his way, shillelah in hand, to the Broad River settlement. I was present at my father's when he stopped to get food and rest. He wore the jump jacket of the last century, and carried under his arm his first manuscript ciphering book. He had taught George Mathews, then Judge of the Supreme Court of Louisiana, Meriwether Lewis, who first explored the wilderness territory of the United States across the Rocky Mountains to the Pacific Ocean, and a few other boys of the neighborhood about their age. The old schoolmaster had returned, after thirty years' tramping hither and thither, to seek employment of his former patrons and their sons. But old things had passed away. The school-house had rotted down; most of those who had known him were dead, and their children gone to other lands. The hickory switch, which had been held up perpetually as the emblem of authority, or plied without mercy to the boys' backs and legs, had been changed for milder means of enforcing knowledge. Printed books had superseded the manuscript. The old field schoolmaster found his occupation gone.

I soon acquired a taste for reading. There were but few books among our people. My father paid me for picking out cotton on Saturdays and other school holidays, by which I made enough to buy Hume's History and Ossian's Poems. My older brothers attended to my father's business, so that I had leisure enough to study my books. My father obliged his sons to be usefully occupied in some way. He was usually content when I was found reading. One consequence of the different habits of my older brothers and myself was, that they were excellent riders, whilst I was quite the reverse. This deficiency I have often felt since. It gave rise to a nickname, which was applied to me for many years. Soon after I learned to read. I found in Scot's Lessons Cowper's John Gilpin, and was so pleased with it, that I learned to read it well, and was frequently called upon to amuse family visitors with it. Dr. Thornton Gilmer was at my father's, and wanting his horse, I went to the pasture with the negro boy who was directed to catch him. I was put upon his back, without saddle. Being a spirited animal, he immediately found that he was uncontrolled, and took to his heels most vigorously until he got to the gate before the house. My father, Dr. Gilmer, and others of the family, being then at dinner, upon hearing the loud clatter of horse's hoofs, ran to the door time enough to see me come up without hat, and holding hard on to the mane with both hands. I had just been showing off my smartness by reading John Gilpin. All cried out, when they saw my rapid approach, Gilpin! Gilpin!

When I was about twelve years old, my brother Lewis and myself went to Mr. Wilson's select classical school, near Abbeville C. H., South Carolina. This was the first change in my life. Until then I had never seen any people but Virginians, and of them few but kinsfolk. Mr. Wilson put us to board with a family of Irish people, who had no children. The old man, his wife, and two nieces, the oldest a very pretty young woman, my brother and myself, slept in the same room, the cabin having but one. It was difficult, at first, to dress and undress before females. We ate mush and milk once, and fried meat twice a day. On Sunday mornings we had hot water, colored with a grain or two of coffee. My father was a lover of good eating. This Irish fare, therefore, went hard with me for a few days. It was, however, soon forgotten when I became interested in my school employments and schoolfellows.

Mr. Wilson, my teacher, was one of the most faultless of men. During the ten months I went to his school he never punished a scholar except by reprimand, and in that way only a few times; and yet his scholars seldom misbehaved, and their advancement was equal to what was made at any school I was ever at.

Mr. Wilson's father had liberated all his slaves. One or two remained with the son, and were great scamps. Mr. Wilson in endeavoring to enforce the laws of South Carolina against trading in slaves, made himself so unpopular that he removed to Ohio, where he was put at the head of a college. Among my thirteen schoolfellows (that being the number to which the school was limited), were John Bull, Joseph Berry Earle, William Taylor, B. Franklin Whitner, and Frank Cummings, all of whom were men of note afterwards.

Soon after the breaking up of Mr. Wilson's school, I went to Dr. Waddel's academy. I boarded with an old Scotchman and his wife by the name of Sutherland. He was from the Orkney Islands, and she from the town of Thurso on the mainland. They had been transferred to the colonies before the revolutionary war by Lord George Gordon, who paid the cost of their removal, upon their giving him their indenture to serve him for five years. He settled with them, and many others in the same situation, on the south side of Broad River, a mile or two above where Col. Taliafero afterward resided. When fighting for independence commenced, Lord George Gordon carried his people to South Carolina, and sold them, there being then nobody in Upper Georgia who had the means to buy servants, and returned himself to the old country to serve his royal master. I have endeavored to find out whether this Lord George Gordon, who preceded the Broad River people in their settlement, was the crack-brained fanatic of London riot memory, celebrated by Sir Walter Scott in the "Heart of Mid-Lothian." I have just received a letter from Grant Thorburn, now upwards of eighty years old, informing me that Lord George Gordon, the fanatic, was somewhere in the Colonies before the revolutionary war. Sutherland and his wife were purchased by Gen. Pickens. They lived on a small, poor piece of land, in a cabin with two rooms, when Dr. Waddel removed his school from the village of Vienna to their immediate neighborhood.

I continued for several years with Dr. Waddel. He persuaded me, when I was prepared for college, and intended going to Princeton, to continue with him. He was for a long time the most useful and successful teacher in the southern country. He devoted his whole life to his calling, and was a most admirable example of the superiority of strong sense of duty and untiring industry in the employments of life, over genius and accomplishments. His family, who were poor, emigrated from Ireland to North Carolina before the revolutionary war. They lived near a school where Latin was taught, of which Moses availed himself at an early age. His retentive memory enabled him to become sufficiently proficient in Latin by the time he was fourteen to aid in teaching. The highest ambition of a poor Irish Presbyterian is for his oldest son to be a preacher. The profits of teaching, with a little addition from his father's means, enabled Moses to pass through Hampden Sydney College, the most southern institution then under Presbyterian direction. He graduated, and prepared there for the ministry. Immediately after he was licensed, he travelled as a missionary to South Carolina and Georgia. He was stout and well proportioned, with a large head, striking features, and quick perceptive faculties. He found a pleasant home during his sojourn in the South at the house of Patrick Calhoun, whose daughter, the sister of the distinguished statesman, John C. Calhoun, he married. He settled in Columbia County, Georgia, where he taught a classical school for several years. He afterwards removed to the village of Vienna, Abbeville, and from there into the country, about seven miles distant, where he taught until he accepted the presidency of Franklin College. When he was appointed to that office, I was requested by the trustees to accompany Col. Campbell, one of their body, to urge his acceptance. In a few years Franklin College, under his direction, became the most flourishing literary institution in the Southern States. When he took charge of it there were neither funds, professors, nor students. Some years after the college commenced prospering, one or two of the trustees, thinking that Dr. Waddel had done all the good which he was fitted to perform, addressed him a letter, in which they expressed the opinion that it was time for him to yield his place to some one of more distinguished literary reputation. He sent his resignation to the Senatus Academicus at its next meeting. I was then a member of that body, as senator from Oglethorpe County. The resignation was received, and a motion made for adjournment, when I offered a resolution expressive of the high appreciation by the Senatus Academicus of Dr. Waddel's value as president, and the desire that he would remain at the head of the college. The resolution was adopted by nearly a unanimous vote. I doubt whether any act of my after life was more cordially approved by the people of Georgia.

I left Dr. Waddel's academy before I was eighteen. Being considered too young to enter a law office, I taught for a year my younger brothers and sisters, and several of the young people of the neighborhood.

CHAPTER II.

WHEN the year of my school-keeping was closed, I set out upon a travelling excursion to Virginia. A young man, named

Muse, who had been keeping school like myself, was my companion. By agreement, we were to meet at Mr. William Barnett's, who lived then on the Savannah River. Mr. Barnett had been my father's neighbor, was his kinsman, and very good friend. Muse did not meet me at the time appointed; I had to wait for him several days. I spent the delay in courting Mrs. Barnett's daughter, Martha Bibb, a young lady rather younger in her teens than myself. The old folks of both families had taken it into their heads to make a match between us; and I suppose would have succeeded, if the young people had been particularly attractive to each other. It was difficult, however to pass days with a very pleasant, familiar acquaintance in the country—the old people keeping out of the way—without saying something that one of the parties would afterwards wish had never been said. As soon as Muse joined me, we set out on our journey. Among the matters which I recollect, was my passing a night in the town of Charlotte, North Carolina; and the evening, until bed-time, with a gold-digger—an Englishman—who had been attracted to that part of the country by the fame of the large lump of gold which had been found some time before, by the Reeds, on the road between Charlotte and Salisbury. He was a very conversable, imaginative man. When he left the room, the taven-keeper informed me, that he had been seeking for gold until he had spent all that he had, and only put on clean clothes by going to bed until those he had on were washed. I have had some cause since to recollect this gold-digger, and his passion for getting gold by finding it.

I travelled with my companion to his home, in Amelia County, Virginia. I went, whilst there, to Amelia Court, saw Benjamin Watkins Leigh—then the most promising and aspiring young man in the Old Dominion—and ate oysters at the tail of a cart, after the fashion of the lower Virginians.

The day I left Amelia, I dined at Cumberland Court House, and heard electioneering speeches for the first time. Cumberland was one of the counties of John Randolph's district. He was then a candidate for re-election. His opponent was using all the means of opposition in his power, before the adjournment of Congress, knowing his inability to contend with Mr. Randolph's extraordinary talents for public speaking.

In the evening, I went on my journey towards the mountains. Arriving at the country tavern, where I had been directed to stop, I was refused admittance, on account of the sickness of the family, and advised to go on about a mile further, to where a gentleman resided, who, I was told, would receive me into his house for the night, when my situation was made known to him. I accordingly applied, and was permitted to stay. Conversing with my host during the evening about the mineral waters of the State, I remarked that Mr. Lewis of the Sweet Springs, was the first cousin of my mother. The gentleman immediately informed me that he was Dr. Trent, and that his wife was the sister of Mr. Lewis and my mother's kinswoman. I was most hospitably entertained for several days. Mrs. Trent was a very pretty and accomplished lady, Dr. Trent a cultivated gentleman, and their children very beautiful. I had been but little accustomed to the society of refined, educated people. The novelty pleased and excited me. I have continued ever since to take great interest in Dr. Trent's family. The day after I left Dr. Trent's, I arrived at Charlottesville, where I found Dr. Marks, the half-brother of Meriwether Lewis. I went home with him, and spent a week at his mother's, who was the sister of my paternal grandmother. During the week I went to Monticello. Mr. Jefferson's last term of office was about terminating. Three rooms of his house were left open, to be shown to strangers who might visit the place. I saw there statuary, fine paintings, and a collection of Indian works. The statuary was very beautiful: I could not be satisfied with looking at it. The paintings did not at all equal the expectations which my scholastic reading had excited. The Indian remains were singular things. Mr. Jefferson's library-room was locked, but the window blinds were thrown back, so that I could see several books turned open upon the table, the inkstand, paper, and pens, as they had been when Mr. Jefferson quitted home.

I was in Charlottesville on the day of the election for members of the Legislature and Congress. It was passed in listening to electioneering speeches from Judge Carr and Mr. Garland, candidates for Congress, and several candidates for the Legislature. Baptist Billy Woods delivered his opinion in the most unique style, for one who was seeking to legislate for a great State. Billy Meriwether said some of his neighbors had insisted upon his offering until he had consented, and took his seat,—the shortest speech I ever heard on such an occasion, and, what is perhaps worthy of remembrance, the speaker was elected, whilst Billy Woods, who held forth an hour or two, was defeated.

From Mrs. Marks's, I went over the Blue Ridge Mountains, accompanied by Dr. Marks. We passed up the mountain by a new-made road, along a considerable creek, sometimes travelling in its bed, crossing and re-crossing it repeatedly. The view from the top of the Blue Ridge, always beautiful, was then wonderful to me, who had never seen a mountain. The vast expanse of country below—the deep blue of the sky—the varied hues of the forest mingling together in the distance—the high mountains, away beyond the valley in the west, losing their inequalities of surface in the obscurity of the view—made impressions upon me which still remain. I passed that evening the birthplace of my mother—then the residence of my uncle, Charles Lewis—and arrived at Lethe, the birthplace of my father—the residence of my uncle, George Gilmer.

I remained two months at this beautiful place, with the best and kindest people whom I have ever known. The house was of brick, situated upon the descent of a hill, about three hundred yards from the Shanandoah River, which was seen over a beautiful meadow, and through thinly scattered sycamore trees, flowing away with strong current. From the top of the hill, back of the house, might been seen exceedingly fertile fields, inclosed in a semicircle, formed by the river, and mountains extending in every direction. In the middle of the valley, between the North Mountain and the Blue Ridge, rose up almost perpendicularly, and to a great height, the Peaked Mountain. In a clear day, many excavations were visible on its side. Upon inquiring about them, I was informed that they had been made by the neighboring Dutch people in search of hidden treasure. A young fellow of the neighborhood, whose father was a man of some wealth and consequence, had a club-foot, and was made a tailor of, as fit for nothing else. In following his trade, he went to many places, and became wise in the ways and some tricks of the world. After a while, he returned to the neighborhood of the Peaked Mountain. The Dutch had heard, and were credulous enough to believe, that a wealthy lord was one of the first settlers of the Shanandoah Valley, had quitted the country a long time before, and returned to Germany, leaving his money behind, hid in the Peaked Mountain. There had been some effort to discover the treasure by digging several places in the mountain side. The tailor told them that, in his travels through Ohio, he had been in a factory of spy-glasses, which so added to the power of sight, that he could see several feet into the earth with one of them. Having excited great interest about these glasses and the hidden treasure by his tales, he proposed to the money-hunters that, if they would make up a sufficient sum, he would go with it to the factory, and buy them a glass, by which they could find the concealed gold.

The required sum was collected, and the tailor went to Ohio. Upon his return, he informed his employers that he had purchased a glass better than he had ever seen before; that he had no doubt but that they could have seen through the Peaked Mountain, if he could have gotten it to them; but unfortunately, as he was travelling home with it, he was obliged to cross a rapid run, which proved more swollen than he supposed. He was washed down by the strong current, lost his saddle-bags, with the glass in it, and came near losing his life. Another sum of money was made up with which the Irish club-footed tailor left the neighborhood of the Peaked Mountain, never again to be seen there. He laid out the money in the purchase of a tract of land, whilst some had theirs sold to repay the money which they had borrowed to supply the tailor with the means to buy the wonderful glass.

Whilst at Lethe, I witnessed an electioneering scene, equally interesting with the one I had been present at in Charlottesville. David Holmes, who had for twenty years immediately preceding, represented in Congress the district of which Rockingham County made a part, had been appointed Governor of the Mississippi Territory by Mr. Jefferson. A new member had to be elected. The republicans and federalists were very equally divided in the district. Mr. Smith (now Judge Smith) became the candidate of the republicans, and Jacob Swope the candidate of the federalists. The Virginians vote *viva voce*. The candidates seat themselves during the day of the election on the judge's bench, in the court-house, and as each voter names the person for whom he votes, he is bowed to, and thanked by the candidate voted for. I was in Harrisonburg, the court-house town of Rockingham, on the day of the election, and saw Mr. Smith and Swope, thus seated and occupied. Smith was of an old Virginia family; Swope was German, and could speak the German language. The farmers of the county were mostly Germans; the lawyers, doctors, merchants, sheriffs, clerks, &c., were Virginians. Mr. Smith and Swope addressed the people on the party politics of the day, British orders in council, Napoleon's edicts restricting commerce, the embargo, and anti-commercial system of Mr. Jefferson. After both candidates had spoken, Mr. Swope commenced addressing the people in German, in reply to Mr. Smith. A huge old German rose, and in broken English, said Mr. Swope should not talk German, because Mr. Smith could not talk German, and stopped Swope. Mr. Swope was a merchant, a handsome man, and usually well dressed. He resided in Staunton, Augusta County. He came to Rockingham, dressed in German fashion. The German succeeded, though the Smith party had the majority in the district; and Mr. Smith was equal, if not superior to Mr. Swope, in qualifications for Congressional service.

Going from Lethe with a pretty cousin to visit Mrs. Gabriel Jones, the sister of our common grandmother, I had to dismount to open a gate which led into a large open field on the Shanandoah River. As I was rising in the stirrup to remount, my horse started, ran at full speed, and threw me. I fell with my weight bearing upon my right hand extended to break the force of the fall, and strained my wrist so badly, that the injury is still felt, adding thereby so much to my previous inability to write legibly, as often to bring down upon me the anathemas of my best friends.

Whilst in Virginia visiting my kinsfolk, I went to Richmond to gratify my desire to see a large town. I arrived there on Sunday. I strolled down to James River, and amused myself, among other ways, with looking at the shad-catchers standing upon the rocks in the currents of the falls of the river, throwing their scoop-nets for fish. The day after I went to the Superior Court, then sitting in a room in the Capitol, and heard the celebrated Edmund Randolph, previously Secretary of State for the United States, defend a criminal accused of horse-stealing. I saw the statue of Gen. Washington, and a bust of Marquis Fayette. During the day, I met with Mr. John Harvie, whom I had seen in Rockingham. Our grandmothers were sisters. He and his wife were on a visit to his mother, the widow of Col. John Harvie. I went with him to his mother's. In the evening, Eliza Grattan, the daughter of Maj. Grattan, of Rockingham, a little girl not yet in her teens, came to Mrs. Harvie's to see me. I pleased her fancy by presenting her with a most beautiful sash. I heard her talk and laugh for the first time, without its entering into my imagination that that talk and laugh would be the chief solace of my after life. She was living with Mrs. Wirt, who was her father's niece, attending a school for young ladies.

The day when I left Lethe to return to Georgia, several of my kinfolk accompanied me to Wier's Cave, which is about six miles from my father's birthplace, and four from my mother's, and near the road travelled to the south, in a high hill, whose base is washed by the Shenandoah River. Madison's Cave, called after John Madison, whose wife was my grandmother's sister, is in the same hill. Its beauty and curiosities were so defaced by making saltpetre in it during the revolutionary war that it attracted then but few visitors. There is a sheet of water in its interior of so great depth that Meriwether Lewis and Maj. Grattan had a small boat carried in and placed upon it. They attempted with the aid of cords to find the bottom, but without success.

Wier's Cave was discovered by a dog pursuing some animal through a hole into the interior, and the Dutchman, his owner, making an opening after him. That opening is still so low, and so confined between masses of limestone rock, that the feeling of restraint comes painfully over visitors, as they pass through it. The cave extends seven or eight hundred yards into the hill, through openings filled with stalactitic pillars. Some of the walls are curtained with thin folding sheets of rocks, which hang down to the bottom from roofs sixty feet high. I have been in Wier's Cave several times since my first visit. An accident happened when I was last there, which has effectually cured me of all desire to visit it again. One part is descended by a ladder of considerable length. Coming to this descent, I assisted my wife down, placed her by my side a step from me, turned round and assisted her companions down. When I again turned to see where I had placed her, she was not to be seen. I heard her moan twenty feet below. There was another descent very near by, which I had not observed. In stepping back she had gone over the precipice. The time which passed from my finding her gone and having her in my arms below was a moment of doubt and dread. She has never entirely recovered from the effects of that fall.

Soon after my return to Georgia, I commenced the study of law with Mr. Upson, of Lexington.

During the Christmas holidays next after, I set off from my father's in company with Daniel Harvie, to visit my brother-in-law Warren Taliaferro, who resided in Pendleton, South Carolina. I carried a led horse, a present from my father to Mr. Taliaferro. We reached McDonald's Ferry, on the Savannah River, just at dark, intending to go to a house about half a mile beyond. The day had been unusually warm. The ferry-boat was scarcely shoved from the shore, when a violent thunder-storm came on, bringing darkness, illuminated by flashes of lightning. The ferry-man was an old diseased foreigner, then nearly drunk. My saddle horse was very spirited, and the one which I led had never been on board a boat before, was young, and had been rode but little, if at all. I had to stand before this spirited horse and the unbroken one, in a crazy boat, directed by a drunken ferry-man. It required all my strength to hold the horses, as they snorted and sprung forward, with every flash of lightning. The current of the river was strong, and the boat very unsteady under the guidance of the old ferry-man. Harvie with great difficulty kept himself and his unruly horse aboard. The boat got entangled for a while in the limbs of the trees and bushes which overhung the water from the South Carolina bank, having fallen below the landing. The rubbing of the bushes against its side, increased the fright of the horses, until we had to compel the ferry-man to stop its motion. We remained in this situation, holding on by the bushes, until the storm abated and the moon rose. The ferry-man then got into a canoe attached to the end of the ferry-boat, and went off for assistance. He came back without bringing any. By this time it was very cold. The ferry-man, whilst he was gone, lost the chain by which he fastened the canoe to its stay. He declared that he would remain where he was all night unless we took his canoe into the boat. The horses had by this time become somewhat quiet. So Harvie and myself left them to take care of themselves. Harvie was very strong, and I was not deficient in that way. By the full exertion of all the force we had, the object was effected, and the canoe lay by the side of the horses' heads. The ferry-man then commenced the use of oars, and the boat slowly ascended towards the landing. We had proceeded but a little distance when Harvie's horse was jostled into the river. The water was deep, and the horse unable to swim, so that Harvie had to hold his head above the water to prevent his drowning. My horses became restless and uneasy. Their moving about knocked one of the oars off its stay, so that it was lost. There was no other in the boat to supply its place. Poles were resorted to, and for a little while with success. But we soon got to water so deep that they scarcely touched the bottom. Whilst struggling to push the boat up, sometimes touching bottom and sometimes not, the boat became fastened on a log. Harvie's horse was failing in strength, and he and I were failing in ours. The ferry-man had given up in despair and would have frozen to death, but that we threatened to thrash him if he did not work enough to keep himself warm. Whilst in this situation we could hear very near us the roar of falls, which the ferry-man informed us were with difficulty passed by a boat in the daytime. An island lay in the middle of the river, a little below where we were. After a while, we got the boat off the log, and made for this island. Numerous rocks obstructed the boat's progress. After many hours' hard work, we got within reach of bushes growing on the bank. The ferry-man then insisted that we should put his canoe into the water, promising that he would make another effort to procure assistance. The canoe was lifted into the water. He got into it, went off and never returned. Before he left us, he said that there was a ford across the river from the island to the Georgia shore. We succeeded, after a long time, in getting Harvie's horse off the rocks into the boat. We then got the boat close up to the bank. My horse in springing from the boat to the bank drove the boat off, so that he fell into deep water. He made several ineffectual efforts to ascend the bank, swam down the river some distance, and still failing to get up, came back to the boat. The bridle reins had been in his way. I cut them off. He then succeeded. After the horses were landed, we went round the island in search of appearances which indicated the place where the river had been forded. We found tracks, and a path to the water, in one place only. After waiting for some time for the return of the ferry-man, and being almost frozen to death in our wet clothes, we determined to try the ford. As Harvie could not swim and knew nothing of the management of his horse, so as to enable him to swim, I went ahead. The water was very cold, and the way full of rocks. The horses were sometimes out of the water, and then plunging into the deep current. It was with great difficulty that I kept my saddle, and held on to the bridle of my led horse. Each moment I expected to struggle for life by getting into swimming water. We continued to plunge forward until we arrived at the Georgia bank. Ascending it to the hut of the ferry-man, we found him nearly frozen to death. He became a cripple for life, had to quit his labor at the oar, and get his bread by begging. It was less than an hour before the light of the morning when we reached the ferry-man's hut. We dried our clothes, fed our horses, and set off at sunrise for a ferry four miles above. We reached my brother-in-law's late in the evening. I became very ill. Harvie returned to Georgia to let my father and mother know that I was probably dead. I got home, after some time, by the aid of my oldest brother, who had joined me for that purpose. I resumed my law studies, and struggled on for some time, endeavoring to overcome the effects of disease. It was all in vain. I went to my father's, where I passed three years in a listless, diseased state.

Chapter III.

RETURNING home in October, 1813, after travelling for some months, I received a commission of first lieutenant in the 43d regiment. Dr. Bibb, whose medical advice I had been following, was then in Congress. He obtained this commission for me without my knowledge, believing, as he said, that service in the army would probably produce some change in my diseased system which would kill or cure me. Col. Long, of Washington, Wilks County, was commander of the 43d. I immediately went to see him. He advised me to accept the commission, promising that he would give me an active command as soon as possible. I took quarters at the barracks near Washington, where Capt. Tatnall was then stationed. Our acquaintance, and subsequent friendship, was the happiest result of my military service. Our strong regard and intimate intercourse was never interrupted for a moment during his life.

As soon as a few recruits were collected, an order was issued by Gen. Pinckney, then in command of the Southern army, that they should be put under a suitable officer, and sent into the Indian territory, where active hostilities were going on against the Creeks. I asked for the command and received it. I marched with twenty-two recruits, without arms, except refuse drill muskets, and a small quantity of loose powder and unmoulded lead. My appointed station was on the banks of the Chattahoochee, about thirty or forty miles beyond the frontiers of the State, near an Indian town, not far from where the Georgia railroad now crosses the Chattahoochee River.

It was an awkward business for one who had only seen a militia muster! who had never fired a musket, and only drawn a sword to govern men who knew no part of their duty. I was ordered to build a fort. I had never seen a fort, and had no means of knowing how to obey the order but what I could get from Duane's Tactics. I went to work, and succeeded very well, so far as I know, or any one else, I suppose, as the strength and fitness of my fortification was never tested.

A few days after my arrival at the standing peach-tree, a ruffian fellow came into the camp with some fine catfish for sale. I had supplied myself with hooks and lines for catching cat in the Chattahoochee before I left home, and had baited and hung them from limbs into the water. I had noticed this fellow the day before gliding stealthily along near the bank of the river, in a small canoe, where the lines with baited hooks were hung. I intimated to him that the fish he was offering to sell were taken from my hooks. With the demoniac look of hatred and revenge, he drew his knife from his belt, and holding it for a moment in the position for striking, turned the edge to his own throat, and drew it across; expressing thus, more forcibly than he could have done by words, his desire to cut my throat. I never saw him afterwards.

One night, immediately after dark, and before any preparations for defence had been made, the Indian war-whoop was heard several times in different directions near the camp. An hour or two after I was roused from my bunk by some of the soldiers rushing into my cabin and crying out that the Indians were upon us. I found, upon jumping up, several of the Cherokee men of the town mixing with the soldiers, and endeavoring to alarm them by assuring them that a large force of hostile Creeks were close by. As soon as possible, I had a barricade constructed in front of the ditch which had been dug for the palisades of the fort. In this ditch, and between the cabins and the barricade, I stationed myself and soldiers.

The Indians went off in the direction in which they reported the hostile Creeks to be. My servant, who had been drinking and was very much alarmed, went off with them. In a short time they returned, accompanied by their women, and carrying off some of their goods to give a show of reality to their feint. From the report of my servant, and the entire conduct of those who had thus attempted to alarm me, I became convinced that their object was to make me leave the country.

At the first cry of Indians, the workmen employed in building boats loosed the horses from the wagons and fled towards the nearest frontier white settlement. To prevent the great alarm which their report would have created among the people of the adjoining territory, I despatched the fleetest runner among the soldiers after them, with orders to pass them if possible. The soldier informed those that had fled, as he passed them, that there was no danger, and then proceeded on to Jefferson, the court-house town of Jackson County, and, through the letter which he carried, prevented the depopulation of the frontier.

At the time of this attempt of the Indians to frighten me out of their country, I had not received the arms and ammunition which was designed for my command. I used bark moulds for running lead into bullets and slugs, and the paper which I carried with me for my own use, for making cartridges. A wagon with a supply of arms was within twenty miles of the encampment. The workmen in passing it so frightened the horses that they broke loose and fled, so that it was several weeks before the arms were received. Whilst I was still unprepared for making much of a fight, I heard one day, about one o'clock, the firing of volleys of rifles in the swamp across the river from my camp. After calling in the men who were in the woods felling timbers for picketing, getting the drill muskets in the best possible order, and putting the men in a position for defence, I ordered a resolute soldier to cross the river and endeavor to find out what the firing meant. He saw several warriors going from cabin to cabin of the town, and meeting the men and women with apparent joy. Soon after eleven warriors, with their town people came to the camp and described to me exultingly as well as they could the battle of the Horseshoe, where they had fought under General Jackson. They brought home eighteen scalps. The night after the day of their arrival the scalps were fastened upon the top of a pole and the men, women and children danced around it all night. I was invited to attend the rejoicing. I sent a soldier that I might be informed of its particulars.

After I had been stationed for several months at the standing peach-tree, I received one morning a visit from a young Cherokee lad, who, in the fulness of his anticipated pleasure, came to communicate to me the secret, that at twelve o'clock the chief men of the town would kill two hostile Creek Indians, who were in huts on the opposite side of the river with a family akin to them. I armed myself, took with me a well armed soldier, and set off for the hut. Upon crossing the river I met several of the members of the family with whom the Creeks intended to be killed were staying. They showed great distress. A little boy belonging to the family had overheard the Cherokees talking of their purpose, and had given information to his relations. The party were going in search of the head of their family. One of them went on; the others accompanied me back to their cabin. One of the Creeks had already left, and the other soon disappeared, I did not perceive where. After a good deal of difficulty their friends found them. All accompanied me to the fort. The soldiers were put under arms. In a few hours the Cherokee men of the town arrived at the fort. They were directed to disarm and enter. After some hesitation they did so. The chiefs were invited into my cabin, where the Creeks were. I knew the leader well. His name was George Proctor. He was one of several brothers and sisters, the children of a white man by that name, and an Indian squaw. I told Proctor that the war was at an end, and that the Creeks were not to be injured. He answered, that the Creeks had killed his brother, and that he must kill a Creek. He was the most respectable man of the town. When he entered my cabin his whole appearance was altered. His usual quiet look had become fixed, intent and demoniac. His clothes, thrown back, hung loosely about him. His knife was stuck in his belt ready for his hand. After a long conversation with the Cherokees of the town who accompanied the Creeks, Proctor consented to defer his revenge until a meeting of the chiefs of the Standing Peach-tree and two or three chiefs of the neighboring villages. Upon the chiefs assembling, the Creeks were assured that they would not be injured.

On the day after this success in saving the lives of two hostile Creeks, I took my departure from the Standing Peach-tree. Upon my arrival at the Washington barracks, where Capt. Hide then commanded, I received a furlough for some weeks. I passed the time most pleasantly with my family friends on Broad River. When I returned to the barracks, I wrote to Col. Long, reminding him of his promise to give me active service. He answered that I should go to the seaboard, then threatened by the British, as soon as I enlisted twenty men, and directed me to seek a favorable situation to effect that object. I went to Carnesville, Franklin County, carrying with me a handsome young recruit, of fine spirit to assist me. I issued circulars, and made speeches, but all in vain. The station had been previously occupied by an officer who used means fair and foul—the people said the latter oftenest—to procure men. He had marched off thirty or forty, leaving the station in bad repute for future recruiting officers. I obtained two recruits, one a maniac, and the other a deserter. My time passed most unsatisfactorily. It was once relieved by the arrival of my old schoolmate, A. Longstreet. We spent a very pleasant evening together, and separated in the morning, he looking for land, I to attend a regimental drill.

The assemblage was of the very rudest people of the country towards the mountains. I was in full dress, and soon found myself a show. The people formed a circle around me as they would have done if they had been looking at a bear or elephant. I addressed them upon the advantages of joining the regular army. Finding that I talked like other men, they soon got near enough to handle my sword and epaulets. Even my whiskers, which were very long and very red, did not escape fingering. It required all my self-command to bear up under such an infliction. But I did, and as I thought when it was over, well; certainly very much to the amusement of Longstreet when I described it to him that evening when we again met at Carnesville. I have warned him against making a Georgia scene of my recruiting efforts, at the Franklin regimental muster.

Finding myself entirely unfit for the recruiting service, I applied to Maj. King for the appointment of adjutant at Columbia, South Carolina. The duty of that office was to take care of the new recruits, and prepare them for service. The appointment was given me. I went to Washington barracks, for the purpose of marching the recruits who were there to

Columbia, South Carolina. Whilst I was at Washington news of peace was received. I went to Columbia, and spent some time discharging the duties of drill adjutant, but with little interest.

War having been declared by the Government against Algiers, I applied to Dr. Bibb to procure me a commission in the marine corps. My service in the army had not improved my health. I was desirous of trying the effect of a campaign on the ocean. My application was not successful. I returned home, and remained with my father, whose health was then very bad, until he died. In the beginning of 1818, I went to Lexington and commenced the practice of law. I soon found that the excitement of business did less injury to my health than the listlessness of inaction.

CHAPTER IV.

WHILST I was temporarily absent from Lexington, a short time before the day for electing members of the Legislature, it was determined by some of the leading politicians of the county that I should be a candidate. The people of Georgia were then divided into the Crawford and the Clark parties. The Crawford party were principally composed of Virginians who had emigrated to Georgia after the revolutionary war; the Clark party of Europeans and North Carolina people, who had settled in Georgia before that time. They were very unindulgent to each other's faults, as most factions are when formed upon personal differences rather than political. I was a friend of Mr. Crawford. On the morning of the election, two or three of my neighbors insisted that I should decline being a candidate, on account of the strong opposition which had been excited against me by charges industriously and secretly circulated by a partisan of the Clark party. Pleasant Compton, Mr. Princes, Capt. Clodpole, then sheriff of the county, a very blount-spoken man, took me by the arm, and insisted that instead of withdrawing, I should vindicate myself, and leading me to the door of the tavern, cried "O yes! O yes! all you who want to hear a speech, come here." I accordingly addressed the people. The greatest excitement against me proceeded from my opposition to private banks, an appropriation by the preceding Legislature for the education of the poor, and my advocation of academies and colleges. At that time there were eleven persons in Oglethorpe County issuing change bills, as they were called, notes for circulation under the sum of one dollar. Many persons in other parts of the State were putting into circulation bills for sums of any amount which they could. I stated to the people, that what had been said of my opposition to private banking, was true; and that if elected I would if possible put an end to what I considered a great evil. I acknowledged the truth of what had been said about my opposition to the poor school fund, and the support which I wished the State to give to acamedies and colleges. At the previous session of the Legislature, an appropriation of $500,000 had been made for educating the poor of the State. I announced that, if elected, the first motion which I would make in the Legislature should be to repeal that appropriation; and attempted to prove (and I suppose did so to the satisfaction of the people) that the interest of $500,000 would not build and keep in repair school-houses for the poor over the large territory of the State, and that the money instead of being expended for the benefit of the poor, would be used for their own benefit, by the irresponsible agents into whose hands it would pass. Whilst I was answering a charge of Federalism, I observed Solomon Jennings and Turner Hamner, friends from Broad River, listening. I pointed them out to the people, stating that they had known me from infancy, had met me for years at the neighborhood post-office, heard me discuss politics, and could say whether the charge was true or false. They cried out "false! false!" I was elected triumphantly.

The embargo, non-intercourse, and war measures, so reduced the price of agricultural products, and lessened the ability of the people to pay their debts, as to induce the Legislature of Georgia to pass laws preventing the collection of debts by legal process. These alleviating or stop laws, were so popular, that very few counties were represented in the Legislature for many years, by members opposed to them. It was long before the advocates of these measures ceased to control the government of the State. They were still in the majority at the session in 1818, when I was first a member. Ben Williams was elected speaker by every vote but mine and one other. He was scarcely able to read or write, was a cut-and-shuffle, three-up card-playing bawdy-house bully, utterly devoid of honesty, of large brawny body, and powerful fisticuff fighting capacity.

In 1808, Linfield Hamner, of Broad River, in Oglethorpe County, purchased of the State fractions 285 and 292 in Putnam County for upwards of $2000, payable in four installments. His father, Richardson Hamner, was his security for the payment of the purchase money, which was further secured by a mortgage lien retained by the State on the fractions. Winfield Hamner was a very handsome, spendthrift fellow, with a wife very much like himself. He provided no means for paying the State, and before any steps were taken to enforce collection, had nothing to pay with. In 1817, Winfield Hamner became indebted to Ben Williams for a small amount, was sued in the Justice's Court of the district in Putnam County, where both resided, a judgment obtained, and the fi fa. founded upon it illegally levied by Ben Williams's order upon fractions 285 and 292. Williams purchased the fractions for $26, subject to the lien of the State. Winfield Hamner's debt to the State, was then less than $4000. Williams soon after sold the fractions for $5000, conditioned that he freed the land from the mortgage lien of the State. To do this he applied to Gov. Rabun in 1818, who in his official capacity had the collection of the State debt against Hamner, for assistance. Gov. Rabun gave the following order:

Executive Department, Milledgeville, 22 Oct. 1918.
Ordered, that Benjamin Williams, Esq., be, and is hereby authorized to attend the sale of property now advertised by the sheriff of Jasper, Morgan and Oglethorpe Counties, whereon the treasurer's execution has been levied to satisfy the first, second, third and fourth instalments due the State, on account of the sale of fractions, Nos. 292 and 285 in the fourteenth district of Baldwin, now Putnam County; and that he be authorized by himself or his attorney to bid in behalf of the State for the property so levied on.
Attest: Edw. Cary, Sect. E. D.

The Governor put into Williams's hands the fi. fas. issued

for the collection of the several instalments. By a provision of the law directing the sale of the fractions, all the property of the principal and securities was made liable for the payment of the purchase money. Williams attempted to avail himself of this provision, to relieve the fractions from the State's lien by collecting the State's debt out of the property of Richardson Hamner, the security for Winfield Hamner, who had died soon after he became security for his son, viz., in 1809, and before any fi. fa. had or could have issued. Upon obtaining this order and possession of the fi. fas., Williams came to Oglethorpe County, and caused the fi. fas. to be levied on the property which had belonged to R. Hamner at his death, and was then in the possession of those who had purchased it at the sale of his effects; and two negroes in the possession of Levi Jennings, the son-in-law of R. Hamner, which he had received for his distributive share of his father-in-law's estate.

The parties interested applied to Mr. Upson and me for professional assistance. Mr. Upson declined on account of its interference with his other business; the defence of the rights of the parties devolved upon me alone. I had commenced the practice of law but a few months before. But the parties were Broad River people, my father's neighbors, whom I had known from childhood. The one most interested, was Wm. P. Culbertson, who had been my first good country schoolmaster. I undertook with a zeal seldom felt by lawyers for their cilents. I caused affidavits of illegality to be made by the parties, setting forth specially, that R. Hamner had died before the date of the executions. These affidavits caused the sheriff of Oglethorpe to suspend proceedings on the fi. fas. I was then a member elect of the Legislature. I carried affidavits of illegality to Milledgeville, and laid them before Gov. Rabun, and urged him to withdraw the levy upon the property which had belonged to R. Hamner. A day or two before the termination of the session of the Legislature, Gov. Rabun gave Williams and myself a hearing upon the case in the Executive office. The result of the meeting was, that on the day of the adjournment of the Legislature, Williams, the speaker of the House, and his brother the doorkeeper of the Senate waylaid me in the streets of Milledgeville for the purpose of doing me some great personal injury. I happened to pass another way.

The Governor ordered the sheriff to suspend proceedings upon the levy in Oglethorpe. A day or two after the adjournment of the Legislature, Williams, not knowing of the Governor's order, wrote to the sheriff, Compton, giving him a false statement of what had passed in the Executive office, and offered him a bribe of one hundred dollars if he would proceed to sell under the levies which he had made. Compton's reply was "that it was unnecessary to offer him a bribe to do his duty, and if it was not his duty he would not do it at all."

Upon my return home from Milledgeville, I proceeded, at the suggestion of the Governor, to procure further evidence of the truth of the facts set forth in the affidavits of illegality. Several letters passed between Gov. Rabun and myself upon the subject. I finally threatened him with impeachment. I wrote an account of the case, and sent it to Mr. Grantland, the Editor of the Journal, for publication. Mr. Grantland answered that he had sold his interest in the Journal, so that the publication was not made.

I addressed the following letter to the Governor:

TO HIS EXCELLENCY WILLIAM RABUN,

Lexington, Jan. 30th, 1819.

Yours of the 20th inst. has just been received. It is with extreme regret that I again trouble you with any remarks on the subject of the case of the State against W. and R. Hamner. If trouble, perplexity and labor, would have stopped my exertions, they would have ceased before this. But I feel that I am contending for justice, and legal right, in opposition to fraud and oppression, defending the poor and honest, against the arts of the cunning and powerful; and endeavoring to prevent the State, in the exertion of its power, from ruining several individuals to enable one to make a very profitable and dishonest speculation. Your Excellency will permit me to say, that I cannot but feel something more than astonishment at the contents of the letter just received. Your Excellency, after you were informed truly of the facts relating to this case, did not doubt as to the course you would pursue. During the session of the Legislature, you informed me that you only delayed making the necessary orders to stop the proceedings against the parties in this County, because Williams had informed you, that the persons who had sworn to the time of R. Hamner's death were not to be believed, and that Hamner did not die until some time after the date of the executions which had been levied on the property which was once his. After Mr. Luckie, Hurdspeth and Pope, who were members of the Legislature from Oglethorpe, informed you of the respectability of the deponents, you stated to me that I should receive the order for stopping further proceedings before the termination of the session. When I went into the Executive office on Friday of the last week of the session, you stated to me, that the office was so crowded with business, that the order could not then be made out, but should be transmitted to me when I returned to Oglethorpe, requesting at the same time that some additional testimony should be obtained, to be filed in your office in proof of the time of R. Hamner's death. When the most indisputable testimony was obtained and placed in your possession, it seems to have produced a strange effect. Whilst it has drawn from you the acknowledgement that the property levied on in this county is not liable to pay the debt of the State, it has changed your purpose to relieve that property from legal process, and determined you to pursue it, compelling the parties interested to all the trouble, expense and uncertainty of a law-suit. Your Excellency ascribes this change in your intention to the want of power, the case having become, as you say, a judicial question. Permit me to inform you, of what I had the honor personally so often to do, that the case has not become a judicial question, and never will, unless you compel the parties to apply to the courts to obtain justice. I know not to whom you applied for legal counsel. I will say, that they were either influenced by the persons concerned in the case, or that the case was very improperly stated to them. Presuming the last to be the fact, and that the statement, so far as it was incorrect, was unintentional on your part, I will endeavor to state it truly.

On the twenty-sixth of May, an execution issued from the treasury directed to the sheriff of Oglethorpe County, against Winfield & Richardson Hamner, which execution came to the hands of the sheriff of Oglethorpe on the tenth of September thereafter, and was levied on a negro woman belonging to Swepson Taylor, and afterwards upon a negro fellow claimed by Levi Jennings, and a tract of land claimed by Solomon Jennings and John McCown. All these parties claimed the property levied on as theirs, and in their possession, and gave their bonds to the sheriff to abide the decision of the proper authorities. Soon afterwards the sheriff discovered that the execution did not come into his hands until after the three months had expired by which the execution became void, and that he was responsible individually for the amount to be collected by it. He then gave up to the parties their bonds, and took new bonds to abide your decision (which last bonds were improperly required by the sheriff of the parties, and without legal counsel) and declined making any entry of the levies on the execution as having been illegally made, and transmitted it to your office as the law required. The affidavits of illegality which accompanied the execution, were made out for the purpose of stopping the sale previous to the discovery that the levy itself was illegal, and were afterwards sent to you, that, from a knowledge of the circumstances of the case, you might be induced to refrain from oppressing the parties, by levying on their property, when it was not liable to that process.

I think it very probable that these affidavits of illegality have been the cause of the erroneous opinion given to you by the legal counsel with whom you advised. They were forwarded for your information, and not your decision. This is a true statement of the case, as you were informed by the letter of the sheriff of Oglethorpe County, sent to you at the same time with the execution which he returned to the treasury office.

Your Excellency will permit me to express my surprise, that you should disclaim the power to control the executions issued from the treasury office against debtors of the State for the purchase of fractions. Suffer me to remind you, that an execution, issued the 17th of June, 1817, for $525.25, exclusive of interest, being the fourth instalment of W. Hamner's debt, was placed in the hands of the sheriff of Putnam County, and levied by him on the fractions 285 and 292, by your directions; and that this execution, at the request, and for the benefit of Mr. Williams, was withdrawn by you. The same execution, only renewed, you ordered to be placed in the hands of the sheriff of Oglethorpe County. It is now in his possession, and is the very execution which you are refusing to withdraw. I will say, that it was legal for you to withdraw an execution out of the hands of the sheriff of Oglethorpe County, by whom no levy had been made, more especially as the three months have expired during which the levy ought to have been made, and as the property upon which you intended it should be levied you acknowledge you think not to be liable to levy. It appears to me that you have as much power to withdraw an execution only designed to be levied on property which once belonged to R. Hamner, as you had to withdraw an execution actually levied on property claimed by Mr. Williams. I know not how it happens that you should have exercised a power for the benefit of Mr. Williams, which power should have ceased to exist when you are called upon to exercise it in opposition to his interest, and for the benefit of the State. Hitherto I was ignorant that there was a difference between the rights of citizens. I will only observe that the executive officer who dares make that distinction dares greatly. As evidence how large executive powers are when exercised in favor of Williams, I transmit to you the copy of an order issued from the Executive

Office, which is so extraordinary that I am strongly induced to believe it a forgery.

That the Executive should authorize any one to purchase lands and negroes for the State is indeed novel. As this order is not immediately connected with the subject of my letter, I should not have mentioned it, but that I am anxious to know of its authenticity.

This subject will be investigated before a different tribunal than the Superior Court.

Finally, permit me to say, that there is a plain and obvious course to be taken. Permit the execution for the first installment to remain in your office, and not again sent to this county; and withdraw the execution for the fourth instalment, which is now in the hands of the sheriff, and never levied, but suspended by your order. If you intend to collect the debt due the State, the executions from Morgan and Jasper must also be recalled—for they are levied on property not liable. There is no property which is liable, except the fractions 185 and 292, as far as I can ascertain,—W. Hamner, the State debtor, owning no property at all. If one execution, and not all, is sent to Putnam, the land will be sold, and the State never received but one instalment. If the fractions should be sold to pay the whole debt due the State, Williams will still make a speculation of $1500 or $2000. I think that numerous citizens should not be driven to the trouble, expense, and uncertainty of a lawsuit, to protect themselves from the means used by the Executive to enable Williams to make a speculation of $5000 or $6000. As you state that the only reason why you did not pursue the course above advised, is that the case has become a judicial question, I must again assure you that such is not the fact. And to convince your Excellency that this statement is the truth, permit the case to remain as it is, and the parties in this county will be satisfied. Suffer the execution which is now in your office (which was returned by the sheriff because it came to his hands after the expiration of three months) to remain there, and the execution now in his hands, suspended by your order, to remain so, and issue no more executions for the particular benefit of Williams; but order the property to be levied on which is known to be liable and sufficient to pay the State's debt, without any regard to the persons holding it, and you will hear no more from me. GEORGE R. GILMER.

Ben Williams having failed to make the money due from W. Hamner to the State, out of the property which had belonged to R. Hamner in Oglethorpe County, so as to free fractions 285 and 292 of the State lien, endeavored to enforce the levies made upon a negro in Morgan County, in the possession of Baber, and eleven negroes in Jasper County, in the possession of Spencer Crane. I went to Morgan County, and had the levy made on Baber's negro dismissed on motion. Williams was present when I addressed the court. Those who knew him supposed my life to be in danger. A pistol was handed me for defence; and the sheriff insisted on accompanying me to the tavern where I boarded. I went to Jasper Court, and succeeded in having the levy upon the eleven negroes of Spencer Crane dismissed. I charged no fees in these cases. I had been so much excited by the interest which my Broad River friends had in them, and the character, station and influence of those with whom I had to contend, that I was amply compensated for my time, exertions, expense, and risk, when I succeeded.

From Jasper Court I wrote to Governor Rabun informing him of the decisions of the courts in the cases in Morgan and Jasper. To that letter I received the following answer:—

{ Executive Department, Georgia.
  Milledgeville, 27th April, 1819.

Sir,—Yours of the 30th ult., by Col. Jones, was handed into this office some time after its date, and lay on my table a considerable time before I was apprised of its arrival. You mention that the treasury executions, which had, at the instance of Mr. Williams, been levied on property in the Counties of Morgan and Jasper, were dismissed by the courts for illegality. The conduct of the courts in those cases was no doubt perfectly correct. I had long been satisfied of the final result; but as Mr. Williams had on several different times assured me that the property levied on would ultimately be found to be liable, I did not feel authorized to refuse him the benefit which the law intended in similar cases. It was therefore my wish that the subject should be fairly investigated in a court of law, in order that, if Mr. Williams's statements were false, they might be exposed, and justice at least would require that he should be saddled with the cost. Had the case in Oglethorpe been brought before the court, it would, in all probability, have shared the same fate. The sheriff of that county has lately returned the execution that was in his possession.

You ask for information respecting the future course that will be adopted and pursued by this department in regard to these several cases; to which I cheerfully reply, that it never was my intention to pursue the parties concerned further than to ascertain clearly that they were not liable, according to existing law, for the payment of a part or the whole of the State's Demands against W. and

R. Hamner. These facts having been satisfactorily demonstrated, the pursuit will be discontinued.

I have long since notified Mr. Williams to make immediate arrangements to pay up the whole amount of principal and interest in these cases, or the State's execution will unquestionably be levied on the land.

The depositions filed in this office by Mr. W. will be retained, and can be used by the prosecuting officer in favor of any of the aggrieved parties.

I have the honor to be, &c.,
WM. RABUN.

I can yet recollect the pleasure I enjoyed when I was assured that my old schoolmaster, and many of my earliest friends, had been saved from ruin by my unassisted exertions,—of self-gratulation at having overcome the Governor and Speaker of the House of Representatives—and, very soon after, shame for having acted and written so rudely to the Governor of the State. I had left home to visit Governor Rabun, to make as ample an apology as possible to him for my threatenings, when I heard of his death. One of the depositions to which Governor Rabun alluded to in the close of his letter, I caused to be placed in the hands of the Solicitor-General of the Ocmulgee Circuit. A man by the name of Stovall, who had gone to Putnam County from Oglethorpe, had been induced by B. Williams to swear falsely as to the time of Richardson Hamner's death. I attended the first Superior Court in Putnam County, after the settlement of the civil cases, to prosecute Stovall. I was accompanied by several Broad River people, so that the falsehood of Stovall's affidavit might be rendered entirely certain. A true bill of indictment was found against him. He put off the trial of the case. In the evening after the continuance of the indictment, whilst I was sitting with several gentlemen of the bar in the balcony of the tavern where I was boarding, Ben Williams, his brother, the door-keeper of the Senate, and two or three others of grog-shop character, were seen coming into the tavern. It was evident that their mission was to insult or injure me. John Walters, a very powerful man, and a native of Oglethorpe County, was present. Some friends requested him to keep his seat, informing him that his county man was in danger. Williams and his party soon made their apperance. He had but commenced his talk with me, when his movements were observed by the Tompkins and other Oglethorpe people, who came to my defence. The talk ended very quietly.

I attended with my Oglethorpe friends at the next term of Putnam Court. Stovall was tried. The solicitor-general, Adam G. Safford, requested me to conduct the prosecution. My exertions were not stinted in exposing the scoundrelism of Williams. The trial was not concluded until some time after night. Whilst I spoke Williams was outside of the bar gritting his teeth. A large party accompanied me to the tavern for protection against him. But it was entirely unnecessary. The exposure of his conduct had taken away his control over others. He was himself harmless, because he felt that attracting the attention of others to himself would but increase the notoriety of his guilt, and add to his shame.

Stovall was sent to the Penitentary, where the speaker of the House of Representatives ought to have been. Ben Williams was never afterwards a member of the Legislature. Public opinion forced him to leave Putnam County. He went to Gwinnett, where he became a constable for the district in which he lived. When I last saw him, he was a poor, shabby creature, exciting only pity for his fallen fortunes.

In 1819 I was re-elected a member of the Legislature. Gov. Rabun having died before its meeting, the duties of Chief Magistrate devolved upon Mr. Talbot, the president of the Senate. The Governor was then elected by the Legislature. Gen. Clark was a candidate. He and his friends were very active in the use of means to secure his success. Gov. Rabun had beaten him but a few votes at the previous election. Parties were so equally divided, that every vote was looked after with great interest. The county of Newton was for the first time represented in the Legislature. The candidate for the House of Representatives who obtained the certificate of election was a friend of Clark. His seat was contested.

The committee on elections was appointed immediately after the organization of the House. The members went into an examination of the right of the sitting member to his seat, so that a report might be made and acted on before the election of Governor.

The opponent of the sitting member, called upon the members of the committee who were opposed to the election of Gen. Clark, and informed them that he was against Gen. Clark, and the sitting member for him. He was threatened with punishment with but little effect. When the committee met, he exhibited affidavits in proof that a sufficient number of the votes given to the sitting member were fraudulent, to entitle him to the seat. The committee reported to that effect. The sitting member was a very simple illiterate man. He acquiesced in the report. A partisan of Gen. Clark rose in the House, and asked that time should be allowed the sitting member to procure evidence in support of his right to the seat. After some hesitation time was granted. The sitting member remained to give his vote for Gen. Clark and then went to Newton, where he obtained satisfactory proof that the affidavits presented by his opponent to the committee were forgeries. As he returned to Milledgeville, his opponent waylaid him, and threatened him with violence if he did not give up the testimony which he had obtained. He contrived however to escape with his papers. When these facts were made known to the House of Representatives, a resolution was passed, directing that the forged affidavits should be turned over to the Solicitor General of the circuit to which Newton County was attached, in order that the forger might be prosecuted. Instead of being indicted he was elected a member of the succeeding Legislature. He proved himself a thorough partisan of Gov. Clark, and as great a knave as ever went unhung.

Soon after the meeting of the Legislature, and the inauguration of the Governor. Jesse Mercer, the celebrated Baptist preacher, was requested by the Legislature to preach the funeral sermon of Governor Rabun, who had been his intimate friend. Our Georgia factions of Crawford and Clark were then flourishing in great vigor. Jesse Mercer was a Crawford man as Gov. Rabun had been. Gov. Clark suspected that this funeral ceremony was intended to do him harm. The sermon was preached in the Baptist Church, which was some distance from the State House. Gov. Clark, Jesse Mercer and the members of the Legislature walked in procession to it. Jesse Mercer did his best in preaching this funeral sermon of his Baptist friend, and enforced the doctrine with great zeal, that when the Lord taketh away a good and righteous ruler, he does it on account of the sins of the people, and will punish them by putting wicked rulers over them, and ended by saying Georgia had reason to tremble. Col. Tatnall and myself had walked together in the procession, and were seated near the principal passway through the Church with Col. Campbell, Gov. Clark's brother-in-law, immediately before us, and John Abercromby, the particular friend of Gov. Rabun a little back—and on the opposite side of the passway. Col. Campbell with a frown on his brow, looked first at the preacher and then at Gov. Clark. Abercromby gazed around with the most approving smile on his face at the leading Clark men, his speaking countenance saying as plainly as words could have done,—How your man gets it; and then at the Crawford men with equally significant tokens of approbation. Col. Tattnall's proud nature scarcely brooked what he considered a gross insult offered to the dignity of the Chief Magistrate of the State. His pent up wrath vented itself in the strongest expressions of disapprobation, as we walked back to the State House, at the conduct of the preacher, the future speaker, and all who approved their words, or looks. A resolution was immediately passed, asking Jesse Mercer for a copy of his sermon for publication. The resolution never returned from the Governor's office. This scene in the Baptist Church showed the state of manners, feelings, and opinions of the times. Col. Tattnall stood alone a party man above faction.

During the session of 1819, Gov. Clark induced Dr. Burton, a member from Clark County to introduce a resolution approving the conduct of Gen. Jackson in writing a very insulting letter to Gov. Rabun, on account of an attack made by a party of Georgia Militia upon an Indian village. Burton had been elected a Crawford man. He was promised for this service, the title of Colonel. Its purpose was to increase the popularity of Gen. Jackson at the expense of the friends of Mr. Crawford. Gen. Clark had a private interview with Col. Thomas Murray, and informed him of Burton's resolution, and its object, and insisted that he should aid in its passage. Col. Murray avowed his disposition to support him, but declined doing any thing to injure Mr. Crawford. When Burton offered his resolution, I moved that it should be laid on the table. The motion was carried, Col. Murray voting for it.

John Abercromby was one of the leading members of the session of 1819. He was a large, fat, pot-bellied man, with his head stuck upon his shoulders without a neck. His mind was uncultivated by books, but quick and intelligent. His passions and prejudices were strong and indulged freely. During the session a kinsman of his by the name of Jernigan (I believe), came to Milledgeville from McIntosh County, where Hopkins had been tried for killing McIntosh. He reported that Judge Berrien, who presided at the trial, had been guilty of great partiality in favor of Hopkins. Abercromby, whose opinion of Judge Berrien was not very favorable, was excited by the report of the judge's conduct to introduce unto the House of Representatives a strongly condemnatory resolution, without any evidence of what it had been, but a short street conversation. A very angry debate took place. Col. Tatnall, who was the Representative and neighbor of Judge Berrien, was very indignant. He and Abercromby were soon in fighting mood. Abercromby reflected upon the lawyers for the support they gave their Brother Chip, as he called Judge Berrien. He and I occupied adjoining seats and were upon very friendly terms. I succeeded in (what I am not very successful at) exciting the laugh of the House at Abercromby, and putting every body into good humor. Col. Tattnall offered a resolution of inquiry into Judge Berrien's conduct, which was referred to a large committee. Judge Berrien was immediately notified of the proceedings of the House, and came to Milledgeville attended by several friends of the Bar. The committee held its meetings in the senate chamber, after the adjournment for the day of the two Houses. A great crowd assembled below in the gallery. Cal. Tatnall, the mover of the resolution of inquiry, was chairman of the committee. Before he took his seat in the President's chair, he told me that Abercromby's violent conduct had so excited him, that he believed he would find it impossible to restrain his temper if it was repeated, and requested me to move as soon as the committee was ready to act, that he should be excused from presiding over it and another chairman appointed.

I did so, and nominated Col. Murray, whose former independent conduct in resisting Gov. Clark's demand that he support Burton's movement against Gov. Rabun, had entitled him to distinction when it could be given him. The investigation was made upon the evidence given by Judge Berrien's friends, and resulted in his entire acquittal by the committee. Abercromby was alone in his attack and without any offensive materials to carry it on. He had to submit, but did so with bad temper.

It may not be amiss to mention here an incident which relates to John Abercromby, which is still freshly remembered by some. In 1824, whilst the House of Representatives was in committee laying off into counties the country ——————— some time before acquired from the Creek Indians, John Abercromby having left the speaker's chair, moved that one of the new counties should be called Butts, in honor of a captain of that name, who had served under General Floyd in the expedition against the Creek Indians, and been killed in a fight with them. Abercromby supported his motion by a very declamatory speech enforced by the most furious gestures, saying that "Captain Butts had marched to the cannon's mouth and died without a grunt." My wife was in the gallery listening. Her Grattan spirit, carried aloft by Abercromby's enthusiastic eloquence, was near being brought to the floor by the spasmodic effect of the word grunt.

During the session of 1819, I offered an amendment to the Constitution, to authorize the Legislature to establish a Supreme Appellate Court. The judges of the Superior Court were then elected for three years, and were of course frequently changed. No reports of decisions were made and published. Lawyers resorted to the law reports of other States and countries, and to their own and others' memories of adjudicated cases in the advocacy of their clients' causes. Declamation and bold assertion perverted the verdicts of juries, and judgments of the judges. The effort to correct these evils by the proposed amendment of the Constitution was without success. The most influential public men in the State were Virginians or of Virginia descent. In former times, the Court of Appeals of Virginia was so constituted, that when a case of any importance got before it the delay became so great an evil as to excite the opposition of the people to the Court itself. It was not until the emigrants from Virginia ceased to govern, that the Court of Appeals was established. I made a speech in support of my proposed measure. It was answered by the leading partisan of Governor Clark. Politics began immediately to enter into the decision of the question. I was requested to publish my remarks as soon as possible. I wrote them out; but the writing was illegible at the printing office. I had not then a faithful copyist ever at my side to mke my writing readable. George Cany, an old schoolmate and fellow-member, offered to copy them. When he returned the manuscript, I found that he had in several places changed the verbiage (which, he said, was so bad that he could not stand it) into redundant terms. As the sense was not altered, I consented to the publication at once. This was my second published speech. I had been still more unfortunate in the first. This was made at the previous session of the Legislature, on the subject of banks, and was printed without any correction at all, and therefore full of mistakes. I sent a newspaper copy of the speech on the Court of Appeals to Eliza Grattan, in a letter, instead of directing the paper to her. This love-letter was opened in search of bank-bills, and its contents exposed to the reading of every curious body at the post office. The postage amounted to one dollar.

Chapter V.

In 1820, I was a candidate for Congress. On Friday, ten days before the election, I received a letter from an acquaintance in Putnam County, informing me that Ben Williams had gone to Milledgeville, to have the correspondence between Governor Rabun and myself published, with the hope that its violence would prevent the friends of Governor Rabun from voting for me. I reached Greensborough, on my way to Milledgeville on the evening after the letter was received. I found Governor Clark at the tavern where I stopped. I had an interview with him and stated what had been communicated to me. He answered, that every citizen was entitled to copies of the papers in the executive office, and that Mr. Williams had only done what other citizens might do. I replied that I was not complaining of the liberty he had given Williams; but that as the Executive Department had furnished copies of the papers belonging to it, for the purpose of impairing public confidence in me, I desired to have the use of the same means for making my defence; and that as I could not get to Milledgeville until Saturday night, I wished an order from him to his secretary, to permit me to go into the Executive office on Sunday, to procure copies of such papers as I wanted for that purpose, so that the publication of my defence might be made with the attack, there being but one paper to be published before the election. Governor Clark answered, that the office over which he presided was not opened on the Sabbath day. I went to Milledgeville the next day. As soon as my arrival was known, the Governor's secretary, Mr. Burch, who had furnished Williams with copies of what he wanted, offered immediately to do the same for me. Upon going to the printing office, I found my hard ride unnecessary, as the editors had refused to print Williams' attack upon a candidate so immediately before the election that no reply could be made.

After the adjournment of the October term of the Superior Court of Oglethorpe, in 1821, I set off for Washington City, by the way of Virginia. I had been corresponding for many years with a Rockingham cousin, whom I had first seen twelve years before in Richmond. In this written intercourse, I had said nothing about marrying. I felt a great curiosity to see her. I wanted to know whether we would fancy each other upon sight, as we had on paper.

I arrived about twelve o'clock on Sunday, at the old Augusta church, which stands on the top of a slight elevation in the midst of a forest of venerable oaks, and near the public road leading from Staunton to Winchester. The doors were closed. I found the son of the sexton, and inquired if Maj. Grattan's family were there. He answered, yes. I opened the door but was unable to go into Maj. Grattan's pew, which was next to the door, and elevated above the seats in front. The owner of the next pew invited me in. I had no power to hear the sermon from my curiosity to see the inmates of the pew behind me. I could hear a stir among the Grattan children. Very soon a beautiful young lady descended from the pew, and went to the stove, pretending that she was cold. I saw that it was not Eliza. When the service was over, I found that Eliza was at my uncle George Gilmer's twenty miles off. I accompanied Maj. Grattan's family home. The next morning, I went to Lethe. As I opened the outer door the door from the passage into the sitting room was opened by Eliza Grattan. When I knew what I was about, my arm was around her waist, and I was pressing her lips; a position which I have been constantly taking ever since, and ever with renewed pleasure. Eliza Grattan and myself settled the matter most interesting to us in a very satisfactory way, agreeing that after the session of Congress was over, we would take each other, for better, for life. During my attendance on the first session of Congress, I wrote to her by every direct mail. During the next session after our marriage, whilst we were separated for three weeks (the longest time we have ever been apart), I wrote to her twice a day. My health became so bad during the winter that I was in great doubt whether I ought to involve any one in my sickly fate. Eliza Grattan considered my doubts a reflection upon her generous devotedness; and for a few days our correspondence was embarrassing. The cloud, however, soon passed away. It was agreed between us, that after the adjournment of Congress I should see Dr. Phisic of Philadelphia, and follow his advice.

During the session, the candidates for the Presidency, and their friends, began to canvass actively. Mr. Adams of the North, Mr. Crawford of the South, and Mr .Clay of the West, were the distinguished, and well-tried politicians of the country, and every where considered best entitled to the office. Mr. Calhoun, and one or two talented and aspiring young men, were showing symptoms of restlessness at their being kept in the background. Gen. Jackson's claims had been advocated by a crack-brained editor of a thumb newspaper in

Georgia, named Minor. Mr. Calhoun considering Mr. Crawford particularly in his way, as they belonged to the same section of the country, was preparing to unite with any one whose success would not put him aside too long. Mr. Clay next after himself preferred Mr. Crawford, but stood aloof, to avail himself of circumstances to secure his own success. Cook, of the House, and his father-in-law, Ninian Edwards, of the Senate, were active partisans of Mr. Adams. Cook introduced into the House a resolution, the object of which was to create suspicions that Mr. Crawford was using the patronage of the treasury department for electioneering purposes. Mr. Crawford was the neighbor and friend of my friends at home. I was very raw, and felt the attack as if it had been an assault upon myself. Whilst Cook's resolution was before the House, I received information that Mr. Calhoun and several members, his own and Mr. Adams's special friends, had been consulting how to give effect to Cook's attack. I offered a resolution of inquiry, whether a conspiracy had not been formed to destroy public confidence in the Secretary of the Treasury. Whilst I was attacking Cook, I saw his father-in-law, Ninian Edwards, come into the gallery and place himself near and rather behind one of the pillars, so that he could see and hear without being conspicuous himself. I pointed at him with my finger, as the skulking scamp who was then acting the part of the conspirator. Every eye in the House was directed at the pillar, with overpowering effect upon the peeping listener. The next day a member from Connecticut, who had been a college mate of Mr. Calhoun, was put forward to assault me in the House. He had scarcely uttered more than a sentence or two before Col. Tatnall called him to order in such manner that he quailed, disavowed intending any discourtesy, and made what he said without point, and unworthy of notice.

The speech from which the following extract is taken, was upon a subject which had at the time lost much of its original interest. The Anti-Democratic party, at first called the Federal, then Federal Republican, and since Whig, had been long using the United States Bank, restrictive duties upon commerce, and appropriations for internal improvements, as means for increasing and rendering permanent in the General Government enlarged legislative powers, and controlling authority over matters which properly belonged to the jurisdiction of the States. The democratic party was at the time making but slight resistance to this departure from the principles which had been the basis of its organization. The urgency of particular sections of the country in favor of making roads and canals to facilitate the transportation of their produce to market, and the demands of large capitalists for the means of safe and profitable investments of their money in banks and manufactures, were hushing up many of its members. The practical operation of the government was thus overstepping, without much difficulty, the theoretic barriers provided by its form for the security of popular rights, and the strict responsibility of the governors to the governed.

'No" (I said) "maxim has been better tested by experience or more strongly urged for our observance, by those who have preceded us than the necessity of a frequent recurrence to fundamental principles as the only means of preserving the original freedom of our institutions. If we go on, regardless of this maxim, is there not reason to fear, that from the gradual operation of causes that never ceased to act, we shall, after a while, find our government in possession of the same controlling authority over the will, the rights, and interests, of the people, and the States, that all other governments have usurped?

"Sir, I consider this power of making surveys, and the consequent right of constructing roads and canals within the large territories of the States, as the most dangerous to the people and the States, which can be assumed by this government. All the wealth of the country may be exhausted in its exercise, and all resistance to lawless authority quieted, in the extended influence which it will give. I deny that this government, has any such power. And believing as I do, that the division of power between the United States and the States, as made by the constitution, should not be altered, it becomes my duty to resist any attempt at such an alteration."

Col. Tatnall and myself left Washington City two days after the adjournment of Congress, for New York. We had for companions Rufus King and Martin Van Buren.

I visited in New York the highest court of law then sitting; saw, heard, and conversed with Mr. Emmet, the celebrated

Irishman, in whom I felt a special interest. On the next day Mr. Van Buren called, and conducted me to the city court, where the young, active, and aspiring lawyers were to be found, with whom he seemed to be particularly intimate. We called upon his tailor, Gen. Mapes, to whom he was very gracious. He gave me a letter to the postmaster at Saratoga Springs, whither I was going. I found a very good landlady by his assistance. I had also a letter to a pleasant gentleman residing at the Springs. He took me with him to Ballston, the county seat of Saratoga, where the superior court was in session. I heard Mr. Van Vechten speak, and dined with Judge Yates, afterwards Governor of New York.

The following letters describe some of the transactions at Washington City in which I took part.

Saratoga Springs, May 24th, 1822.

If I mistake not, I mentioned to you in a former letter, that I had been very much vexed at some occurrences which took place in the last two days that I remained in Washington City. I received the papers on the same day that I received your letter relative to these occurrences. * * * * *

The report which as chairman of a select committee, I made on the subject of Indian lands in Georgia, was not taken up for consideration by the House of Representatives, as it never became the order of the day. I was enabled, however, to obtain an appropriation of $30,000 for the purpose of holding treaties with the Cherokee and Creek Indians for the extinguishment of their title to lands in Georgia. The law containing this appropriation passed on Tuesday, the last day but one of the session. On the evening of that day, the members of Congress from Georgia had a meeting, for the purpose of agreeing upon the persons who should be recommended to the President for the appointment of commissioners to hold treaties. We drew up a written address, recommending to the President Gen. Floyd, Maj. James Meriwether, Col. Warren Jourdan, Freeman Walker, Richard H. Wild and Joel Crawford, from whom he was requested to select three. On Wednesday morning, it was determined that we should wait upon the President, and name to him the persons whom we preferred for commissioners. Accordingly, Col. Ware, Judge Reid, and myself, called upon him, and requested that he would nominate Gen. Floyd, Maj. Meriwether, and Col. Jourdan. The President stated that he was pleased to see us, being unacquainted with the passage of the appropriation. We asked him if he would nominate the commissioners to the Senate before its adjournment, or would he appoint them during the recess. He answered, that he did not think it right to delay making appointments until the recess of Congress which could be made during the session, and that they would be made during the day. Whilst the Senate was still in session, the President sent for Col. Ware, who is a member of that body, and informed him, that Mr. Calhoun had communicated to him after the conversation with us, that he had recommendations in his office from Gov. Clark of Georgia, the President of its Senate, the Speaker of its House, and a large number of the members of the Legislature, of Gen. Newman and John A. Cuthbert, of Georgia, and Gen. Preston, of Virginia, for Commissioners, and that he could not therefore make any nominations to the Senate. Col. Ware sent for me. I requested an audience of the President, which was granted. I stated to him that the recommendations which had been mentioned by Mr. Calhoun, proceeded only from the efforts of a party, to get their creatures into office. That Gen. Newman was a man of broken fortunes and character, and Mr. Cuthbert had no knowledge of Indian character or manners. Gen. Preston having been appointed to the office of Commissioner in Florida, it became useless to say any thing of him. After a long conversation, in which the President showed more restlessness than disposition to hear, he informed me that he could not make the appointments then, but that such persons should be appointed during the recess, as he supposed to be most agreeable to public opinion in Georgia. Congress having adjourned in the morning, I called at the Presidents house in the evening for the purpose of seeing the recommendations. The President informed me that he had not himself seen them, that his knowledge of them was from the statement of Mr. Calhoun, but that I should be furnished with copies. He sent for Mr. Calhoun, who had left upon my entering his room. Upon his coming in, he directed him to have copies made out for me. Mr. Calhoun commenced a conversation, or rather attack upon me, which continued until, from its peculiar nature, the President had to stop it, at the same time saying to me very politely, that he would receive any thing from me, verbally or written, with pleasure. You may have some idea of the conversation between Mr. Calhoun and myself by what I am about to tell you. He stated, among other things, that his conduct in making the treaty with the Cherokee Indians in 1819, had been very much misrepresented in Georgia. I told him that the people of Georgia believed that injustice had been done them by that treaty. You may see the objections to that treaty in my report. He stated that those who believed so only showed their ignorance. I told him that the treaty had been protested against by a unanimous vote of the Legislature of Georgia. "Sir," says he, "I repeat it, they knew nothing of what they were doing." He said that the treaty had been made by the particular advice of Mr.

Crawford. Mr. Crawford informs me that the statement is entirely false, that he was confined to bed by sickness, at the time of the making of the treaty. Mr. Calhoun asked me if Col. Jourdan was not the brother-in-law of Mr. Crawford, thereby insinuating to the President, that the members of Congress were influenced in their recommendations, by a regard for the interest of Mr. Crawford. Mrs. Crawford's maiden name was Gerdine, and is usually called in the same manner as Jourdan. He stated that the recommendations from Georgia must have been known to myself and other members. I answered him, that they had been kept secret even from the President, and that the only member who knew any thing of them, was Mr. Alfred Cuthbert, the brother of the person recommended, to whom he had stated at his own house, in a private conversation, that his brother John could be appointed a commissioner; (I had drawn this information from Alfred Cuthbert a few hours before) that this had been several months before, and that the recommendations had continued unknown to the other members.

On Tuesday morning, Col. Ware, Judge Reid and myself directed a note to the President, inclosing the first written recommendations, for the purpose of showing to the President that we had no political view in making them. I also addressed a note to the President, inclosing one to myself from a highly respectable merchant of Georgia, who had arrived in the city the evening before, in which he stated, that Gen. Newman had become insolvent and had gone to Tennessee, it was believed never to return, leaving his securities to pay his debts. Mr. Calhoun stated the evening before, that the paper containing the recommendations from Georgia could not be furnished before nine or ten o'clock next morning. Before that time I expected to have left the city, and therefore directed them to be sent to this place. Afterwards finding that I should be detained by the sickness of Col. Tatnall, I wrote to Mr. Calhoun, requesting that they should be sent to me in the city. They were not, however, received until I arrived here. You may imagine my surprise, when, upon examining them, I found that the statements of Mr. Calhoun to the President, with regard to them, had been entirely different from the facts. Gen. Newman had been recommended by no one from Georgia for the appointment of Commissioner; Mr. Cuthbert only by the Governor, the President of the Senate, and the Speaker of the House.

I have a letter addressed to the President, a copy of which is inclosed to you. From all these circumstances you will be better enabled to form some opinion of the state of politics at Washington City. When ambition can produce such effects upon men, who, in private life are its brightest ornaments, we are warned to quit politics. GEORGE R. GILMER.

Saratoga Springs, May 20th, 1822.
To Mr. Monroe, President of the U. States:

The papers which you directed the Secretary of War to have copied for me have been received. I must confess that I am very much surprised to find that the statements made by the Secretary to the President were very incorrect. The President was informed that Gen. Newman, John A. Cuthbert, and Gen. Preston, had been recommended for the appointment of commissioners to hold treaties with the Indians in the State of Georgia, by the Governor of the State, the President of the Senate, Speaker of the House, and a large number of the members of its Legislature. It appears that the statement with regard to Gen. Newman was wholly unfounded. Mr. Cuthbert has been recommended by the Governor, Mr. Talbot, President of the Senate, and Gen. Adams, Speaker of the House, but by no others of the Legislature. Gen. Preston is recommended by the Governor alone. I know of no excuse for the conduct of the Secretary. The papers have been in his possession for several months. He stated in the presence of the President, that their contents were so publicly known, that the members of Congress could not have been ignorant of them, notwithstanding my assertions to the contrary. I regret that nominations about to be made upon the recommendations of the Representatives of the State, of men selected alone for their capacity to perform the duties of the office to which they were to be appointed, should have been prevented by a mistake, which could have been so easily avoided.

So far as regards Gen. Preston and Gen. Newman, there is no probability that either would accept the appointment of Commissioner. I have already stated to the President that Mr. Cuthbert is a man of respectable character and talents. The objections to his appointment are, that he has none of the peculiar qualifications necessary in public agents who would transact business with the Indians. He has no knowledge of Indian character and manners, and nothing in his own character or manner would be very imposing upon savages. There is another strong objection to the appointment of Mr. Cuthbert, arising from the manner in which he has been recommended. The President cannot be ignorant of the violence of the parties which agitated the State of Georgia in the late election of its Governor, and the attempt which has been made to connect those parties with the more extensive parties which are now forming throughout the Union. Mr. Cuthbert took an active part in favor of the present Governor. Immediately after the election, recommendations were sent to the Secretary of War by the Governor and two of his most active partisans, for the appointment of commissioners to hold treaties with the Indians, long before any such office was created, or any appropriation made for that purpose, or indeed any report made to Congress upon the subject of Indian land in Georgia. There can be no mistake with regard to the motives which have produced the recommendations of Mr. Cuthbert, and of his being pressed as he has been upon the President. Individually, and in the name of my constituents, I protest against the appointment of any man under such circumstances.

The President will have discovered by the written communication sent him on the 9th inst. by Messrs. Ware, Reid, and myself, that the Representatives from Georgia had intended sending the names of more persons than were communicated when we had the honor of waiting upon him personally. This change took place in consequence of the belief that Gen. Floyd, Maj James Meriwether and Col. Warren Jourdan, from their acquaintance with the Indians, and their high reputation among them, would probably serve the country more effectually in treating with them than any other persons. Gen. Floyd has the reputation of being a man of talents, and high honorable character. His success in the expedition which he commanded against the Indians, is calculated to give him great weight with those people. I have never known of his having been engaged in political, or party strife. He has never been in the Legislature, or held any office of public importance in Georgia, except military, since I have had any knowledge of public affairs. He was appointed a commissioner to hold the treaty with the Creek Indians in 1820, but from some family misfortune could not accept. The difficulty when then existed is now removed.

Maj. James Meriwether is the son of Gen. David Meriwether, who has been employed by the Government to hold treaties with the Indians on several occasions, and who would again have been recommended but for the state of his health. Maj. Meriwether is a trustee of the University of Georgia, a member of the Legislature, a man of talents and integrity. For the last twenty years he has resided within a few miles of the Creek and Cherokee frontiers. He commanded a company in the expedition against the Creek Indians, under Gen. Floyd.

Col. Warren Jourdan has been frequently a member of the Legislature, is a man of talents and character, with person and manners peculiarly calculated to render him useful for the service required. He was recommended to the President for the same appointment in 1820.

I have been thus particular, that the President may be satisfied that the members of Congress from Georgia were actuated by no motives but public duty, in recommending Messrs. Floyd, Meriwether and Jourdan. Messrs. Walker, Wild and Crawford are, either of them, equal in every respect to Mr. Cuthbert. These last gentlemen were withdrawn, because it was believed that those who were recommended possessed some qualifications for the appointment of Commissioners, which those gentlemen did not. If we had been governed by the motive which the Secretary of War intimated when he asked me in the presence of the President, whether Col. Jourdan was the brother-in-law of the Secretary of the Treasury, we would certainly have recommended Messrs. Walker, Wild and Crawford, as having far more political influence than the gentlemen who were recommended.

I have written thus much from a sense of duty to my constituents. I have myself taken great interest in the extinguishment of the Indian title to lands in Georgia, both as a member of the Legislature of that State, and a member of the present Congress. I believe the difficulties in removing the Indians from Georgia are continually increasing. I therefore protest against any political intrigue interfering with the accomplishment of that important object.

I inclose a copy of the papers sent me by the Secretary of War, lest the President might not be informed of the extraordinary mistake committed by the Secretary, and continue to act under it.

I trust that the interest which I have taken in the subject of this letter, will be my sufficient excuse for making such large claims upon the attention of the President.

With highest respect,
Your obt. servant,
GEORGE R. GILMER.

After remaining at Saratoga a few weeks, I went to Virginia. I was soon afterwards married. This event, the happiest, and the only one of any really great importance to myself which had happened to me, was too engrossingly selfish from the circumstances which attended it to be of any importance to others. My wife and myself were first cousins. We were with mutual friends who were the best of people, and with whom we were special favorites. Time passed away without any measure for its fleeting moments. After a while we came to Georgia. The evening we arrived at my mother's, we were expected. The family were assembled. All the negroes about the house. They set up a great shout, "Massa George is married and come home." They took my wife from the carriage and carried her in triumph to the house. My brothers had all married by the time they were twenty-one, and my sisters much younger. I had grown old enough to make my marriage unlooked for.

I went to professional business with eagerness, supposing that what had happened to others would be our fate, and that labor would have its rewards increased by the objects of care for whom the exertion was made. Our anticipations were not realized. I doubt not, happily for us. Time has never dragged. We can never be without matters to interest us whilst we are spared to each other. Exertion finds its best compensation in contented, happy spirits. As to its profits, Madam disposes of them easily, and with great pleasure.

The courts over, I returned to my service in Congress. During the Christmas holidays I visited Mr. Taliaferro, of Orange, Virginia. There I found my wife and her sister, Lucy Grattan. They accompanied me back to Washington City. Lucy Grattan was seventeen, and the most perfect sample of youthful beauty and joyous hilarity which belonged to the romantic valley of the Shenandoah. She attended, with my wife, the winter parties, and for some weeks astonished the modish beings of conventional society by her freedom from form, the sprightly, elastic step with which she danced; and occasionally startled the Senate and House of Representatives by a laugh so loud and joyous as to attract all ears and eyes.

I had been living with a mess not very well suited for ladies: Hardin, of Kentucky; Blair, of Carolina; Thompson and Abbot, of Georgia; Smith, of Virginia, and Allen, of Tennessee. I took rooms at Dowson's, in the mess of Mr. Randolph, Macon, Col. and Mrs. Benton Tatnall, Elliot, Archer, Burton and Jones, of Virginia. Mrs. Benton and my wife were from the same part of Virginia, and had been friends and schoolmates when young ladies. Archer had been in the same society with my wife in Richmond some years before. He was under an hereditary obligation to be specially civil to every one of the Gilmer family. His father was a member of the Virginia Legislature when Col. Tarleton dispersed that body when sitting in Charlottesville, and was cut down in the street by a dragoon, and his life saved by Mrs. George Gilmer running from her house to where he was in possession of the British soldiers, begging for his life, having him carried into Dr. Gilmer's house, and nursed until he was able to go to his home. Col. Eliot and Tatnall were old Georgia friends. Col. Randolph, of Tuckahoe, married the daughter of Col. Harvie (afterwards Mrs. Dr. Brokenbrough, of Richmond), my kinswoman, with whom Mr. John Randolph was very intimate. Mr. Macon was the special friend of Mr. Crawford, my father's neighbor and friend.

In the summer we returned to Georgia. My wife went to housekeeping, and I to the law.

Chapter VI.

In 1824, Gen Jackson, Mr. Adams, Mr. Crawford, and Mr. Clay contended for the presidency. I went into the Senate from Oglethorpe County for the purpose of aiding to elect electors who would vote for Mr. Crawford. Mr. Crawford's body and mind had been very injuriously affected some months before by an attack of paralysis. His advocates in Washington City assured the public, that the effects of the attack would not disqualify him for the discharge of the duties of the presidential office if elected. I believed what they said. Some time before the election of electors came on, I received a short letter from Mr. Crawford, written cornerwise instead of across the paper, and seemingly with a blunt stick instead of a pen, requesting me, as his known friend, to introduce resolutions into the Legislature to alter the constitution, so as to give to Congress the power to make internal improvements in the State, for the purpose of removing objections to him on account of the course pursued by his political friends on that subject. The manner of this letter was as bad as it well could be; but the matter was still worse, because he knew my opinions to be against the proposition which he desired me to make. I had been sent to the Legislature by the people of Oglethorpe for the purpose of voting for him after his sickness was known. In my embarrassment I called upon Mr. Peter Crawford, the Senator from Columbia County, his kinsman, stated to him my difficulties, and showed him the letter which I had received. He pulled from his pocket a similar one, and confessed himself equally at fault. We concluded that nothing could then be done but go on and do what our constituents had elected us to do.

On our way to Milledgeville and a few miles from town, John Abercromby overtook us. He requested me to take a seat in his carriage, for the purpose of consulting about some public matters. When we arrived at the river, I returned to my carriage. I found my wife very much put out. She said that she was ashamed to be seen alone by the crowds that passed her carriage; and that she was not accustomed to be left by her escort, for the company of gentlemen. It took hard courting to reconcile her to the necessities of a politician. Col. Hamilton invited Mr. Peter Crawford, Mr. Prince and myself, to dine with the electors of President and Vice-President at his house on the day they gave their votes, as the special friends of Mr. Wm. H. Crawford. I left the Senate Chamber in time to go to my boarding-house, to see my wife, whilst Mr. Prince went on to Col. Hamilton's. During my absence, Col. Tom Foster called to see my wife. When he went into the drawing-room, it was evident that she had been in tears. He was alarmed, lest some great family misfortune had happened; and being a very intimate friend, took the liberty of asking her what was the matter. She frankly told him, that she could not bear for her husband to leave her, in search of pleasure. The Colonel explained to her, that I could not well avoid doing what I had done. When I returned, she sat down on my knees, put her arms around my neck, and told me how Col. Foster had found her crying, and of her telling him the cause. And although she was then acknowledging that she had behaved like a child, she said, My dear George, whilst I live, I must live with you. And yet whenever duty or business called me, she never delayed or prevented my going, but always urged me on, and aided me in getting ready. I never lost a day from the Courts, the Legislature, Congress, or the Executive department, at her intercession.

When I was last in Congress, the celebrated actor, Powers, was performing in Washington City. Mr. B. W. Leigh requested me to accompany him one night to the theatre, where a play particularly suited to Powers' talents was to be acted. When I proposed to my wife to go, she said that the church to which she belonged did not tolerate plays at all, and that she could not offend it; but insisted that I should go. I did. But my enjoyments had so long derived their relish from sympathy with her, that I returned home tired, and with the opinion that I had seen many a schoolboy act better than

Powers. These are the only times when I have voluntarily sought pleasure in the society of others, apart from my wife, for the thirty-two years we have been married.

From 1824 to 1827, I was engaged in the practice of law, without any interruption from public business. In newly settled countries, all are in movement. Each one presses eagerly forward. Expectation is ever on the tip-toe for coming events. Nobody has time or inclination to look back, or examine into what has been done. All die, though nobody seems to think so. Many persons in Georgia availed themselves, in former times, of the loose administration of the estate of deceased persons, to appropriate property to themselves which did not rightfully belong to them. There was no settled public opinion, to control the dishonest by a sense of its supervision. Under the full press of the universal struggle for money, unsecured rights were often lost. It was the observation of one of the shrewdest old Georgians, that the administration of two large estates, in the hands of a skilful and unscrupulous administrator, was worth a fortune. Administrators moved off to newly acquired territories, to Alabama, Mississippi, or elsewhere, before they could be called to an account, or the children themselves dispersed before they received what belonged to them. Very few understood how to examine into the accuracy of the returns of administrators and executors. Lawsuits were formerly seldom resorted to for the settlement of the estates of deceased persons.

In 1822, William B——— died. He was an old man, a bachelor and wealthy. He left no will. His estate belonged to Jonathan, his only brother then living, and the children of numerous deceased brothers and sisters. Jonathan B———, the brother, and Henry B———, a nephew, administered on his estate. Jonathan B——— was a very old, weak and inefficient man. Henry B——— was in the full vigor of life, had some property, and a large family. He was a drinking, turbulent, fighting, smart, unprincipled man. The management of William B———'s estate was monopolized by him. Instead of distributing, he sold the whole estate for the purpose of getting five per cent. upon the entire sum of its value. Most of the kin, entitled to share it. lived in distant States, were poor, ignorant, and without the means of enforcing their rights, if they had known them. Those in Oglethorpe and the neighboring counties, purchased property at the sale of the estate, at very high prices, and fully equal to their shares; and being poor, were all in the administrator's power. Henry B——— kept the money for which the estate was sold for years, without making any movement towards the distribution, and until it entered into his head that he might keep the whole, or most of it, without making any distribution at all. The nearest distributee out of the State was Henry B———'s own brother-in-law. He came to Georgia, and applied to him for his share, or rather his wife's share, of her uncle's estate. Henry B——— denied any knowledge of him.

After long delay, a few of the distributees applied to me for the enforcement of their rights. In bringing the bill for that purpose, it was necessary to make all the persons in interest parties. The distributees who were suing, had no desire to share the estate with those who were so distant that they might never know anything of their rights. If permitted, they would have sued without them. It required time and labor to ascertain the names and residences of all who were interested. After much unavoidable delay, I brought a bill in equity for the distributees, against Henry B———, returnable to the Superior Court of Oglethorpe at the April term, 1826. At the trial term, thereafter, Henry B——— suffered me to take a judgment against him without defence. At the trial term of the appeal, October, 1828, he made an effort to engage counsel to assist the novice whom he had employed; but the fee he offered was so insignificant, that no lawyer would accept it. The case was tried by a special jury, composed of the best informed, and most upright citizens of the county. I had applied great labor to the investigation of all the particulars of the case, and was fully prepared to explain its merits to the jury. It was the most important, for the amount of property involved, which had ever been tried in the up country. Henry B———'s brothers, Richard and Thomas, had been frequently sheriff of the county, and its Representatives in the Legislature. I was forced, by the pressure of my responsibility, to the exertion of whatever capacity I had to bring the suit to a favorable issue. When I addressed the jury, I pointed out each instance of the administrator's betrayal of his trust in the strongest terms. Whilst I was speaking, Henry B———stood near me with a large stick in his hand, which he was accustomed to apply with great power to the heads of others. As I exposed his rascality, he repeatedly appealed to Judge William H. Crawford, for the protection of the court against my abuse. The judge answered as often, "Take your seat, Mr. B———. It is no abuse. Sir, it is no abuse." The jury brought in a verdict for the full amount of all I claimed for my clients, and fourteen per cent. damages for a frivolous appeal.

The result of Henry B———'s administration of his uncle William B———'s estate, became well known. Administrators and executors perceived that the time had passed by when they could acquire fortunes out of the management of their trusts, at the expense of widows and orphans, and became content with their lawful fees. Few acts of my life have been so beneficial to society as the disgrace which I caused to the administrator, B———, for his knavery.

I went to Virginia in 1825. Whilst there, I visited Mr. Jefferson at Monticello. He was still erect, his reddish hair but slightly gray, his complexion florid, and his countenance intellectual. He described his plan for making the University near Charlottesville, then under his particular direction, the great seat of learning for the Southern States. His advanced age and valuable public services, eminent abilities, social qualities, and controlling influence in organizing and giving direction to the democratic republican party, made him an object of special interest. It was indeed surprising to see one so old, who had been so industriously employed in discharging the most difficult public duties, so intent upon what he had yet to do.

Col. Tatnall's health became so bad in 1827, that he resigned his seat in Congress. I was elected to fill the vacancy. He was born at Bonaventure, four miles below the city of Savannah. His father, Josiah Tatnall, was one of the most popular and patriotic public men who had ever served the State of Georgia. He was a youth at the commencement of the

Revolutionary war. The kinsman who had charge of him (his father being dead), carried him aboard the vessel which was to convey himself and family to England. He jumped into the Savannah River, before the vessel got to sea, and swam ashore. He was, however, forced away, and never found an opportunity of returning until near the close of the war. His patriotism was rewarded by the unlimited confidence of the State. He was the Representative of the people in Congress, their Governor, and might have had any other office in their gift, had he so desired. He died in the prime of life, leaving two sons, Edward Fenwick and Josiah, and one daughter. Edward Fenwick received his early education in England. He was at a school in Hampstead, in 1802, when Napoleon was threatening England with invasion. I have heard him tell with renewed excitement, how he felt the desire to fight, as he listened to an English yeoman marching for the coast, talking of his resolution to stand by his country to death, against her foes, the French. Col. Hamilton, who commanded the English mulatto regiment in the service of the British Government in the Revolutionary war, was his uncle. He resided in London, where Col. Tatnall had other relations of wealth and distinction. I do not know at what time Edward F. Tatnall returned to Georgia. He finished his collegiate education at Princeton College, and afterwards attended the law school at Litchfield. He was licensed to practise by the Superior Court of Chatham, in 1813, and was soon afterwards appointed Captain in the 43d regiment. In 1814, he was ordered with his company to the seaboard, and stationed at Point Peter, under the command of Major Massias. Several British war vessels were then on the Georgia coast. An attack was made on Point Peter. Massias fled, notwithstanding the strongest remonstrances from Captain Tatnall. He was pursued by a British detachment. A skirmish ensued, in which Captain Tatnall, by constantly fronting the enemy, exposing his person every where, and setting an example of indifference to danger, was severely wounded.

Whilst Captain Tatnall was at Point Peter, the Spanish officer on Amelia Island gave a ball to the merchants and their families. The place attracted to it at that time many persons, on account of the facilities which it afforded for carrying on trade. The officers at Point Peter were invited. The ball was opened offensively to the Spanish Commandant, by the omission to place his wife at the head of the first dance. The Spanish soldiers were ordered into the ball-room, accoutred with their full complement of arms, and commanded to disperse the company. The utmost alarm prevailed among the ladies and their husbands. Some hid in one place and some in another. Captain Tatnall and Lieutenant Holt defended themselves as they could, whilst they made for the seashore, where they had left the boat in which they had passed the strait from Point Peter with a squad of four soldiers. With these soldiers they returned to the ball-room, drove the Spanish officer and his men from the house, collected the affrighted company, and attempted to renew the dancing; but the spirit of jollity was gone. Tatnall sent a challenge to the Spanish Commander. Upon his declining to fight, he made a representation of his conduct to the Governor of Florida, who put his inferior into chains, and sent him to old Spain to be tried for cowardice.

Captain Tatnall resigned his commission in the army upon the return of peace.

On the 14th of July, 1818, he and myself made our first political speeches; he in Savannah, and I in Lexington. We were both members of the Legislature for the first time in 1818. We belonged to the same political party, and usually acted together with cordiality in the support of the same measures. In 1820, Colonel Tatnall and myself were elected members of Congress by almost the same number of votes, there being only the difference of four after twenty thousand had been counted. The leading men of Chatham were at that time disposed to undervalue the men of the up country, and showed it by inducing the people to vote only for gentlemen of the low country when they were candidates with citizens of the up country. At the election, when Colonel Tatnall and myself first offered for Congress, Alfred Cuthbert, of Savannah, was also a candidate. On the day of the election, Colonel Tatnall was dangerously ill at his home, several miles below Savannah. So certain were his friends that he would die, that some one proposed to him that his name should be withdrawn from the canvass; to which he would have consented if his withdrawal could have been made known at all the other places of election throughout the State. In the evening, whilst there was scarcely a hope of his living, he inquired if an arrangement had been made for having his friend voted for. Being answered in the negative, he insisted that they should go up to the city, and canvass for him.

The treaty with the Creek Indians, made by Meriwether and Campbell, which had produced great excitement throughout the country, was quieted by the amendatory treaty of Washington City. Feelings of ill-will had, however, been excited among the members of the Georgia Delegation, on account of the different course pursued by them when the treaty was under consideration. The opposition to the first treaty, on the part of the President and members of Congress, was occasioned, as they avowed by the large sums expended by the commissioners in bringing it about, though what was done was much after the manner of making previous Indian treaties. The members of Congress who understood and acted under the obligation created by the contract of the United States to extinguish for Georgia the title of the Indians to lands within its limits, were in danger of losing their seats, by taking an active part in favor of the first treaty. They persuaded the members from Georgia to have a meeting and agree to let what had been done by the commissioners pass sub silentio. Mr. Forsyth, however, said he would speak. When the treaty was before the House of Representatives, Colonel Tatnall rose and observed, that the Georgia Delegation was not prepared to discuss it. Mr. Forsyth spoke. The people of Georgia lauded Mr. Forsyth to the skies for doing what endangered their interest, whilst Colonel Tatnall became unpopular on account of his forgetfulness of himself in serving his constituents and the friends of Georgia.

Colonel Tatnall's person was erect and perfectly formed, with delicate hands and small feet. Our people, from the President down, are all men of work, and show it more or less. Looking at Colonel Tatnall, you knew that he had never labored with his hands. He appeared much larger than he was. His walk was always with a lofty, military gait, and measured tread. He was something more than fearless. His spirit was the essence of chivalry. He preferred death to the slightest discoloring of dishonor. He risked his life, and was near losing it several times, that he might be considered above wrong doing. He stood by his country and his friends as he stood by himself. He would have gloried in offering up his life, if his country's safety had required the sacrifice. If his bravery, generous unselfishness, noble gallantry, and vigorous execution, had been accompanied by corresponding ready conception, and forcible ratiocination, he would have been the great man of his country. He was fitted for command rather than popular service—for rank rather than equality. He died before middle manhood, prostrated by disease in mind and body.

Chapter VII.

INCREASED experience and observation of the world made public service, upon my return to Congress, much more agreeable than my first term had been. The wiry edge of political zeal had become tempered. I had learned that the country was not ruined by the Government pursuing a course of policy different from what I thought best. I associated freely and cordially with the members of opposite party opinion.

There was a great contest for mastery between Napoleon Bonaparte, at the head of the French people, and the Government of Great Britain, from the latter part of the eighteenth century to some time in the nineteenth. They acted as if no countries had rights, or were worth consideration, but their own. The British King passed orders in council, announcing that the coast of France was under blockade; so that American vessels should not carry supplies to the French without being made subject to be made British property. Bonaparte, on the other hand, made liable to capture all American vessels which should enter the ports of Great Britain. Between the two, the people of this country appeared to be in a bad fix for carrying on commerce. But the Yankees—our traders —were full of expedients. Though they lost often by the

British orders and French edicts, their losses were usually made up by their fortunate ventures.

Our Southern people got on their high horse on account of the insolence of the King of Great Britain and the Emperor of France. They insisted that the Yankees should not trade with the English or French, unless upon equal terms and aboveboard.

Congress passed embargo and non-intercourse laws to shut up the Yankee vessels in their own harbors to rot, to prevent their capture and confiscation by Great Britain and France. The big talk of the Southerners, the insolence of Great Britain, the lawlessness of France, and the tricks of the Yankees, brought on war with Great Britain.

The embargo, non-intercourse, and war, so changed the profits of labor in the United States, that new avenues were opened to wealth. The Northern people, cut off from foreign trade, employed their money at home. Instead of exchanging the cotton of the South for goods of the British and French, the Yankees made goods for themselves for the supply of pressing demands of the Southern people. When the war ended, they insisted that, as the Southerners were the authors of the measures which had caused the destruction of their vessels, and the loss of their foreign trade, they ought to be made to buy the goods which the Yankees had been forced to make. The Northern, Middle, and Western States made common cause against the South. Laws were passed by Congress to compel the Southern people to buy Northern manufactures, by imposing so heavy a tax upon the same kind of goods when brought from foreign countries, as to make the home-made the cheapest. One of the legislative tricks used for this purpose was to tax imported goods upon a valuation greatly beyond their cost, instead of the merchants' invoices. It was somewhat in this fashion: Imported cloth, costing twenty cents a yard, by a tax of thirty per cent. ought to have paid six cents, but actually paid twelve cents, by being valued as having cost forty cents; so that Southern laborers paid for cloth twenty cents for the original cost per yard, twelve cents for duty; fifty per cent. upon that sum to the importer, making seventy-two cents if they used foreign goods; and, as the

Yankees always got as much as they could for their manufactures, but little less for the home fabric. The Yankees urged that, as the Southern people had their power in Congress enlarged by the representation of their slaves, they, the Yankees, ought to have the benefit of clothing them. To this argument the Southerners replied, that, as the Yankees had kidnapped the Africans, brought them from their native country, and sold them in this, on account of their aptness to serve, by taking advantage of the indisposition of the Southerners to making the fires on cold mornings, black shoes, catch horses, wash clothes, and other dirty work, they had already got their advantage, by their great accumulation of wealth from the traffic.

The vexation of the Southerners increased, as the measures of the Yankees became more and more oppressive. They became quite furious after the passage of the Tariff law of 1827-28, particularly in South Carolina and Georgia. Public meetings were held every where in those States. The people passed resolutions that they would dress in their own homespun, instead of Yankee cloth, eat their own hominy without the aid of Kentucky hogs, and walk, rather than ride Western horses. The Southern ladies, naturally touchy, took fire at being dictated to about the dress of their servants. They insisted that their husbands, sons and brothers in Congress, should hold out a flag of defiance to the Northern members, by dressing in cloth made by their own constituents. All the representatives of the people of the up country of South Carolina and Georgia appeared in the Congressional Hall, at the opening of the session of 1828, dressed in homespun. There was a marked difference in the appearance of the members from the two States. The Georgians had Virginia mothers and wives, practiced in making Virginia cloth. The South Carolina people were later from the old country, and less skilful in the peculiar fabrics of the new. The very becoming coats of the Georgia members, threw into the shade the antiprotective show-off of the South Carolinians. This difference was immediately observed and felt. Georgia and Carolina had been for some time before, rivals in their political strife, South Carolina to make Mr. Calhoun President, and Georgia to give the distinction to

Mr. Crawford. Two celebrated combatants had written, fought and bled in this cause. Mr. McDuffie was then a member. His suit was made principally of cotton, and so fine, that one felt chilled looking at him. Nuckols' coat was wool, dyed with copperas and bark, or leaves of some fruit or forest tree, and so coarse, that it stood off and around him like a laboring woman's petticoat. My coat was of cloth made of fine wool, dyed with indigo, and mixed in the carding with black silk. It was presented me by one of my female constituents. I had it made by a tailor of taste. The cape was covered with the finest black silk velvet. It was always worn with a rich silk vest. It was put on when I attended the sessions of the House, and doffed as soon as I left it.

During the winter of 1829-30, whilst I was Governor, I occasionally wore this homespun coat of mornings, as a negligee, until I went to the executive office. One morning, a French gentleman came to my house in great haste, knocked at the door, and upon being admitted by myself in this coat, and other shaving fix, asked to see the Governor. I requested him to walk up stairs, the drawing-room of the house in which I lived being in the second story. Upon getting into the room, he turned to me, and repeated his request to see the Governor.

My wife had the prettiest feet in the world, such as a Chinese lady would have envied. They were small, delicate, and symmetrical. I have threatened a thousand times to kiss them, and as often expressed a wish to have them painted as a model for the painters and sculptors of our country. When we went to Milledgeville, she could get no shoes except the shapeless things made for girls before their teens. I wrote to my friend Col. Tom Foster, then in Washington City, to have made for her a dozen pair by the shoemaker whom she had employed whilst I was in Congress, and have them sent to me in Milledgeville by the first safe conveyance. He executed the commission, by making the acquaintance of this French gentleman, who was then on his way from New York to New Orleans, through Milledgeville, getting him to take charge of the packet which contained the shoes, and his promise to deliver it himself to the Governor. Whilst the Frenchman was looking at me in my homespun, doubtfully, I was opening the packet.

Upon exposing the contents I said, "Some shoes for my wife." He dodged as if some plebian missile had been sent at his head, and was off in a moment, losing all his anticipated pleasure of telling to his coffee-house companions in New Orleans, how he had acted as agent between the authorities of the U. States, and the Governor of Georgia.

Nuckols, the South Carolina member, whose copperas and walnut-dyed coat made so great a display, was very young for his station, and very raw, with the taste for attracting notice, so strong in the Irish people and their descendants. He had very thin light flaxen hair, and a full, high forehead extending far back. We belonged to the same mess. Some time during the session of 1827-8, Nuckols appeared at the dinner-table with a very black wig coming down near his eyebrows. No one knew him. During dinner Judge Smith, who was one of us, and Nuckols' neighbor at home, asked where Nuckols was. Nuckols answered, "Here am I." Every eye was upon his black head. Archer of Virginia, who was sitting next him, turned fully round, and asked, "Why, Nuckols, is this you?" Nuckols' look of simplicity and strangeness, and Archer's unaffected surprise was too much for restraint. The laugh would no doubt have been loud and long, but for the utter confusion of Nuckols. It took some persuasion to keep his big fist from being applied to Archer's head.

My wife and myself were both taken dangerously sick in Athens at the commencement of the summer of 1828, whilst I was attending the Board of Trustees of Franklin College. My physician had no knowledge of my peculiar constitution, and administered medicines according to his usual practice. I was prostrated at once. My wife was so ill that she was unable to take care of me. Fortunately for us, Dr. Henry Branham came to see me immediately upon hearing of my situation, took charge of my case, and never left me day nor night until a change for the better took place. After going as far as Watkinsville on his way home, he came back, upon being informed that I was considered worse.

It is one of the pleasures of life to remember such obligations, and to have the opportunity of returning them, as I have since had to Dr. Branham, in a matter of great interest to himself and family.

I was re-elected to Congress in 1828. My wife and myself left Georgia before the result of the election was announced. The health of each continued so feeble, that I considered it of importance to go on towards Washington City before the weather became very cold. I forgot the required formality of signifying to the Governor my acceptance. Gov. Forsyth, without giving me any intimation of his purpose, declared the seat in Congress, to which I had been elected, vacant and ordered a new election. I was then a member of Congress, attending to my duties in Washington City. I had offered for re-election by a public notice to the people, so that there could have been no doubt on the part of the Governor of my acceptance. I had no acquaintance with Mr. Forsyth, and had taken a decided part against his election to the Senate of the United States in 1818. A newspaper altercation took place, which ended by my making the following address to the people:—

I have been waiting to ascertain the state of public opinion, in order to put an end to the uncertainty in relation to my right to a seat in Congress. I am now satisfied that the people desire another election, although the law under which the Governor is enforcing may be unconstitutional. The office of Representative of the people was created for their benefit, and according to the principles of our Government, ought to be exercised in pursuance of their will. Although I have no doubt about my right to that office, I cannot consent to exercise its authority contrary to the opinion of those by whom it has been conferred. It is therefore resigned into their hands. The people are thus relieved from any embarrassment in voting for a Representative at the time ordered by the Governor, and the person whom they may select may take his seat in Congress, instead of finding it constitutionally occupied by another.

Nothing has been so unpleasant to me, as the opinion I find to be entertained by many, that in defending the right of the people to choose their Representative without restraint except from the Constitution, I have been endeavoring to sustain myself in office. The most important power retained by the people, had been violated in my person. My situation imposed upon me the duty of resistance. I have just the same interest that every good citizen has in preserving unimpaired the principles of our Government. If the people, however, desire the enforcement of a law violative of their most invaluable constitutional privileges, I cannot oppose their wish, especially as it is intended to operate exclusively upon myself. I accepted the office which I now resign, because I believed it to be the duty of every citizen to devote a portion of his time to the public service; and because others, whose opinions I was bound to respect, believed that I could be useful. I stand in no need of assistance from the public treasury, for my support. I am not conscious of having had any selfish ends to answer, in any act of my public life. No office in the gift of the people, or the Government, was so gratifying to me as at which I have been compelled to resign, because I believed that my opinions in relation to the constitution and the policy of the Federal Government really represented those of the people of the State; and because I had flattered myself with the opinion, that if I could be useful in any office it was in that. I have always believed that the rights of the people and the State, the continuance of our Union, and the preservation of our freedom, depended upon the uniform adherence to the principles of the Constitution by all the authorities of our country. My conduct has conformed to that belief. The very first act of my political life, was the refusal to comply with an unconstitutional law of the Legislature; and my last is of the same character. I may have been mistaken; and may yet be so. There is, however, one thing about which I cannot err, and that is in doing what I believe to be right. It is a principle of action that never varies, and which I hope shall always have the firmness to pursue.

Influenced by the desire to conform my conduct to public opinion, I should be a candidate for re-election, but from the conviction that my services would be useless. The manner in which I have been deprived of the right of representing the people, after an election duly made, will be familiar to every member of Congress, and will be considered unconstitutional by all. Were I, under such circumstances, to accept of a seat by virtue of another election, any effort on my part to defend the constitutional rights of the people, would be met with ridicule. My case has no precedent in the history of our Government, and would be quoted upon me in answer to all arguments upon such subjects. My conduct has been too uniform and decided to admit of any doubt as to the course I ought to pursue. I must either not serve at all, or serve in conformity with those principles of which I have been the steady advocate. I must become a selfish politician before I can accept of an office with the knowledge that no benefit could be rendered to the country; and believing that much the largest part of the misdirection and corruption which has occurred in our Government has proceeded from that class of men, I prefer becoming a private citizen.

I cannot quit public life without expressing my regret at the manner of its termination. The people have always confided in me far beyond my capacity to serve them. I have felt the strongest obligations to them for their kindness, and have to the best of my abilities endeavored to discharge that obligation by honest service.

Your fellow-citizen,
Lexington, May 9th, 1829.   GEORGE R. GILMER.

The session of Congress of 1828-29 was one of great interest. Gen. Jackson's election was bringing into office a new set of aspirants, who were as busy as bees, in obtaining their places. Having no part or lot in the seeking, I enjoyed the scene highly.

Among the various matters which took place at the time, was a call made through a partisan of Mr. Adams, upon the war department, for information, so as to afford Col. Barbour, the Secretary of War, a pretence for sending to the House in answer a literal copy of a letter of Gen. Jackson, written carelessly, a long time before, in which he spelled several words wrong. To revenge this petty exposure of Gen. Jackson's deficiency in learning, a pasquinade was written, which represented Mr. Adams occupying the country schoolmaster's chair, with the members of his cabinet standing around him, after the fashion of boys when exercised at spelling on evenings before they are dismissed from school.

Mr. Clay stood head, with the other members of the cabinet following according to rank, in a circle around. Mr. Adams's bald head, weeping eyes, and short dumpy person, seated on a split-bottom chair, made him an admirable representative of the class of old-field teachers. He held a book in his hand, from which he selected the words for spelling. He rose and said that his administration had called public attention to Gen. Jackson's want of knowledge in spelling, and that it behooved them all to mind their P's and Q's, and that he had assembled them for the purpose of exercising them in spelling. He then took his seat, and commenced giving out words, saying, Spell female. Mr. Clay, femail; Southard, feemale; Barbour, phemale; Porter, phemail; McKinney, who stood foot, and being a sort of cat's-paw for the cabinet, had put himself there without being asked, when Mr. Adams nodded to him, spelt at the top of his voice, pheemual. Mr. Clay, who had by this time recovered his self-possession, and being very familiar upon the subject, spelt it right. The next word was negro, which was given out to Southard, who having once been a schoolmaster, and taught Latin to two or three boys in Virginia, spelt it niger. The lord of the empty barrels, as Mr. Barbour was popularly called, was at home with the word, and spoke out with his full or a rotund voice, "nigger," that being the Virginia way of calling negro. Porter, nigro. Mr. Adams, bursting with pent-up rage, threw the book at McKinney's head and dismissed the class—McKinney going off blubbering out, that Mr. Adams could not spell Michilimackinac.

To accommodate the great numbers who had come to Washington City to witness the inaguration of Gen. Jackson, it was determined that the official oath should be administered in the eastern portico. Seats were prepared there for the senators, judges of the Supreme Court, and foreign ministers, whilst all others were to stand off and around.

It soon became obvious, that those on the outskirts of the crowd would not be able to see what was done. Some of the young ladies present, who showed a very strong desire to observe and be observed, were placed on the sculptured projections of the pillars a few feet from their base, and held up by their attendants. Gen. Floyd's daughter, a young lady of about fourteen, thus stood, with one arm around a pillar, and a hand on my shoulder. Near the front of the portico, Gen. Jackson was seen, without his hat, his stiff gray hair giving length to his striking features. Near by was Chief Justice Marshall, with his long, spare legs, small head, and eagle eyes. The long flight of steps which led up into the portico were barricaded, so as to keep off the crowd. George Kreamer, the Representative of the German mass, ignorant and honest, was at the foot of the steps with his hand on it. Gen. Jackson drew forth a leaf of manuscript, read from it with trembling hand and inaudible voice, a few sentences. He then took the oath of office, which was administered by the Chief Justice of the U. States. The two then shook hands. This was just done when George Kreamer, who had leaped the barricade, had hold of the President's hand, shaking it heartily. The shout, which was raised by the thirty thousand spectators below, showed that they viewed this shake as no hollow-hearted ceremony.

The President's house was open for the reception of all who desired to pay their respects to the new Chief Magistrate. From one o'clock the populace and dignitaries were constantly pressing into the building. When Gen. Floyd, with Mrs. Gilmer, Mrs. Floyd, and myself attempted to penetrate the crowd, we should have failed, but for the bold and strong push of Gen. Floyd's two stout sons, who went before and made way for us. We took the hand of the President, already sinking into listlessness from exhaustion, and after seeing, among other things, the hundred and fifty dollar official chairs profaned by the feet of clodhoppers, attempted to get out; but the current still set in so full that it was impossible. We passed through a window or two to make our exit; in doing which I had to sustain the weight of Mrs. Floyd, equalling three hundred pounds, with a leg weak from a fracture scarcely healed. Many persons discovered that a Presidential inauguration, though of universal attraction, does not give unmixed pleasure.

At the college commencement in Athens in 1829—(the great assembling place of the active politicians of the State)— I was pressed to be a candidate for chief magistrate of the State, and consented. Major Joel Crawford was my opponent The Clark party had no candidate. The majority of its members voted for me. I was consequently elected by a very large majority.

In the morning before I was inducted into office, the leading editor of the Clark party insisted that I should divide the patronage of the Executive Department equally between the two parties. The day after an active Clark man, who was particularly hostile to the Crawfords, urged me to subscribe money for the benefit of a widow of a Clark partisan, who had been killed in a duel by one of the Crawfords. I declined these and all similar proposals, and thereby excited the ill will of the leading Clark men, as I had of many of the Crawford party, by my success over one of the family. I soon found that to be chief magistrate of the State, when party politics are violent, without party support, is to run barefooted over a thorny way. I attempted to perform what I declared in my inaugural address to be my purpose—give employment to integrity, talent and industry. The factions which had long distracted the State were then objectless. I thought it was time for them to end; but, having never acted with the Clark party, I probably judged those who wanted office through a deceptive medium. They showed that they were of that opinion, or became dissatisfied for some other cause, as they very soon united in the most active opposition to me.

A day or two before the termination of the first session of the Legislature, after I went into the Executive office, I received information that a large number of pamphlets, whose matter was calculated to excite the negroes to insurrection, had been sent from Boston to Georgia. A bundle of them was soon after found in possession of Burret, a Yankee editor. They purported to have been written by a negro in Boston. Burret had been to that city just before, and was suspected of having written them himself—a suspicion which was confirmed by his subsequent conduct.

I come now to the time in my public life when I had to struggle with great difficulties, and was the object of the vilest abuse. The extension of the jurisdiction of the State over the territory occupied by the Indians; the punishment of religious missionaries, and other white men who lived within that territory, who refused to obey the laws; the survey of the land, and the removal of the Indians to the west of the Mississippi, were subjects which attracted the attention of every body at the time. The political censors knew enough of their office, in working for party success, not to make their attacks upon the State. Invectives were directed specially at the Governor, who was the public agent for doing what was done. I was pictured as fiendish as possible, that the good and humane might be deterred from any connection with such a horrid fellow.

The question was tauntingly put to Georgians, Why not let the Cherokees remain among you?—Why not foster and improve them, and let them add to your numbers and wealth? Our villifiers seemed, in their clamor against us, to have forgotten that there was no interchange of the productions of labor between the Indians and others; that they were without wealth, and were incapable of acquiring any; and that they had remained ignorant savages, notwithstanding the constant efforts to change them into better beings. They expressed great surprise that the Georgians felt no sympathy for the poor aborigines.

To appreciate fully the motives, and understand the causes which induced the public men of Georgia to adopt its Indian policy, it is necessary to know what sort of people Indians were, and the relations which existed between them, the State, and the United States. The race seems destined soon to pass away, and leave no trace behind, except in the discolored skin and revengeful temper of their descendants from the crossings with other races. The curious are puzzling themselves with conjectures about the intent of the Almighty in making such beings,—whether they are the descendants of Adam and Eve,—and if they are, when and from whence they came to America.

For a long time the appearance, manners, and habits of the Indians, strangely affected the imagination of all those who talked or wrote about them. Travellers, missionaries, and government agents, magnified their own consequence in giving importance to those of whom they wrote, by describing them to be what they were not. According to their accounts, some of the chiefs were as crafty as Ulysses, others as brave as Achilles, and here and there one as eloquent as Demosthenes. Facts were so slightly investigated, or so perverted by pictures of the imagination, that the truth was seldom perceived, and constantly exaggerated.

Though the Indians made upon sight impressions the most difficult to forget, they have been found upon examination to be the least worthy of remembrance of any human beings. The men were erect of stature, with slender arms and stout legs. Their shoulders were never rounded, nor their backs bent, by habitual stooping to labor. They usually stretched themselves out at length upon logs, or upon the ground, when not stalking after game, or pursuing or flying from enemies. They could run further, and endure hunger longer, than any other people. Indian women were the least inviting of their sex. They lost by drudging what the men gained in comeliness by freedom from it. They hoed the corn at home, and carried packs when travelling abroad. Their hair was coarse like the hair of a horse's tail. They greased it with rancid bear's oil—too offensive for other beings to bear—to keep down the increase of vermin. They effected the same object for their children's heads by aid of their teeth. Men and women went with unwashed hands, faces, and bodies, except when they cooled themselves in the streams in warm weather. Salt was so difficult to be had, and so little used, that most of their food was eaten in the state preferred by the buzzards. Their wigwams were of unbarked poles, with unswept earthen floors, Their beds were of badly dried skins, whose scent added to the other vile smells about their cabins. Most of them could count ten; few could number a hundred. They had no genius for invention, and have added nothing to the stores of human knowledge or instruments. Stone axes and hickory clubs were their tools for work and weapons of war. Their wealth was without money, and its greatest accumulation extended only to wigwams, skins, and canoes. Their gods they worshipped when they desired to do evil, and found them in the worst of their kind, low animals, sticks, and stones. They were the least obedient of all men to the divine commands—do unto others as you would they should do unto you—love your neighbor as yourself; forgive your enemies. Many of them professed Christianity, under the teachings of the Jesuits and others; but their profession was followed by but slight evidence of conversion. Social affections were scarcely felt. Children were uncared for when they became old enough to take care of themselves. They relieved their habitual apathy by occasionally warring upon men and beasts. Their master passion was revenge, which they indulged in as their greatest luxury. They sought no social meetings, nor enjoyed any greetings. They lolled about their cabins smoking and looking at the clouds. They talked but little, and that little of what happened yesterday or to-day. They were never seen walking side by side one with another. Their paths were all single. They indulged in no wants but such as each could supply himself with. If any one became dependent, he died. They seldom asked questions—not because they believed in the adage, Ask me no questions, and I will tell you no lies—for they loved to act by trick, deceit, and stratagem; but from the absence of the desire for information. They were called eloquent, because they followed the vagaries of their imagination in speaking, without investigating facts, or elucidating principles;—heroic, because their insensiblity enabled them to bear torture wthout complaining;—hospitable, because they laid up no provisions for the future, and consumed what they had without care;—and dignified, because they were calm and indifferent when others would have been excited. They described heaven with vehement gestures and excited voice, not because they conceived it to be a place free from sin and sorrow, but where plenty of game would be had. They stuck light-wood splinters into the bodies of their prisoners, and set them on fire, and danced and shouted around them as they burnt, not to overcome the suffering of the dying, but to feast upon a spectacle which relieved them from their accustomed apathy. They delighted in no melody, and remained unmoved by any concord of sweet sounds. Neither the thrilling notes of the violin, nor the exalted strains of the organ, made any impression upon them. They danced with slow uniform steps to their own humming, the striking of sticks, or the rattling of pebbles in terrapin shells. They worshipped at the shrine of Cupid with less fervor than any other animal. The squaw which the Indian took to his side one day, he often kicked the next. He looked at her toiling for him, without sympathy and without assistance. The Indian women learned from their first intercourse with white men, the superior results which followed from choosing them for husbands. The half-breed children, consequent upon such connections, have changed the character of all the tribes among whom white men have gone. Whilst the unmixed Indians have remained what they ever were, and will ever be, until they finally pass away—the most thoughtless, listless, least lovely, of human beings—the half-breeds are making a show of civilization among all the tribes where they are. Their insensibility may be imagined from the following incidents:—

That part of the County of Wilks which is now Oglethorpe,

bordered on the Cherokee country. Not many miles from where I now reside, a man by the name of Bridges lived in 1791. He had sons, and daughters, and grandchildren living with him in the same house. Old Bridges was going into the forest one day to hunt. A grandchild seeing her grandsire, with whom she was a pet, leaving the house, commenced crying to be tken into his arms, and to go with him. This could not be done, as the Indians had been doing mischief, and were known to be upon the frontiers. He carried her to a mulberry tree, then in full bearing with ripe fruit, in a field close by, and after filling her hands and mouth with the berries, went back towards the house. Before he reached it, a party of Indians rose from their concealment in the wheat, then growing in the field, shot down old Bridges, and running up to him, seized the child, and, carrying it out of gunshot from the house (where the father of the child was looking out, having been startled into attention by the firing of the gun), stripped it naked, and, whilst one of them held it up by its little feet to the gaze of the father, another opened it, and took from within its body the lobes of the heart, which they threw at him.

An aged, respectable woman stated on oath, in Elbert Superior Court, that a party of Indians came to her house about the close of the revolutionary war, and after taking whatever of her goods they fancied, seized her infant baby, carried it into the yard, and beat its brains out against a stump.

Who can sympathize with creatures who habitually act thus? The answer may be given in the language of the Indian chief, Logan, "Not one."

At the close of the revolutionary war, Georgia was the weakest of the old thirteen States; for though its people were not the fewest in number, its territory was the most extensive, and occupied by the most numerous and warlike Indian tribes. The other States had gotten entirely rid of Indians, or their numbers had become so reduced, or their temper so subdued, that but little inconvenience was felt from their presence.

Many of the tories who had aided the efforts of their royal

master to subjugate the Colonies, by exciting the Creeks and Cherokees to massacre the people, when the war was over, very fitly preferred remaining among their king's allies, to becoming outcast citizens of the State. Independence, which secured peace to the other States, gave no peace to Georgia. Murderings, and plunderings, continued to be committed by the Creeks and Cherokees through the instigation of the tories. Attempts were frequently made to conciliate them. Treaty after treaty was entered into, without securing safety. The frontiers were too extensive to be defended by its scattered inhabitants. The Indians had easy access into the country, every where. The people endeavored to protect themselves by fortifications of their own making. Block-houses were erected, and manned by voluntary service. The inhabitants, just arrived from distant parts of the United States, with scanty means of support, suffered greatly.* They lost their slaves, horses, and cattle, when such property was all important to them, and could not be replaced. The country had to be cleared of its forests, to fit it for cultivation. Labor was not to be hired. There were no surplus negroes, horses, nor cattle, in the country, nor surplus money to buy them, if there had been. The exuberance of the natural vegetation of the soil, the great

*The following returns of depredations committed by the Creek Indians show what their character and extent must have been.

Whites killed	72
Do wounded	28
Do taken prisoners	30
Blacks killed	10
Do taken prisoners	110
Horses taken off (their value, £3,395 10s)	184
Horses taken off not valued	459
Horned cattle taken off	984
Hogs destroyed	387
Houses burnt	89

Sundry household furniture, farming utensils, wearing apparel destroyed.

"Office of Sec. of Council, 5th Oct. 1789.

"I do hereby certify, that the above estimate of losses sustained by the Indians, since the commencement of hostilities, is taken from returns made on oath, and filed in this office.

"F. MERIWETHER, Sec. E. C."

inducement to the settlement of the country, occasioned the greatest losses to the people by exposing their houses and stock to the depredations of the Indians. The State applied to the General Government for protection. It was answered, by permission to raise troops. A corps was accordingly formed, of its citizens, and the service rendered. The United States deferred, or neglected, to pay its members, for thirty years, though continually urged to do so by their Representatives in Congress. In 1790, a delegation of Creek Indians went to the seat of government, then in New York. They were under the lead of Alexander McGilvray.

Lackland McGilvray whilst yet a lad, showed the instincts of the Scotchman, by leaving his country and family, in search of adventures and wealth. Upon arriving at Charleston, he met with a party of singular looking men, dressed in wrappers belts, leggins and moccasins; having high cheekbones, sedate countenances, and following strange ways. They reminded him of home. They were Creek Indians, who had brought deer and fur skins to market, to exchange for blankets and whiskey. He accompanied them to their wigwams on the Coosa. He soon saw that the Creeks were very indifferent about accumulation. His Scotch propensity found an ample field to operate in. He engaged in trade, as most Scotchmen in his day did, when they left their country for other lands. To add to the facility of doing business with the Indians, he took to his side an Indian girl, the child of a Frenchman and a Creek squaw. The result of this union was Alexander McGilvray, whose loyalty to the British crown, and instinct for making money,—whose faithlessness and malignity, gave obvious indications of his Scotch, French, and Indian descent.

When the spirit of liberty inspired the people of the Colonies to throw off the yoke of the mother country, Lackland McGilvray returned to Scotland. Alexander showed his inherited bent, by sticking to the crown, and staying in the woods. He aided the cause of royalty, by inducing the Creeks to take part with his master, King George, against the Georgians. The Legislature put Lackland and Alexander McGilvray upon the list of tories whose property it confiscated for the use of the State. Alexander repayed himself for his losses by the injuries which he inflicted on the Georgians, through the Creek Indians. The British government, deeply aggrieved by its forced relinquishment of control over its colonies, endeavored to bring the States under its power, by destroying their capacity for warring against it. The Indians were excited to harass the frontier people, by plunderings and murders. Alexander McGilvray was the chosen instrument for doing this vile work in the South. He was made a colonel, and given the pay which belonged to his rank. He availed himself of his advantageous position among the Indians, and his British pay, to form a copartnership in trade with the mercantile house of Panton, Lesly & Co.

The Spanish Government claimed a considerable portion of the territory of Georgia. With the hope of making its claim good at some future time, McGilvray was taken into its pay, and appointed a general. He and his partners were permitted to carry on trade through Florida and other Spanish dependencies, with advantages allowed to no others. The importance which McGilvray acquired among the Creeks through his connection with the British and Spanish Governments, aided by his talents, enabled him to obtain, though a half-breed, the speakership of the Creeks, and rule them to his purposes. He also acquired great influence among the Cherokees, stirred them up to hostilities against the whites, and endeavored to unite them with the Creeks and other southern tribes against Georgia. The Government of the United States was fully informed of McGilvray's intriguing character. His exciting the Creeks to make inroads into the States, and his being in the pay of the British and Spanish Governments. Following in the footsteps of Great Britain and Spain, the government attempted to attach him to its interest, by flattering courtesies, and creating him a brigadier-general with a salary of twelve hundred dollars. He induced the United States, in making the treaty of New York, to take from Georgia, a large extent of land which the Creeks had previously ceded to it, and to agree that the Indians might put to death any Georgian who should be found upon the land, without being accountable to the United States. He offered his services to the General Government, if it would make another State out of the western territory of Georgia. He said to Dr. White, United States Superintendent of the southern Indians, "If that honorable body (meaning the Congress of the Confederation) can form a government to the southward of the Altamaha, I will be the first to take the oath of allegiance thereto." The agent of the Confederation in reply says, in the spirit which has ever since governed the conduct of many in the same matter: "The territory of Georgia is amply extensive, and this Confederation is a security for the Indians, that there will be no further ground of complaint in future, as it cannot be an object to disperse its subjects still more widely, while there is so much internal room for cultivation. I can take upon me to assure you, that measures are adopted with strict security, for curbing the licentiousness of any who may be disposed to give offence to this people."

When Gen. Clark and his associates took possession of the country between the Oconee and Ocmulgee in 1794, and attempted to organize a republic, the Indians looked on quietly, supposing that the new State was what Dr. White and McGilvray had agreed should be established for the purpose of limiting the power of the Georgians; and were surprised when Gen. Washington gave no support to Gen. Clark, as they supposed from the treaty of New York that the new government would assent to any thing which the Creeks agreed might be done in their territory to the injury of Georgia.

The treaty of New York did not stop the thieving and plunderings of the Creeks. When they ceased, after four or five years, the State advised its citizens to prove by such testimony as they could, the particulars and amount of their losses. The peculiar circumstances under which these injuries had been sustained rendered certainty impossible. The property was taken or destroyed when apprehension of massacre made the owners fly from their homes. They could not retake it, or follow the plunderers, so as to know certainly who they were, and what they had taken, but at the risk of their lives. How poorly they were compensated will be seen by the sequel.

The confederation and the United States succeeded in procuring from most of the States the relinquishment of their unsettled lands. Repeated efforts were made to induce Georgia to cede, in the same way, its western territory. Politicians who want to effect an object, are not very ready to obstruct the doings of what will lead to it. The protection which the people of Georgia was entitled to from the General Government was given so slowly and inefficiently, that the massacres of the Indians were perpetrated and they gone before the United States troops were in force to defend them. The State, being unable to defend its citizens, or procure from the Indians cession of their occupant right to the soil, found its extensive territory, wealth without profit. It therefore, in 1802, conveyed its title to what now makes the States of Alabama and Mississippi to the United States, in consideration that the United States would extinguish the Indian title to the remainder of the land which they then occupied in the State. The General Government thus became bound, by positive contract, to remove the Indians from Georgia whenever it could be done peaceably and upon reasonable terms.

In 1808, the Cherokee Indians proposed to the United States to permit them to examine, and if pleased, to settle upon the public land on the west of the Mississippi. The permission asked for was given. They found a country which suited them very well, and many immediately emigrated to it. Although the means were thus afforded to the United States Government to execute its contract with Georgia, it neglected to avail itself of them. When the Creeks were conquered, and sued for peace in 1814, the United States had the rightful power to demand of them a cession of the land which they occupied in Georgia, in repayment of the expenses of the war. What it did, was to take land in Alabama, which it sold for its own benefit. When, by the urgency of the representatives of Georgia, money was afterwards appropriated for holding a treaty with the Cherokees for a cession of land, the government appointed two Tennesseans and one Georgian, commissioners. The consequence followed, that the most valuable land which the Indians relinquished was in Tennessee instead of in Georgia.

But the State might not have complained if the treaty had been fully complied with. The wealthy half-breed Indians who owned slaves, cultivated large farms, kept ferries, and taverns, and had other means of acquiring wealth in Georgia, were unwilling to lose their advantageous positions. They sent a delegation of their own class to Washington City, in 1819, and induced the Secretary of War to change the terms of the treaty so as to let them remain in Georgia. The United States took from Georgia the benefit of the previous treaty under the plea of the great importance of civilizing the Indians. The Secretary of War was lauded to the skies by the Indian sympathizers, because he granted to the chiefs large tracts of the most fertile land in Georgia, in fee, though the fee was known to be in Georgia, and the consent of the State was not asked for nor given.

In 1821, a treaty was made between the United States and the Creek Indians, by which it was agreed that $250,000 of the money which the Indians were to receive for the land sold, might be applied by the United States to compensate the citizens of Georgia for the negroes, horses and cattle which had been previously taken from them by the Indians. These claims amounted to $280,000, according to the testimony which had been taken by the losers, and recorded in the executive office of the State. The proofs were exhibited to the United States commissioners and the Creek chiefs at the making of the treaty, by the commissioners from Georgia specially appointed for that purpose. Although the losses sustained by the frontier people from Creek spoliations were suffered under circumstances which greatly increased the extent of the injury; though the losers had waited in vain for near thirty years in expectation that the United States would perform its duty, by compelling the Creeks to return the property, or make compensation for its loss; such strict rules for their adjudication were enjoined by the United States upon the commissioners appointed to investigate them, that only about a hundred and ten thousand dollars were awarded in satisfaction of them. Those whose claims were allowed to be sufficiently proved, then insisted that they should be compensated for the delay in making payment by the application of the remainder of the $250,000 to that purpose. The question was referred by the United States to its own law officer. The Attorney-General decided that nations did not pay interest to each other for delays in making compensation for spoliations. The representatives of Georgia in Congress applied to that body in behalf of their unjustly treated constituents. In the discussion which followed, ex-President Adams, then a member, and an admirable exponent of the feeling and opinions of his class, spouted a most violent philippic against any further allowance to the Georgia claimants· "Sir," said he, "these Georgians are the most extraordinary people in the world. They put their hands into the public treasury as no others ever did. Sir, it comes within my personal knowledge that these claimants have been paid three times for their losses."

In 1825, a treaty was authorized to be held with the Creek Indians. The government of Georgia being forewarned, became forearmed. They procured the appointment of Georgia citizens for commissioners. A cession of land was made in the form and manner which had been customary. The treaty was laid before the Senate by Mr. Adams, then President. Upon the pretence that unwarrantable means had been used by the commissioners in making the treaty, his first message was immediately followed by a message to prevent its ratification. The whole country was put into an uproar because what had always been done in Indian treaties had been again done. The President sent an agent, a subordinate clerk in one of the departments under his control, to procure evidence that money and other presents had been given to the Indians. The agent took the testimony of those who had failed to make as much profit as they desired, or who feared some loss from it. Whilst the country was agitated by the pros and cons, Governor Troup took possession of the land, and notified Mr. Adams that the people of Georgia would stand by their arms in defence of their rights. Mr. Adams was a candidate for re-election at the time. He and his friends made a great effort for success, by exciting sympathy for the poor Indians. They would most probably have gained their end, but that Gen. Jackson's victory at New Orleans secured for him more votes than the cry of poor Indians did for Mr. Adams.

A few weeks after I went into the Executive Office, I received the report of the commissioners who had been appointed to investigate the facts in relation to the claim of the State to possess at once a territory of considerable extent, which had been previously occupied by the Creeks, abandoned by them, and taken possession of by the Cherokees.

The following is an extract from my message to the Legislature, upon the subject of this claim.

Permit me to recommend to the Legislature the most liberal and forbearing course, in relation to our right to the territory in dispute. Delay, and thorough investigation will not weaken our title, if valid. Representing as we do a great community, and having for dependants, a weak tribe of Indians, subject to our legislation, it becomes us, not only to act justly, but to avoid the appearance of violating right. The immediate possession of the disputed territory, is comparatively of small importance; the removal of all the Cherokees beyond our limits is an object of the very greatest. Until it is effected, our population must remain unsettled, our policy wavering, and improvements of all kinds, whether they contribute to the enjoyments of society, or the advancement of the wealth of the State, unexecuted to their fullest extent. We are assured that the exertions of the present Administration of the General Government will be used to enable the State to arrive at this very desirable end. The obligations of the United States, to extinguish the Indian title to all the lands within the limits of the State, we may now hope will be complied with in good faith. No one understands better the Indian character, and the nature of the peculiar relations which exist between them and our government, than the President of the United States. It is believed that the efforts of the Government to remove the Cherokees, will be strengthened by the truth which is becoming more evident, that the cause of humanity requires it. Long experience has satisfied all, except sectional and party zealots, that the Indian tribes, when surrounded by white men, continue to disappear, until they become extinct. The government proposes to remove all who are within the limits of the State, to an extensive territory, which belongs to it, beyond the Mississippi, where they can be protected and aided in their advancement in civilization, so far as that object can be effected. The humane and intelligent are every where concurring in the proposed measure. In pursuing the course recommended, we shall avoid the unpleasant necessity for acting as the sole judge in our own cause, and collision with the present Administration of the General Government, which is so much more favorable to the rights of the State than that which immediately preceded it.

The following extract from a letter to the President of the United States, will further explain this claim to the immediate possession of a part of the territory which was in possession of the Indians.

Executive Department, Milledgeville, Dec. 29th, 1829.

Independent of any knowledge derived from individuals, it is probable that we could have accounted for the change of possession of the disputed territory from the Creeks to the Cherokees, from the alteration of the habits of life which has been for a long time taking place in both tribes. Within the last thirty or forty years the Creeks and Cherokees gradually became less and less capable of subsisting by hunting. Very many of the half-breeds of each tribe exchanged hunting for herding. But even these were but little accustomed to provide, by cultivating the earth, food for the support of their cattle during the winter, but rather trusted to the cane and other natural productions. Both tribes therefore inclined to progress to the south, where the lands on the streams were richer, and the cane more capable of sustaining their cattle. That portion of the Cherokee tribe in particular, who inhabited the high, mountainous, cold and sterile country about the head-waters of the Savannah and Chattahoochee were disposed to leave it for one further to the south, and more suitable to the change that was taking place in their habits. The truth of this opinion is verified by the talk delivered by the Cherokees, in 1808, to the President of the United States, in which they represent the scarcity of game in that part of their country, and their intention to leave it. In addition to the superior advantages of a more southern country for the support of their cattle, was added the inducement of approaching nearer their markets, rendered important by the increased value of their beef and hides.

It is probably known to the President, from personal observation, that the country in dispute was formerly occupied by the Creeks entirely, and that they gradually relinquished their possession, until at the close of the late war, there were very few of that tribe remaining on it; and, that, at the same time, and in the same manner, the Cherokees by degrees obtained almost entire possession. The fact that all the streams and remarkable places bear Creek names, prove certainly that it was but lately occupied by the Creeks, and that there has been no general and simultaneous transfer of its possession from one tribe to the other, and that the Cherokees must therefore have intermingled with the original inhabitants, so as to have adopted their proper names. The Cherokees' talk, the testimony of the Indians, and the information of the original white settlers on the frontier, prove that this occupation of the country by the Cherokees was permissive on the part of the Creeks, and so considered by the Cherokees until 1820, when General McIntosh procured the consent of the Creeks to make it a matter of right.

The country was said to have been loaned by the Creeks to the Cherokees. The first claim of the right to possess it at all, on the part of the latter tribe, was derived from success at a ball-play, at which the stake was the disputed country, and at which play the Cherokees were successful. This ball-play took place some time between the years 1816 and 1820.

I understand that the President is of the opinion that the United States Government is bound, by its contract of 1802 with Georgia, as well as upon general principles, to permit no transfer of territory after that time from the Creeks to the Cherokees, or rather to disregard any contracts which may have been made between the two tribes. The Creeks having been the occupants of the country in 1802, and having parted with possession, it now belongs to Georgia, as the rightful owner of the soil. The wisdom and prudence of the President will direct the time and manner in which the State shall take possession of the country. We are desirous that the President shall so manage the matter as not to interfere with the efforts of his administration to obtain for Georgia, through the measures proposed to be pursued by Congress during its present session, the whole of its Indian territory. The people of Georgia, and those who administer its government, are fully apprised of the opposition which the President has to encounter in the management of Indian affairs. They know that in discharging his high duty, to advance the real interests of the Indians, and secure the rights of Georgia, he will be opposed by the prejudices, the ignorance, and the feigned sensibility of affected philanthropists, and still more by the party seeking to succeed him in office. The Legislature of the State and its Executive have therefore endeavored to pursue such policy, in relation to every thing connected with the Indians, as to aid the President in sustaining his measures. He will be satisfied of this by the accompanying report and resolutions of the Legislature, and the message of the Executive.

It is my duty to state to the President, that I have lately received information from a highly respectable source, that Gen. Coffee, the United States Agent for taking testimony in relation to the disputed line, has been subjected to an attempt to have palmed upon him much corrupt testimony.

Mr. Gates, the Georgia Commissioner, who lives immediately upon the line of the disputed territory, writes me thus:—"I am informed that Major Ridge, a Cherokee, had some old drunken Indians, heretofore chiefs, drilling for a month, and then introduced them to General Coffee, as competent evidence." The constant and active efforts of Ridge to thwart the views of the Government renders this account highly probable. It is, however, less regarded, because it is believed that the President himself is well acquainted with the facts connected with the present possession of the Cherokees, Indian habits, and the character of their principal chiefs. I have requested Mr. Gates to endeavor to procure some evidence, in a more authentic form, of the truth of his statement as to Ridge's conduct.

Georgia considers herself entitled to the immediate possession of the country claimed, but is willing to have the right postponed for the attainment of a more important object. If that object is not affected by the means adopted during the present session of Congress, the State expects that the President will, so far as his own power extends, do her justice, by having the Cherokees removed from so much of the territory as is included in the treaty lately made with the Creeks.

These remarks are submitted to the President with sentiments of the most respectful consideration.

GEORGE R. GILMER.

To the President of the United States.

Soon after this correspondence with the officers of the General Government, the Cherokee chief, Ridge, with a large party of Indians under his command, entered the disputed territory, and dispossessed the whites, by burning all the houses occupied by them. The Indians were armed and painted. The weather was exceedingly inclement, the earth being covered with snow. Two women in childbed were exposed to its severity. The difficulty of preserving peace when the frontier people wanted protection from the Indians, and the Indians were redressing their imagined wrongs by shedding the blood of the whites—excited as both whites and Indians were by the contest about this disputed territory—will be understood by the following correspondence. That only a single life was lost when so many were perilled, is a matter for wonder.

Executive Department, Milledgeville, 15th Feb. 1830.

Sir,—I have just been informed by express, that a party of Indians, headed by Ridge, have entered into the territory now in dispute between this State and the Cherokees, and destroyed fourteen or fifteen houses occupied by our citizens. The houses were formerly possessed by the Cherokees. They were purchased of them by the treaty of 1821, and paid for by the United States. The Indian occupants had also received a valuable consideration for them from the ctiizens who were in possession at the time they were burnt. It is understood that very few Cherokees remain upon any part of the disputed territory. The conduct of Ridge and his party was without justification in this matter, on account of their knowledge of the determination of the President not to interfere with the present occupants of the disputed territory, either white or Indian, until the possessory right shall be determined to be in one or the other. The Indians are represented to have been painted and armed, and to have acted under the order of their principal chief. The whites, excited by this outrage, have endeavored, in a very informal way, to have the trespassing Indians arrested. Application has been made to me for the aid of the military authority, to defend the citizens of the frontier from attack. It has not been granted, from the belief that the Indians will not attempt any further violence. This, however, is far from being certain. I shall request the commanding officer of the United States troops at Fort Mitchel, to march with a sufficient force for the protection of that part of our frontier where danger seems to be apprehended. The President will perceive, in this state of things, additional inducement to comply with the request which has been hitherto made him, to remove the Cherokee Indians from all the lands within this State to which they have no clear possessory title. Very respectfully yours, &c.

GEORGE R. GILMER.

To the Hon. John H. Eaton.

Executive Department, Milledgeville, 15th Feb. 1830.

Dear Sir,—From the information received by express this day, I learn that the Cherokees have burnt the houses occupied by the whites in the territory, the right to possess which is now in,dispute between them and the Georgians, and that the whites have revenged themselves by killing one Indian and confining another in Carroll jail. I also understand that the sheriff of Carroll, and twenty followers, are about to enter the Cherokee country, in search of the Indians who destroyed the houses. It is very important to the interest as well as the character of the State, that these acts of violence should be stopped. The law extending the civil jurisdiction of the State over the Cherokee country will not go into operation until next June, and does not therefore affect the rights of the Indians. The Cherokees have been for a long time in possession of the territory which is now claimed by Georgia, and many of them yet occupy it. The houses burnt were within the disputed territory. The white occupants were considered by the United States intruders, and subject to be driven off. The General Government has only deferred the orders to its troops until the right of Georgia to the country can be examined into and determined upon. Its final decision is looked for daily. It is therefore exceedingly important that no acts of violence should be committed by our citizens. If the Indians who burnt the houses have committed any violence upon the personal rights of our citizens, they have rendered themselves liable to be arrested and punished. But this does not seem to have been the case. An inquiry was made of the War Department, by direction of the last Legislature, as to the ownership of the houses. The answer was, that the Indians could not convey the houses to our people. This answer was communicated to the Legislature, and acquiesced in.

My object in writing is to inform you of the facts, and to request the interposition of the civil authority in suppressing any further violence on the part of our citizens.

I write in great haste.

Very respectfully yours, &c.
GEORGE R. GILMER.
To the Hon. Walter J. Colquit.

Executive Department, Milledgeville, 11th March, 1830.

Sir,—I have received your letter, inclosing the report of the committee on Indian affairs, for which, please to accept my thanks. The deepest interest is felt here for the success of the measures proposed by the committee. Their failure will produce a most unpleasant state of things in Georgia. The mutual irritation between the people of the State and the Cherokees, renders it improbable that our laws can be executed without acts of violence. The whites and half-breeds, who are most capable of understanding and valuing the benefits of civil government, are the most active in opposing the jurisdiction of the State. Their conduct, together with the constant abuse of the State and its people, by the opposition to the present administration, under the guise of sympathy for the Indians, will draw upon them the most rigid enforcement of the laws. The officers of the frontier counties, who will be the instruments for their execution, reside in a community too much excited, to expect that their conduct will be uniformly conciliatory. A late occurrence has added very much to the excitement among both whites and Indians. You are aware, that early in the last year the Legislature caused an investigation to be made into the title of the State to the immediate possession of a part of the country in the occupancy of the Cherokees, and a survey to be made of it for the purpose of ascertaining its extent. Soon after, most of the Cherokees, who resided upon the land, accepted of the terms offered them by the treaty of 1828, received the valuation for their possessions, transferred them to citizens of Georgia, and removed to the West. In this manner the disputed territory became settled almost entirely by the whites. The President declined complying with the request of either, until it should be determined by an investigation (which he ordered to be made), to whom the right of possession belonged. With the knowledge that the investigation was not completed, and that the President had ordered the whites on the disputed territory should not, for the time, be treated as intruders, Ross, the principal chief of the Cherokees, directed Ridge (known to be the most active and malignant enemy of Georgia), to destroy all the houses occupied by the whites, on a day when the earth was covered with snow and sleet. The order was executed by burning the houses. A number of women, with infant children, were thus deprived of shelter from the severity of the coldest and most inclement weather. Such has been the excitement produced by this outrage, that it has been with the utmost difficulty that the people have been restrained from taking ample vengeance upon the perpetrators. All the influence of the Executive of the State has been used to prevent any further violence. It is hoped that every member of the United States Government will perceive, in this state of things, sufficient reason for the use of the most effective means for the removal of the Indians. The occasion does not admit of the discussion of mere abstract questions. It is required by the interests of all the parties concerned, and especially that of the great body of the Indians.

With sentiments of the highest respect, yours, &c.

GEORGE R. GILMER.

Honorable Hugh White.

Executive Department, Milledgeville, 6th May, 1830.

Dear Sir,—Your letter, together with the documents from the War Department, which you have so obligingly had copied for me, have been received. I do not understand the object of the President in withholding from the Executive of the State the official communication of his determination in relation to the disputed territory.

Your opinion, that the possessory right of the Cherokee tribe to the places occupied by individuals who have received value for their improvements, and agreed to emigrate, is extinguished thereby, and the corresponding policy of the administration, in determining not to consider the white persons who have settled upon those improvements, intruders, opens to the State the most certain prospect of insuring the enforcement of her laws, and acquiring her entire territory.

I am in doubt, as to what ought to be done with the gold diggers. They, with their various attendants, foragers and suppliers, make up between six and ten thousand persons. They occupy the country between the Chestatee and Etowah Rivers, near the mountains, gold being found in the greatest quantity deposited in the small streams which flow into these rivers. There are no Indians residing in that section of the country. The quantity of gold is said to be very great. It is intimated, that the gold diggers intend procuring the consent of the Cherokee Council to the continuance of their operations, if the United States Government should attempt to remove them as intruders, thereby evading the non-intercourse law.

The State considers itself entitled to all the valuable minerals within the soil of the Cherokee territory, by virtue of its fee-simple ownership, and is now permitting itself to be plundered of its wealth, from the strong desire of its authorities to avoid any collision with the General Government. If, however, the gold diggers should attempt to evade the operation of the United States laws, in the manner suggested, it may become necessary for the State to protect its property by taking possession of the gold country. If it should, it is hoped that it will be under circumstances which will prevent any opposition on the part of the General Government.

I have not issued a proclamation, ordering the gold diggers to cease their operations and to depart from the Cherokee territory, because the laws of the State give the Executive no power to enforce such a proclamation. I cannot call upon the General Government to enforce the non-intercourse law, because I do not believe that it has the constitutional right to do so. All that I can do, is not to resist the exercise of an authority which has been uniformly acquiesced in by the Legislature of the State, and all of my predecessors.

Very respectfully yours, &c.
GEORGE R. GILMER.

Honorable John McPherson Berrian,
Atty. Gen. of the United States.

When this letter was written to the Attorney-General, a community was forming in the gold country scarcely ever paralleled any where. Many thousands of idle, profligate people flocked into it from every point of the compass, whose pent up vicious propensities, when loosed from the restraints of law and public opinion, made them like the evil one, in his worst mood. After wading all day in the Etowah and Chattahoochee Rivers, picking up particles of gold, they collected around lightwood knot fires, at night, and played on the ground and their hats, at cards, dice, push pin, and other games of chance, for their day's findings. Numerous whiskey carts supplied the appropriate aliment for their employments. Hundreds of combatants were sometime seen at fisticuffs, swearing, striking and gouging, as frontier men only can do these things.

About the last of May, the Congress of the United States passed a law, authorizing the President to exchange with any Indian tribe the lands occupied by them in any State or Territory, for lands of the United States west of the Mississippi. This law was passed by a majority of five votes only. It was opposed most violently in both Houses, although its enactments were altogether favorable to the Indian tribes, and was the most certain way by which the Government's contract to extinguish the Indian title to the lands occupied by them in Georgia could be extinguished. The sectional interests of the Northern and Middle States, and the partisan opposition to the Administration, resisted every effort made by the United States and Georgia to place the Cherokees in a situation more favorable to their civilization, and improvement than that which they then occupied, surrounded and mixed up as they were with the whites, who corrupted their morals, and lessened their attachment to each other, by lessening their identity.

Immediately after the time, when by the Act of the Legislature, the laws of the State became of force in the Cherokee territory, I gave notice of it to all whom it concerned, by the following proclamation, forbidding trespasses upon the gold mines in the Cherokee territory, and notifying the Indians, and whites living among them, of the extension of the State's jurisdiction over them. So much as is supposed to be necessary to understand what is said about it, is copied here.

> Whereas, it has been discovered, that the lands in the territory, now occupied by the Cherokee Indians, within the limits of this State, abound with valuable minerals, especially gold: And whereas, the State of Georgia has the fee-simple title to said lands, and the entire and exclusive property in the gold and silver therein: And whereas, numerous persons, citizens of this and other States, together with the Indian occupants of said territory, taking advantage of the law of this State, by which its jurisdiction over said territory was not to be assumed until the first day of June last past, have been, and are now employed in digging for gold in said land, and taking therefrom great amounts in value, to the injury of its public resources: And whereas, the absence of legal restraint, and the nature of their pursuits, have caused a state of society to exist among said persons, too disorderly to be permitted: And whereas, an Act of the Legislature has added the territory occupied by the Cherokee Indians, included in the limits of this State, to the counties of Carroll, DeKalb, Gwinnett, Hall and Habersham, and rendered void all Cherokee laws: And whereas, the jurisdiction of the State is now extended over said territory, and all persons therein, made subject thereto.—Now, for the purpose of removing all persons from the lands of the State, in the territory aforesaid, except such as are permitted by the laws or assent of the State to occupy the same; to secure to the State its property in the minerals therein,

and to put an end to the lawless state of society which has hitherto existed among the gold diggers in said territory; I have thought proper to issue this, my Proclamation, notifying all persons whom it may concern, that the jurisdiction of this State is now extended over all the territory in the occupancy of the Cherokees, included within the limits of the State.

The following letter was written to the President of the United States, immediately after issuing this Proclamation, informing him of the policy which the authorities of the State were pursuing, upon the subjects of the Indians and gold mines.

Executive Department, Milledgeville, 15th June, 1830.

Sir,—I transmit to the President, for his information, a proclamation, which is designed to notify the Indians within this State, of the extension of its jurisdiction over them, and to require white persons as well as Indians, to desist from trespassing upon the property of the State, by taking gold or other valuable minerals from its ungranted land. Before this proclamation reached the part of the State occupied by the Cherokees, the United States troops had driven from it all persons except Indian occupants.

The President is aware, that such an exercise of power, without the consent of Georgia, is believed to be unauthorized by the Constitution of the United States, especially since the passage of the law, by Georgia, extending the jurisdiction of the State over all its Indian territory. It is, however, so important an object with the State to obtain from the United States the execution of its contract of 1802 to remove the Indians from within its limits that it has been unwilling to create the least embarrassment by any assertion of its rights, in opposition to the policy of the General Government. This disposition has been increased, by the special confidence reposed in the present administration.

From information just received, there is much reason to apprehend considerable disturbances, and perhaps bloodshed, from the manner in which the order of the President to remove the intruders, has been executed by the officers commanding the regular troops. The persons who have been removed by them were engaged in mining for gold. Thir numbers amounted to several thousand, most of whom had found their employment exceedingly profitable. The Indians in their immediate vicinity, so far from objecting to the occupation of their country by the gold miners, favored their presence. They were not interrupted in the accustomed enjoyment of their country, by the taking gold from its soil. The gold country is situated very near the thickly inhabited part of the frontier of the State. When the gold diggers were removed by the troops, although much discontent was felt, they retired to their homes with-the mines from which they had been driven were immediately taken possession of by the Indians and the whites connected with them, and that they were permitted to take the gold without any resistance from the troops. Very great excitement is said to be the result. There is much reason to apprehend that the Indians will be forcibly driven from the gold region, unless they are immediately prohibited from appropriating its mineral wealth.

Georgians think they violate no law except that of the State, in digging for gold within its limits; and that after the passage of the law extending its jurisdiction over the Cherokee country, the Government of the United States has no authority to enforce the non-intercourse law. What effect the Executive proclamation may out any actual resistance. It, however, soon became known, that have in allaying this excitement, is very uncertain. It is probable that it may prevent an immediate attack upon the Indians, from the expectation that they will be restrained by the authorities of the State.

I shall be compelled to resort to the tedious process of the courts, for this purpose, the laws of the State not having invested the Governor with the power to protect the public property by military force. In the mean time, it is very desirable, that the President should direct the officers commanding the United States troops, to prevent intrusion upon the property of the State by the Indians, at the same time they are defending the occupant rights of the Indians from intrusion by the whites. The President will perceive, that in the proclamation forbidding all persons, both whites and Indians, from taking gold from the territory of the State in the occupation of the Indians, that the right of the State to all the gold and silver in its ungranted lands is asserted. All the European nations who made discoveries and conquests and retained possession of any portion of this continent, claimed the exclusive right to all the gold and silver mines within their possessions. This was, in fact, the first and strongest inducement to the enterprise of the early adventures to this country.

In addition to this right assumed by all European nations, the King of Great Britain claimed, by virtue of the common laws of England, to be the sovereign owner of all the lands within his kingdom, and especially in the American Colonies. Upon the independence of the States, their Governments became entitled to all the rights of sovereignty over the territory within their limits, which had before belonged to the Kings of Great Britain. The State of Georgia is therefore entitled to the gold and silver in its territory occupied by the Indians, as well by the customary law established by the nations by whom the country was settled, as the fee-simple or paramount title which it derives from the crown of Great Britain.

The Courts of this State have uniformly determined that the State is the proprietor of all the ungranted lands within it, including those in the occupancy of the Indians. This right is claimed by each of the original States of the Union. It is certainly the right of Georgia, according to the decision of the Supreme Court of the United States.

If the Indians take possession of the gold mines through the assistance of the United States Government, they will be fixed upon the soil instead of being removed. It is said that preparations are making by a large number of the wealthy Cherokees to remove into the gold region for the purpose of participating in its mineral riches. If they can be protected in so doing by the United States, we shall thus not only retain the Cherokees who have hitherto occupied the lands of the State, but many of those who reside in Tennessee, Alabama, and North Carolina. The United States is bound by contract to prevent this state of things. No doubt is entertained of the disposition of the President to perform the obligations of the Government in good faith. The State of Georgia cannot permit her rights to be violated by persons subject to her jurisdiction, as the Indians are acknowledged to be, without applying a remedy adequate to the removal of the evil. In exercising this power, if it should unfortunately become necessary, it will be the object of the State to do it in such manner as to aid, rather than thwart, the policy of the present administration, and carefully to guard against violating the rights intended to be secured to the Indians.

Very respectfully yours, &c.,
GEORGE R. GILMER.

To the President of the United States.

P. S.—I have this moment received information which may be relied on, that when the Executive proclamation was received all the Indians left the mines, but that most of the whites and wealthy half-breeds continued digging for gold. I have not yet understood what effect the proclamation has had upon the intruders who have been driven off, and who have evinced a disposition to act with violence. An agent of great discretion and firmness will be immediately sent to the gold country with directions to enjoin, by process from the courts, all persons who may be found trespassing upon the rights of the State., In this way hopes are entertained that peace and order may be restored to our frontier.

GEORGE R. GILMER.

Whilst I was harassed by the difficulty of preventing trespass upon the land where the gold was found, and enforcing the jurisdiction of the State upon the Cherokee people, I received the following letter from Mr. Wirt:

Baltimore, June 4th, 1830.

Sir,—A just respect for the State of Georgia, and a desire to avoid a misconstruction which might be attended with evil consequences, seems to me to call for a communication which, under other circumstances, might well be deemed officious and intrusive. The excitement with regard to the Indians within your borders is already so high, and in this state of feeling measures of the most innocent character are so easily misapprehended and converted into causes of offence, that I persuade myself your Excellency will at least approve the motive of this letter as a measure of peace.

The Cherokee nation have consulted me professionally as to their rights under their various treaties with the United States. Among other questions, they have asked me whether, under the Federal Constitution, laws, and treaties, the State of Georgia has the right to extend her laws compulsively into their nation; and whether this question can or cannot be carried for decision to the Supreme Court of the United States. I am fully aware of the serious import of these questions, and regret exceedingly that they have arisen. I foresee distinctly the disastrous consequences which may be made to flow from giving the controversy this direction; and yet if it be met and conducted with proper temper, as I trust it will, it is quite as apparent that it may prove the means of peace and reconciliation.

I have not sought this consultation. It has been cast upon me in the common and regular practice of my profession, and according to my understanding of my professional duties, I am not at liberty to refuse either my advice or services to any one who comes to consult me on his legal rights, and who has nothing more in view than the assertion of those rights according to the course of the law of the land.

It is my misfortune to differ with the constituted authorities of the State of Georgia on the question of her power to extend her laws into the Cherokee nation; and the late debates in Congress will have satisfied your Excellency that in this opinion I am not singular, but that I hold it in common with many of the most distinguished lawyers on our continent. We may be wrong; and, as infallibility is not the lot of mortals, those who hold the opposite opinion may be wrong. Fortunately, there exists a tribunal before which this difference of opinion may be quietly and peacably settled, and to this tribunal I think it may be regularly referred. I perceive that in the debates to which I have alluded, a mistaken humanity has been supposed to warp the judgment on one side of this question, and interest on the other. In the Supreme Court of the United States we shall find a tribunal as impartial and as enlightened as can be expected on this earth; or, if partiality can be supposed to find its way into that high tribunal on any occasion, it is not on such a one as this that the Cherokee nation have a right to expect it in their favor. To them the courts of the United States are foreign courts, while they are the domestic tribunals of the States of the Union.

I have told these people that I am willing to assist them in bringing their rights for final decision before the Supreme Court of the United States, on the condition that they conduct themselves peaceably towards the people of Georgia and of the United States, and that they make the question purely a question of law for our courts; but that I will abandon them and their cause on the first aggression by violence on the white people around them which shall be authorized by their nation. It is but justice to add, that in those of the nation who have been with me, and who compose the delegation that have been at Washington, through the winter, I have not discovered the slightest disposition to violence. They are civilized and well-informed men. They wear our dress, speak our language correctly, and in their manners indicate all the mildness and much of the culture and courtesy of our own best circles. They assure me that their people at home have abandoned the habits of savage life, and subsist by agriculture and the other usual and peaceful pursuits of civilized societies. They profess, and I believe with entire sincerity, to be willing to make the question of their rights under their treaties, questions of pure law for the decision of our courts; and as I perceive by the reported debates in Congress that a measure of this sort has been anticipated, and that one of your enlightened senators in that body expressed a strong, and without doubt, sincere conviction that the decision of the judiciary would, if it should ever be asked, be in favor of the right of the State to legislate over the Cherokee nation; I cannot but indulge the hope that in proposing to bring this question before the Supreme Court, I shall have advised a measure rather pleasing than otherwise to the State of Georgia.

Be this as it may, I cannot reconcile it to my sense of propriety to have any agency in this affair without apprising your Excellency, frankly and respectfully, of what is intended. I desire to have it distinctly understood on every hand, that neither these people nor their counsel aim at any thing more in this movement than an open, peaceable, and respectful appeal to the opinion of our own courts, the courts of the Union.

Your Excellency will not understand me as asking or expecting that you will take the trouble to answer this letter. My object is single and sincere; it is simply to avoid all appearance of concealment, and all misapprehension or surprise on the part of the State of Georgia, by advising your Excellency fairly and openly of the measure in contemplation, and by assuring you that there is no other purpose in view than a quiet, peaceble, and respectful reference of the questions of law and right in dispute between the State of Georgia and the Cherokee people to the highest court of our nation, the Supreme Court of the United States.

Your Excellency will permit me to assure you further, that in the future measures which may grow out of this controversy, so far as they shall be under my direction, care will be taken to give as little trouble as possible to the constituted authorities of the State of Georgia, that the discussion will be conducted with all the respect for that State and its laws which may consist with the proper assertion of what I consider the rights of this unfortunate people.

The decision may be expedited by making a case by consent, if that course should suit the views of the State of Georgia. It is not asked, however, but suggested merely for your consideration, with an assurance that if it should meet your approbation, the Cherokees will cheerfully concur in the measure.

The motives which have led me to trouble you with this communication make it equally proper, I think, that I should submit a copy of it to the President of the United States; and I shall place another copy in the hands of the Cherokee delegation, in order that they may distinctly see and remember the conduct which is expected from their people, and what alone they have a right to expect from me.

I have the honor to remain, sir, most respectfully,
Your obedient servant,
WILLIAM WIRT.

To this letter of Mr. Wirt's I wrote the following answer:—

Executive Department, Milledgeville, 19th June, 1830.

Sir,—Your communication addressed to the Governor of Georgia, has been received, informing him of your employment by the Cherokee Indians to defend them against the operation of the laws of the State, and proposing a reference of what you have thought proper to call the dispute between the Cherokee Nation and the State of Georgia to the Supreme Court of the United States. The Governor of Georgia knows of no reason why he should be notified that professional duty required of you to take fees of all who ask your advice. Georgia claims no jurisdiction over the lawyers of Maryland. Your justification will have become appropriate when that State interferes with your professional business. Why it should be the misfortune of a citizen of Maryland (as you say it is yours) to differ with the constituted authorities of Georgia, is not very clearly understood. You are neither responsible for the legislation of the State, nor subject to its control. There is no doubt but that many lawyers, like yourself, profess to believe that the State has usurped authority, and violated the faith of treaties, by passing laws for the protection of the rights, and punishing the crimes of the Indian people who reside within its limits. It is known that the extent of the jurisdiction of Georgia, and the policy of removing the Cherokees and other Indians to the west of the Mississippi, have become party questions. It is not therefore surprising, that those who engage in the struggle for power, should find usurpation and faithlessness in the measures of the Government, accordingly as the loss of office or the hope of its acquisition, may enlighten their understandings. What you say of the fallibility of the constituted authorities of Georgia, is a truism of universal application, and can have no meaning but your intention to render the application particular.

You say the Supreme Court of the United States is a high, impartial, and enlightened tribunal. Why such commendation?

The promise you make to use your professional influence to prevent your clients, the Indians, from committing violence upon the people of Georgia, is very kind—coming as it does from a private citizen of another State—and will, without doubt, create an obligation upon the people, whose safety is intended, commensurate with the favor to be received.

There are no fears felt in Georgia of Indian violence, although it is highly probable that your efforts will be productive of some mischief. It is believed that the Cherokees in Georgia had determined to unite with that portion of their tribe who have removed to the west of the Mississippi, if the policy of the President were sustained by Congress. To prevent this result, as soon as it became highly probable that the Indian bill would pass, the Cherokees were persuaded that the right of self-government could be secured to them by the power of the Supreme Court, in defiance of the legislation of the General and State Governments. It was not known, however, until the receipt of your letter, that the spirit of resistance to the laws of the State and views of the United States, which have of late been evident among the Indians, had in any manner been occasioned by your advice. Although insurrection among the Indian people of Georgia may be the consequence of your proceedings, and those who act in unison with you, the constituted authorities of the State disclaim all right to interfere with you in any manner, so long as you keep yourself beyond the jurisdiction of the State.

You have thought proper to give the Governor of Georgia an account of the civilization of the Cherokees—describing those whom you have known to be polished gentlemen, and those whom you do not know to have ceased to be savages. What you say of the intelligence of the members of the Cherokee tribe who were in Washington City last winter, is partly true, and equally descriptive of many others. They are not Indians, however, but the children of white men, whose corrupt habits or vile passions have led them into connection with the Cherokee tribe. It is not surprising that the white men, and the children of white men, have availed themselves of the easy means of acquiring wealth, which the Cherokee territory has presented for thirty or forty years; nor that intelligence and spirited activity should increase with their increasing wealth; nor that, when wealth, intelligence, and industry are confined to the whites, and the children of white men, that the power over the tribe should become centered in the same hands. But that these causes are calculated to produce similar effects upon the Indians—the real aborigines—is disproved by every example among the thousands which the experience of the two last centuries has furnished in every part of this continent. The Cherokees have lost all that was valuable in their Indian character—have become spiritless, dependent, and depraved, as the whites and their children have become wealthy, intelligent, and powerful. So long as the Cherokees retained their primitive habits, no disposition was shown by the States, under the protection of whose government they resided, to make them subject to their laws. Such policy would have been cruel, because it would have interfered with their habits of life, the enjoyments peculiar to Indian people, and the kind of government which accorded with those habits and enjoyments. It was the power of the whites and their children among the Cherokees that destroyed the ancient laws, customs, and authority of the tribe, and subjected the natives to the rule of that most oppressive of governments, an oligarchy. There is nothing surprising in this result. From the character of the people, and the causes operating upon them, it could not be otherwise. It was this state of things that rendered it obligatory upon the State of Georgia to vindicate her rights of sovereignty, by abolishing all Cherokee government within its limits. Whether intelligent or ignorant, the State of Georgia has passed no laws violative of the liberty, personal security, or private property of any Indian. It has been the object of humanity and wisdom to separate the two classes among them, giving the rights of citizenship to those who are capable of performing its duties and properly estimating its privileges; and increasing the enjoyment, and the probability of future improvement of the ignorant and idle, by removing them to a situation where the inducements to action will be more in accordance with the character of the Cherokee people.

Your suggestion, that it would be convenient and satisfactory if yourself, the Indians, and the Governor, would make up a law-case to be submitted to the Supreme Court for the determination of the question, whether the Legislature of Georgia has competent authority to pass laws for the government of the Indians residing within its limits, however courteous the manner, and conciliatory the phraseology, cannot but be considered disrespectful to the Government of the State. No one knows better than yourself, that the Governor would grossly violate his duty, and exceed his authority, by complying with such a suggestion, and that both the letter and spirit of the powers conferred by the Constitution upon the Supreme

Court forbid its adjudging such a case. Your suggestion is but an evidence of the state of that contest in which the advocates of power are exerting themselves to increase the authority of the departments of the General Government, whilst the friends of liberty and the rights of the people are in opposition, endeavoring to sustain the sovereignty of the States. It is hoped that the efforts of the General Government to execute its contract with Georgia—to secure the continuance, and advance the happiness of the Indian tribes—and to give quiet to the country—may be so effectual as to prevent the necessity of any further intercourse upon this subject.

Yours, &c.,
GEORGE R. GILMER.

I had never felt so indignant as I did upon reading Mr. Wirt's letter. Some explanation may be necessary to understand why, and the spirit of my reply.

Mr. Wirt's first wife was my kinswoman, the daughter of Dr. George Gilmer of Albemarle, the brother of my grandfather. Mr. Wirt was poor, unknown, and undistinguished, when Dr. Gilmer took him into his house, gave him his daughter, and introduced him into the society of his friends—then the best in that part of the country of his residence. Soon after the death of his first wife, Mr. Wirt removed to Richmond, and then to Norfolk, and was in danger of being utterly ruined by dissipation, when he again prospered by marrying the daughter of Colonel Gamble of Richmond, my wife's first cousin. My wife lived with Mr. Wirt's family in Richmond, when she was a little girl going to school. Mr. Wirt had been so great a favorite with my own family friends, that he was named for his executor by my grandfather Gilmer. His niece, a young lady who had resided with him during the life of his first wife, was, after Dr. Gilmer's death, taken into his house by my wife's father, Mr. Grattan, with whom she remained until her marriage with Mr. Dabney Minor.

All these circumstances induced me to believe that Mr. Wirt expected that his age, high-standing, and intimate relationship with my family friends, would induce me to do at his request what I would refuse to another. A fee of twenty thousand dollars was certainly a very urgent inducement to every means for success.

This letter to Mr. Wirt was published in the papers of Milledgeville, without my approval. It produced the most united expression of popular approbation which I received whilst I was in the Executive Department. The people assembled en masse the night after, paraded before my house with drum and fife, and noisy acclamations. A very different expression from what I received when I recommended the appropriation of the gold mines to public purposes.

To the judges whose circuits included the Cherokee country, and whose duty it was to enforce the laws of the State upon the Indians, and the white people residing among them, I addressed the following letter:—

Executive Department, Milledgeville, 7th June, 1830.

Sir,—I send you a Proclamation, giving notice of the extension of the jurisdiction of the State over the Indian territory—a part of which is within your judicial circuit—requiring obedience to our laws from all persons residing therein. I believe myself, that the principles of humanity and policy require that no violations of our laws by Indians should be noticed for the present by our courts, except the particular offences specified in the law extending the jurisdiction of the State over them, and that these should be punished with the utmost rigor and certainty. The effect of this course will be to drive from the State all those Indians and Indian people who are unwilling to become subject to the laws of the State, and to leave the ignorant and peaceable, free from the action of their chiefs, to choose whether they will accept the offers of the General Government, and remove to the West, or remain where they are. I have no doubt but that the great body of them will remove, if their refractory chiefs can be strictly governed, and that their situations will be greatly improved by such removal. I believe that justice entitles those to remain where they are, who will be satisfied with the lands which they have improved and occupy, and so much more as may be necessary for their use. For the government of these, laws ought to be passed, as well to guard and protect their weakness and ignorance, as to punish their vices.

Very respectfully yours, &c.,
GEORGE R. GILMER.

Hon. Augustin S. Clayton.

Note.—A letter similar to the above sent to Judge Colquitt.

Executive Department, Milledgeville, 6th July, 1830.

Dear Sir,—A short time ago, I received a formal notice from a very distinguished lawyer of Maryland, (a partisan of the opposition), that he was counsel for the Cherokee Indians, and suggesting the advantage of making a case for the determination of the Supreme Court, upon the right of the State to pass laws for the government of the Indians residing within its limits.

The suggestion has been rejected as highly insulting. I understand that the President concurs with me, in deprecating the interference of the Supreme Court with this question. Nothing but the most disastrous consequences can flow from the determination of the Federal Courts, that they have appellate jurisdiction in cases brought in the Courts of Georgia, against the Indians residing within its limits. We desire no decision of that Court to sustain the sovereign rights of the State. They rest upon higher authority—the power which necessarily belonged to the State when it became independent, and which it retained, when the Constitution of the United States was formed.

The Indian question is too excitable, and of too partisan a character for the interference of the Supreme Court. The judges are men, and members of the community, subject to the same frailties and passions with others. If they could be impartial, their decisions would not be so considered by those to whom their opinions might be adverse.

There is, too, a love of power, which tempts men to be the arbiters of the destiny of others. Of all the departments of the General Government, the Judiciary alone is irresponsible. The members sacrefice no personal interest by their decisions. All men are disposed to believe that power is more safely deposited with themselves than others. All men naturally interpret instruments concerning their own power or interest most favorably to themselves. Is there not danger, therefore, that the Supreme Court may assume to itself powers which are not conferred upon it by the Constitution, and destructive of the Governments of the States? Talented men can always give plausibility to their ambitious purposes. The Supreme Court ought not, therefore, to be tempted to assume so high a power as prescribing limits to the jurisdiction of the States in all cases, for such would be the power if it could restrain the State's authority from passing laws for the government of the Indians residing within its limits,

There is, too, no probability that the State of Georgia would submit to the orders of the Court if it should determine that the laws of the State in relation to the Indians were void. It is, therefore, important that no case should be transferred from the courts of the State to the Federal Courts. I have been induced to write thus freely and fully, because it is understood at Washington City that you are desirous that the Federal Court should assume the jurisdiction of determining the extent of the right of the State to govern its Indian people. I have no doubt but that the opposition are very desirous of bringing that question before the Federal Court, in order to keep up the resistance of the whites and the half-breeds to the removal of the Cherokees. Our lawyers ought to know the object of the opposition, and refuse to be concerned in such a case.

Very respectfully yours, &c.,
GEORGE R. GILMER.

Honorable Augustin S. Clayton.

Judge Clayton, to whom this letter was addressed, was related by marriage to Mr. Wirt in several ways, and his association with Mr. Wirt and family very intimate.

The Legislature conferred upon me no authority sufficient for the prevention of trespassers upon the gold mines. I was, therefore, obliged to use such expedients as I could for that purpose. I found paper bullets but light artillery against masses of men who could not read. The proclamation giving notice of the extension of the jurisdiction of the State over the Cherokee territory, and forbidding trespasses upon the gold mines, made but slight impression upon heads ccustomed to hard knocks. I added to these the authority of a Superintendent of public lands, whose business it was to restrain trespassers by writs of the courts. I conferred this new-fangled agency upon Col. Yelverton King. The following letter explains what he was required to do.

Executive Department, Milledgeville, 21st June, 1830.

Dear Sir,—You will receive with this letter the appointment of Superintendent of the public lands in the occupancy of the Cherokees, together with instructions as to the duty which you will have to perform. I am very desirous that you should accept this appointment, and immediately. I am confident that the presence of a person of your character and firmness in the Cherokee country will be calculated to prevent riots dangerous to its peace, to preserve to the State valuable public property, and obtain from the Indians an acquiescence in the extension of the laws over them.

The Cherokees were prepared to have submitted without resistance to the laws of Georgia and the policy of the General Government, upon their failure to obtain protection from the majority of Congress. As soon, however, as it became highly probable that Congress would sustain the President in the course which he had recommended for the removal of the Indians, the opposition induced them to believe that they could find protection from the operation of the laws of Georgia and the power of the President and Congress, by appealing to the Supreme Court. A formal notice was received two days ago, from the former Attorney General of the United States, that the Cherokee Indians were his clients, that Georgia was not infallible, and that her laws exercising jurisdiction over the Indians, are in violation of treaties. It is highly probable, that the first effort to resist the authority of Georgia will be by an endeavor to secure to the Indians the gold mines. With the possession of this source of wealth, the removal of the Cherokees may be delayed a great while. The enforcement of the powers of the State to protect from trespass the gold in the lands occupied by the Cherokees, through the jurisdiction of its courts, is, therefore, the question upon which most probably the contest is to commence between the State, the Cherokees, and their allies.

The duty which you have to perform will, therefore, be of the highest importance, not only to Georgia, but the whole Union. If the State can, by any act of the General Government, be deprived of its sovereign jurisdiction over all persons residing within its limits, the whole character of our institutions will be changed, and the powers, the retention of which are most valuable to the people, because the best security for the preservation of their rights, will have been lost. The contest is one in which the country has a right to claim the services of all her citizens, and especially the patriotic and talented.

Very respectfully, yours, &c.,
GEORGE R. GILMER.

Col. Yelverton P. King.

It was ascertained very soon, that the Superintendent of public lands could do but little by writs of injunction and suits of law. The bayonets of the United States troops were found far more effective. The difficulty which remained was, that although the troops removed the citizens of Georgia and those of the adjoining States from the Indian country, the Cherokee half-breeds and the whites licensed to live among them, continued to collect gold. It was a sore trial to frontier Georgians to keep away from the golden treasure in the land which they considered theirs, whilst it was plundered by others who had no right at all. There was great danger that the frontier citizens, the Indians, and licensed occupants of the Indian country, would battle for possession of the gold mines. The following letters will give a glimpse of this danger:—

Executive Department, Milledgeville, 28th June, 1830.

Sir,—I have just received intelligence, that the Militia of Hall County are about to be marched into the country occupied by the

Cherokees, for the purpose of making prisoners of those who are engaged in digging for gold. If this information be true, and any of the Indian people are arrested, you will cause them to be liberated immediately. Explain to the Inferior Court of Hall County and to all other Magistrates, so far as you can, that it is not considered a criminal offence for the Cherokee people to dig for gold in the lands occupied by the tribe, and that they are not liable to an arrest therefor: That the title to the gold belongs to the State in consequence of its fee-simple title to the soil, and that the violations of that right can only be redressed by the Superior Court, because of its exclusive jurisdiction of all cases respecting titles to land. Endeavor to convince the Militia officers and those under their command, that the Governor alone can call them into the service of the State, except in case of sudden invasion or insurrection, and then only through the Commanding Officer of the county; that to commit acts of hostility upon the Cherokee people, without such orders, will be a very high offence; and if the death of any one should be occasioned thereby, each concerned will be guilty of murder. Endeavor to convince every one, both Georgians and Cherokees, that the public property in the gold regions will be protected. Considerable excitement is said to have been occasioned by the arrest of a number of citizens of the State by the United States troops, without legal process. Perhaps some indulgence is to be granted to acts immediately resulting therefrom. If, however, you shall find any persons persisting in violating the rights of the Indians, spare no exertions to cause such to be arrested and punished.

Much anxiety will be felt, until it shall be known with certainty whether an attack upon the Indians was really made by the Militia of Hall. Very respectfully, yours, &c.,

GEORGE R. GILMER.

Col. Yelverton King.

Executive Department, Milledgeville, 5th July, 1830.

Dear Sir,—I send you copies of communications from the War Department, by which you will perceive, that the United States troops are ordered to restrain the Indians from taking gold, and other minerals, from the lands of Georgia.

You will oblige me by showing these papers as soon as possible to the commanding officer of the United States troops, and requesting his earliest attention to their contents. It is desirable that the most cordial co-operation should exist between the United States and State Governments, upon the subject of our Indian affairs.

You are aware, that it would be contrary to my opinion of the rights of this State, to recognize by any official act, the power of the United States Government to remove the Indians from the

Cherokee lands. I believe, however, that their presence in the Cherokee country is very useful, in restraining the whites from trespassing upon the public property, and committing violence upon the Indians. The President has been informed that the Indians will be protected if possible.

A report has reached here, which I suppose to be true, that Col. Harden, of Hall County, has been arrested by the United States troops, and is now a prisoner, and that the commanding officer is at a loss to know what to do with him. It is very desirable that his release should be effected, without the determination of the courts upon the right of the troops to arrest. The effect of their presence in restraining our citizens, ought not to be lost, if it can be avoided. Present this view of the subject to the commanding officer. If you have obtained any writs of injunction against the Indians to stay waste, you will stop their service, and all further proceedings, until it is discovered whether the Indians will be restrained by the United States troops, under the orders which have been issued. I feel great interest upon this subject, because it is important to prevent any interference on the part of the Federal Court. The transfer any suit to the Federal Court, although the hope of success might be very small, would operate very injuriously, by keeping up the resistance of the whites and half-breeds. Such is no doubt the object of the opposition. The President, I am assured, unites with the authorities of the State, in deprecating any connection between this highly excitable party question, and the Supreme Court. Nothing but the most injurious consequences can follow from such an interference. Endeavor to convince the members of the profession, of the law, upon the frontier, of the injury which may result from their being instrumental in transferring from the State Courts, any suit relative to her rights of jurisdiction over the Indian people, or the Federal Court.

Very respectfully, yours, &c.,
GEORGE R. GILMER.

Col. Yelverton P. King.

The first difficulty which occurred in the enforcement of the laws of the State over the Cherokee territory, was the liberation of a squad of gold diggers, arrested by the United States troops for a violation of the laws of the United States, by the Judge of the Superior Court of the Circuit. The removal of white men from the Cherokee territory by the troops of the United States, was, at the time, the only means by which such removal could be effected. None had been placed in the hands of the Governor, or other officers of the State, sufficient for that purpose.

Chapter IX.

The impossibility of restraining trespassers upon the gold mines by any means at the command of the Governor, and the difficulties which the United States troops created by the manner in which they removed the whites from the Indian territory, induced me to call the Legislature together earlier than the prescribed time. This was done by the following proclamation.

> Whereas, thousands of persons have entered upon the lands of the State, in the occupancy of the Cherokees, and are now, and have been for some time past, employed in taking great quantities, in value, of gold therefrom: And whereas, this state of things was unforseen by the Legislature, and therefore no laws have been passed for the prevention thereof: And whereas the powers vested in the Executive Department by the Constitution and laws, do not sufficiently enable the Governor to remove or restrain such trespassers:—It is therefore considered that an extraordinary occasion has occurred, for convening the General Assembly of the State at a period earlier than that prescribed by law. I have therefore thought fit, and by virtue of the power vested in me by the Constitution, do hereby require the members of each House of the General Assembly of this State, to convene at the State-House in Milledgeville, on Monday, the eighteenth of October next, then and there to deliberate and decide on such matters as the public welfare may render necessary. GEORGE R. GILMER.

The following extracts from my message to the Legislature, will show the policy which I recommended in relation to the public lands, the gold mines, the government of the Cherokee territory, and the white persons residing among the Indians.

> In the early part of the year, gold was discovered in great quantities in the Indian lands. The Act of 1829 having fixed upon the first of June, as the time when the laws were to be extended over that part of the State, all persons seemed to consider themselves at liberty, in the mean time, to appropriate as much of its mineral riches to themselves as possible.
>
> The whole community became very much excited by rumors of the great profits made by those who were engaged in searching for gold. The love of gain became stimulated to excess. All classes of people, but especially the idle and profligate, pressed into the mineral country, with the hope of acquiring wealth with little labor. The thousands of persons thus collected together, operated upon by motives which lead to most of the disorders of society, and freed from the

restraints which the laws impose upon the evil dispositions of men, exhibited scenes of vicious indulgence, violence, and fraud, which would not have been tolerated for a moment if means could have been used to prevent them. The rights of occupancy belonging to the Indians were wholly disregarded, and they were not permitted to participate in the riches of the earth, which circumstances made common to all for the time.

So far as the United States, our sister States, and foreign Governments are concerned, the rights of jurisdiction and soil are perfect as exercised by the State over the Cherokees, and the lands occupied by them. These rights have, however, their correspondent duties. If you subject the Indians to our laws, they have a right to our protection. If the exigencies of the State require that the gold mines in the country occupied by them, should be taken possession of, such exercise of power should not be extended further than the public necessity requires. The desire of acquiring land for individual profit ought not to be the operative motive in directing what may be done. It is also due to our own character that we should have a jealous care, lest we press that necessity beyond what the public interest, the preservation and use of the public property, and the enforcement of the laws, require. Even the measure of surveying the Cherokee territory, however useful for the proper administration of the laws, may be, on account of the sensitive feelings of the humane, excited as they have been, by the selfish and improper statements of political partisans, so liable to misconstruction, that it would be magnanimously forbearing, in the Legislature, perhaps wise, to delay the adoption of that measure for the present.

In removing intruders, it will be expedient to consider all white persons such, without regard to their length of residence, or the permission of the Indians. The citizens of this and other States, who have taken refuge in the Indian country to escape from the punishment due to their crimes, or connected themselves with their society from unfitness to live in civilized communities, have not thereby acquired any claim upon the State to peculiar privileges. Much of the opposition of the Cherokees to the extension of the laws of the State over them, and to the offers made by the United States, to induce their reunion with that part of the tribe who have removed to the west of the Mississippi, have proceeded from the influence of these persons. At the same time we acknowledge that it would be harsh to compel the Indians to leave the country which they have always occupied, yet, believing that their removal to the West would be advantageous both to themselves and the people of the State, it is proper that you should take away any extrinsic causes which prevent their voluntary action. It may be proper, as well as expedient, to exempt individuals of good character from the operation of such law, upon their taking the oath to support the

Constitution and other laws of the State, and giving security that they will discharge the duties of citizens of the State. The number of white men residing among the Cherokees within the limits of the State, is estimated at two hundred and fifty, exclusive of missionaries, traders, and pedlers. About one hundred are living with Indian women; fifty have permits from the Cherokee Chiefs, and one hundred from the Cherokee Agent. Twenty-four are possessed of negro slaves.

The law extending the jurisdiction of the State over the Indians, contains no provision prohibiting white persons from entering upon their lands. The Indians will be exposed to continual vexation and disturbance, unless their rights are so secured as to enable them to obtain certain redress for their violation. Hitherto intruders have been kept off their lands by the force of the General Government. However justifiable the exertion of this power may have been formerly, it cannot be continued any longer consistently with the right of jurisdiction which has been assumed by the State. It becomes therefore an imperative duty to afford to the Cherokees, by your enactments, the same protection from intrusion which they formerly received from the United States.

The tract of land from which the Cherokees have been removed by order of the President, is supposed to contain 464,646 acres, and is now subject to be disposed of in such a manner as you may think expedient. The great object to be effected by the State in the appropriation of its lands, is the increase of its population, the excitement of its people to industry, and the accumulation of wealth. The lottery system, which has been hitherto adopted, is believed to be better calculated to attain these ends than the disposition by public sale. In an unimproved country, where capital is scarce, interest high, and every trade and employment demand labor and wealth, the surplus money in the possession of the people can be laid out more usefully in making improvements, and otherwise adding to the riches of the country, than if drawn from them to be placed in the public treasury. It has always been found more difficult to restrain improper expenditures, arising from a full treasury, than to obtain, through the powers which belong to the Government, the money which may be really required for public purposes. There are valuable gold mines in the lands to be disposed of. The public interest demands that the lots of land which contain valuable minerals shall be exempted from distribution. The spirit of speculation, which the disposition of the public lands by lottery excites, is the great objection to that system. The knowledge that the land to be disposed of contains gold, would increase that spirit to the most injurious extent. The community would become highly excited, by the hope of acquiring great wealth without labor. The morals of the people would be corrupted by the temptation held out by law, to the commission of innumerable frauds. Regular industry and economy might be suspended by restless idleness and imaginary gains. In most instances, even the successful drawers of the rich prizes would not be benefited. Prodigality is the usual result of riches suddenly and easily acquired. Mines, like the accumulation of the people's money in the public treasury,. should be managed for the general and not for individual advantage. If they prove exceedingly profitable, the State will be enabled thereby to relieve the people from taxation, improve the public roads, render the rivers navigable, and extend the advantages of education to every class of society.

Executive Department, Milledgeville, 29th Oct., 1830.

Sir,—By an act of the Legislature of Georgia, passed at its last session, all the Cherokee territory, and the persons occupying it, were subjected to the ordinary jurisdiction of the State after the first of June next then ensuing. This act has not gone into operation. The acknowledgment by the President of the right of the State to pass such an act, renders it unnecessary to say any thing in its justification. The object of this letter is to request the President that the United States troops may be withdrawn from Indian territory within Georgia. The enforcement of the non-intercourse law in the limits of the State, is considered inconsistent with the right of jurisdicion which is now exercised by its authorities and must, if continued, lead to difficulties between the officers of the United States and State Governments, which it is very desirable should be avoided. No doubt is entertained, that the object of the President in ordering the United States troops into the Cherokee territory was the preservation of the peace of the Union. The motive is duly appreciated.

The Legislature of the State is now in session. The special object of its meeting is the enforcement of the laws of the State within the Cherokee country, and the punishment of intrusion into it, by persons searching for gold. Its power is amply sufficient for that purpose. The law for the punishment of trespassers upon the public lands will go into operation within a few days; the President is therefore requested to withdraw the troops as soon as it can be conveniently done. The conduct of Major Wager has been very severe to the gold diggers. In some instances, unoffending citizens have been made the subjects of punishment in violation of the rights and the authority of the State. Complaints have been made to this department and redress asked for. The removal of the troops is believed to be the most effectual means of preventing the repetition of such injuries. Information has also been received at this department, that the digging for gold is still carried on in various parts of the Cherokee territory, and that the extent of country containing mines is so great, that it is wholly impossible to prevent it by the use of military force alone. It is said that the Indians are even more extensively employed in taking gold than before the arrival of the troops. This proceeds from their residence within the country, intimate acquaintance with it, and other means of avoiding the operation of the troops. The fear of the whites restrained them previously.

The President is assured, that whatever measures may be adopted by the State of Georgia, in relation to the Cherokees, the strongest desire will be felt to make them accord with the policy which has been adopted by the present administration of the General Government. Very respectfully, yours, &c.,

GEORGE R. GILMER.

To the President of the United States.

Upon receiving an answer from the Secretary of War, that the order had been issued to the commanding officer of the troops to retire from the Cherokee territory, I made the following communication to the Legislature:—

Executive Department, Milledgeville, 29th Oct., 1830.

I transmit to both Houses of the General Assembly, copies of a communication received from the War Department, in answer to a letter requesting of the President the withdrawal of the United States troops from the territory of the State occupied by the Cherokees. The Legislature will perceive, in the conduct of the President in this matter, as well as in others, the disposition to accord to Georgia all her rights. The removal of the United States troops from the territory occupied by the Cherokees, creates an immediate and pressing necessity for the passage of such laws as may effectually restrain all persons from entering into that territory for the purpose of taking possession of the public lands, or taking valuable minerals therefrom, without license from the State.

GEORGE R. GILMER.

Soon after I recommended to the Legislature to authorize the President to grant fee-simple reserves to the Cherokee Chiefs, in making a treaty with them for the lands of the State, as follows:

Executive Department, December 8th, 1830.

From information received from various sources, it is believed that the efforts of the President to remove the Cherokees from within the limits of the State would be essentially aided by the passage of resolutions by the Legislature, giving its assent to the President's granting to the Cherokees fee-simple reserves, in any treaty or contract which he may make with them. It is known that there are two classes among the Cherokees, very widely separated from each other. One consists of white men with Indian families, and the half-breeds. This class have both wealth and intelligence, and now control the tribe. Some of them are qualified to discharge the duties of citizens, and are said to be desirous of doing so, provided they can have secured to them fee-simple titles to reasonable portions of their lands. Others would be willing to remove with the tribe beyond the Mississippi if they could receive lands in the same way, so that they might be enabled to sell them for their value, either to individuals or to the United States. They are now, or soon will be, convinced that their love of power cannot be gratified if the tribe remains in its present situation. If, therefore, their cupidity can be satisfied, the chief difficulty to its removal will be overcome. The other class of Cherokees are composed of unmixed, aboriginal people, deprived of their former pride of character and love of enterprise, debased into slavish dependence upon their wealthy chiefs, and corrupted by the degrading vices which they have contracted from their intercourse with vicious white men. This entire class would willingly remove to the country prepared for the tribe by the United States upon the terms which are now offered, if the consent of their principal men could be obtained. The President cannot offer to the principal men reserves with fee-simple titles, as the fee belongs to the State. For the purpose, therefore, of placing at the control of the President the means which are believed to be most efficient in making a treaty with the Cherokees, permit me to recommend that you pass resolutions authorizing the President to make such reserves as has been done in former treaties, conditions that the United States pay to the State their value. This is due to the Indians who understand the peculiar advantages which their country presents for acquiring wealth, and how to use them for their own benefit. It will aid the President in his efforts to remove the Indians, and if successful, will be of incalculable advantage to the State in relieving it from its embarrassing relations with the Cherokees.

Permit me to avail myself of this occasion to suggest to the Legislature the expediency of not interfering with the right of the Cherokees to occupy their territory for the present, as the policy best calculated to obtain their peaceable removal.

GEORGE R. GILMER.

Executive Department, Milledgeville, 18th January, 1831.

Sir,—Your letter of the 12th of November last was duly received, in which you suggested the importance to the success of future negotiations with the Cherokees for the relinquishment of the lands occupied by them, that the State of Georgia should authorize the President to grant fee-simple reservations to their principal men, upon condition of the United States paying to the State a reasonable price therefor.

An extract from your letter containing this suggestion was laid before the Legislature during its late session. It was not acted on, because at that time, and until very near the termination of the session, a bill was pending, the object of which was to dispose of all the lands within the State in the occupancy of the Cherokees, in such manner as would, if it had passed, have made the consideration of your proposition entirely unnecessary. After that bill became a law, although it passed in a different form from that which was originally proposed, yet found it difficult among the hurried proceedings of the close of the session, to procure the united consent of the members of the Legislature to the particular conditions upon which such reservations should be made. No resolutions whatever were, therefore, introduced upon the subject, and especially as the Legislature had, at two former sessions (1826 and 1827) granted to the President the authority asked for. Copies of these resolutions are sent you.

The people of the State, and its constituted authorities, have entire confidence that the President, in contracting with the Cherokees for their removal from Georgia will use no means adverse to the interest of the State, or which may not be necessary for the accomplishment of that object.

Humanity to the Indians, the maintenance of the rights of the State, and the preservation of the Union, require that every exertion should be made to put a speedy termination to the Indian question. The spirit which has manifested itself in Congress, and among the people of some of the State in opposition to the measures pursued by the President to execute the contract of the United States with Georgia for the removal of the Cherokees, and the improvement of their condition, has produced the most serious alarm, lest the strength of the Constitution and our free institutions may not be able to resist the machinations of party fraud and violence.

From information received from various sources, there is but little prospect of procuring the immediate consent of the Cherokees to remove beyond the Mississippi. The leaders of the opposition have been completely successful in producing the belief among their influential men, that the Supreme Court will make a foreign and independent nation of their tribe, and thereby exempt the Indian people from the laws of Georgia. Until they are convinced that this is a mistake, it will be useless to treat with them. If the Supreme Court should fail to make its decisions correspond with the designs of those opposed to the Government, my information is, that the

Cherokees will at once agree to relinquish their right of occupancy, and remove from the State.

> Very respectfully yours, &c.,
> GEORGE R. GILMER.

Hon. John H. Eaton.

The law which was passed for the protection of the gold mines, directed the Governor to take possession of them without placing at his command any adequate means for obeying its injunctions.

I communicated to the Legislature upon that subject as follows:

Excutive Department, Milledgeville, 4th Dec., 1830.

The United States troops having been withdrawn from the Cherokee territory, it is expected that numerous persons will be again tempted into the gold country. The law which has been passed for the protection of the gold mines requires the Governor to take possession of them, without prescribing the means to be used, or placing any at his control for that purpose. Although I am authorized to use military force to defend the mines, it will be in vain to attempt to do so, until that part of the law which makes the digging of gold a crime goes into operation.

Permit me, therefore, to ask of the Legislature that it will devise some effectual and immediate means for the protection of this public property. Even after the taking of gold shall have become a highly penal offence, the law will be continually violated, if no other means of prevention are provided than what are pointed out in the law which has been passed. I would, therefore, respectfully recommend to the Legislature, either to organize an efficient guard to be stationed at the mines, or to place all the mines in the possession of individuals, under such contracts as may induce their occupation.
GEORGE R. GILMER.

The case of the Indian, Tassels, who committed a murder within that part of the Cherokee territory which had been added to Hall County, for the purpose of giving jurisdiction to the courts of the State over the Indians and the whites residing among them, excited the notice of the whole country, and in some sections violent abuse of the authorities of Georgia. Tassels was arrested, indicted, and tried with all the caution observed by our courts in such cases, found guilty, and hung just as if the deed had been done on the eastern instead of the western side of the Chattahoochee River. The judge before whom he was tried, suspended passing sentence until he consulted the convention of judges upon the question which was made, whether the court had the legal and constitutional power to try the case. The judges in convention decided unanimously that the power belonged to the court.

All that the Indians asked of the whites when Tassels was arrested was, that they should be permitted to put him to death in their own way.

Application was made to the Chief Justice of the United States, on the part of the Indians, to interpose the authority of the Supreme Court, to prevent the execution of the sentence. The Chief Justice granted a citation to the Governor of the State, and to the Sheriff of Hall County, to appear before the Supreme Court to have the case examined into.

The Chief Justice knew when he granted the writ, that it was impossible for the officers of his court or the Indians upon whose application it was granted, to serve the process upon the officers of Georgia, whose duty it was to hang Tassels. The citation was sent through the mail to the Governor. No process reached the Sheriff of Hall, so that he would have had no excuse if he had failed to execute the judgment of the Court. The whole proceeding could have had no purpose, except to excite doubts in the public mind about the propriety of the conduct of the authorities of Georgia, and raise popular clamor against them.

What would have been done if the writ of error granted by the Chief Justice had been regularly served may be conjectured from the following message sent to the Legislature, and the resolutions consequent upon it.

Executive Department, December 22d, 1830.

I submit to the Legislature for its consideration the copy of a communication received this day, purporting to be signed by the Chief Justice of the United States, and to be a citation to the State of Georgia to appear before the Supreme Court on the second Monday in January next, to answer to that tribunal for having caused a person, who had committed murder within the limits of the State, to be tried and convicted thereof.

The object of this mandate is to control the State in the exercise of its ordinary jurisdiction, which, in criminal cases, has been vested by its constitution exclusively in its Superior Courts. So far as concerns exercise of the power which belongs to the Executive Department, orders received from the Supreme Court for the purpose of staying, or in any manner interfering with the decisions of the Courts of the State in the exercise of their constitutional jurisdiction, will be disregarded; and any attempt to enforce such orders will be resisted with whatever force the laws have placed at my command.

If the judicial power thus attempted to be exercised by the Courts of the United States, is submitted to or sustained, it must eventuate in the utter annihilation of the State government, or in other consequences not less fatal to the peace and prosperity of our present highly favored country.   GEORGE R. GILMER.

Resolved, by the Senate and House of Representatives of the State of Georgia, in General Assembly met, That they view with feelings of deep regret, the interference by the Chief Justice of the Supreme Court of the United States in the administration of the criminal laws of this State, and that such an interference is a flagrant violation of her rights.

Resolved further, That his Excellency the Governor be, and he and every other officer of this State is hereby requested and enjoined, to disregard any and every mandate and process that has been, or shall be served upon him or them, purporting to proceed from the Chief Justice or any Associate Justice, of the Supreme Court of the United States, for the purpose of arresting the execution of any of the criminal laws of this State.

And be it further resolved, That his Excellency the Governor be, and he is hereby authorized and required, with all the force and means placed at his command by the Constitution and laws of this State, to resist and repel any and every invasion, from whatever quarter, upon the administration of the criminal laws of this State.

Resolved, That the State of Georgia will never so far commit her sovereignty as an independent State, as to become a party to the case sought to be made before the Supreme Court of the United States, by the writ in question.

Resolved, That his Excellency the Governor be, and he is hereby authorized, to communicate to the Sheriff of Hall County, by express, so much of the foregoing resolutions, and such orders as are necessary to insure the full execution of the laws in the case of George Tassels, convicted of murder, in Hall County.

The Senate concurred with the House of Representatives in the passage of the foregoing preamble and resolutions.

Whilst I was stationed among the Indians, in 1814, in command of a detachment of United States troops, I became acquainted with a white man by the name of Rogers, whose wife was a half-breed Cherokee woman. He was an active, sensible, thriving man, and his sons promising young men. William was afterwards Clerk to the Cherokee Council, and to the Delegation sent by the tribe to Washington City. When the State extended its jurisdiction over the Cherokee territory, I wrote the following letter to Rogers. The free and familiar expression of my feelings and opinions about the Cherokees, the policy which was best for them to pursue, and the account of passing events which this letter gives, does better what is one of the purposes of writing this book than any account which I might write now.

Executive Department, Milledgeville, March 10th, 1831.

My Dear Sir,—I wish it had been possible for you so to have complied with the laws of the State, in relation to the Cherokee territory, as to have avoided any embarrassment to yourself and family, and all danger of loss of property. I have always had great respect for your character, as an honest man, and was chiefly induced to recommend the Legislature to permit white men to continue their residence among the Cherokees by my knowledge of yourself and family. I sincerely regret that my object should have been defeated, by the construction which you have put upon the obligation which you suppose you would incur by taking the oath required by the law. I am exceedingly anxious that the present disturbed and unsettled state of our Indian population should be quieted as early as possible. My desire is that the State should act justly and humanely towards you and those with whom you are connected. To do this will be extremely difficult, so long as the present opposition is continued to the Government of the State, and those of your people who are industrious, intelligent, and honest, are mingled with the mass of the Aborigines. However well fitted many of the whites, half-breeds, and their children may be for the support and preservation of an orderly and well-conducted Government, the Indians are not so, and never will be until their present situation is changed. I am fully convinced, that the happiness of every Indian will be advanced by the removal of the tribe beyond the limits of the State. I am also convinced, that the sooner this can be done, the greater will be the advantage which the Cherokees will derive from it. I am in the situation which enables me to form more correct opinions of the probable future course of the legislation of the State than your people are. I have incurred a great deal of ill-will from our own citizens, by my determined opposition to the passage of laws which would have oppressed you. I claim the right, therefore, of being

listened to as a friend, whose intention is to serve his country, and
all classes of its population faithfully. You are perhaps aware,
that but for a provision inserted in the law of the last session, in
its last stage, the Cherokees would have been deprived of the whole
of their territory without any equivalent or pay for it: You, and all
others, therefore, who wish to secure for yourselves reserves or
compensation for your improvements and the right of occupation,
ought to be convinced, that by resisting the offers of the United
States Government to give you lands to the west of the Mississippi
for your present possessions, and reserves to those who may have
made actual improvements, or desire to remain where you are, and
become citizens of the State, are essentially injuring yourselves. I
tell you what I know to be true, that every act of opposition on the
part of the Cherokees to the exercise of the jurisdiction of the
State, or the policy of the General Government, but renders their
removal more certain, and with less regard to their feelings and
interests. All hopes of resisting the Government of Georgia through
Congress, the Supreme Court, or the President, are now at an
end. The Choctaw Treaty has been ratified by the Senate by a vote
of 33 to 12, and the appropriation to carry it into effect made by
both Houses by large majorities. Congress has refused to order your
annuities paid to the tribe, instead of to individuals, as the President has directed. The President has sent a message to the Senate,
stating that he has no right to interfere with the legislation of Georgia, or to enforce the non-intercourse law, since the State has extended her laws over the Cherokees within its limits. I know how
much your people have been deceived in the protection you have
sought from the Supreme Court. You have thrown your money to
the winds; for not the slightest respect will be paid by the authorities of the State to the orders of the Court, if its decisions should be
different from what I am almost sure it will be. What then does
duty to yourselves require, under such circumstances? Surely to
acquiesce in the necessity, which no exertion can overcome, and to
attempt which would be inevitable ruin. The sooner, the more
certainly will you be able to make a contract with the United States
satisfactory to all parties. Many of the respectable white men and
half-breeds who have families, are desirous of remaining in the
country, and of becoming citizens of the State, rather than remove
to Arkansas. I believe you are mistaken. However respectable,
industrious, and intelligent your children may be, they never can
associate upon an equality with our people. Many individuals
among us may be free from prejudices against the Indian people,
but it will be long before our society will become so. I believe you
to be an excellent citizen. I have heard the most favorable accounts
of your two oldest sons, for whom I have an affectionate remembrance. Yet, my advice to you, and to them, is to accompany the

Cherokee people in their move. You can be more useful, and consequently happier, with them than with us. You will find that many of those who have been most active in effecting your removal, will be your surest friends in securing to you an independent Government, and every other advantage tending to the improvement and happiness of your people.

Cherokees are naturally jealous of what comes from Georgia. Dr. Reese, of Jasper County, the member of our Legislature, is, however, a cousin of Boudinot, Adairs, and others among them, and they know he will not deceive them. Let them consult him as to the course they ought to pursue. If your son William will visit me, he shall be treated with kindness, and I will give him all the information in my possession which may enable you to determine what may be the best course for you to pursue.

I shall regret very much to see injustice done to the Cherokees, and so far as I can, will prevent it. I am bound, however, to defend the rights of the State, and cannot but hope that the time will soon arrive, when, in doing so, I shall meet with no opposition from our Indian people.
Your friend,
GEORGE R. GILMER.
Mr. John Rogers.

Shortly after the execution of Tassels, I received a notification from John Ross, the Cherokee Chief, that his people were about to apply to the Supreme Court of the United States, for an injunction to restrain the State of Georgia from exercising jurisdiction over the Cherokee territory, accompanied by a printed paper, without signature, purporting to be a bill in equity, brought by the Cherokee nation, against the State of Georgia. The case thus made was, however, dismissed by the Supreme Court, its only purpose seeming to be, to give to the opponents of the Administration an elevated stand from which they might be heard by the people in their denunciations. The Court, in pronouncing its decision, instead of confining itself to the examination of the question, whether the Cherokees were a foreign nation, and capable of suing the State of Georgia, made a statement wholly irrelevant, without proof, and contrary to the truth. The following extracts from a message to the Legislature may aid others in understanding this matter.

The Court affirms, that no case could be better calculated to excite its sympathy than the conduct of Georgia to the Cherokees: That they have been continually deprived of their lands, until they at present retain no more than what is necessary for their comfortable subsistence: That they form a State capable of governing themselves: That the acts of the Government recognize them to be a State, and that the Courts are bound by those acts: That they have the unquestioned right to the lands which they occupy; and intimate to them that it will redress their wrongs when the application is made in proper form.

What wrong has Gerogia done to its Indian people to call for this extraordinary sympathy of the Court? They are in the peaceable possession of their occupant rights. Intruders have been removed from among them by severe penal laws. None of the burdens of Government have been imposed upon them. Instead of being reduced to a remnant of the land not more than sufficient for their comfortable subsistence, they are in the possession of near five millions of acres in this State alone, of which the Aborigines do not cultivate more than five thousand. They are indeed becoming more and more destitute. Not, however, from want of land, but because their situation is unsuitable for the improvement and happiness of our Indian people.

Is it true that the Cherokees have an unquestionable and hitherto unquestioned right to the lands which they occupy? These lands form portions of the territory of the States of North Carolina, Tennessee, Alabama, and Georgia. That portion which is in Tennessee was ceded by North Carolina to the United States, upon the express condition that it should form a common fund for the benefit of the Union, and be applied to the payment of the public debt. That portion which is in Alabama, was sold to the United States by this State for a valuable consideration, and before any attempt had been made to exercise jurisdiction over them. In consequence of which sale, it was made a condition of the admission of the State of Alabama into the Union, that it should disclaim all title to the Indian lands within its limits, the United States declaring by law that it had the sole and exclusive power to dispose of them. The United States has acknowledged that this State has both the right of soil and jurisdiction over that portion which is within its limits.

It is difficult to conceive of any proposition tending to more absurd consequences than that laid down by the Court, that any Indian tribe with which the United States form contracts to which the term Treaty may be affixed, becomes a nation capable of governing itself, and entitled to the recognition of the courts as states. It would bring into being hundreds of states utterly incapable of self-defence, or exercising one attribute of national sovereignty. If the opinion of the courts be correct, then all the territory which was acquired by the original thirteen Provincial Governments, of various Indian tribes, is yet the property of the Aborigines, because the treaties by which it was obtained were invalid, not having been made by the King of Great Britain, who alone had the power of entering into national compacts.

Another difficulty, equally embarrassing, would arise out of our relations with the Cherokees themselves. A few years ago the United States removed a portion of that tribe to the west of the Mississippi, placed them upon the public land, and have since made several treaties with them. Which is now the Cherokee nation, the Indians who reside on the lands of the United States, or those within Georgia? But whatever obligations the United States may have incurred by its contracts with the Cherokees, it has no constitutional authority to limit, or in any manner alter the territorial rights which belonged to this State when it became a member of the Union.

Upon no subject has there been more misrepresentation than in relation to the government of the Cherokees, and the civilization of the people of that tribe. Upon examination, it will be found that the Aboriginal people are as ignorant, thoughtless, and improvident, as formerly; without any of the spirit and character which distinguished them when war was their employment, and their support derived from the forest: that none of them in this State, with the exception of one family, have acquired property, or been at all benefitted by the improvements which have been made by others among them; that the chief, the president of the council, the judges, marshal and sheriffs, and most other persons concerned in the administration of the Government, are the descendants of Europeans, and many of them citizens of this and the adjoining States; and that the Indians, instead of living under their own simple usages and customs, have been compelled to submit to a system of laws and police wholly unsuited to their condition

After the passage of the law for removing white persons from the Cherokee territory, who had no license to remain, and for extending the State's jurisdiction over the Cherokee territory, the missionaries and their assistants, to the number of twelve, held a public meeting in the Indian country, where they passed resolutions, calling upon the people of the United States to take part with the Indians in resisting the laws of Georgia, and declaring that they considered the removal of the Cherokees to the west of the Mississippi, an event most earnestly to be deprecated. I mention this fact, to show the spirit which directed the conduct of the missionaries who resided among the Indians, and to justify the course pursued by the authorities of the State in removing them.

I found it impossible to protect the Indian country from

intruders, and the gold mines from trespassers, by the means provided by the laws. I asked the Legislature for the authority to form a guard to execute that duty. It was granted. The guard was authorized to arrest any person guilty of the violation of the laws of the State in the Cherokee territory. It consisted of forty men, under efficient officers, and was stationed among the Indians near the gold mines.

I addressed letters to every white man of any influence who lived among the Indians, whose name and residence was known, especially to every religious missionary, urging them to take the oath to obey the Constitution and laws of the State, and take licenses, to remain in the State. I also caused one hundred copies of the laws in relation to the Cherokee country and people, to be distributed among them, so that no one might be punished for offences ignorantly committed.

Two hundred and three white men took the required oath, and were licensed to remain among the Cherokees. Some removed, and others were arrested.

The guard found great difficulty in preventing trespassers upon the gold mines. The frontier people of the State, who had been engaged in mining before the passage of the law making it penal to do so, were greatly irritated by the clause which excluded them from any participation in the distribution of the public lands. The people of the adjoining States, were in a hurry to get what gold they could, before the lands were appropriated.

Soon after the guard entered the mining districts, a number of persons were made prisoners for taking gold contrary to law, and marched off to the nearest judicial officer for commitment. A large body of trespassers followed them for the purpose of rescuing their arrested associates. They attacked the guard. One of the attacking party was wounded. The guard was at the time under the command of Col. Nelson, a brave but violent man. I wrote the following letter upon the subject to Gen. Sanford:

Executive Department, Milledgeville, 27th Jan. 1831.

Dear Sir,—I am well aware of the difficulties which you have to encounter in preventing trespass upon the gold mines by the lawless people upon the frontiers, although I had not anticipated the resistance which it appears you have met with from the citizens of this State. I feel perfectly confident that your command will succeed in protecting the public property. The danger, toil and embarrassment, which it may encounter, will but add to the honor of success, and the extent of public favor which it will deserve.

Col. Nelson and the members of the guard under his command, have united great prudence and spirit in the manner in which they have arrested the violaters of the law. Be pleased to express to Col. Nelson my decided approbation of his conduct, and the high sense I entertain of his gallantry, and to the members of the guard under his command, my thanks for the soldier-like manner in which they executed the orders of their commanding officer, and for the efficient service they have rendered to the State.

I think it highly probable that the resistance you have met with from citizens of the State, has proceeded entirely from those who are, by the late law, deprived of a draw in the land lottery, on account of their previous trespass upon the mines. It would be useful to inform this class of people that, as the law is yet subject to alterations, the only probable means of restoring themselves to the right of which they have been deprived, will be by aiding the guard in the discharge of its duties. It is important that the guard should so act as to avoid, if possible, any confirmed hostility on the part of those who are disposed to see the laws enforced. I rely with full confidence upon your judgment and prudence in discharging the duties of your command.

Very respectfully, yours, &c.,
GEORGE R. GILMER.

Col. John W. Sanford.

The following letter to an influential lawyer in the Cherokee country will exhibit some of the obstructions which had to be overcome in enforcing the jurisdiction of the State:

Executive Department, Milledgeville, 3d Feb., 1831.

Sir,—Your letter, with an affidavit of Mark Castlebury inclosed, was received last night. I had previously known of the reports put into circulation, as to the conduct of the guard. Its officers and men are citizens of the State, and equally with others answerable to individuals and to the State, for any offences which they may commit. After the taking of gold from the ungranted lands of the State was made highly penal by law, I believed that I would have the assistance of every good citizen in bringing to punishment those who should trespass upon this public property. The commander of the guard was so informed. I regret exceedingly to understand that I have been mistaken, and that the disposition has been shown to protect and rescue from prosecution the guilty. I am aware that much discontent prevails among those who were engaged in digging for gold previous to the passage of the law forbidding it, on account of their having been excluded by its provisions from participating in the benefit of the lottery. If they expect to obtain compensation by continuing their employment in defiance of its injunctions, and the means placed at my command to prevent it, they will deceive themselves. Punishment will at some time or other be the certain consequence of such conduct. A different course may, and most probably will, induce the next Legislature to repeal that part of the law which excludes them from draws. In fact the entire law is at present in abeyance, except so much as requires the survey of the lands. The lottery will not take place until after the next session of the Legislature, even if the Indian right of occupancy should be purchased previous to that time. Though the gold diggers may disregard the laws of the State and the danger of punishment, their own interest ought to dictate to them the policy of aiding the Executive in preserving the gold mines from intrusion.

I have been informed that the lawless people from other States are not only determined to persist in taking gold if they are not prevented by force, but that they are using their influence to excite the Cherokees to resist the jurisdiction of the State. Whilst the opposition to the President and the administraion of the Government are attacking the rights of Georgia through the Supreme Court, and by other means, with the greatest energy and virulence, is it possible that any citizen, who deserves to be so called, can be found aiding or giving countenance to those who are trespassing upon its authority, violating its laws, and defying its power? The united and determined support of the people can alone sustain the State in enforcing its jurisdiction over the Cherokees, and in exercising the right of ownership over the soil which they occupy within its limits. I know that many respectable persons were concerned in taking gold from the Cherokee territory previous to the passage of the late law. It is very certain, however, that a large part of those from other States who were so employed, and many from this, were of the most dissolute and abandoned class of society, and that, such persons cannot be restrained from continuing to search for gold, notwithstanding the prohibition by law, but by force and punishment. Is it therefore patriotic to endeavor to excite the people to enmity against the guard, who are required by their duty to arrest and bring to punishment these lawless persons? The guard has other important duties to perform besides the protection of the gold mines. The white men who reside among the Indians, and who have been opposing the jurisdiction of the State, must be removed; the Indian Chiefs must be controlled; and the surveyors, who are now about commencing their work must be protected. Under such circumstances, I cannot but hope that it will meet with support instead of opposition.

I have minute information as to the affair at Leathersford, and it differs in every respect from the statement in Castlebury's affidavit. It is not at present so important to inquire into the accuracy of these different accounts, as to unite the people in protecting the gold mines. I have great reliance upon your prudence and integrity. If any member of the guard has done wrong, I have no power to punish him; that belongs to the courts. The motives of those who have urged you to send to me charges against the guard, may have been the hope that it will be withdrawn. If they had such an object in view, they have deceived themselves. Increased vigilance and force will be used, if necessary, for the protection of the mines, and to bring to punishment those who trespass upon them.

Very respectfully, yours, &c.,
GEORGE R. GILMER.

Robert Mitchell, Esq.

This affray became rather famous as the battle of Leathersford. I thanked the guard for its conduct by a letter written in a style suited to the battle and the combatants.

During my service in Congress, two years afterwards, one of the young ladies of the mess to which my wife and myself belonged, played Governor Gilmer's march. A Scotch gentleman who was travelling in this country, and passing the evening with us, asked my wife on what occasion the march had been composed. He was answered by Colonel Jones, with the quickness so instinctive with him, "The battle of Leathersford!"

I endeavored to procure the services of the most active and intelligent gentlemen of the counties which bordered on the Cherokee territory, to sustain the authority of the State by enforcing the laws, as will appear from the following circular letter:

Executive Department, Milledgeville, 26th Jan., 1831.

Sir,—From the operation of various causes, it is highly probable that the Cherokees will resist the enforcement of the laws of the State. Obedience must be compelled. The gard which has been organized and stationed among them, under the command of excellent officers, will be a most efficient instrument for this purpose. It is not, however, sufficient, encouraged as the Cherokees have been by the opposition to the administration of the General Government, and the late proceedings of the Supreme Court. Will the people aid the Executive Department in defending the honor and character, and preserving unimpaired the rights and sovereignty of Georgia? If so, let them organize volunteer companies in every frontier county near the Cherokees, for the special object of compelling the Indians to submit to the authority of the laws, and of removing vicious and refractory white men residing among them, whose influence has been directed to excite them to disobedience.

You are requested to encourage the formation of a volunteer company in your county. If one can be raised, it is desirable that it should be done as soon as possible, that organization and discipline may be acquired before it is called into service. The company must be infantry. It is important, however, that it should be able to act as mounted infantry if necessary.

Very respectfully, yours, &c.,
GEORGE R. GILMER.

Note.—A letter similar to the above was sent to the following gentlemen, viz.:—William Ezzard and Maj. Hines Holt of DeKalb, Col. Nathan S. Hutchins of Gwinnett, Col. Allen Flambrough, Col. I. W. A. Petit, and Col. Andrew Moore.

Executive Department, Milledgeville, 4th Feb., 1831.

Sir,—I am of the opinion, that the law does not authorize the granting of licenses to any white person to reside among the Cherokees, except those who were residents at the time of its passage. The object of the Legislature was not to increase the number of white persons among the Cherokees, but to remove those whose presence might be injurious to the interests of the State.

The time from the passage of the law until the first of March was allowed to the white men residing among the Cherokees to remove, or to comply with its requirements.

I concur in your opinion, that postmasters in the Cherokee territory are not the agents of the United States, who are exempted from punishment for their residence among the Cherokees after the first of March. If the postmasters think differently, the question can only be determined by the Courts; and to that tribunal you are directed to carry it, if those postmasters to whom you may not grant licenses may think proper not to remove.

The missionaries who have publicly taken part with the Cherokees, in opposition to the rights of the State, must not receive licenses.

I am very much gratified at the information derived from the expedition to the Sixes. It is very important to keep the Indians quiet. Their rights should not only be respected, but protected with vigilance from violation. You are requested to assure them, that this is the disposition of the State, and that you will arrest every white man who may commit crimes affecting them. The State requires of the Cherokees submission to its authority, and is bound in return to protect them.

I have received complaints from the people at Leathersford, of the conduct of the guard. I have no doubt but that you are correct in supposing, that those who intend to violate the laws will, if possible, excite opposition to the guard. This state of things increases the necessity for prudence in its intercourse with the frontier people. It would, perhaps, prevent collisions, if the guard would keep within the Cherokee territory in their expeditions, unless when engaged in actual pursuit of intruders, or in making commitments, and attending to prosecutions.

I am now satisfied that I was mistaken in supposing that you would have the aid of all the citizens of the State. Increased vigilance and energy will therefore be necessary. I send you a copy of the information received in relation to the guard. In order to prevent enmity on the part of its members against those who have made these charges, I would suggest the propriety of confining the knowledge of them to yourself and Col. Nelson.

Very respectfully, yours, &c.,
GEORGE R. GILMER.

Col. J. W. A. Sanford.

By a clause of the law, all agents of the United States were exempted from its operation. The judge of one of the circuits which included the Cherokee territory, the relative of Mr. Wirt, imagined that he had read somewhere, that missionaries among the Cherokees were agents of the Government. He charged several missionaries who were brought before him upon a writ of *habeas corpus*, upon his own assumption that missionaries were agents of the United States Government, and therefore exempt by law from arrest. His judicial imaginings were not true. The missionaries heard the plea made for them by the Court, knew that it was not true, yet held their tongues, and took the benefit of the mistake. I immediately wrote the following letters, to the Secretary of War, and Postmaster-General, sent their answers to the guard and ordered the discharged persons to be again arrested:

Executive Department, Milledgeville, 20th April, 1831.

Sir,—By a law of this State, all white persons, except agents of the United States, are prohibited from residing within the territory occupied by the Cherokees, unless authorized by license from the Governor.

This law resulted from the active influence which that class of persons were exercising in opposition to the humane policy of the General Government, and the rights of Georgia. Fugitives from justice, outcasts from society, and trespassers upon the gold mines, had an interest very readily understood in preventing both the removal of the Cherokees beyond the Mississippi, and the operation of the laws upon themselves. Some of the missionaries who were stationed among the Indians refused to obey. Individuals among them acted the part of political incendiaries, misdirected the Indians, misstated facts, and perverted public opinion, so as to embarrass the Administration of the General Government in doing its duty to the State. Among those who have been arrested for violating the laws, is a man by the name of John Thompson, reported to be a clergyman, and a missionary from some religious society in the New England States. He was, upon his arrest, carried before one of the judges of the Superior Court, by writ of habeas corpus, and discharged upon the ground that he was a missionary, and that missionaries were agents of the United States, and consequently not subject to the penalty of the law prohibiting the residence of white persons among the Indians. It is not necessary to say any thing about the correctness of the decision. It is due both to the United States and Georgia, that its effects should be obviated. Mr. Thompson is reported to have been very active in stirring up the Indians to their attempt to sustain an Independent Government, and no doubt will feel secure in continuing his mischievous exertions, unless the laws of the State can have their proper operation upon him. For this purpose, I must request from you an official assurance, that this Rev. John Thompson is not an agent of the United States, and that religious missionaries, as such, are not agents of the United States Government.

It is very desirable that your answer should be received as soon as possible. Very respectfully, yours, &c.,

GEORGE R. GILMER.

Honorable John H. Eaton.

Executive Department, Milledgeville, 79th April, 1831.

Sir,—At the last session of the Legislature of this State, a law was passed, making it highly penal for white persons, except agents of the United States, to continue their residence within the territory of the State occupied by the Cherokees, after the first of March then next ensuing, without taking the oath to support the Constitution and laws of the State, and obtaining a license for such residence, from the Governor or his agent. The object of this law was to remove from among the Cherokees, fugitives from justice, trespassers upon the gold mines, and those who under various pretences of attachment to the Indians, had obtained lucrative situations for themselves, and were using their influence in opposing the policy of the General Government, and the rights of Georgia. Immediately after the passage of the law, means were used for making its provisions known to all upon whom it might operate. Of the number of white persons who were residents in the State among the Cherokees (reported by Col. Montgomery to be 300), 250 have taken the required oath, and received licenses.

Two Presbyterian clergymen, Samuel Worcester and John Thompson, who are understood to have exercised extensive influence over the Indians, and been very active in exciting their prejudices against the Administration of both the General and State Governments, have refused either to leave the territory reserved to the Indians, or take the oath required of white persons. They have consequently been arrested in the same manner as others thus acting. Worcester has been discharged by the Superior Court, because he was postmaster at Echota; and Thompson, because it was reported that he was a missionary; the Court deciding that postmasters and missionaries were agents of the United States, and consequently exempted from the penalties of the law. It is wholly unnecesary to inquire into the correctness of this decision. The General Government will certainly not permit its postmasters to use a privilege arising from their official stations, to thwart its operations, or defy the jurisdiction of the State. The object of this communication, is to request you to dismiss Samuel Worcester from the office of postmaster. If you consider it important to continue the postoffice at Echota, I would recommend William Tarvain, who is said to be a respectable white man, to fill the place of S. Worcester. If Worcester is not now removed, he will, without doubt, consider himself authorized to continue his seditious conduct. No disposition is felt, in executing the laws of the State, to prevent the diffusion of the light of knowledge and Christianity, among the Indians. It is due to the State, however, that those who under the cloak of religious ministry, teach discord to our misguided Indian people, and opposition to rulers, should be compelled to know, that obedience to the laws is both a religious and civil duty.

I transmit to you for your information a correspondence between this Department and the Board of Directors of the United Brethren's Missions, in relation to one of their missionaries, Mr. Byhan, who is postmaster at Spring Place. Mr. Byhan is said to be a respectable man, and I have no doubt will hereafter, under the direction of the pious men who employ him, confine himself to his duty.

I have no objection to his continuing in his present office, if such should be your desire. We ask only for the removal of political incendiaries.

The Baptist missionary has taken the oath, and those employed by the Methodists have removed from among the Georgia Indians.

A letter will be immediately addressed to the Secretary of War,

requesting an assurance from him, that religious missionaries are not, as such, agents of the United States, and specially that John Thompson is not its agent. Your early attention to this subject is requested. Very respectfully, yours, &c.,
GEORGE R. GILMER.
Hon. William T. Barry.

Executive Department, Milledgeville, 13th April, 1831.

Gentlemen,—Your letter of the 30th ult. upon the subject of the missionary employed by the Board of Directors of the United Brethren's Missions among the Cherokee Indians residing in Georgia, has been received.

I have the highest respect for the general character of the United Brethren, and entire confidence that their Board of Missions have, in its efforts to improve and Christianize the heathen and savage Aborigines of our country, been directed by the most pious and benevolent motives. I regret that your missionaries should have found any difficulty in complying with the requirements of the laws of the State. The principal object of these laws has been to remove from the Cherokees white men of bad character, and those who, from mistaken views of the rights and powers of the State, have been engaged in exciting the Indians to sedition, and opposition to the policy of the Government. The guard which has been stationed among the Cherokees, to protect the public property from trespass, and to arrest violators of the law, has been directed specially to bring to trial, every white man, who in any manner commits an injury upon our Cherokee population; and it is a source of high satisfaction to believe, that under the present administration of the laws of the State, the rights of liberty, personal security, and private property, belonging to the Indians, are far better protected than they have been heretofore.

According to your request, and in full confidence that your missionaries will conform to your directions, the commanding officer of the guard will be directed to wait with them, until they can conveniently remove from the State, or take the oath required by law.

I cannot close this letter without expressing the fullest conviction that the removal of the Cherokees to the west of the Mississippi will result to their advantage, and the hope that such removal, instead of embarrassing the efforts of Christians in communicating to them the light and saving influences of the gospel, will prove the efficient means of obtaining for them the most satisfactory success.

Very respectfully, yours, & c.,
GEORGE R. GILMER.
To the Board of Directors of the United
    Brethren's Missions.

The preceding letter is the first written to the missionaries who were residing among the Cherokees. As the treatment of this class of men for continuing to reside among the Indians, in opposition to the laws of the State, produced great excitemen against its authorities, I insert it with much satisfaction; because it shows that all who evinced no determination to disregard the laws, were treated with due consideration and kindness.

Executive Department, Milledgeville, 14th May, 1831.
Sir,—I inclose to you the copy of the answer of the Secretary of War to a letter of mine, upon the subject of the missionaries residing among the Cherokees, by which you will perceive that none of them are really the agents of the United States, although the Moravian and Baptist missionaries receive a portion of their support from the fund appropriated for the civilization of the Indians. As, however, the expressions of the Secretary of War leave it doubtful, whether he does not consider the Moravian missionary at Spring Place and Oachgalogy under the superintendence of Gilbert Byhan, and the Baptist missionaries at Valley Town and Notley, under the superintendence of Evans Jones, as agents of the Government; you will, for the present, consider them such, taking care to report to this department any opposition which may be made to the laws of the State, or the policy of the United States, by any white person connected with those establishments. The missionaries of other Christian denominations, who may be found within the territory appropriated to the occupancy of the Cherokees, without having taken the required oath, you are directed not to recognize as agents of the United States.

Since writing the above, I have received from the Postmaster-General a letter, of which the inclosed is a copy, by which you will perceive that Samuel Worcester is no longer protected by his office of postmaster in his seditious conduct among the Indians.

I inclose to you unsealed letters to S. Worcester, Thompson and other missionaries, which after reading you will cause to be delivered to them. If after receiving notice to leave the State, they should continue their refractory conduct, you will cause them to be arrested, and turned over to the civil authorities for punishment. If they show no disposition to mislead the Indians or oppose the policy of the Government, treat them with kindness and liberality, and permit them to remove from the State in such manner as may be most convenient and agreeable to them. Independently of the general disposition of the Government to induce men to obey the laws, in preference to the infliction of punishment, it is important that the Cherokees should not be further excited, by harsh treatment of any whom they may be disposed to consider members of their community. I am fully convinced, that their future distinct existence, prosperity, and happiness depend upon their speedy removal beyond the Mississippi. Every thing, therefore, which is done to them should tend to the accomplishment of that object.

The letters of the Secretary of War and the Postmaster-General, are on file in this office. That the copies of them sent you may be used as evidence in any future prosecutions against the missionaries, I have had the seal of this office annexed to the certificate of their correctness.

Dr. Reese, who is known to have the confidence of the Indians, is about visiting them at their request, to advise with them as to the course which their situation requires them to take. He is thoroughly convinced of the necessity which compels their removal, and that the sooner it can be made, the more beneficial for them. He goes by my advice, and will no doubt receive an agency from the President to remain among them for some time. It is necessary that his connection with the General Government should be secret for the present, in order to avoid the suspicions of the Indians. It is now mentioned to you, for the purpose of requesting that you will give him any information, and afford him any assistance in your power.

Very respectfully, yours, &c.,
GEORGE R. GILMER.

Col. John W. A. Sanford.

Note.—The letters without direction, you are requested to direct to any missionaries who may be found residing among the Cherokees contrary to the laws of the State.

Executive Department, Milledgeville, 16th May, 1831.

Sir,—Sufficient evidence has been obtained from the Government of the United States, to convince the Courts of this State, that the missionaries employed among the Cherokees by the American Board of Foreign Missions, are not its agents, and therefore not exempted from the operation of the law forbidding white persons to reside among the Cherokees without license. In continuing so to reside, you must have known that you were acting in violation of the laws of the State. The mistaken decision of the Superior Court upon this subject, in the late case determined in Gwinnett County, has enabled you for a time to persist in your opposition to the humane policy which the General Government has adopted for the civilization of the Indians, and in your efforts to prevent their submission to the laws of Georgia.

However criminal your conduct in this respect may have been, I am still desirous that you should have an opportunity of avoiding the punishment which will certainly follow the continuance of your present residence. You are, therefore, advised to quit it with as little delay as possible. Col. Sanford, the commander of the guard, will be directed to cause to be delivered to you this letter, and to enforce the laws, if you should persist in your disobedience.

Very respectfully, yours, &c.,

GEORGE R. GILMER.

Rev. John Thompson, and others.

Executive Department, Milledgeville, 16th May, 1831.

Sir,—It is a part of my official duty to cause all white persons residing within the territory of the State occupied by the Cherokees, to be removed therefrom, who refuse to take the oath to support the Constitution and laws of the State. Information has been received of your continued residence within that territory without complying with the requisites of the law, and of your claim to be exempted from its operation on account of your holding the office of postmaster at New Echota. You have, no doubt, been informed of your dismissal from that office.

That you may be under no mistake as to this matter, you are also informed, that the United States Government does not recognize as its agents, the missionaries acting under the direction of the American Board of Foreign Missions.

Whatever may have been your conduct in opposing the humane policy of the General Government, or in exciting the Indians to oppose the jurisdiction of the State, I am still desirous of giving you, and all others similarly situated, an opportunity of avoiding the punishment which will certainly follow your further residence within the State contrary to its laws. You are, therefore, advised to remove from the territory of Georgia occupied by the Cherokees. Col. Sanford, the commander of the guard, will be requested to have this letter delivered to you, and to delay your arrest until you shall have had an opportunity of leaving the State.

Very respectfully, yours, &c.,

GEORGE R. GILMER

Rev. Samuel Worcester.

I omitted no opportunity of making impressions upon the Cherokees favorable to their removal to the people of the Mississippi, and re-union with their people already settled there.

Executive Department, Milledgeville, 14th May, 1831.

Sir,—I have learned, through various sources, that since the late decision of the Supreme Court, the Cherokee Indians are in the most unsettled state as to their future course. It is exceedingly important, that the Government should immediately send an agent among them, who has their confidence, and who may be qualified to give direction to their measures. Such an agent may be procured by the appointment of Dr. David A. Reese, of Monticello, Jasper County. He is a gentleman of intelligence, high respectability, a member of the Legislature of the State, and as such, very efficient in opposing the effort made at the last session to deprive the Cherokees of the occupancy of their country without their consent, and without compensation. He is the relative of Boudinot, the Adairs, and Charles Reese, and acquainted with many of their principal men, having visited his relations during the last summer. He has lately received letters from them, giving an account of the distracted state of their councils, and urging him to visit them, and assist them with his advice. He is thoroughly convinced that it is to their interest to exchange the territory which they at present occupy, for lands on the west of the Mississippi, and that the contract for that purpose should be entered into as early as possible. He wrote to me upon the receipt of the letters from his Indian friends, desiring to know whether it was probable that his peculiar situation would enable him to be useful to the State. I have seen him, and requested that he would immediately comply with the invitation of his Indian friends. I have stated to him, that if he will do so, I did not doubt but that the President would confer upon him such an agency as would authorize him to remain among the Cherokees for such time as he could be usefully employed in giving success to the policy of the Government, with such compensation as would be an equivalent for the pecuniary sacrifice he would make. He will, in compliance with my advice and desire, visit the Cherokees immediately. I consider it important that no time should be lost in giving the proper direction to their present unsettled purposes.

Permit me, therefore, to request that you will present to the consideration of the President the propriety of employing Dr. Reese as an agent of the Government. If such an appointment should be conferred upon him, I will take upon myself the care of forwarding any communications you may make him. Dr. Reese has had with him for some time past an Indian boy, a relation of his, who is now desirous of returning to his home. This circumstance, together with others which have been mentioned, will enable him to visit the Indians, consult with them, give them correct views of the humane policy of the President, convince them of what they may expect from the legislation of the State, if they should obstinately persist in opposing its wishes, what are its present designs and probable future course, without exciting the suspicions which would be certain to interfere with the exertions of any other agent.

The deep interest which is felt by the people of this State in the immediate acquisition of the Cherokee lands, will, I have no doubt, excuse me with the President for pressing upon his attention such information as may possibly aid him in executing the contract of 1802, and of giving success to his liberal policy in placing all the

Indian people within the States beyond their jurisdiction, where the means of the Government may be used to advance their happiness and civilization.

As connected with this subject, and calculated to throw some light upon it, I send you the copy of á letter to the officer commanding the guard stationed among the Cherokees, with his answer.

Very respectfully, yours, &c.
GEORGE R. GILMER.

Hon. John H. Eaton.

Executive Department, Milledgeville, 17th May, 1831.

Sir,—Some days ago I received a letter from Dr. David A. Reese, stating that he had received letters from his Indian relations, representing the Cherokees to be very unsettled as to their future course, and requesting him to visit them and aid them with his counsel, and desiring to know of me whether, in complying with their request, he could serve the State. I have urged him to visit the Cherokees immediately. He is thoroughly convinced that the Cherokees ought for their own advantage, to exchange their lands with the United States, and without delay. To authorize his continuing among them during such time as may be necessary to explain to them their true situation, the policy of the President, and the probable future course of the legislation of this State, I have written to the Secretary of War, requesting him to obtain from the President for Dr. Reese, an agency for this purpose. Whilst we had the pleasure of your company in Milledgeville, I recollect having stated to you that I knew of no individual in the State so peculiarly qualified for such an agency as Dr. Reese. If you should concur with me in this opinion, will you oblige me so far as to write to the President, and request of him the appointment of Dr. Reese to such an agency.

Various accounts state that the Cherokees are restless, disturbed, and undetermined, since the decision of the Supreme Court. The chiefs are very active in representing to the Indians that the decision is in favor of their right of self-government. I believe that no measure is better calculated to prevent the success of the designs of the chiefs, and to convince them of the advantages which they will derive from acceding to the terms which the United States is disposed to offer them for their lands, than the knowledge of what was done at the last session of the Legislature, and the certainty that the efforts of those who are disposed to award to them the rights of humanity, cannot long prevent their removal from the State, whether they consent or not. It is specially on this account that I am so desirous that Dr. Reese should be among them.

Very respectfully, yours, &c.,
GEORGE R. GILMER.

To the Hon. John McPherson Berrien.

I sought for information as to the temper and wishes of the Cherokees, whenever and wherever it could be had, that what could be done might be done, for their removal from the State. The following letter was written to the surveyors upon their return home from running off the Cherokee territory into districts and lots:

Executive Department, Milledgeville, May, 1831.

Sir,—I am desirous of procuring from you whatever information your late employment of surveyor among the Cherokees may have enabled you to obtain, as to their present temper and designs, and probable future course.

You are fully aware of the importance of this subject to the happiness of the Indians, the success of the present administration of the General Government, the peace and quiet of the people, and the character of the State of Georgia. Permit me, therefore, to ask of you answers to the following queries:

What effect has the late decision of the Supreme Court had upon the Cherokees?

Are the chiefs now disposed to cede their occupant rights in Georgia?

Are the body of the Indians more or less disposed to do so than their chiefs?

Do the chiefs retain their former influence over the people?

Which would the chiefs and the people prefer, ceding the whole of their lands by treaty, or for each individual to receive of the Government the value of his improvements?

What number of them have left the State of Georgia on account of the extension of its jurisdiction over them?

What additional numbers could probably be induced to remove from Georgia by the Government's paying to each individual the value of his improvements?

What effect has the guard had upon them?

Do they now hold councils, pass laws, or hold courts?

What effect has the law compelling the white men among them to take an oath to support the constitution and laws of the State had upon their conduct?

Could commissioners now be sent among the Cherokees with any prospect of successfully treating with them for their lands?

Do you know of any person who has the confidence of the Indians, who could be induced to go among them, and inform them fully and correctly of the views of the Government, and their own situation?

Very respectfully, yours, &c.,
GEORGE R. GILMER.

Executive Department, Milledgeville, 31st May, 1831.

Sir,—By the treaty of 1819, between the United States and the Cherokees, it was stipulated, that thirty-one persons, whose names were attached in a list to the treaty should be entitled to fee-simple reserves, on condition that they would, in six months thereafter, signify in writing to the agent their intention of residing permanently upon them.

I am desirous of ascertaining from you the number of the Cherokees mentioned in that list, who complied with the conditions of the treaty so far as to notify the agent of their intention to remain upon their reserves, and who afterwards sold the same and gave fee-simple titles to the purchasers, and who are now residing within the limits of this State upon the lands reserved to the Cherokees for their occupancy. I am specially solicitous to know whether Walter S. Adair, John Martin and Richard Taylor, who are now acting as Chiefs among the Cherokees, and residing within Georgia, are the same persons to whom reserves were granted by the treaty of 1819, and whether John Ross received an additional reserve to the one mentioned in the treaty, as a citizen of the United States?

Will you also inform me what relationship by blood, John Ross has to the aboriginal Indians? Who was his father, how much of Indian blood his mother had? &c., &c. Similar information will be very acceptable about John Martin, Richard Taylor, John Ridge, and Coody.

I have heard in various ways, that the Cherokee chiefs are very active in holding secret councils, the object of which is to persuade the Indians to continue their resistance to the laws of Georgia, and the policy of the United States. As the holding of such councils violates the laws of this State, it is my duty to have the chiefs who may be present at them, arrested and punished. If you have any information upon this subject, permit me to request that you will communicate it to this Department as early as convenient.

I write to you freely upon this subject, because the enforcement of the laws of this State, accords with the opinions and policy of the Administration of the General Government, and is believed to be required, both for the quiet of Georgia, and the peace and happiness of the Indians.

I am also desirous of knowing from you, what course you think it probable the Cherokees will now pursue. Can the chiefs be induced to cede their lands to Georgia? and if so, when, and upon what terms? Are the Indian people willing to emigrate if the Government will pay them a fair value for their improvements? Whether can they be most readily removed from Georgia by treaty, or by paying them the value of their improvements?

Very respectfully, yours, &c.,

Col. Hugh Montgomery.   GEORGE R. GILMER.

Executive Department, Milledgeville, 15th June, 1831.
Sir,—I consider it of some importance in order to give the proper direction to public opinion, to know something of the particular history of the chiefs of mixed blood, who are at present influencing the conduct of the Cherokees. You are therefore requested to ascertain with as much accuracy as possible, who was the father of John Ross, to what state or country he originally belonged, what cause induced his connection with the Cherokees, what portion of Indian blood John Ross's mother had, where John Ross was educated, &c., &c. It is desirable to have similar information as to Richard Taylor, Coody, Ridge, John Martin, the two Adairs, Daniel, and other half-breed Chiefs in this State.

Very Respectfully, yours, &c.,
GEORGE R. GILMER.

Col. John W. A. Sanford.

The answers to these two letters enabled me to communicate to the Legislature upon the subject of them, as already stated.

In my intercourse with the Cherokee chiefs, at Washington City, and elsewhere, I never knew but three of any distinction who were not descendants of white persons. I regret that I have not the means at hand of giving with accuracy a genealogical tree of each dsitinguished chief. The father of John Ross, Lewis Ross, and their brothers and their sister, the mother of Coody, was a Scotchman. The father of John Ross's mother was a Scotchman. Martin's father was a Virginian. The fathers of the Adairs were Irishmen, or South Carolinians of Irish descent.

The conduct of Worcester and Butler, as described in the following letter, exhibits a most singular contest between the State and two very insignificant individuals, swelled into great importance by being instruments used by the northern section of the Union to prevent the increase of the population and consequent political strength of the South, aided by religious fanatics every where.

Executive Department, Milledgeville, 17th June, 1831.
Sir,—I inclose to you copies of letters from Samuel A. Worcester and Elizur Butler, two white men, who are missionaries among the Cherokees, in answer to my letter notifying them that they would be arrested if they continued to disobey the laws of the State by residing among the Cherokees, without taking the oath to support the constitution and laws.

You will perceive that they deny the authority of the State to pass laws to govern them, notwithstanding their residence within its limits, and express the determination to abide its penalties. Let them feel their full weight, since such is their voluntary choice. Spare no exertions to arrest them, and all other similarly situated and offending. If they are discharged by the Courts, or give bail, continue to arrest for each repeated act of continued residence in violation of the law. If resistance is made, call upon the militia of the counties to aid you in enforcing the laws. Although I am disposed to execute the laws with the utmost forbearance upon our Indian people, I owe it to the Sovereignty of the State, to punish with the utmost rigor the injurious and insolent conduct of the whites who deny its power and oppose its authority.

Your duty is laborious; but I know your zeal in supporting the just rights of the State, and hope that your efforts may be soon rewarded with the most complete success.

Very respectfully, yours, &c.,
GEORGE R. GILMER.

Col. John W. A. Sanford.

Executive Department, Milledgeville, 17th June, 1831.

Sir,—The information received through your letter, by Col. Jordan, upon the subject of the feelings and views of the Cherokees in Georgia, is exceedingly discouraging. I pity the poor and ignorant Indians, for the fate which their misguided leaders and our own dishonest political partisans will be certain to bring upon them, unless, indeed, it can be yet prevented by the exertions of the Government, and the friends of humanity.

On the 14th of May, I wrote to the Secretary of War, requesting that the President would confer upon you such an agency as would authorize your remaining for some time among the Cherokees, for the purpose of convincing them that their own interest requires them to cede their lands in Georgia. To that letter I received no answer. This has probably been owing to the present vacancy in the office of Secretary of War, and the absence of the Attorney-General.

I cannot ascertain from your letter whether you have still any hope that you could render service to the Government by procuring the consent of the chiefs to cede the lands which they occupy by treaty, or inducing the mass of common Indians to enroll for emigration. Write me fully and freely, so that I may be enabled to communicate your views to the President.

Very respectfully, yours, &c.,
GEORGE R. GILMER.

Dr. David A. Reese.

The following letter to the President, exhibits the urgent spirit with which the authorities of Georgia pressed upon the General Government its right to require that all proper and availble means should be used to execute its contract of 1802. Those who know the evident disposition of the preceding Legislature of the State to take possession of the Cherokee territory, and the earnest exertions used to prevent it, until that course should be obviously just to the right-minded, can alone understand fully the cause of that urgency.

Executive Department, Milledgeville, 20th June, 1831.

Sir,—Circumstances have enabled me to collect much information as to the present temper, designs, and probable future course of the Cherokees. The great interest felt by the people of this State in having them removed from its limits, and the contract of 1802 finally executed, have induced me to communicate directly to the President, so much of that information as may possibly be useful to him, in his endeavors to effect these objects. Strong hopes were at one time entertained, that if the decision of the Supreme Court should be against the application of the Cherokees for a writ of injunction to stay the jurisdiction of Georgia, that they would immediately treat with the United States for an extinguishment of their present occupant rights. It is known, that previous to that decision, and during the pendency of the case before the Supreme Court, all classes had expressed their belief, that such would be the course pursued by them. These hopes have, however, proved illusory. Since that decision, the wealthy and influential half-breed chiefs have been exceedingly active in persuading the people to continue their present residence, in opposition to the desire of the General Government to extinguish their title, and in defiance of the rights and power of Georgia. These efforts have unfortunately been very successful. This has resulted from the extra-judicial opinions of the Supreme Court, in determining that the Cherokees formed a distinct political society, capable of managing its own affairs; and that they are the rightful owners of the soil which they occupy. Meetings of the Indian people have been called in most of the towns, at which their chiefs have used these opinions to convince them that their rights of self-government and soil were independent of the United States and Georgia, and would be secured to them through the Supreme Court, when the change (which they represented to be certain) in the Administration of the General Government was made.

From all the information which I have received, I am satisfied that the President would fail in any immediate efforts to execute the contract of 1802 by treaty with the chiefs, and that the attempt would only expose the Government to their insults, and increase their confidence in the unfortunate measures they are pursuing.

It is most respectfully suggested to the President, that no measure can at present be successfully adopted for the execution of the contract of 1802, except inducing individuals, families, and towns to emigrate from the State, by paying them for their improvements, or giving them such other advantages as may be found acceptable; and the President is earnestly requested to try the effect of this measure as early as possible.

The great body of the common Indians are without wealth or power. Nothing prevents their acquiescence in the policy of the Government to unite them with that part of their tribe who are on the west of the Mississippi, but their habitual submission to the control of their chiefs, and their inert, and listless character. What is said of their strong desire to remain with the bones of their fathers, are but the expressions of those whose ancestors' bodies are deposited in Europe. The confidence of the common Indians in the rule of their chiefs, has been somewhat impaired by their appropriation of the wealth of the tribe to themselves. Their listlessness of temper and indifference about the future, may possibly be in some degree overcome, by the fear of unknown evils from the operation of the laws of Georgia. The guard which has been stationed among them, has been successful in preventing any trespasses upon the gold mines, in putting a stop to their legislative councils, their courts, the execution of their laws, and in removing all white men from among them, disposed to excite their opposition to the government of the State.

The chiefs can no longer prevent the people from enrolling for emigration, by the fear of punishment. It is thought probable that the very attempt to remove the people in that way will tend to produce a willingness on the part of chiefs to treat for an exchange of their lands. They know, that by the removal of the common Indians, they will lose their power, the exclusive possession of the country, and become subjected to the prejudices of the white population with whom they will be mingled.

I have inclosed to the Secretary of War, with the request that the same may be laid before the President, the copy of a letter just received from Dr. Reese, a respectable gentleman of this State, who has lately returned from a visit to the Cherokees, and whose connection with some of the influential half-breed chiefs, has enabled him to acquire an accurate knowledge of the designs of that class; and a correspondence with the surveyors who have been lately engaged in dividing the country occupied by the Cherokees into sections and districts, and whose employment led them into very unreserved intercourse with all classes of the Indians. The opinions expressed by these persons, in favor of the plan of removing the Cherokees by enrolling individuals for emigration, rather than by treaty with the chiefs, is confirmed by information derived from various other sources.

This subject is of great importance, not only to the peace, prosperity, and quiet of the State, but to the character of its Government. The obstructions which have been thrown in the way of the execution of the contract of 1802, the long-continued indifference and neglect of the General Government, and its actual opposition in 1825-26; the constant abuse which party violence has poured upon the authorities of this State and its people, on account of the measures which have been adopted for the support of its rights of soil and jurisdiction; the influence which that partisan violence is now exercising over the Cherokee chiefs in inducing them to continue their opposition to the laws of Georgia, and in exciting their expectation that by a change of the present administration of the General Government, they will be secured in the rights of self-government; the conduct of the Chief Justice of the United States in interfering with the administration of the criminal laws of the State, and the intimation given by the Cherokees in his decision, that the laws of Georgia were exceedingly oppressive; that the State had neither the right of jurisdiction nor of soil; have all conspired so to irritate the public mind here, that it will be extremely difficult, perhaps impossible, to prevent the Legislature from disposing of all the lands of the State assigned to the Indians for their occupancy, except so much as may be in their immediate possession, or required for their support, unless the President shall be enabled during the present year, to adopt such measures as will give assurance that the Cherokees will be certainly and shortly removed from the State. It is important that the Government of the State should know, whether it has become impossible for the United States to execute the contract of 1802, so that its policy in relation to the Cherokees may no longer be influenced by the expectation of that event.

Hitherto the Indians have neither been compelled to pay taxes, nor perform any civil duties. The only operation of the laws since the extension of the jurisdiction of the State over their territory, has been to protect them from injury, by the removal of the whites who had been tempted into their country by the attraction of the gold mines, to escape punishment for their crimes, or to indulge in vice. The State is at this time maintaining a guard at great expense, for the purpose of preventing the exercise of assumed authority on the part of the chiefs, from the expectation that the President will be enabled during the present year, to succeed in removing the Indians beyond its limits, and the strong disposition felt by its authorities to avoid the adoption of any measures which might have even the appearance of violating the laws of humanity, or the natural rights of the Indians.

If tha Cherokees are to continue inhabitants of the State, they must be rendered subject to the ordinary operations of the laws with less expense and trouble, and more effectually, than heretofore. The State must put an end to even the semblance of a distinct political government within its territory. It has hitherto been permitted, from the belief that the happiness of the Indians required it, and that such condition was not then inconvenient, nor injurious to the rights of Georgia. The agitation which the Indian question has excited throughout our country, and the manner in which it has endangered the most important political rights of the State, require that what is insisted on shall be done. The millions of acres of land which are now of no value, except to add to the gratification of the idle ambition of the chiefs, must be placed in possession of actual cultivators of the soil, who may be made the instruments for the proper administration of the laws.

It is hoped that the President will concur in the necessity of making such efforts for removing the Cherokees, as will ascertain whether it is practicable by any means whatever.

I trust that the importance of the subject will be my sufficient apology for the manner in which it has been pressed upon the consideration of the President.

With sentiments of the highest consideration,
I am most respectfully, yours, &c.,
GEORGE R. GILMER.

Andrew Jackson,
President of the United States.

In the month of August, 1831, I wrote to the Secretary of War, urging the appointment of several persons to enroll the Indians for emigration. He appointed Col. Montgomery the Cherokee agent, an old, inefficient man, whose residence was in Tennessee, at a distance from the Indians most disposed to emigrate. The following letter points out the mistaken course pursued by the officers of the General Government, and the difficulties which the authorities of Georgia had to encounter in the efforts made to acquire all the territorial rights of the State. Nothing was done voluntarily, and upon its own suggestions, by the Government of the United States for executing its contract with Georgia. Every measure for that purpose had to be proposed and urged again and again, or nothing was done. Great sympathy was evinced for the Indians by the people of those States in which there were none. All effectual means for removing them from Georgia were unpopular. It was more politic and easier to conciliate the greater number, than do justice to one. Even Gen. Jackson, with his thorough knowledge of the subject and bold, fearless spirit, had to be stirred up, and coaxed into the humor to do any thing worth doing.

Tennessee was much more interested in removing the Indians from its own territory than from Georgia. Gen. Jackson was a Tennesseean, and never forgot it in all his transactions with the Cherokees. And yet even this injustice (for it was injustice to put Tennessee upon an equality with Georgia in the measures to be taken for removing the Indians) operated incidentally to the advantage of Georgia. Without it, Gen. Jackson might have been as forgetful of the obligations of the General Government's contract as those who preceded him and the President who followed him.

The following letters to the President and to the Secretary of War show how urgent the authorities of the State had to be with Gen. Jackson to induce him to act.

Executive Department, Milledgeville, 20th August, 1831.

Sir,—Some time ago, I had the honor of addressing letters to the President, and your predecessor in office, urging the expediency of attempting to remove the Cherokees from the State, by paying individuals and families the value of their improvements, with such advantages as might be thought proper, upon their consenting to emigrate beyond the Mississippi. I have been convinced by information received from various persons, that no treaty can be formed with the chiefs but through the measures proposed, and that though this should fail to effect the entire object, a large proportion of the unmixed Indians may be thus removed. The President answered, that orders would be given to the agent to enroll the Cherokees for emigration after the plan proposed. The laws of the State give authority to the Governor to have the places which may be relinquished by the Indians occupied by citizens. It is, indeed, this circumstance which renders the plan that the President has consented to adopt, so well calculated to secure success. With the aid of those who may be thus settled every where among the Indians, the organization of the territory as portions of counties, and the election and appointment of civil officers, it is believed that the controlling influence of the chiefs may be destroyed, and thereby the principal difficulty overcome which prevents the execution of the contract of 1802. Permit me, therefore, respectfully to urge upon your department to press this policy immediately, and to its full effect.

The obstructions which have been thrown in the way of the execution of the contract of 1802 by former administrations, the attempt of the half-breed chiefs to create an independent Government, and their active resistance to the efforts of the President to do justice to Georgia, have added great excitement to the desire of the people of this State to acquire the immediate possession of the lands occupied by the Cherokees. Measures may, in consequence, be adopted by the State which, under other circumstances, would be considered highly injudicious, and which will be prevented if the plan which the President has consented to pursue should create a probability of success.

It has been suggested that it will be important to have several persons engaged at the same time in enrolling for emigration in different parts of the territory, and that they, or the Indian agent, should be supplied with funds to pay at once for the improvements of such individuals and families as may enroll for removal.

It is probable that the Indians on the south and east side of the Etowah River, can be more readily induced to enroll than those on the borders of Tennessee and North Carolina, on account of the number of citizens who are among them, and the means thereby afforded to the Government to render them entirely subject to its authority. The immediate possession of that part of the territory is also particularly desirable to the State, on account of the gold mines which it contains. I would, therefore, request that the enrolling officers be directed by you to make their first efforts to remove the Indians from it.

Permit me, also, to request that you will communicate to this Department the success of your measures upon this subject, that the same may be laid before the Legislature at its session in November next. Very respectfully, yours, &c.,

GEORGE R. GILMER.

Hon. Lewis Cass.

P. S.—I send you copies of several letters lately received, which may possibly contain information useful to your Department.

Executive Department, Milledgeville, 24th August, 1831.

Sir,—I received by the last mail, your letter of the 12th inst., together with a copy of your instructions to the Cherokee agent, upon the subject of enrolling the Cherokees for emigration.

Some disappointment has been felt at the delay which has occurred, the cause of which was unknown until the receipt of your letter.

On the 20th inst., I wrote you, urging various reasons why the policy which is about to be pursued, should be pressed to its fullest effect as soon as possible.

I perceive from your instructions to the Cherokee agent, that the business of enrollment is intrusted exclusively to him. Col. Montgomery is a worthy man, but I do not consider it injustice to him to say, that he is too old, indecisive, and uninfluential to produce the effect which the Government desires. Besides, his agency is in Tennessee where the Indians are not subject to the jurisdiction of the State, and the white men who reside among them under no special restraint and interested in preventing the successful accomplishment of the policy of the Government.

I suggested to you in my letter of the 20th, the propriety of establishing several offices for enrolling emigrants. I again repeat the suggestion, convinced, as I am, that its adoption is of the greatest importance to insure success. The contract of the United States to extinguish the Indian title to all lands within the limits of Georgia, authorizes me to request, as an act of justice, that the Cherokees should be first removed from this State.

If there is but one office of emigration, and that at the agency, it will be difficult to induce the Indians from this State to go that far to enroll, inert as they are, and subject to the controlling influences of their chiefs. Those who reside within our limits are most probably readier than others to enroll on account of the extension of its laws over them, and their apprehension of suffering therefrom unknown evils. It is indeed believed, that the indications of a desire to emigrate have been almost exclusively confined to the Indians in this State, and principally to those who reside on the south and east of the Etowah River. They may, also, enroll without fear of injury from the influence of their chiefs, on account of the protection which the Georgia guard will be enabled to afford them.

If any difficulty should occur in procuring proper agents, I would respectfully recommend to you the persons who are mentioned as suitable for such services in my letters of the 14th of May and the 21st of June, and the accompanying communications.

You may be assured that I have no desire to give undue importance to this subject. The evils which are anticipated from an inefficient or dilatory employment of the means of the Government to remove the Cherokees may be very great; I would, if possible, avert them. Very respectfully, yours, &c.,

GEORGE R. GILMER.

Hon. Lewis Cass.

When it was known that preachers of the Gospel had been arrested for illegal residence among the Cherokees, and subjected to the restraints of prisoners, great sympathy was felt for them by their brethren throughout the State, and elsewhere. I received a letter from one of the oldest and most respectable Presbyterian preachers of the Southern country, asking why Presbyterian clergymen were treated by the Governor as knaves.

The sensitiveness of the Methodists may be inferred from the following answer to a letter received from the Rev. John Howard, making complaints of the treatment of Methodist missionaries.

Executive Department, Milledgeville, September 1st, 1831.

Rev. Sir,—I have just received your letter of the 29th ult., in which you call my attention to the publication in the Advocate and Journal of the 12th inst., upon the subject of the conduct of the Georgia guard.

I thank you for the direct course you have pursued in this matter, and the freedom with which you have expressed your feelings and opinions. I have no desire whatever to avoid any scrutiny into my official conduct.

McLeod's statements concerning the orders which I have given to the guard are wholly destitute of truth.

Immediately after the passage of the law which made it criminal for white men to reside among the Cherokees, without license, I caused one hundred copies to be published and distributed among those upon whom it was to operate. By this means every white man who resided among the Indians, was informed of the provisions of the law in time to make up a deliberate resolve whether he would obey or not. Between two and three hundred persons have continued their residence by taking the oath to support the laws. A few have left the State. The missionaries alone have publicly denied the power of the State to extend its jurisdiction over them, and expressed their design to disregard the law, and abide its penalties. One of them was arrested, and discharged by the Superior Court, upon the ground that missionaries were agents of the United States Government, and therefore not liable to arrest. This person was a Mr. Thompson who knew at the time that he was not an agent of the United States Government, as he has since acknowledged in a letter to me. The decision, however, furnished an excuse for the missionaries to continue their illegal residence. I procured from the United States Government proof that the missionaries, as such, were not agents of the Government. Instead of ordering Col. Sanford to arrest them immediately, as would have been lawful, and I think justified by their conduct, I wrote to all the missionaries, notifying them that they would be arrested, if they did not remove. Orders were given to Col. Sanford, that if they showed no disposition to oppose the policy of the Government, to treat them with kindness, and liberality, and permit them to remove as might be most convenient and agreeable to themselves. I received aswers from Worcester and Butler, denying the authority of the laws of the State, and refusing to obey them. Copies of their answers were sent to Col Sanford, with directions to spare no exertions to arrest them, that they might feel the full weight of the law, since such was their choice.

There has been no expression, or intimation whatever in any order or letter, or otherwise from me, to treat those who might be arrested, in any other manner than as the law directs. You cannot regret so much as I do, that any members of the guard should have been so much excited by the improper conduct of these men, as to put them into chains. That they were in the constant habit of speaking in the most opprobrious terms of our Government, laws, and public authorities, I have positive proof. And the account of McLeod himself, shows how far he was disposed thus to act. Although I cannot excuse the severity with which he was treated, it is certain that the guard acted under excited feelings, created by the abuse of those under whose orders they were acting.

But you, my dear sir, and many others, are entirely mistaken both as to my power over the guard, the kind of authority which has been conferred upon it, and the manner of its organization.

It is composed of citizens of the State (forty in number), who have been employed upon wages, to perform a particular duty. They are but assistants to the civil officers, and are substituted for sheriffs and constables, only because they can act more efficiently. They are neither soldiers, nor subject to military law. If they violate the rights of any person, whether missionary, or Indian, they are liable to be sued, or indicted like other citizens. I have no authority to punish them, whatever may be their conduct. My power extends only to the appointment of the agent or commissioner (as the commander is called in the law), and the organization of the guard. The agent himself cannot punish a member of the guard himself for disorderly conduct or other offence, not even by dismissing him without pay. However improper the guard may have acted, Col. Sanford is not answerable for it. Worcester, Trott, and others were arrested, whilst he was in Milledgeville in the discharge of his duty making his quarterly report. He did not return, until after the persons arrested had been confined for several days at his station, waiting for the evidence which he had in his possession, to prove that the missionaries were not agents of the Government.

I must refer you to the publications in the Georgia Journal of this day, for further evidence of what has been my official conduct.

In conclusion, I would observe that the missionaries have not been compelled to 'desert their religious labors, by any conduct of the authorities of the Government, but by their improper connection with political parties, and refusal to obey the laws. Had they submitted to the jurisdiction which rightfully belongs to the State, they would have received its protection, and had my best wishes for their success in enlightening the Indians.

The law does not punish missionaries for residing among the Cherokees, but every white man who so resides contrary to its provisions, and if missionaries will act illegally they must suffer the consequences.   Very respectfully, yours, &c.,
GEORGE R. GILMER.
Rev. John Howard.

Executive Department, Milledgeville, 3d Sept., 1831.

Sir,—A few days, I read in the Cherokee Phoenix, statements from Worcester and Trott, charging Col. Nelson and some of the guard with the use of irons in confining them, and other illegal and unnecessarily severe treatment.

The flagrantly criminal conduct of those two men induced me to discredit them. I have since, however, received through a friend, the New York Advocate and Journal, containing a letter from McLeod corroborating the account given by Worcester and Trott. The character of the Government, and the good of that portion of the public service committed to your particular charge, require that the facts should be inquired into, and if found true, efficient means used to prevent their occurrence.

That you may know how to direct your inquiry, I inclose to you the paper which contains the publication to which I have referred.

You are requested to inquire particularly into the fact, whether irons were used to confine the prisoners arrested by the guard, the necessity which existed for the use of such means, the causes which led to the arrest of McLeod, and the severe treatment of himself and other prisoners.

I am aware that these things occurred, if they occurred at all, during your presence in Milledgeville in the discharge of your duties. The highly efficient and honorable manner in which you have executed the service which has been assigned you, and your own character, are sufficient security that you have not sanctioned any unauthorized oppression of prisoners.

You are requested to report both the conduct of the guard and of the persons arrested.

It will be proper for you to instruct the guard, that in the arrest of those who may have violated the law, their duty is confined to the certain delivery of their prisoners to the civil officers, and that no other severity is authorized by the law, but what may be necessary to effect that object.

Very respectfully, yours, &c.,
GEORGE R. GILMER.
Col. John W. A. Sanford.

Great vigilance was necessary to prevent the continuation of the misdirected influence of the missionaries over the Cherokees. The following letters will show the spirit of the missionaries, and how it was met.

Executive Department, Milledgeville, 8th Sept., 1831.

Sir,—In answer to your letter of the 5th ult., you are informed, that the Executive officers of the State are not authorized to make any distinction between persons, on account of their religious opinions or employments. No white person, whether a citizen of Georgia or Tennessee, can now be permitted to reside in that part of the State occupied by the Cherokees, who was not an inhabitant of it previous to the first of March last, and had not at that time taken the oath to support the laws and constitution of the State. All ministers of the Gospel who resided among the Indians when the law upon this subject passed, had an opportunity afforded them of continuing their religious services, by complying with its requirements.

Those who have thought that they were under higher obligations to act according to their own opinions of the rights of the Cherokees, than to submit to the policy of the General Government, and obey the laws of the State, have found that obedience to rulers is a positive duty. White persons who continue to move about from one place to another among the Cherokees, are considered as much within the mischief which the law intends to remedy, as if stationary, and will be arrested in like manner.

Very respectfully, yours, &c.,
GEORGE R. GILMER.

Rev. D. C. McLeod.

Executive Department, Milledgeville, 5th Sept., 1831.

Sir,—Your letter of the 30th inst., tendering the resignation of your appointment as sub-commander of the guard, has been received, as has been your report, in answer to the inquiries directed to be made into various charges which have been published against yourself, and the members of the guard under your command, in the arrest of certain missionaries.

I have uniformly found you exceedingly active and faithful in the discharge of the public service which has been assigned to you, and although I have not altogether approved of the means which were employed on one or two occasions, in enforcing the laws, I have never doubted but that your object was the performance of what you considered your duty.

The avidity with which those who are opposed to the Administration of the General and State Governments seize upon every thing which can be made to operate upon public opinion injuriously to their success, renders it necessary that those efforts should be promptly met.

From the belief that your resignation has been tendered from chagrin at the inquiry which has been ordered, I have returned it to you with the expression of my wish that you will not, when the State most requires your exertions, leave its service.

Your report is deemed satisfactory.

The rule to be observed relative to prisoners is, that they be confined in such manner as to prevent their rescue or escape. Whatever is necessary to effect this object is justifiable. Confinement is never to be rendered severe upon prisoners for the purpose of punishment.

I shall take no steps to supply your place, until I again hear from you. Very respectfully, yours, &c.,

GEORGE R. GILMER.

Col. Charles H. Nelson.

An unexpected obstruction was placed in the way of protecting the gold mines from trespass, and removing intruders, by the decision of one of the judges, declaring the law to be unconstitutional which made it penal for the Indians to take gold from the lands of the State.

The law which the judge pronounced unconstitutional, made it the special duty of the Governor to prevent the Indians from trespassing upon the gold mines.

As the Executive and Judicial Departments are by the Constitution made separate and distinct, I did not consider that the authority belonged to the judges to direct the Governor how he was to enforce the laws. I, therefore, obeyed their requirements, rather than the opinion of the judge.

Upon being notified that a violator of the law who had been arrested by the guard, had been liberated by the Court, I wrote the following letter to the commander of the guard:

Executive Department, Milledgeville, 19th Sept., 1831.

Sir,—I have just learned, that the judge of the Western Circuit has decided that the law for the protection of the mines in the territory occupied by the Cherokees is void; and that he has discharged an Indian from confinement, who had been arrested by the guard for its violation. As the effect of this decision will be to create the opinion among the Indians, that they are now licensed to plunder the State of this valuable property, I have thought proper to give you express instructions to defend it, that you may be justified in that course.

I have no doubt that the Legislature has the authority to take possession of the mines, and the constitutional right to pass laws to protect them from trespass. By the law which has been passed, the Governor is directed to take possession of the mines, and to cause all persons to be arrested who may attempt to violate that possession. The special object of your appointment, and the organization of the guard under your command, was to enable the Governor to obey these requirements. You are not an officer connected with the Judiciary Department, but the agent whom the Legislature has authorized the Executive to employ, to perform a public service which was imposed by law upon that department. You will therefore arrest every person who may be found attempting to take away gold from the mines. You will give general information in the Cherokee Country of the determination of the Executive Department to enforce the law, so as to avoid if possible the necessity of making any arrests.

The peaceful acquisition of our Indian territory, and the preservation of the rights of the State, may depend essentially upon your prudence and firmness, in executing the duty which has been assigned you. Very respectfully, yours, &c.,

GEORGE R. GILMER.

Col. John W. A. Sanford.

Another difficulty between the officers of the Judiciary and Executive Department occurred about this time, which embarrassed me quite as much as the decision of the judge of the Western Circuit. Gen Charles Floyd of Camden, was charged with the commission of a violent assault upon a man who had killed his brother. The officers of the judiciary were unable, or failed to arrest him. The presiding judge of the Superior Court of the county where the offence was committed, instead of ordering out the posse comitatus, or such force as would have insured the arrest, if it could have been made, applied to the Governor to make it. I was the intimate friend of Gen. John Floyd, whose son's violent death was the immediate cause of the offence charged upon Gen. Charles Floyd. I was at the time a candidate for re-election. The most personal and abusive opposition made to my election proceeded from some of the officers of the court by whom this singular application was made. The matter is as inexplicable now as it was then. It was at once known that I had refused to do the duty of sheriff of Camden County. An application was made to me by those opposed to my re-election, for a copy of my letter upon the subject. It was given to them. They declined publishing it. The seekers for matter to defame the Chief Magistrate, determined that their account of the contents of this letter was better fitted to effect their purpose than what was in the letter.

This is a copy of the letter.

   Executive Department, Milledgeville, 19th Sept., 1831.

 Sir,—I received some days ago your letter of the 7th inst., together with various inclosures in relation to the prosecution and failure to arrest Gen. Charles Floyd.

 Bad health has prevented an earlier reply. I undertsand from your letter, that you have pursued the direction of ———— in inclosing the papers to me, and that his direction to you is the consequence of the opinion given to him individually by the judges, whilst they were assembled in convention in this place.

 Before I can form any definite opinion or answer you distinctly upon this subject, it will be proper to understand the reasons which induced the judges to advise the course which has been pursued, or rather the opinions which have influenced Judge ———— to adopt them, and what he expects from the Executive authority.

 The Constitution declares, that "the Legislative, Executive and Judiciary Departments of the Government shall be distinct and each Department shall be confined to a separate body of Magistry. And no person or collection of persons, being of one of these Departments, shall exercise any power properly attached to either of the others, except in the instances expressly permitted."

 I am disposed to give the most respectful conisderation to any suggestion which I may receive from Judge ————, as to what he and the other judges suppose to be my duty. So far, however, as I can perceive from an examination of the papers alone, I am not aware that I have any authority to interfere in the case.

      Very respectfully, yours, &c.,
        GEORGE R. GILMER.

To ————, Solicitor-General of the Eastern circuit.

Many persons were arrested by the guard, for illegal residence in the Cherokee territory. Twelve were indicted, found guilty, and condemned to confinement in the penitentiary. When the convicts arrived in Milledgeville, and before any of them were degraded by being placed within the penitentiary, pardon was offered to all who would promise not again to violate the laws of the State; as the following letters to the keeper and inspectors of the penitentiary show.

Executive Department, Milledgeville, 22d Sept., 1831.

Sir,—You are requested to cause the persons lately condemned in Gwinnett County for violating the laws of the State, for illegal residence within Cherokee country, not to be received into the penitentiary, until the record of their convictions can be examined, and a decision made, whether they or any of them are entitled to Executive clemency.   Very respectfully, yours, &c.,
GEORGE R. GILMER.

Maj. Philip Cook,
P. Keeper of the Penitentiary.

Executive Department, Sept. 22d, 1831.

Gentlemen,—I understand that a number of persons have been lately convicted in Gwinnett County for illegal residence in the territory occupied by the Cherokees within the State, and will very soon be placed within the penitentiary, unless they shall be considered proper subjects for the exercise of Executive clemency. As it is probable that some of these persons may have committed the offence of which they have been convicted under mistaken opinions of duty, or of the powers of the Government; I am desirous of pardoning such of them as may have thus acted, and will now give assurances that they will not again violate the laws of the State.

You are requested to see each of the prisoners, converse with them alone, and ascertain from them whether they are disposed to promise not again to offend against the laws, if they should be pardoned. You are also requested to ascertain as accurately as you can, what has been the general character of each of the convicts, and the motives which have influenced their opposition to the authority of the State. The result of your inquiries, and conversations, you will oblige me by communicating as early as convenient.
Very respectfully, yours, &c.,
GEORGE R. GILMER.

The Inspectors of the Penitentiary.

The Methodist clergyman who was stationed at the time in Milledgeville, waited upon the convicts, and urged the propriety of accepting the offers of pardon upon the terms made by the Governor.

The following letters to the commander of the guard, exhibit the spirit of my entire conduct to the missionaries among the Cherokees.

Executive Department, Milledgeville, 23d Sept., 1831.

Sir,—I am assured by Benjamin F. Thompson, one of the persons who has been pardoned for illegal residence in the territory occu-

pied by the Cherokees, that he has a brother, John Thompson, who has not been arrested, and who will now remove from the territory. He wishes to do so without arrest. You will give him that permission, if done immediately. You will arrest no one for illegal residence after he has left the territory. Those who continue obstinately to remain contrary to law, you will spare no exertions to arrest. They have had sufficient warning, and if they will not profit by it, they ought to suffer. Very respectfully, yours, &c.,
GEORGE R. GILMER.
Col. John W. A. Sanford.

Executive Department, Milledgeville, 23d Sept., 1831.
Sir,—All of the prisoners who were lately convicted of illegal residence within the Cherokee territory, at Gwinnett Superior Court, have been pardoned, except Dorcester and Butler, upon their giving assurances that they will not again violate the law. I am entirely satisfied of their sincerity in this matter. The State has no object to effect, by punishing persons whose examples are not calculated to operate upon others. All persons must now perceive, that the State intends to exercise its jurisdiction over its territory, and that resistance on the part of individuals is folly.

The prisoners who have been pardoned, and have families (and all have except DeLesure), assure me that they will immediately proceed to remove them out of the territory occupied by the Cherokees. Those who have plantations (and all have except DeLesure and Trott) say, that it is important to them, that they should have the liberty of passing into the territory occasionally, for the purpose of saving and disposing of their crops, and selling and removing their cattle. You are directed to allow them the liberty which they ask for, and to instruct the guard accordingly.
Very respectfully, yours, &c.,
GEORGE R. GILMER.
Col. John W. A. Sanford.

Worcester and Butler, who were acting under the direction of some missionary board at the North, refused to be the subjects of the offered clemency, and voluntarily went into the penitentiary.

No official act of mine occasioned so much abuse at the time, or was so little understood, as the punishment of religious missionaries by imprisonment in the penitentiary. An impression was made upon the public out of Georgia, that ministers of the gospel were thus punished for making efforts to Christianize the Cherokees. The subject excited great interest throughout the country. The newspapers gave currency to the greatest misrepresentations of the facts. Georgia people travelling in other States, were every where subjected to the mortification of listening to the most malignant strictures upon the conduct of the authorities of the State, and particularly its Governor, who was specially abused by name.

In North Carolina where all the facts ought to have been known, the Presbyterian Synod passed a strongly condemnatory resolution of my conduct.

At a Presbytery held in the county of Rockingham, Virginia, the birth-place of my father and mother, and where many of my immediate relations then resided, a Presbyterian clergyman proposed a similar resolution, though domiciled in the house of my brother-in-law, Mr. Grattan, and might have succeeded, but for Dr. Speece, a special friend of my wife and myself, who took upon himself to be answerable for the propriety of my conduct.

Travelling through North Carolina the summer after I left the Executive office, I stopped to get dinner at a house between Charlotte and Salisbury. The landlord abused very freely the tyranny of the Governor of Georgia for his conduct in putting ministers of the gospel into the penitentiary for preaching. I explained to him what had been done by the Governor. The old man said it was impossible that what I said could be true, and would not believe me until I told him that I was the person he had been abusing, and knew all about the matter. His face would have made a good picture just then, for the confounded.

It was very painful to know that I was an object of dislike to great numbers of my fellow-beings, especially as many of those who thus felt towards me, were distinguished for their benevolence. The following circumstance made a strong impression upon me at the time.

David B. Ogden of New York, attended the session of the Supreme Court of the United States in 1834. I was then a member of Congress. We boarded at the same house. When he first came into the mess, and for some time after, he appeared disposed to keep aloof from me, though naturally very social. Before he left Washington City we became quite intimate. I liked him very much, which he appeared to reciprocate very warmly. The day after he left Washington City, he wrote to me from Philadelphia, expressing great friendship for me, and saying that he could scarcely forgive himself for his dislike, previous to our acquaintance, arising from the strong impressions which newspapers and other statements, in relation to my conduct to the Indians and missionaries, had made upon him. Mr. Ogden intended by his letter to give me pleasure. Its effect was very distressing. I had not been aware, that sensible, well informed and good men, had viewed my conduct through the same prejudiced medium as the ignorant, or that the organs for diffusing information at the North, and in the Middle States, had refused or neglected to publish any of the official documents, or other matters, tending to set public opinion right upon the subject.

A large delegation of the Cherokees were in Washington City after Mr. Ogden left there. They were endeavoring to obtain an extension of their territory on the west of the Mississippi. I called to see John Ross and the other chiefs, to understand their wishes and to state to them my information about the country which had been assigned to them. John Ross replied to me, that they had as much confidence in me as any other public man; that they had received as much kindness and protection from me when Governor as was possible for one in my situation to give them; and that if I would visit the territory, and would then say that it was what the agent of the Government had represented it to be, he would make no further contest about it.

Whilst I was in the Executive Department, in the spring of 1838, several Indians, among them two or three women, came to Milledgeville to ask my assistance in procuring for them an infant child, the daughter of one of the women, who had been carried off secretly from its mother, by a white man, and concealed in the country some distance south of Milledgeville. The Cherokees were then on their way to their new country beyond the Mississippi. Cherokee women inherit property equally with the men. This child was entitled to considerable property, which the white man wished to obtain possession of and keep in Georgia.

I ascertained where the child was, wrote letters to the neighborhood, and instructed the mother how she was to act to get possession of her child. She pursued my directions, succeeded, and brought her little daughter to my house, where she was dressed by Mrs. John Gilmer, the party entertained, and sent on their way home rejoicing.

Some time after the laws of Georgia were extended over the Indians, a set of knavish white men among them attempted to get possession of the property of their wealthy Indian neighbors by forging notes, and suing them in the justices' courts, then established in the different parts of the Cherokee country. By the laws of the State, an Indian could not be a witness in a suit to which a white man was a party. Information was given me of these attempts to oppress the Indians. I wrote a circular letter to the magistrates, advising them to permit the Indians to deny on oath the making of the notes upon which they were sued, so as to put the plaintiffs to the proof of their signatures: That such an oath was a form of pleading, and not considered in law as evidence. My advice was followed, and with success.

The conduct of the State in extending its jurisdiction over the Indians excited so much animadversion at the time where the facts which led to that policy were unknown, that great injustice was done to her public authorities. What was done continued to be spoken of and written about without any knowledge of the truth, and in the most abusive terms. And yet every one is now obliged to acknowledge that the policy of Georgia has tended to the improvement and happiness of the Cherokees. That policy was expressly based upon the conviction such would be the result. All now admit that the public men of Georgia showed their wisdom in what they did, and their slanderers their folly. Motives were scanned, and those who knew nothing of the peculiar state of the Cherokee people, passed judgment of condemnation upon the conduct of those who had the means, and whose duty it was to understand it well. It is a source of pride and pleasure to those who were responsible for the conduct of Georgia towards the Cherokees, to know that what they did has tended to the good both of the Indians and Georgians: That the Cherokees, instead of being controlled in their public affairs, and corrupted in their morals, by profligate white men, as they were when within the limits of Georgia, are now in a country the best suited to their peculiar instincts and habits of living: And that the Georgians have already converted the Cherokee hunting grounds into the most beautiful, highly cultivated, and populous region of the South. For the information of those who may desire to know something more upon this subject than is found in this exposition of mine, I insert here a paper published at the time of the transactions referred to, containing statements from two distinguished members of the Georgia Legislature, Mr. Nesbitt, Maj. Stocks, and the editor of the leading paper of the State, Mr. Camak. Maj. Stocks had been for a long time President of the Senate, Mr. Camak was some time previously a professor in Franklin College, and Mr. Nesbitt is now a Judge of the Supreme Court of the State.

THE CHEROKEE QUESTION.

Albany, 20th June, 1892.

Mr. Croswell,

Sir,—I was desirous that the following article should appear in the New York Observer, as that paper has been particularly industrious in circulating statements to the prejudice of Georgia. Having been refused admission to its columns, I must beg the favor of you to permit me to use yours.

If you can, without inconvenience, publish this note, together with the papers which accompany it, during the approaching session of your Legislature, you will confer a favor on,

Sir, yours, very respectfully,

JAS. CAMAK.

To the Editor of the N. Y Observer.

New York, June 1, 1832.

Sir,—Since I left home I have conversed with many persons on the subject of the missionaries who are confined in the penitentiary of the State of Georgia. I have been greatly surprised at the opinions entertained and expressed, in relation to the course that has been pursued by Georgia; and the more so, as these opinions appear to me to be founded on an apprehension of the facts of the case, altogether erroneous.

To dispel error, and to give to those who sincerely desire to know the truth, an opportunity of gratifying that desire, I request the publication, in the Observer, of the inclosed document, and the notes annexed thereto. Permit me to express the hope that it will be attentively read, and patiently examined.

In the Baptist convention lately held in this city, the writer of this article is informed, that the question concerning these missionaries was agitated. Mr. Stocks, president of the senate of Georgia, being one of the delegates, had the report and notes printed and circulated among the members of the convention. The result was an unanimous vote in favor of Georgia, as the writer has been informed.

The author of the report, E. A. Nesbitt, of Morgan County, is a member of the Presbyterian church; and, as a jurist, a man and a Christian, will not suffer any thing by a comparison with any man of his age in the country. The author of the notes is a distinguished member of the Baptist church; and has been, for many years, president of the senate of Georgia—the second officer in the State government.

As to the right of Georgia to extend her laws over the Cherokee territory, the writer refers confidently to the report, to the note (a), and to the treaty between the government of Georgia and the government of the United States, in 1802. So also does he refer to the report as to the expediency of such a measure, on the part of Georgia; but more particularly to the note marked (b) as containing a statement of fact, among many others of a like character that might have been made, the force of which, he thinks, is irresistible.

Very respectfully, your obedient servant,
JAS. CAMAK,
Of Milledgeville, Georgia.

Report of the Committee on the State of the Republic, presented to the Legislature of Georgia, December 15, 1831

The committee, to whom was referred so much of his excellency the Governor's communication as relates to the enforcement of the law, making it penal, under certain restrictions, for white persons to reside within the limits of the Cherokee nation, together with the documents in relation to that subject, have bestowed upon the subject much reflection, and given it such investigation, as its importance merits. It does not appear to your committee, so far as the people of Georgia are concerned, at all necessary to enter into a defence of this measure of the government. Our people with one accord, your committee believe, approve both the policy of the law and the manner of its enforcement. The policy of the State towards the Cherokee tribe of Indians, in regard to the unsettled lands within her limits, and particularly in reference to the missionaries who have made themselves obnoxious to the penalty of the act of the last legislature, has been and still is already (abroad) the subject of misrepresentation, and the theme of vituperation. We have been represented as usurping rights which belong to the Indians, as exercising dominion over a people free and independent, and as disregarding the sacred character and holy functions of the missionaries of the cross. A regard for the moral sense of the people of the Union, and a just respect for the character of the State, your committee believe, require that, upon this subject, facts should be exhibited, and the principles of action which have governed the State should be well understood.

By a law of the State, passed at the last session of the General Assembly, all white persons, except agents of the United States, are prohibited from residing within its territory occupied by the Cherokees, unless authorized by license from the Governor or his agent, on taking an oath to support the constitution and laws of this State. The right of the State to pass this law, results as a necessary consequence to the right which she has to the soil, and jurisdiction over the Cherokee lands. Her right of jurisdiction is co-extensive with her chartered limits, and embraces the persons and things within those limits. No enlightened jurist of the present day; no one familiar with the custom which has governed all the States of the Union who have had Indian tribes within their limits (a); or who is conversant with the policy of the federal government since the administration of Mr. Monroe, will for a moment doubt the right of the State to extend her criminal laws over the whole of her chartered limits. This is not a vexed question. At all events, its elucidation does not constitute a part of the duty of your committee upon the present occasion.

(b) The reason and necessity of the law are as obvious as the right to enact it. A leading object with the general government has been, for many years, the removal of the Cherokee Indians west of the Mississippi. This has been held by the most benevolent, and also the most distinguished of our statesmen, the only means left to the government to save the wretched remnants of this once numerous and powerful nation from moral ruin as individuals, and total extinction as a tribe. Year after year, the tribes within the States have been seen to decrease in numbers, and to sink lower and lower in crime, depravity and sin. The parental arm of the government has been extended to their relief, and the federal and state governments have united their efforts to remove them from their present habitations, and locate them beyond the Mississippi. There, under the protection of the government, and free alike from the crimes and the cupidity of the white man, to live in their own peculiar way, the happy and lordly masters of the forest.

It was an object of peculiar interest to Georgia to acquire a speedy possession of her Cherokee lands. Too long had the government delayed to liquidate the Indian possession. She had become justly jealous of her rights, and her people had become impatient of the restraints imposed by the delay of the federal government to fulfill her treaty obligations. The Cherokee tribe had assumed the attitude of an independent nation, with government and laws distinct from, and independent of the State authority. The discovery of immense mineral wealth within the limits of the nation, acting upon the avarice and cupidity of men, had brought into the territory a numerous body of men, lawless, abandoned, and hostile to the policy of the State. (c) These circumstances imperiously asked of the State decisive and prompt action; and on these accounts she enacted laws, abrogating the Cherokee government, making it penal to dig gold, and punishing a resident within the territory, unless the resident would take an oath to observe the constitution and laws of the State. The exclusion of all white persons from the Cherokee lands was the dictate of policy and necessity. It was well ascertained that the efforts of whites resident in the nation were directed to a prevention of the removal of the Indians. They dissuaded the Indians from emigrating, encouraged them in their ideas of independence, misrepresented the policy and intents of the government, and thwarted by all the means within their power, the views of the State. It became necessary, therefore, that the State should abandon her policy, and cease her efforts to remove the Indians, or rid herself of the selfish and corrupt whites who had settled among them. Hence the passage of the act making it penal to reside within the limits of the land occupied by the Cherokees, without a license, and without taking an oath to observe the constitution and laws of the State. The oath and the license, it was thought, would be sufficient protection of the policy of the State, from any attempts to defeat it by such as might think proper to remain. To such as were well disposed to the benevolent views of the State, the oath would be no stumbling block, whilst it would exclude such as were hostile to her interests and her policy. And the fact of permitting a residence there, upon such terms, proves conclusively that the law was intended to operate upon such only as were defeating the great objects of the State. Removal of the whites was not so much desired, as the destruction of that influence which was at war with the interest of Georgia.

It is worthy of remark, that the federal government, acting "in loco parentis" to the Indians, delegated to her Indian agents more power over whites, resident in the nation, than Georgia seeks to exercise, in the enforcement of her law. They were instructed, by order from the War Department, in the following words: "You are to allow no white person to enter and settle on the Indian lands within your agency, who shall not, on entering, present to you approved testimonials of his good character for industry, honesty and sobriety; nor than, without the consent of the Indians. And if, after permission is given under such testimonials, the person or persons to whom it is given shall become lazy, dishonest, intemperate, or in any way setting vicious examples before the Indians, exciting them against each other, or inflaming their jealousy and suspicion against the general government, or any of its acts towards them, or attempting to degrade in their eyes the agents of the government, thereby destroying their influence over the Indians by false accusations or otherwise, you will forthwith order such person or persons out of the Indian country." It is here seen, that Georgir, in her sovereign character, has scarcely assumed as much power cver these persons, as the federal government thought proper to commit to her agents, who were to a great extent irresponsible. Both governments had mainly in view the same object, in the suppression of any influence among the Indians adverse to their benevolent designs towards them; and yet, not a few of those who admit and justify the measures of the general gcvernment, condemn and reprobate the law of this State. Your committee are of the opinion that when this matter is understood, it will be admitted that all which Georgia has done was made necessary in order to effect the removal of the Indians.

Let those, too, who clamor so much about Indian rights, and who weep so over Indian sufferings, know, that this law was necessary to the protection of the persons and property of the Indians, from the violence, the intrigues, and the corruptions of the whites. Here it is well understood, that white men are the greatest enemies to the Indians, whether in the character of the selfish, avaricious, and ambitious resident within their limits, or the character of the political knave, or canting fanatic without their limits. At no time have Indian rights been better protected, and at no time has the Cherokee tribe exhibited more evidence of peace, quiet and protection, than since the extension of our laws over them. The Georgia jurisdiction has been their shield. Not only so, but the law excluding the whites, was intended to extend, and does now extend, protection to those who are willing to evade its penalties, by complying with its terms. The laws and character of the State are a guarantee to such of more right than they ever enjoyed there. By a strange perversion of principle, or a wretched ignorance of facts, a mild and benevolent policy has been corrupted into the veriest despotism, and that law, which created a right for the white man in the Cherokee country which he had not before, and protected him in the enjoyment of it, has been denounced as arbitrary, unjust, and unholy. At no time, under the intercourse laws, have the Indians been so effectually protected, and at so little cost, as under the laws of Georgia. Your committee have said, that the act of the General Assembly was necessary to carry into effect the benign policy of the State, in reference to the Indians that it operated as a protection to them from the rapacity and violence of the whites; and that, so far from its being an unwarrantable proscription of them, it actually conferred privileges which, of right, they had not before possessed. The latter position is made manifest, by adverting to the fact, that before the passage of the act, no white citizen could claim his residence there as a matter of right; but the moment he complied with the reasonable requisitions of the law, he became ipso facto entitled to such residence, and all the benefits it conferred. It is true, that many were upon the soil at the moment of passing the act; but their residence was assumed, and only tolerated by the State: they were only residents at the sufferance of the State. The missionaries themselves will not deny but that their condition in the Cherokee nation, under the jurisdiction of Georgia, was greatly preferable to what it was under the dominion of the agents of the United States.

The law which has excited so much feeling among our brethren of the Eastern States, is not partial or exclusive in its operation. The first citizen of Georgia, the most abandoned of the refugee adventurers for gold, as well as the meek and law-abiding Moravian missionary, are within its provisions—all classes, all grades, and all professions, are alike liable to its penalties. Our law in this, as well as all (other) cases, aims at no individual or individuals, and recognizes no exemptions; and had the most talented or the most dignified of our sons resided within the limits of our lands in the possession of the Cherokee Indians, without having taken the oath, the law would have been administered upon such a one with unsparing rigor and unrelenting severity. Your committee, therefore, declare that no objection can be urged against the State, with any propriety, upon the score of its inequality, for the State made all "men equal under the law."

The law of the last Legislature, herein adverted to, did not, according to its provisions, take effect immediately. The commencement of its operation was fixed at a time sufficiently remote to put all persons interested upon their guard; and ample opportunity was afforded for a knowledge of its existence and of its provisions. No man was entrapped; and all who offended against it, sinned against the authority of the State, with a perfect knowledge of the consequences. Most of those persons who were residents in the Cherokee country, either removed from the State, or submitted to the requirements of the law (d). The board of directors of the United Brethren's mission at Salem, believing that the object of their mission to the Cherokees, under the peculiar circumstances of the State and the Indians, could not be effected, instructed their missionaries to remove from the country. Acting, as your committee believe, from a sense of respect to the laws and authorities of Georgia, they were unwilling to interfere with her laws or her policy. In the conduct of these unobtrusive and devoted missionaries of the cross, is exhibited in bold relief the pure and suhlime principles of our holy religion. Some there were, however, who refused to remove from our limits, and who refused to comply with the conditions of residence prescribed in the law. These individuals were either missionaries, or persons who were under their influence, and acted under their advisemnt. The most conspicuous and talented of these individuals, are the Rev. S. Worcester and Dr. E. Butler, missionaries of the American Board of Foreign Missions.

These persons had long been conversant with the policy of the general government, and with the rights as well as the laws of Georgia. The law, to whose penalty they became obnoxious was known to them. The law had raised, within their hearing, its warning voice, and admonished them of their duty; but the Governor of the State, reluctant to enforce upon them the penalty of the law, respecting their sacred profession, and respecting still more the most holy cause in which they were engaged, kindly and politely, and in the spirit of forbearance, warned them yet again of their crime, and invited them away from their own ruin. A perscnal address was made to each of them by his excellency, and ten days given for their removal—all this did not avail. They not only persisted in their illegal residence, but ventured upon the justification of their crime in an address to the executive of the State. Orders were then given to arrest them, that they might feel the full penalty of our laws, "since such was their voluntary choice." They were arrested, tried, convicted, and now, inmates of the state prison, they suffer the melancholy doom, which their perverse obstinacy or misguided zeal has brought upon them.

What reproach could be cast upon the State for their conviction, and what justification or exemption can be had for their violation of the laws of the State? None. No man would hesitate to pronounce them the wilful perpetrators of their own misfortunes. If it be said that they were residents upon those lands by permission of the United States' government, and therefore the State had no right to punish them; your committee answer, that the government has no power to bestow a right which is adverse to the rights of Georgia, and that this permission was good to them so long as the State acquiesced in it, and no longer (e); and the enacting of the law, making the residence criminal, is a declaration of the State's dissent to it. If it is said that their residence was by permission of the Indians, and therefore the State could not make it penal—your committee answer, the Indians, it is true, have a right of occupancy; but this right of occupancy is personal to themselves, and cannot be delegated to any person whatever; therefore their consent to a residence is no justification. The ultimate fee to the lands is in Georgia; and so far as Georgia and all the world (except the Indians) is concerned, she is the absolute, unqualified owner. As your committee before remarked, the right of jurisdiction is in Georgia, and of consequence there is no limit to her right of penal enactment. The State owned the lands, and it was perfectly competent for her to prescribe such terms to residence upon them as she deemed fit and expedient. It will not be denied that the State has the right to prescribe such conditions to a residence upon the Statehouse square in the town of Milledgeville, as she may think fit. So far as all the world (except the Indians) is concerned, there is no difference between the title which the State has to her Statehouse square and her title to the Cherokee lands. In either case the grant is in her, and can never be divested but by her own act. If it is said that the State did require the missionaries to take an oath which in conscience they colud not take, or suffer the penalty of the law; your committee answer, that the State involved the missionaries in no such desperate dilemma. If the oath was taken, it was a voluntary act, and the oath could have been avoided by removal from our limits (f). If the penalty was suffered it was a voluntary act, which might have been avoided either by taking the oath, or removing from the limits. The missionaries were left free to choose between the oath, the penalty of the law, and removal; and they chose the penalty of the law. Why then should the State be censured for an act, which was the result of choice on the part of the missionaries; and which your committee fear was sought by them, either for the purposes of political effect, or to exhibit themselves to a sympathizing fraternity, as sufferers for righteousness' sake.

They surely cannot claim for themselves exemption from the operation of the laws of the State by reason of their profession or their vocation. The laws of Georgia interfere not with the religious privileges, or conscientious opinions of men; and the State lends her aid to all efforts for the dissemination of the truths of revelation: she is the auxiliary of the missionary, in teaching the heathen the great truths of Christianity; and her constitution and laws are based upon the principles and doctrines of Him who spake as never man spake. Still the law is no respecter of persons: and he who violates it, whether Jew or Gentile, Christian or Infidel, Mohammedan or Pagan, must expect to meet its sanctions, and feel its penalties. It is for the missionaries to reconcile their precepts with their practice, and to prove to the world that the religion which they profess allows, much less encourages, disobedience to laws, insubordination, and resistance to the powers that be. It remains for them to show that resistance to rightful civil authority is either a Christian duty, or a Christian privilege; that things which are Caesar's are not to be rendered to Caesar; and that conscientious scruples can defeat the operation of laws, or stay the hand of government. If the opinion of every subject, as to the constitutionality of the laws under which he lives, can exempt him from their operation, then is government a mockery, and lawgivers, judges, and governors, the merest toys to be sported with according to the whims and caprices of individuals. In the letters of these individuals to the Governor, the reason of their refusal to obey the laws of Georgia, is assigned to be that they did not believe the State had the right of jurisdiction over the country; and believing as they did, they could not do violence to their consciences by taking the oath. Your committee believe that scruples as to the oath should have removed all scruples as to their duty to remove. They cannot deny the right of all men to judge for themselves the constitutionality or propriety of any law; but it is a new idea, that the law, as to such a one so judging, is to fail of its effect and become a nullity. Those who do assume this original, natural right, and act upon it, as the missionaries have done, must expect to suffer as they are suffering the consequences of their rash judgment.

The Rev. Samuel A. Worcester and Dr. Elizur Butler were warned of the existence of the law they have violated. They were politely invited to remove, and time given for their removal. They resisted the authority of the State, and repelled with disdain the kind offices of the Governor in their behalf. They were arrested, defended by enlightened counsel, tried before a court distinguished for its legal wisdom and benevolent feeling, and convicted and sentenced. Still, the authority of the State followed them with anxious solicitude to relieve them; still kindness and mercy and forbearance would have stayed the execution of the sentence. At the gate of the penitentiary they were met with the offer of pardon, upon the easy terms of removal from the territory, or taking the oath. This offer they repelled—these overtures of mercy they heeded not, and entered the penitentiary; a living monument to fanaticism, political knavery, or egregious folly. Notwithstanding all these things, Georgia has been ranked among the despotisms of the east; and her late benevolent, honest, and talented Governor placed among the Neros, Dionysiusses, and Dracos, of infamous memory. From the enlightened, the candid and the pious, of all parties and all creeds, the State must receive a judgment not only of acquittal of error or crime, but of high commendation.

Resolved, That this committee recommend, and do hereby recommend to the General Assembly, the printing of forty copies of this report for each member of the State delegation in Congress, and that his excellency the Governor, be, and he is hereby requested to forward to our delegation in Congress forty copies each of the report.

Read and agreed to.   THOMAS STOCKS, Pres.
Attest I. L. HARRIS, Sec'y'

In the House of Representatives, concurred in, Dec. (24) 1831.
ASHBURY HULL, Speaker.
Attest, W. C. DAWSON, Clerk.
Approved, Dec. 26, 1831.
WILSON LUMPKIN, Governor.

NOTES—By Thomas Stocks.

The foregoing Report was drawn up by a distinguished jurist and esteemed member of the church, and unanimously agreed to by both branches of the Legislature.

(a) New York and other States had done the same. Extract from the law of New York in 1822:—"The several courts of justice, organized under the constitution and laws of this State, possess the sole and exclusive jurisdiction of trying and punishing, in the manner prescribed by law, all persons, as well Indians as others, for offences and crime committed within the boundaries of the State," &c.

"For a long succession of years," says the Supreme Court of New York, "we have exercised entire supremacy over all the tribes within the State, and have regulated by law their internal concerns, their contracts, and their property."

(b) There was no safety to persons travelling through the nation, and no authority to punish for the most enormous crimes. Two white men wantonly murdered another who was residing within the limits of the nation. They were arraigned before the Superior Court of an adjoining county; but the judge could not punish them, because the constitution of Georgia requires all criminals to be tried in the county where the crime was committed; but the Cherokee country was not a county. Unwilling, however, to let such an infringement of personal rights pass without punishment, the judge bound the prisoners to appear before the United States Court for the district of Georgia. There the judge decided that he had no power to punish them, and they went at large! When these decisions were made known, the number of outlaws and villians was greatly multiplied, and they swarmed into the Cherokee Nation.

(c) These men, together with chiefs, controlled the whole body of Indians. It was their interest to retain possession of the country, and impose on the ignorance of the great mass of the population. The chiefs, most of whom are nearly destitute of any Indian blood at all, received and made use of the annuities paid by the general government, for themselves, and expended it for their own interest. Lately, however, the President has directed these annuities to be paid to each family; and hence the head men, in order to fee lawyers, have resorted to the speech-making plan among the Northern States. A few years ago, some hundreds accepted the offer of the government, and removed west of the Mississippi; but to prevent further immigration, the chiefs passed a regulation making death the punishment of any family that would enroll for this purpose! The common Indians felt it was their interest to remove, and all would have gone ere this, had it not been for the despotism of their rulers. Their game is gone; and it is well known they are too indolent to labor, and many of them are in a most wretched condition.

(d) Rev. Mr. O'Bryan, a Baptist missionary, was in the nation; but he did not think it was his duty to defy the laws of Georgia, lecture on politics, and insult the government. Nor did he lose the confidence of the Indians for his respect to the laws. More than eighty families begged him to go west with them; he has consented, and they have now probably arrived beyond the Mississippi.

(e) The right of soil and jurisdiction was in Georgia previous to the formation of the federal constitution. She permitted the United States government to regulate intercourse with the Indians, until it became necessary for her to assume jurisdiction.

(f) The missionaries could have removed if they disliked the law, a few miles, either into Alabama, Tennessee or North Caroline, and there, within the same tribe, pursued their benevolent labors. There is nothing in the Georgia law which infringes at all their rights of conscience, or hinders them from preaching the gospel. Should it be said that the taking of the oath would destroy all their hope of doing good with the Indians, it may be answered, that it is not true; for Mr. O'Bryan's obedience did not unfavorably impress the Indians towards him.

Let is be asked, would Massachusetts suffer the Mashpee tribe within that State, to declare itself an independent nation? Would New York, or any other State suffer it?

If it should be said that Georgia is wresting the lands from the Cherokees, it is not true: she has directed the survey of them, in expectation that the general government will soon induce them to remove beyond the Mississippi; but she does not intend to dispossess them of the right of occupancy. They may remain as long as they please.

This report, and these few notes and remarks, have been reprinted to correct the many erroneous impressions that are abroad on this subject. Had the presses at the North given publicity to the report and other documents, refuting the many slanders cast upon Georgia, this pamphlet had not seen the light.

THOMAS STOCKS.

New York, April, 1832.

Chapter X.

THE proper application of the public money appropriated by the Legislature for the support of free schools, and the education of the poor, was a matter of great difficulty when I was in the Executive Department. Society was so loosely organized, whilst the State was acquiring from time to time possession of its Indian territory, and its public lands settled up with people from hither and thither without the knowledge of each other, or any principles of action in common, that the trial to educate the poor by the public money through the people of each neighborhood proved a wasteful expenditure.

The following letter was written upon the same subject at the time.

Executive Department, Milledgeville, 8th April, 1830.

Sir,—I have been requested by the Legislature to correspond with the distinguished and intelligent gentlemen of our country upon the best practical plan of extending the benefits of education to the children of the poor, at the public expense. Large appropriations have been made to effect this object for several years past, with but very little success. It is important that the causes which have produced this failure should be ascertained, so that they may be obviated hereafter, or if the object be found impracticable that the present wasteful expenditure should be no longer continued.

I am desirous of obtaining your opinions upon this subject, and hope that the request of the Legislature will be my sufficient apology for asking their full expression in answer to this letter.

The policy of making appropriations by the government to effect ends which are within the means of individuals has always been considered questionable. Is it not true that active enterprise, love of distinction, and the selfishness of men, will effect whatever improves their condition within their own means to accomplish, more certainly and economically than when undertaken by the government? Is it not one of the most beneficial results of free governments that the people are permitted to enjoy according to their own will and taste the largest possible share of the profits of their labor? Are not the means of the people for the education of their children lessened by supporting common schools out of the public treasury, just by so much as the money which they pay in taxes for that purpose is decreased by the expense of collection, loss of interest, and the unfaithfulness of public agents? Is not public opinion so impressed with the value of education in our country, as to render it sufficiently certain that the people will of their own accord apply their means to the support of schools? In those cases where this may not be true, can the government by any vigilance or expense overcome the neglect of parents but at an expense greater than any consequent advantage to the community?

If you are of the opinion that the education of the people should be conducted at the public expense, ought not the children of all classes to receive an equal benefit? Is it not contrary to the spirit of our government to make distinctions by the laws, between the rich and the poor, or to extend advantages to one class which are not given to the other? Will not improper jealousies be thereby created among the people? Are we not by such a system inducing the poor to be contented in a state of poverty? Ought we not rather by our policy to stimulate them to industry?

If you are of the opinion that the poor alone should be educated at the public expense, are there not insuperable difficulties in making beneficially such an expenditure, arising from the peculiar locality and population of the State? Whilst one-third of our territory has a population exceeding twelve to the square mile and another third not equal to two, is it possible to adopt any system which will operate equally in every section of the State, and profitably to all? Is not our population too sparse, if it were equally distributed, to enable the government to render any plan useful? Are not the present habits of our people too migratory to have the constant advantage of experienced agents for disbursing the public money or of acquiring and retaining any tolerably accurate knowledge of the poor children who are proper subjects of the bounty of the government? Can we create any civil divisions subordinate to the counties in which agents can be found capable of properly directing the education of the poor within them? If notwithstanding the obstacles in the way of success, you should be of the opinion that our present system ought to be continued, how shall its defects be corrected? I suppose them to consist principally in making the Trustees draw the money to be expended by them from the Treasury of the State; the want of responsibility in the Trustees; not requiring the Trustees to report to the Executive office, and to have their accounts passed upon there; the imperfect manner in which the numbers of poor children are ascertained; the smallness of the sum appropriated for their schooling; and its not being annually made and certain in amount.

The inconvenience of drawing money from the Treasury, according to the requirements of the law, especially by the Trustees in the distant counties, is so great, that many of the counties do not draw their proportion at all. It is now more than three months since the dividend of the Poor School fund for the years 1828 and 1829 was declared, and not more than one third of the counties have applied for their allotments. Would it not be more convenient and equally safe, to authorize the Trustees to draw upon the County Treasurer, or the Collector of the Taxes, the amount being first ascertained at the treasury and duly published? Might not the responsibility of the Trustees be better secured, by requiring them to submit their accounts to the County Treasurer, and there passed upon? They are never accompanied by any vouchers, so that the Governor cannot know whether the expenditures have been made at all, nor is it possible for him to judge of their propriety, if made, because the subjects of them and their attendant circumstances cannot be known to him. All that is required of the Trustee, is to report. If it were his duty to exhibit his accounts to some officer in the county where the public money is disbursed, to be examined and passed upon, or rejected by him, and then filed in his office, where they would be subject to the examination of every person, would not improper accounts be more easily detected and certainly exposed than at present?

Would it not be a still more convenient and efficient plan, to provide that no money shall be drawn by the Trustees, but make it their duty to contract with the schoolmasers for the educaion of the children to be taught, and on the execution of the contract, give to them orders upon the State or County Treasury for whatever may be due them? At present the Trustees may receive the money allowed their counties, and hold it for a long time without the knowledge of those interested in its disbursement. This could scarcely be the case, if they received the money of the County Treasurer, or Collector of Taxes, and would be effectually prevented by the schoolmasters drawing the money as has been suggested.

The present law requires that the Justices of the Peace in each captain's district shall make out a list of the children in their respective districts, whose indigence entitles them to a participation in the poor school fund, and report the same in writing to the Trustees, &c. It attaches no penalty to a failure on the part of the Trustees to comply with its requirements, and the consequence has been that reports have been made by very few. Must not this difficulty be overcome in some way before any thing can be effected of any use? What do you think of making it the duty of the Grand Jury in each county, to investigate this matter, and requiring of that body to present defaulting Justices? Or, if this should be supposed harsh or calculated to deter respectable men from accepting the office of Justice, could it not be made the duty of the Receiver of Tax returns to make out a list of the poor children as a part of the business of his office giving him an adequate compensation for his additional labor?

The sum hitherto appropriated has as yet equalled $20,000. But as some of the sources from which it is derived are failing, or uncertain, it may in some years be less than that sum, and when that shall be the case, according to the present law, no distribution can take place.

Is it not absolutely necessary for sustaining such a system of education as ours, that it should be kept constantly in operation? How are teachers otherwise to be had, the poor children to be known, or experienced agents found who will act

Estimating the extent of the State at 60,000 square miles, and allowing 16 square miles to each school, the number in the State would be near 4,000. According to this calculation, $5 would be received by each school for the education of the poor children.

Is not $20,000 wholly inadequate for the purpose of educating the poor in a territory so extensive as ours? Ought not the sum appropriated to be sufficiently large to authorize the maintenance of a school in each neighborhood for at least a part of the year?

These various suggestions and inquiries have been made for the purpose of drawing your attention to the whole subject without any expectation that each will be specially answered.

The education of the people, as well as the appropriation of large sums of public money for purposes within the attainment of individual exertion, are important subjects of consideration for the Legislature of the State. It is hoped that yourself and other gentlemen whose intelligence and weight of character have the power of directing public opinion upon such matters, may throw so much light upon this subject as to enable the Legislature to correct the defects of our system of educating the poor, or to justify it in putting an end to the public expenditure for that object altogether.

Very respectfully, yours, &c.,
GEORGE R. GILMER.

Col. William Cummings, Dr. Henry Jackson,
Dr. John Wingfield, Col. Joseph H. Lumpkin.

Executive Department, Milledgeville, 29th March, 1830.

Sir,—By the request of the Legislature of this State, I have addressed letters to gentlemen residing in different States of the Union for the purpose of collecting all the information possible upon the subject of the best practical system of educating the poor of the State at the public expense. I have taken the liberty of directing one of these letters to yourself. I am desirous that you should extend your remarks beyond the particular subjects of inquiry in that letter. Your intimate acquaintance with our people, their habits and wants, and your knowledge of the local peculiarities of the State, will enable you to do this in a very acceptable manner to us.

Can we make an application of the public money for the education of the poor sufficiently beneficial to justify such an expenditure? Is not the extent of the State too great and the population too sparse, too unequally distributed and too unsettled? It is on this part of the subject that your opinion is particularly desired. I must confess my want of confidence in the success of any system of free education that could be devised for Georgia at the present. All admit that the money which has been hitherto been expended for that purpose has been wasted. The importance of education in a free Democratic Government like ours is so strongly impressed upon public opinion, and the cause of the poor so popular, where all officers depend upon the voice of the people, that it is extremely difficult to pursue such policy as the true interest of the State requires.

At present, the annual product of the bank stock and other property pledged for the education of the poor scarcely equals $20,000. Of that sum, it may be estimated that not more than half has its proper application, and of that half, that its usefulness is not equal to one half of the same amount applied by the people to the same purpose from their private resources, and according to their own judgments. This proceeds from a variety of causes, besides those already suggested, especially from the fact, that we have no such class as the poor. Our lands are so cheap, and the absolute necessaries of life so easily obtained, that the number of dependent poor are scarcely sufficient to give exercise to the virtue of charity in individuals. A beggar is almost as rare with us as a prince. Children instead of being an encumbrance to the poor of our country, are their riches. It has also been found that from the smallness of the sum appropriated, it has been either so temporary in its application or so local that no general benefit has resulted. The smallness of the sum appropriated, as well as the uncertainty of receiving any portion of it for any certain length of time, has prevented (what was very desirable) any increase in the number of teachers. I have no doubt, myself, that as much money is drawn from the poor by taxation (for those who have nothing are subject by our laws to poll tax) as is ever returned to them for the education of their children. I have as little doubt but that the cause of general education would be as much advanced by relieving the people of the payment of $20,000 in taxes, as from the application of that sum by the Legislature to that purpose.

Perhaps the very highest blessing of a free and enlightened government is, that each individual is secured in the enjoyment, according to his own taste and will, of the profits of his own labor. Governments may be considered oppressive in proportion to the authority which they exercise in arbitrarily controlling that enjoyment. It yet remains to be tested (it seems that our own country is not to furnish the example), what extent of prosperity and happiness would result from the establishment of a government without revenue, except for its administration and for defence from foreign enemies. It appears to be extremely doubtful whether a government like ours ever did beneficially execute any measure which would be effected by individual exertion. The vigor of execution, the enterprise, industry, ambition, and economy which result from every individual in society having the use of all his own means, would most probably accomplish in the best manner every thing required by the interest or happiness of the community.

The benefit derived from permitting society to use its means according to its will would seem to apply as well to education as to any other improvement.

When to the truth of these general principles is added the practical objections arising from the peculiar situation of our State and people, are not appropriations of the public money for the purpose of general education rendered questionable?

Our poor school system has been in operation six years, and we have been unable to procure lists of the poor children from one fourth of the districts of the State.

It is believed that not one additional school has been kept on account of the assistance furnished by the State.

The Trustees draw the money to be expended by them through a warrant from the Executive office, and account only to that department for their conduct. The money is, consequently, obtained with great trouble, and afterwards expended with little or no responsibility.

These suggestions are made for the purpose of calling your attention to an examination of the whole subject. My apology for asking such an examination is to be found in the high respect known to be entertained by our people for your character and talents.

Very respectfully, yours, &c.,
GEORGE R. GILMER.

Rev. William T. Brantly.

The legislation of the State and the opinions and practice of men have been so various about banking; the buying and selling of coin; the lending of money and the rate of profit charged for its use, that it may be worth while to give here the copy of a letter which I wrote upon the subject, in answer to one received from a tax collector or receiver, asking for my opinion to aid him in the discharge of his official duty.

For many years after the age when men usually receive of their father their allotted share of his estate, I declined taking any from mine, from the probability that I might never have health sufficient to employ it profitably. When my father died, my brothers gave me money or their notes for my share of our inheritance. I have never owned land and negroes, beyond what was sufficient for household purposes and wants. Although I was born in Georgia, and belonged to a prosperous tobacco and cotton-making family, I have never made a pound of these staple productions. My property has always been in the hands of others. I have been offered ten, twelve, sixteen, twenty and twenty-five per cent., and even more, for the use of my money. I have never received more than the law determined to be the proper rate of interest.

I have six brothers, all of whom are much richer than myself. Not one of them has enjoyed his estate so much, or had so little trouble in its management, or been so entirely satisfied with its increase as myself. One day in the year suffices to ascertain what I am worth, so as to report to the receiver of taxables for Oglethorpe County. I take but little further trouble about it. When I am from home for a long time, my neighbor and friend L. J. Deupree, takes charge of my moneyed concerns, and reports them in a better state when returned, than when received. I make my profits and expenses tally, except when my wife wants a large addition to her house, a new carriage, an additional supply of hothouse plants, new carpets, china, silver, &c., &c. The overdraws thus made, I have usually paid out of some family legacy, or old fees, so that my estate is about equal in amount to what it was when I quit professional and public business. The Legislature to be sure has made a strong inroad into my income of late years by lessening the rate of interest from eight to seven per cent. But as I consider this change of the law right, I have endeavored to accommodate my expenditure to my lessened means, though it operates a little hardly, upon my wife's love of new and pretty things. As she has the happiest temper in the world, and makes her husband well satisfied as his constitution will allow, he is Cauderized but little on account of the deficiency of money to supply her wants.

The letter alluded to is as follows:

Executive Department, Milledgeville, 16th March, 1830.
Sir,—I received, this morning, your letter, requesting my opinion as to the construction of the Tax Act of 1829, and particularly whether money-lenders are subjected by it to the payment of a tax.

It is not a part of my official duty to expound the Acts of the Legislature. Any opinion which I may give upon such a subject can have no more weight than that of any private citizen. In most wealthy and commercial communities, the business of brokerage and private banking are well known. It is the employment of brokers to exchange one kind of banknotes for others, or for coin, or one kind of coin for another, for profit. To carry on this business properly, requires a collection of the various sorts of money, as the trade of the merchant does of many kinds of goods. It is really the trade of buying and selling money. The stock on hand for the purpose of taxation can be as easily ascertained as a stock of merchandise.

Private bankers differ only from public bankers in this—that public bankers act by the authority of law, and private bankers without it. Whoever keeps a bank, or office of discount and deposit, or office of discount only, is a banker. Whoever makes a business of issuing negotiable paper in such a manner as to form a part of the circulating medium of the country, may also be considered a banker, such as McKinne & Schultz formerly were, and the many issuers of change bills.

Money shaving is an employment never perhaps dignified by the notice of a Legislature before the Tax Act of 1829. Since the great decline in price of most of the staple productions of the State, the heavy duties upon imports, and the consequent suffering and want in our community, this trade has been but too sensibly known to our people. It consists in the buying of promissory notes, or bills, at a deduction, or by shaving off a part of their amounts, or paying for them less than is actually due. If the money lending about which you ask my opinion, is conducted either in the form of banking, brokerage or shaving, it comes within the meaning of the act.

If by money lending you mean the act of a man's putting his own money out at interest, and taking a bond or note of the borrower as the evidence of the debt contracted, and to enforce payment, it does not come either within the words or spirit of the law; nor do repeated acts of this kind make a man a banker. A man taking a bond or note from one to whom he has loaned money does a very different act from issuing notes to others, upon their paying him money therefor. The banker keeps money, and issues notes upon the credit of it; the lender parts with his, and takes notes for the purpose of getting it back with interest. The community derives great advantage from the circulation of all the money within it. The State cannot, therefore, intend to suppress the lending of money, except at usurious interest. The issuing of bills of private bankers has always been considered highly injurious to the State, because it renders the quantity of the circulating medium sometimes too great for the purposes of the people, and at other times too little, and gives rise to speculation, and most commonly to the failures of bankers, and consequent loss to the community.

As you have stated no particular case, my remarks could not be more precise. Very respectfully, yours, &c.,
GEORGE R. GILMER.
John Smith, Esq.

The power of pardoning convicted criminals is the distinguishing authority which belongs to the Governor. It is sometimes exercised with too much rigor to answer the end intended, and at other times with so much clemency as to defeat it. How I exercised this peculiar executive prerogative may be judged of by the following answers to applications for pardons.

Executive Deparment, Milledgeville, 31st December, 1829.

Nothing is more natural to human beings than pity for those who suffer, and the wish to relieve them. It is not, therefore, a matter of wonder that petitions for the pardon of convicts in the penitentiary should often be signed by great numbers of persons, without regard to the guilt of the convict. The petition for the pardon of Henry R. Rodgers is a striking instance of this fact. It is said that Rodgers has a wife dependent upon him for support. So much the greater his guilt, in forgetting what was due to her. His belonging to a respectable family still further proves that the ordinary restraints upon men could not prevent him from committing crimes. His good behavior in the penitentiary, is but a very slight reason in favor of his pardon, because his obedience to the laws of the penitentiary, is a matter of constant compulsion. The reasons assigned in the petition for his pardon are not those for which the Governor was invested with the extraordinary power of forgiving offences against the State. There seems to be no doubt but that Rodgers has been guilty of taking away the life of a fellow-being, without the justification of self-defence, and under the influence of vile passions. I should feel the guilt of blood upon my own conscience if I were to pardon him. GEORGE R. GILMER.
To the Petitioners, &c.

Executive Department, Mlledgeville, 26th January, 1830.

Sir,—Your letter, requesting the pardon of H. I. Brewer, a convict in the penitentiary, has been received.

During the session of the Legislature a petition was received from a large number of the most respectable citizens of Elbert County, making the same request. After the most deliberate consideration which my situation enables me to give to this application, I feel compelled to reject it. It must be grateful to Brewer's feelings to know that you have forgiven him the injury done you, and does honor to your character as a benevolent man. But the State, in punishing crimes, does not look to the particular injury done to the individual. Its object is to secure the peace and happiness of society by deterring bad men from the indulgence of their evil propensities. The Governor of the State cannot, consistently with his official duty, permit his respect or regard for individuals to influence his conduct. It is his duty to execute the sentences in all cases, except where alleviating circumstances accompany the commission of offences. There was nothing of the kind in Hendly I. Brewer's case. He disregarded the early precepts of a pious father, and the obligations he owed to an aged mother. His offence did not have the justification of immediate and pressing temptation. Were I to pardon Brewer, I know not how I could refuse to grant most of the many applications for pardon which are made to me. I can, however, fully appreciate the motives which induced you to write in his behalf. Very respectfully, yours, &c.,

GEORGE R. GILMER.

James J. Banks, Esq.

Executive Department, Milledgeville, 2d February, 1830.

Sir,—No application that has been made for the exercise of the pardoning power has occasioned me so much painful difficulty and hesitation as that for Moon. This has proceeded very much from the opinion expressed by yourself, and one or two other friends, who I am certain would not intentionally mislead me in the discharge of my official duties. I have also not been able to avoid sympathizing with the distress of his respectable father; I cannot, however, satisfy myself that I should act correctly in granting his pardon. He has been guilty of a very heinous offence, in taking away the life of a fellow-being. I cannot pardon such a crime, unless committed under the strongest excitement of passion, produced by greatly irritating insults or injury. I have not been able to find any very palliating circumstances in the conduct of Moon. The whole riot in which he deliberately connected himself with others of acknowledged vicious and desperate character, was violent and criminal.

The state of society in our country seems to require that offences of this kind should be suppressed, if possible. Scarcely a week passes without some death by the hand of violence. I am convinced that reformation will only be the consequence of certain and exemplary punishment. In exercising the high prerogative vested in me by the constitution of pardoning crimes, I consider it my duty to be governed by no consideration but the public interest. I dare not consult my own feelings and wishes, the desires of my friends, or the entreaties of the friends of the criminals. Influenced by these considerations, I have not, as yet been able to find it consistent with my duty to pardon Moon.

Very respectfully, yours, &c.,
GEORGE R. GILMER.

Frances Meriwether, Esq.

The following letter is upon a subject which still calls for investigation, and the hand of reform. The power which the courts exercised at the time when this letter was written, of punishing personal injuries done to the officiating judges, without the intervention of a jury, or the express authority of law, is a remnant of the barbarous despotism of the English judiciary in old times. The will of the judge is uncontrolled by any limits defined by law. The injured party sits in judgment on his own case, and uses his official power to punish his enemies or insulters.

The punished persons can obtain no relief from hardship or oppression through the pardoning power. The conduct of the court in the case to which the letter alludes, may have been proper as the law then was, and yet the law be very wrong. The Legislature has since defined the offence of contempt, but still in a very loose manner.

Executive Department, Milledgeville, 12th June, 1831.

Dear Sir,—In the letter lately received from you upon the subject of Philpot's case, you say you have no earthly doubt of my having the power to pardon for contempt. I regret that neither your suggestions, nor my own investigations, have brought my mind to the same certainty.

The very first, and one of the most important principles of government adopted by the people of this State, is that the Legislative, Executive and Judiciary Departments shall be distinct. The Executive Department has no power to interfere with so much of the Government as has been by the constitution and laws committed to the Judiciary Department. Before the Governor can exercise the power of pardoning, a crime against the State must have been committed and the criminal sentenced by the Judiciary. If the sentence of the court be interlocutory in its nature, and of such character as to look to other results connected with the administration of the laws than the punishment of the offender, and the Executive Department were to pardon such a case, the object to be effected by the Judiciary Department would be defeated. The facts in the case which you have presented to me seem to be these:

A man by the name of Philpot many years ago purchased a negro boy as a slave. In the month of October 1829, he resold the negro. Soon after a writ of habeas corpus, granted by the Inferior Court of Richmond County was served upon him, directing him to produce the body of that negro. This he failed to do, and was ordered by the Superior Court upon an attachment for contempt therefor, to be imprisoned until he produced the negro. This order not having been made a part of the record sent me, I am unable to know what were its terms but from other parts of the record.

After the order of the court directing the imprisonment of Philpot until he should produce the negro, it seems that Philpot himself prayed a writ of habeas corpus of the Superior Court, to inquire into the legality of his imprisonment under the order of the court, which was granted to him, and upon examination, he was re-ordered to prison to be confined under the original order.

The following inquiries suggest themselves, upon the statement of facts. Does it appear that Philpot committed any crime against the State? and if so, what? Was it for lying? for selling a negro? or failing to produce the negro as required by the writ of habeas corpus, without proof that the negro was in his possession at the time of the service of the writ Do these proceedings show that Philpot was convicted of a crime against the State, and sentenced by the court therefor? If so, by whom was he tried, by the Inferior or Superior Court, and what is his sentence? Was his crime contempt of the Inferior or Superior Court? Is the order of the Superior Court for the imprisonment of Philpot until he produces the negro, the sentence of the court upon conviction? Is it a final sentence, or can the court again take cognizance of the same offence? Can the court hereafter order the discharge of Philpot?

A single consideration, arising from these inquiries, goes very far to convince me that the pardoning power does not authorize under present circumstances, the discharge of Philpot. It does not seem to be doubted by yourself or others, that the Superior Court can at any time hereafter discharge Philpot, or in other words, do the act which you are requesting the Executive Department to do. It is very certain that the courts have no power to pardon criminals after conviction and sentence. By what authority, therefore, can the judiciary hereafter interpose so as to discharge Philpot? Evidently (considering the proceedings otherwise legal) because the order under which Philpot is imprisoned is not a sentence upon conviction, but an order auxiliary to other proceedings, for the determination of some individual right. If the Superior Court had considered its order for the imprisonment of Philpot to be a sentence passed upon summary conviction for a crime of which he had been guilty, then the court could not have granted to him, as it did, the writ of habeas corpus to inquire into the legality of that sentence, because that writ is not issuable upon the application of persons in confinement, upon conviction or for execution. I take it for granted, therefore, that the Superior Court in passing its order that Philpot shall be imprisoned until the negro James is produced, did not consider such order a sentence upon conviction, but as the most efficient means of producing obedience to the mandate of the writ of habeas corpus directed to Philpot, requiring him to produce in court the negro which he had sold, and which, according to an allegation in the writ, was not a slave.

It would be foreign to the object of this letter to inquire whether the writ of habeas corpus designed by the Constitution and laws of the State to be the effectual means of preventing the violation of the personal liberty of its citizens, can be used for their continual imprisonment upon such allegations as those made in the writ directed to Philpot. It would be equally so to express any opinion as to the power of the courts of the State to assume the jurisdiction over contempts, summary convictions, and punishment therefor, as exercised by the Superior Courts in England. These matters belong exclusively to the Judiciary Department.

Very respectfully, yours, etc.,
GEORGE R. GILMER.

Augustus B. Longstreet, Esq.

Extract of a letter to the same person on the same subject.

It is not my purpose to investigate at large the doctrine of contempts, as determined by the English Courts. It is sufficient to say that it is the most arbitrary and tyrannical power now exercised over the liberty of the subject in that country.

I think you are mistaken in saying that the common law of England is the law of this State. It is the law only so far as it is consistent with our Constitution, laws, and form of Government, and as had been adopted in practice during the Colonial Government. The courts of England have determined that the power to punish for contempts results from necessity, and that their dignity and authority could not be otherwise maintained. This may have been true when this determination was made, and may yet be so in some degree. But the great object of the British form of Government is to secure its own existence. The object of ours is to secure individual rights. The power of the courts in England to punish for contempts, results from no public law. The courts which have no criminal jurisdiction exercise this power equally with those that have. Crimes, in this State, consist in the violation of some public law. No other acts can be punished as such by our courts. Can any thing be more inconsistent with the nature of our institutions, than that a judge should determine the extent of his own personal dignity, its value to the community, preside in the trial of an offence against it, make the law, determine the guilt, and award the punishment? I repeat, however, that these are all matters that properly belong to the judiciary.

You say that the power to remit the order of imprisonment may be concurrent in the court and the Governor, and analogize it by the power of pardoning which in England may be exercised both by the king and the parliament. But the analogy is directly against your conclusion. In this State the Legislature cannot pardon, because the departments of the Government have been made separate and distinct by the Constitution, and the pardoning power has been conferred upon the Executive Department.

You conclude your letter by asking, if a judge should order a citizen to be cropped, branded, or put to death for a contempt, whether I would not remit the sentence or respite? I answer without hesitation, no. I would no more pardon in such a case, than I would if a judge should, whilst walking the street, order a citizen to be incarcerated for life, for moving in his sunshine.

The Executive Department has no authority to correct the errors of the judiciary. Very respectfully, yours, &c.,
GEORGE R. GILMER.
Augustus B. Longstreet, Esq.

Chapter XI.

THERE are few situations more trying than to remain in office after one has been turned out: to meet the jests of successful exulting opponents: to shake hands with friends who have just lost political power by one's mistakes or unpopular doings. Not many public men have gone through a more severe trial than I did in leaving the Executive office.

By my election, I had offended a large party of my accustomed political supporters. I was defeated by those who had been previously my most clamorous advocates. Those who had voted for me for selfish purposes when I was successful, had not got what they desired. Those who had opposed my election, were compensated for their mortification at my success, by my defeat. However strong may have been my determination to do what was right in office, and however conscious I was of having done so, I could not avoid feeling my situation was very uncomfortable.

My wife, who had stood by me with her smiling face and

cheering voice during the most slanderous abuse, sank in spirit, when she met the chap-fallen looks of old acquaintances, as they assembled at the meeting of the Legislature, and the inauguration of my successor. She thought she had gloried in my defeat for attempting to do what the public good required in opposition to immediate popular impulse. But she found that it was a glory that they had to wait for its exultation until the pageant of the day had passed away.

The party by whom I was supported in the canvass insisted that I should accept of a public dinner. The members thought it would strengthen their re-orgnization. It required the greatest exertion of self-command, to overcome my reluctance to take part in the celebration of my own defeat. I had, however, received their support, and, therefore, consented to their demands. The dinner was on the day when I left the Executive office. Every moment of my time was fully occupied with matters connected with official business. I dined with friends at a private house, so that I had no opportunity to prepare my thoughts for what I was to do or say at the public dinner. None but those who have encountered similar difficulties can enter into the feelings of my very absurd position. Occupying the seat of honor at the dinner table, I was called upon to say how, and why, I had contrived to deprive those by whom I was surrounded of the public offices to which they considered themselves entitled. I made the effort, hemmed, hawed, stammered, stopped, went on by fits and starts, and finally concluded, without saying what might have been very well said in justification of what had been done. We went towards my home in the morning; that night I put upon paper a sketch of what I imagined I had said, and sent it back to the managers of the affair.

This is the sentiment which I expressed when called upon for a toast, and part of the speech.

Honor and success to those servants of the people who have the firmness to execute what judgment directs and conscience approves.

Extract from the speech:

Notwithstanding the difficulty which I find of expressing myself in my present embarrassment, I am yet anxious to add something further in explanation of the measures of my administration. In opposing the immediate survey and distribution of the Cherokee lands, I was influenced not only by what I considered justice to our Indian population, but due to the present Administration of the General Government. The firmness with which Gen. Jackson has sustained his policy of removing the Indian tribes from the States, and placing them in the only situation in which their existence can be continued, or in which they can acquire the arts of civilized life; his prompt acknowledgement of the rights of this State to extend its laws over all its territory, and the exertions which he had made, and is now making, to remove the Cherokees from beyond our limits, imposed upon the State the strongest obligation to avoid the adoption of any policy which would conflict with that of the United States. Upon no subject have stronger efforts been made to excite the prejudices of the people against Gen. Jackson, to prevent his re-election, than his efforts to do justice to Georgia. And shall we give effect to these unprincipled efforts by adopting such measures as must either sacrifice our best friends, or force them, under the pressure of public opinion, to resist their execution? Gratitude and policy both forbid.

The disagreeable circumstances which accompanied my defeat were soon forgotten in the pleasurable sense of relief from the labor, excitement, and exactions of office, and in the sense of gladness created by home, kind neighbors and friends, and the power of doing as inclination led me.

I was soon after put in nomination by the State-rights party, for one of the representatives of the State in Congress.

My wife and myself spent part of the next summer in Virginia. We had been separated from our affectionate relatives and friends there longer than we had ever been before. We greatly enjoyed the meeting and social intercourse with them. Whilst we were in Virginia, Robert Grattan, my wife's brother, married Martha Minor, daughter of Peter and Lucy Minor, of Albemarle. The bride was a capital addition to our family circle, giving a foreshadowing of what an admirable wife, fond mother, and kind kinswoman she has since proved herself to be.

Whilst I was in Rockingham, I read in the newspapers the copy of a letter which had been addressed to me as one of the candidates for Congress, by a meeting of a portion of the citizens of Richmond County, demanding my opinions of the political doctrines then being disseminated by the party in South Carolina, headed by Mr. Calhoun, and known as the Nullifiers. The following is my answer:

Rockingham, Virginia, Sept. 7th, 1832.
To the Citizens of Richmond County.

I have seen published in the Augusta Constitutionalist of the 21st of August, the proceedings of a meeting of Richmond County, at which a committee were appointed to ascertain by direct correspondence with the candidates for Congress "their sentiments in regard to nullification." My absence from Georgia has probably prevented my receiving the communication of the committee. I have therefore thought it my duty to address you directly, lest the object of the call upon me should be defeated. My answer is, that I do not believe that a State can render a law of Congress null and void, which has been passed upon a subject over which Congress has, by the Constitution, the exclusive power of legislation. I am, therefore, no advocate for the adoption of nullification to remedy the evils of the tariff.

This answer might be misconceived, were it not extended to the other important matters embraced within your resolutions.

I cannot concur with you in the opinion that "the tariff recently enacted is a decided amelioration of the system." Its inequality and want of uniformity has certainly been increased.

I cannot agree with my fellow-citizens of Richmond County that the evils of the tariff have been greatly exaggerated. It would, indeed, be difficult to exaggerate the injustice and tyranny of our present system of taxation and public expenditures, which has been made so to operate upon different sections of our country, as to render it an object of eager desire with the majority, for the purpose of enlarging their individual profits, to increase rather than lessen their amounts; and especially when that system has been adopted in violation of all the obligations which bind us together as one people. Georgia suffers more oppressively from the system than any other State in the Union. I do not, therefore, think that its evils ought to be palliated by any portion of her citizens.

I cannot agree with you, "that it is advisable for the present to leave the subject of the tariff to the State Legislature," because all that can be done has already been tried, by resolutions, threats and protests, without producing the slightest effect upon the fixed majority in Congress. I consider it more advisable to refer the subject to a State convention, as recommended at the meetings which have been held in many counties, with the hope that it may lead to one united effort on the part of Southern States, to procure a repeal of the tariff, as the only practicable means by which that object can be effected. I, however, entirely coincide with you in the opinion, that the acts of such a convention will not be obligatory upon the people, without their subsequent approval.

I have thus, in answer to your requirement, given you briefly, and, I hope, with sufficient distinctness, my views upon a subject of great interest to us all. I have not thought that the occasion called for any elaborate reasoning in their support, or that they should be extended beyond the matters in your resolutions.

With sentiments of great respect,
Your fellow-citizen,
GEORGE R. GILMER.

In the election which followed, I received but little support from the union party. The nullifiers, though not satisfied with my answer, could not very well avoid giving me their votes. Although elected, it was evident that my moderate opinions, when everybody else was talking furiously, were creating distrust. Circumstances soon after developed what had been for some time the tendencies of the political parties in the State. The protective tariff policy of the General Government was then the great subject of interest.

Judge Berrien, Judge Clayton, and other adherents of Mr. Calhoun, were soon after found actively engaged in collecting the people together, making speeches and using other means of opposition to General Jackson's administration and the existing tariff laws. They succeeded in getting up a great convention, with the design of effecting their purposes, through what it might be induced to do. The friends of Mr. Van Buren were equally active in their preparations for defence. They endeavored to secure ascendency in the proposed anti-tariff convention, when they found that they could not prevent its assembling. The nullifiers and union-men met in Milledgeville, in November, 1832. I was absent from the State when the preparations for the struggle were making. I was selected for one of the members of the convention, by the people of Oglethorpe County, without having been consulted upon the subject. It was known that my political principles were democratic, that I was thoroughly opposed to the existing protective tariff laws, and that I had long been opposed to the election of Mr. Calhoun to the Presidency. The first act of the convention was the selection of its presiding officer. Both parties being somewhat distrustful of their strength, concurred sufficiently in choosing me, to prevent an immediate trial of their relative strength. Mr. Forsyth was the controlling spirit of the Van Buren, or union party. Judge Berrien and Judge Clayton directed the course of the nullifiers, or friends of Mr. Calhoun. Mr. Forsyth exerted his extraordinary eloquence and tact to prevent the organization of the convention. When he discovered that the friends of Mr. Van Buren were in the minority, he induced them to withdraw. This separation did not secure unanimity among those who remained. Many of the democratic members, who had gone into the convention for the purpose of uniting public opinion at the South against the tariff, and devising plans for its repeal, concurred with me in dissenting from the doctrines of the nullifiers. The convention broke up without doing any thing satisfactory to any body.

A few days after my return home, I received a letter from James Liddell, a leading member of the Legislature, in which he stated that he had heard a portion of my remarks against the doctrine of nullification, that he did not understand the subject, wished to be informed, and asked me to give him my views fully, saying that my letter should be considered strictly confidential. I wrote to him what my opinions were about the resolutions which had been adopted by the convention, particularly that which set forth the extreme opinions of Mr. Calhoun, of the power of a State to control the legislation of Congress on the subject of the tariff, stating to him that they were given to himself, and not for others, or the public. I was thus cautious, because I wished to avoid writing any thing which could be used against my party friends. I kept copy of my letter. When the democraitc State-rights party were about selecting a candidate for Governor in 1837, those who were opposed to my being a candidate, and desirous that Judge Clayton should be, obtained a mutilated copy of my letter to Liddell, and used it to excite the nullifiers into opposition to my nomination. I was in Virginia whilst this intrigue was going on. Upon being informed of it, I wrote to Liddell, that I had heard of his having communicated to others the contents of my letter, and asked him to send me a copy. The sorry fellow, having no suspicion that I had kept a copy, answered that he thought the letter did me great honor, and sent a copy of the part which he knew to be offensive to the nullifiers, and omitted that which qualified what made it so, averring that his eyes were so sore, and he so unwell, that it was as much as he could do to copy what he sent. I soon after saw Judge Clayton and General Harris, who had been very busy circulating Liddell's mutilated copy of my letter, showed them the entire copy, and convinced them that they had been mislead.

Those who are engaged in politics in highly exciting party struggles, are usually driven by experience to keep their bump of caution well rubbed. I met with many other difficulties in going on in my own way during the excitement which preceded the convention, distinguished its discussions, and followed its adjournment. To maintain the position of middle-man, which is generally assumed to avoid responsibility and curry favor, required all my fortitude. As the hubbub passed away, I was cheered by the approving voice of those whose approbation was most agreeable to me.

In May, 1833, a convention of the people of the State assembled in Milledgeville, to consult about the best manner of reducing the number of the members of the Legislature, and equalizing the representation of the people in that body. William H. Crawford and myself were two of the members for the County of Oglethorpe. Mr. Crawford was voted for by the State-rights party to preside over the convention. He was beaten by Judge Wayne, the candidate of the Van Buren party, by nearly two votes to one. Judge Wayne received 151, and Mr. Crawford 88. The amendments to the Constitution for the ratification of the people, being intended for securing party ascendency instead of the rights of the people, were rejected at the polls. The time chosen for assembling the convention proved to be very unpropitious for arriving at beneficial results. The anti-tariff nullification convention which preceded it, had created a state of factious party spirit, which controlled every effort for the general good.

My wife accompanied me to Milledgeville. We passed our time very pleasantly among many excellent friends. Indeed, the difficulty was to find leisure enough, from my necessary attendance upon the convention, to enjoy their hospitality. Before we left home, we agreed to go to Alabama, on a visit to my relations there. My wife insisted that I should direct the time and place of our visitings, as I had always urged upon her to do when we were among her relations in Virginia. The day we left home, she began to prescribe where we should dine, and where we should sup, &c. I laughingly reminded her of her previous proposal, that I should control our visiting until our return home. She replied, that she did not intend that my absolutism should commence till we got to Alabama; but that, if I so desired, she was content. She declined accepting any invitations, referring every one to me. When the applications were accordingly made, I did not know what she wanted, and, as that was which I wished to do, I was very much bothered. The third night after we retired to bed, I told her I was tired to death doing as I pleased, and that if she ever told me again to do so, I would not forgive her. She has constantly kept in mind this injunction.

When the convention adjourned, we went on our way to Alabama. As we passed from Columbus to Montgomery, through the Creek territory, I saw many collections of the people of that most numerous tribe of Southern Indians. I found them less civilized, and uglier in features, than the Cherokees. They showed the same mixture of the blood of the whites in their influential chiefs, and well-dressed and best-looking women. White men occupied many of the public houses on the road, and productive plantations. The United States had shortly before made a treaty with the chiefs for a cession of lands, in which a great many reservations were secured to individual Indians. These reservations had been, from the time of the making of the treaty, the subject of eager speculation on the part of the whites.

I found the fertile lands of Montgomery settled up with active, intelligent, wealthy citizens, who had been drawn there from the old States, by the many great advantages which these afforded to those who desired to increase their riches. The rapid accumulation of wealth whetted the appetite for getting more money, until the people could not be satisfied with any quantity acquired. It was a subject of wondering cogitation for me, who had for many years been constantly taken up with the affairs of government, and the strife of party politics, to listen to my Montgomery friends talking without ceasing of cotton, negroes, land and money. I had never bought negroes, or made profit out of their labor, accumulated any money by speculation, cultivated cotton, or been engaged in any way in the occupations which were stimulating them to incessant exertions. The spirit of devotion to politics and the strong desire to accumulate wealth, find but few common subjects of interest.

Great as were the advantages for money-making, which belonged to this new country, the people were not contented. Every body was agog, and ready to sell out, and move off. When any one breaks away from his native homestead, and goes among strange people, he seldom finds what he seeks for, but goes on hunting for a better home, until his resting-place is under the sod.

I found a kinsman of mine there, who had been my schoolfellow and neighbor in Georgia. He married there, cultivated a good plantation, and was growing rich in the country of his birth. The temptation offered by the rich lands of Alabama, made him sell out. He acquired a large tract of land of the greatest fertility, and made money rapidly beyond example. His land increased in value, until he was offered ten dollars an acre for it. He heard that lands of equal production could be purchased in Texas for twenty-five cents per acre. He had left his house and family to search for lands in Texas, then inhabited by Spaniards and Indians, and was the receptacle of robbers and cutthroats of all sorts. This money mania proved so contagious, that my carriage driver was overheard offering to bet a fellow driver forty thousand dollars.

I returned to Lexington pleased with having seen the prosperity of my kinsfolk, convinced that a great quantity of land, many negroes, and much money were not necessary for my happiness; and thankful that I was permitted to enjoy where I was born, a competency of these good things.

The lawsuit of which I am about to give an account, developes a case of fraud and oppression, more after the fashion of the finished vice of Europe, than what we are accustomed to in this country.

Many murders have been prevented by the adage, "Murder will out." If the maxim, "Fraud will be punished," was as universally believed in, the amount of consequent good might be beyond calculation.

Francis Meson, an Irishman, taught school for many years in Oglethorpe County, and until his savings, and the credit which he acquired by his honesty, capacity, and industry, enabled him to become a merchant. He traded so successfully, that when he died in 1806, he left an estate of near $40,000; one portion of which he bequeathed to William H. Crawford, his lawyer; another to George Phillips, his physician; another to Robert Allison, his countryman and friend; another to a boy who was reputed to be near akin to him; and the remainder to endow an academy in Lexington. Robert Allison's legacy amounted to about six thousand dollars. The legatee was an honest, hard-working, economical man. He laid out his legacy in the purchase of negroes, and went on thriving until his death. He left a widow, two sons, and two daughters. One of the sons married, moved away, and died. Robert, the other, became a sot, and soon after insolvent. Nancy, one of the daughters, was equally unfortunate in getting rid of her property; so that the widow, and Margaret, the other daughter, after a few years, owned whatever of the estate was left unsquandered.

Bob F——'s father, and old Robert Allison, were near neighbors. Bob F—— and the Allison children were schoolmates and associates, as they grew up. When Bob F—— became a man and a merchant, the Allisons traded almost exclusively with him. When he left off selling goods and moved from Lexington into the country, the Allisons by his persuasion rented a part of the land on which he lived, so as to be close by him. They owned at the time twenty very likely negroes, whom they regarded, Irish people like, as a part of their family. These twenty negroes Bob F—— coveted, and determined to make them his own.

The widow and her daughter became very much involved in debt, principally on account of the liabilities which they incurred for their drunken son and brother. They were very plain, hard-working, and economical. The debts which they made on their own account, were for their plantation, which was very profitable. Bob F—— constantly pressed his counsel and assistance upon them, took the entire management of their affairs, supplied them with whatever they stood in need of, bought their crops of cotton, hired many of their negroes and bought others, agreeing that the amount due therefor should be applied to Robert Allison's and their debts. Neither the widow nor daughter could write, or read writing understandingly. They trusted their pretended friend so implicitly, that they were in the habit of putting their mark to whatever papers he presented to them for signature. It was his practice to prepare the papers which he wanted them to sign at his own house, carry them to their's, and request them to make their mark, saying that "the papers are all fixed," so that they might have no suspicion how their amounts were made up. They had no relation, neighbor, or friend, to whom they could look for advice or assistance, except Robert Allison, whose conduct only increased their difficulties. Bob F—— having cut them off from all association with those who could be of service to them, often told them to trust entirely to him, and not to let their left hand know what their right hand did. In this way, and with many other contrivances carried on for ten years, he finally got their marks to a note for $3,700, and a mortgage deed for thirteen negroes to secure its payment, though he was at the time in debt to them.

The widow and daughter took of Robert Allison for the large amount of money which they paid for him, seven negroes. Bob F—— made them believe that these negroes were liable for other debts of Robert Allison which were still unsatisfied. When he found them sufficiently alarmed for his purpose, he bought a small execution against Robert Allison, placed it in the hands of the deputy sheriff, who was a creature of his, took him to the widow's home, beckoned Peggy aside, told her that he had found out that the sheriff had come to levy upon the negroes which she and her mother had bought of her brother, advised her to secrete them, promising that if she would send them to him, he would keep them out of the sheriff's way. When the negroes were accordingly put into his possession, he made the widow and daughter believe that it had become impossible to save them from the sheriff's hands without rendering himself responsible for Robert Allison's debts, and so excited their fears of losing the negroes entirely, that they sold them to him for about half their value. When he had thus stript them of all their property, except the negroes mortgaged him to pay the note of $3,700, he threw off the mask of devotion to their interest, foreclosed the mortgage, had the negroes levied on, and advertised for sale. Horror stricken at his perfidy, the loss of the negroes to whom they were affectionately attached, and the prospect of poverty, they applied to me to aid them with such protection as could be had from the law. I brought a bill in equity for them against Bob F——, in which I stated the various frauds and impositions which he had practised upon them. How he had won their confidence and love by his pretended friendship; how he had got them into his power, by inducing them to put their marks to papers the contents of which were unknown to them; how he had charged them twenty-five per cent. upon the several sums he advanced them in payment of theirs and Robert Allison's debts, and again and again, the same per cent., as they had renewed their notes from time to time; and that the consideration of the note of $3,700 for the payment of which their negroes were about to be sold, if founded upon any consideration at all, was made up partly of charges of interest at twenty-five per cent., and compound interest at the same rate. The bill further stated that the widow and daughter were so poor and friendless that no one would be their security: that they had endeavored, but in vain, to comply with the law requiring security upon injunctions, and that they had offered to let the negroes remain in the possession of Bob F——, where they then were, until the suit should be determined, in lieu of the security which they were required to give.

At the first term of the court, after the service of the bill on Bob F——, he moved that the injunction should be dissolved for want of security. I urged upon the court in opposition, his possession of the negroes, and renewed the offer of the widow and her daughter that he should keep them as he had expressed his willingness to do, till he had discovered their inability to give other security. I stated how he had secluded them from all intercourse with others until they were entirely without friends; how he had preyed upon their property until they had none; and all his other rascally arts to get them into his power. I met only with rebuff from the judge for my denunciations. His honor, though one of the shrewdest of men in judging of character, and himself perfectly honest, had, like everybody else, failed to look through Bob. He was his nearest neighbor, and very good friend. He appreciated him highly as an active member of the Legislature, and a political partisan of the right sort. He ordered the injunction to be dissolved. The negroes were soon after sold by the sheriff, and for far less than their value.

When I was about preparing the bill in equity, I went to the house of the widow and her daughter, to make myself familiar with the facts upon which it was to be founded. I asked them for all the accounts, notes, bonds, and executions which Bob F—— had paid off for them and their brother, and any other papers in their possession, which might in any way relate to the case. They told me that Bob F—— had requested them to put all such papers into the fire. After a good deal of conversation and inquiry, Peggy recollected that there were some papers in the rag box under the bed. The rag box was brought out, and searched. I found a slip of paper having on it calculations at twenty-five per cent., in the figures and handwriting which I knew to be Bob F——'s, of the several debts of Robert Allison, the widow, and her daughter, which made up the note of $3,700. I had, therefore, charged in the bill with perfect confidence, that the debt which Bob F—— was collecting from the widow and her daughter was partly made up of sums of interest calculated at twenty-five per cent.

Bob F——, ignorant of the existence of the paper which I had found, and supposing that all had been burnt which had passed between him, the widow and her daughter; in his answer to the bill, perjured himself, by swearing that he had never charged them more than lawful interest but twice, and then upon inconsiderable debts. I was a member of Congress elect at the time. My health became so bad, whilst I was at

Washington City, and during the next summer, that I did not return home. I put the papers which proved Bob F———'s perjury into the hands of the lawyer who represented me in my law cases in Oglethorpe County, and requested him to use it to make Bob F——— do ample justice to my clients. When my representative showed Bob F——— the paper on which he had calculated interest at twenty-five per cent., he surrendered at discretion, pleaded poverty, and told all manner of lies, so that he was not only permitted to escape the penitentiary, but got off without doing much more than half justice to my injured clients. Though he was the richest man in the community, he tried, before the trial came on, to excite the sympathy of the people, by walking to town and telling those whom he met, that he was about to be made so poor by the Allisons that he could not allow himself a horse to ride.

On the first day after my return home from Washington City, Bob F——— came to me in the court yard, and asked me to go with him into a private room near by. He was stouter than I, and accustomed to striking. I felt my hand grasping my stick, expecting to have a fight, with all the disadvantages arising from his full preparation for the combat. When we got into the room, he turned upon me with a very submissive countenance, and said, in a conciliatory voice, that if he should ever be again a party to any law case, he asked me to consider myself retained counsel for him. My hand let go the grasp upon my stick. It was evident that he felt his knavery to be too well known to fight for it. When he found that he had worked out his row of rascality in the field of Oglethorpe, and that no future crops from cheating were to be gathered there, he determined to move away. His first wife had been long dead, and he married again. He had no feeling for his wife, but jealousy. He had no children. He made his will, by which he bequeathed most of his property to his own kin. Fearing lest his wife might find the will, and discover its contents, if kept in his house, and being without a friend, he put it into the hands of a negro woman, who had been his property, lived with him all his life, and whom he trusted more than any one else. To keep his wife in the dark about what he had done, he told her and every body else that he had no will. When it was found in the possession of the negro woman, after his death, he had so discredited it by his own words, that his kin, after endeavoring for a long time to establish it, became fearful that they would get nothing, compromised with the widow, the lawyers coming in for nearly ten thousand dollars for their share of his ill-gotten gains. His wife and his kin are yet at law; contention and ill-will having been Bob's only certain bequests to those who would have loved his memory if he had followed the injunction, Do unto others as you would that they should do unto you. Before his death, his conscience became very much disturbed about what might follow the final judgment. When he felt his health to be failing, he took to praying, and became a professed Christian. But cheating had been so long practised, that whenever he got rid of the imagination that the devil's claws would be upon him to plunge him into the depths below, he renewed his evil doings. Whilst in a repenting mood, he determined to move away from the place which constantly recalled to his memory each instance of his guilt. He sold his land for six thousand dollars. He ascertained soon after, that the purchaser would have given him eight thousand if he had insisted upon that price. He could not bear to lose so large a sum. He forged a note upon the purchaser for two thousand dollars. His executor was compelled, for his own safety, to sue for the recovery of its amount. At the trial, the plaintiff, the lawyers, judge, and jury concurred in the belief, that the note was of Bob F——'s own making, so that the fact of his guilt was fixed upon his memory by the record of the court, where he had passed all his days, until a few months before his death.

No one who heard his prayers and confessions, or saw the streaming tears of contrition running down his face, doubted the sincerity of his repentance. The forged note, the will made, concealed, and lied about whilst he was thus penitent, proved the overpowering force of the long confirmed habit of deceiving, upon one only convicted of sin, but not converted from it, and adds another convincing example to the innumerable instances recorded in the history of society, of the hopelessness of the struggle by the weakness of advanced age, to change into virtue the vices of an ill-spent youth and manhood.

Chapter XII

In December, 1833, I went to Washington City, and took my seat as a member of the House of Representatives. This was my third term of service in Congress. The interval from the last had been sufficiently long to novelty one of its pleasures. I met many old acquaintances, for whom I had great respect and regard. I had been so constantly engaged in public affairs at home, that I had kept up with the course of politics. My wife preferred Lexington to Washington City. She accompanied me, however, without scolding, because I was there in compliance with the wish of my constituents rather than my own. I had voted for General Jackson for President without being his special adherent; was very indifferent about my relations to parties as they then existed, and yet sufficiently interested in whatever affected the state of the country to take an active part in what was doing. I had felt too much the weight of government on my own shoulders when I was first initiated into the public service. I was now easy in the harness. I occupied a position whose duties were familiar to me. My previous official stations had made me acquainted with the character of the Indians and created an active concern in their well-being. I had associated with me on the committee on Indian affairs, Horace Everett, of Vermont, a plain, sensible man, who was always ready to do the work of writing. A scheme was concocted for changing the idle habits and listless nature of the Indians into activity, by giving them inducements to labor; and of civilizing them, by elevating the objects of their ambition. It was proposed that all the Indian tribes west of the Mississippi, bordering immediately on the frontiers of the United States, should be united into a general government, with power to establish schools; regulate the intercourse and trade between the tribes of the confederacy, and with the United States; and to do whatever else could be done by themselves for the improvement of the people of the confederacy. The United States was to be represented in the general council of the confederated tribes by an agent, and obliged to keep a garrison at the place of its assembling, to secure peace and the enforcement of the laws. The Indian territory was to be represented in Congress by a delegate. It so happened that many of the chiefs of the Northern, Southern, and Western tribes were in Washington City at the time. Among those who met the committee, and entered into the discussions of the plan for the improvement and government of their people were John Ross, Major Ridge, and John Ridge, of the Cherokees in Georgia; Taylor and Van of the Cherokees west of the Mississippi; Chilly McIntosh, of the Creeks; and the principal chief of the Choctaws, whose name I have forgotten. When the Indians first met the committee, John Ridge rose, and addressed me in the declamatory manner and figurative expressions of his people. His father, Major Ridge, spoke English so badly, that he conversed with the members of the committee through an interpreter. He was a very large man, with features indicative of clear perceptions. His conduct was dignified, and his whole demeanor distinguished for propriety. He was the noblest specimen I ever saw of an Indian uncrossed with the blood of the whites. His son John described him to be the most eloquent of all his tribe, and, in proof of what he said, repeated to me the speech he had made to his people when he left them for Washington City. John's description was certainly very good. John Ross is better known than any other Indian in our country. He was only one-fourth Indian by his descent—the other three fourths being Scotch and American. He had all the calculating shrewdness indicated by the European race from which he was descended. The Choctaw chief was equal in ability, if not superior, to John Ross, and with less of the blood of the Indian. McIntosh was sprightly, as was also Taylor, of the Western Cherokees. I wish I could give in detail what passed between the committee and the chiefs, in consulting about the formation of a general government for the tribes. But as I took no notes, the time is too long past to remember with sufficient accuracy what occurred to justify the attempt. I remember that the chiefs concurred in the opinion, that the education of their young men among the whites was injurious to them, and the tribe to which they belonged. They said that such Indians were almost always discontented and dissipated, and did harm by their example. They desired that the laws relating to Indian trade and intercourse should be repealed, from the opinion that trade could be beneficially carried on by their own people. The proposition to allow the territory a delegate in Congress, afforded the chiefs especial gratification.

In October, 1774, the Virginians and Western Indians fought at Point Pleasant, on the Kanawha River, the greatest of all their numerous battles. The fight commenced in the morning, and continued until evening. The Virginians kept possession of the battleground and the slain. A treaty of peace was concluded in 1777, between the tribes engaged in that battle and the Government of the Confederation, through their commissioner, Thomas Lewis, my grandfather. That treaty promised to the Indians a delegate in Congress. The tribes with whom it was negotiated, were some of those whose organization into a general government was the object of the bill. The committee was not, however, entitled to the credit of attempting to execute in good faith the promises of the treaty of 1777. It was not known to the members, at the time when the bill was reported, that any such obligation had ever existed. It was indeed a singular incident that I should have unconsciously attempted to execute a promise made by my grandfather seventy years before.

On the morning of the day when the bill was to be acted on by the House of Representatives, I went early to the hall to prepare some materials for its discussion. I found Mr. Adams in his seat. I paid my respects, mentioned to him the subject of the expected debate, and asked if he would aid in getting the bill passed. He made no answer. I saw the imps of mischief dancing in his eyes, and was unable to draw him from the course he intended to pursue. Judge Wayne, who was then a member of the House, spoke first, in advocation of the bill. Mr. Adams amused himself by a violent philippic against its passage;——denouncing the scheme as the most perfect despotism that had ever been imagined since the tyrannies of ancient times. He dwelt with peculiar severity against the clause which authorized the United States to keep a detachment of troops in a fort to be built at the place of holding the great council. The invectives evidently proceeded from the recollection of the abuse which he had received from the Georgians, on account of his endeavors to prevent the execution of the Creek treaty of 1825. I had no opportunity of replying to him. Meeting him the next morning, I asked him if he remembered that the United States had then a garrisoned fort within the limits of the proposed Indian territory? He said he did not. I then informed him that a fort had been erected there, and a detachment of troops stationed in it, during his administration, and apparently by his orders. The information amused him very much. Whilst he was addressing the House, many of the Indian Chiefs were in the gallery, listening very attentively to him. Before he concluded, John Ridge wrote, and sent me a note, in which he said, that the Northern people had been for a long time shedding tears over them, on account of their degradation; but that now, when the time had arrived for elevating them, they were the first to desert their cause.

In the session of 1827-28, Congress passed a bill authorizing a subscription of $1,000,000 to the Chesapeake and Ohio Canal Company. Mr. Mercer was the mover of the bill, and its very active supporter. The only speech in opposition was made by myself. After stating many objections to the proposed appropriation, the difficulties to be overcome in making the canal, and the improbability that it would yield any profit, I observed that one portion of its route was through the valley between the Blue Ridge and the Alleghany Mountains, a country unsurpassed in richness of soil, salubrity of climate, picturesque scenery, and the industrious habits of its people. It was, indeed, I said, a most lovely land, rendered dear to me by a thousand tender and happy recollections.

In the same speech I compared the expenditure of the twenty millions of money—the conjectural amount which it would take to make the canal—to supply the market of the District of Columbia, to Col. Nick Johnson's scheme to create a fortune for his first son, by planting 100,000 walnut trees along the lane through his plantation, to make coffins for the rich people of the neighborhood.

The long session, continued confinement, and hard labor, tired out all the members, and especially those who had been accustomed to the country and active life. Towards its close a party was gotten up by Mr. Mercer and the Canal Company, for Harper's Ferry. From the opposition which I had made to the Government appropriation for the canal in 1828, I was not entitled to be one of the invited. Mr. Mercer was, however, the special friend of my wife's kinsfolk, the Gambles of Richmond, among whom he had met her in former days. So I was invited, and my wife authorized to invite any ladies of her acquaintance. We availed ourselves of the days when the two Houses adjourned for cleansing their halls, to make the expedition. A fine band of music attended the party. The weather was charming. Every thing was novel, the boats, the canal, and the country. The change from the constant employment in business during a long session, prepred the members for enjoying every incident and sight with peculiar relish. The party left Washington City in the morning, and arrived at Harper's Ferry in the evening. The next day was spent in examining the public works, and enjoying the many picturesque views created by the wonderful pass of the Shenandoah River through the Blue Ridge Mountain, and the vast piles of rocks on each side of it. We ascended to the top of the high hill to the south of the town, where we saw the Shenandoah and Potomac Rivers approaching each other, until their currents united and passed through an opening in the mountain which the Shenandoah had for a hundred miles sought for without success.

I felt a sort of selfish right to enjoy the scene. My great-grandfather was the first white man who dwelt on the headwaters of the Shenandoah. Mine and my wife's ancestors for the previous hundred years, had lived and died on its banks. Many of our nearest relations still resided there. It was my wife's native place, where she had always lived until she accompanied me to Georgia. A public dinner was given to us, where the clever people of the town and neighborhood assembled to do us honor. The workmen at the armory had holiday and added by their merriment to the pleasures of the day. Whilst some of the men were washing their hands at the run of water near the shops, I happened to pass by, and overheard one commenting upon the visitors. He observed that the Adams men were the lean and ill-favored folks at Gen. Rust's, and that the fat, good-looking men at the public-house were Jackson men. When I joined our party and told in the presence of Mr. Adams what I had overheard, he felt it very sensibly as an expression of popular good will for Gen. Jackson, at his expense. It passed away, however, in a moment, the only moment when Mr. Adams was not ready to do his full share of talk and laugh during the trip. The next day we returned to Washington City, with all the necessary accompaniments for fun and frolic. We had with us Hawes, a member of Congress from Kentucky, a western rowdy boatman, who drank brandy, talked and made speeches all day. Mr. Adams never quitted his company, laughing most of the time as if fun was his peculiar enjoyment. Going into the House of Representatives early the next morning, I paid my respects to him and asked how he was. He answered smilingly by holding his sides to indicate their soreness from laughing.

The removal of the public deposits from the Bank of the United States by President Jackson, excited a long and animated debate in both Houses of Congress, and great agitation throughout the country. The measure was high-handed, and the means used not according to rule. But Gen. Jacksons' conduct had never been controlled by what others had said or done. The bank was the most influential instrument of the Aristocratic party, for defeating the Democracy, and controlling the President. Gen. Jackson took from it the deposits of the money of the government, when he ascertained that their use was abused. The contest for rechartering the bank, and for party ascendency, was carried on with all the materials which could be made to bear upon the subject. The managers of the bank created dismay among the merchants and others accustomed to use its money and credit for carrying on business, by curtailing its circulation. The classes injuriously affected thereby, instead of endeavoring to change the direction of the bank, sent deputation after deputation to the President, to represent to him the ruinous condition of the business men of the country, occasioned by his act of removing the public deposits. Gen. Jackson's temper gave way. The deputations were increased in numbers and frequency, so as to drive him to desperation, resignation, or such acts as might change the state of parties.

I went to wait upon the President, to introduce a friend,

whilst these deputations were making their calls. I heard him answer the set speech from the rich merchants of Philadelphia with such fury of feeling, that froth began to gather about his mouth. Though thus maddened in his temper, his purpose was not to be shaken. His friends succeeded, after a while, in stopping the reception of suppliants for the bank.

I was opposed to rechartering the bank, and yet did not approve of the means used by Gen. Jackson for putting it down. Most of the Georgia members of Congress who had been elected on the same ticket with myself, were favorable to the bank, and partisan opponents of Gen. Jackson. I had to mark out a course for myself. The speech which I made upon the subject was prepared with unusual care for me, whose speaking had been usually but impromptu efforts. I give extracts from it because the question discussed has been of continued interest from the commencement of the government.

Mr. Gilmer, of Georgia, addressed the House in substance as follows: He said that the interest excited by the subject under consideration was not confined to the great commercial cities, or to particular sections of the country—it was felt every where.

Those who were of the opinion that the bank was entitled by contract to the public deposits, inferred the obligation from the bonus of $1,500,000 which the bank paid to the government for the exclusive privilege and benefits conferred upon it by the law of its incorporation. That inference, however, disregarded what had been clearly shown to be true, that the public money was deposited in the bank, not for the benefit of the bank, but for the purposes of the government. The inference did not follow from the premises for another reason. The control of the public money was a trust, which the government could not part with; which it had no power or right to sell to the bank or other corporate body, or to any individual. The depository of the public money must, like the money itself, be kept continually within the controlling power of the laws. For what, then, it was asked, did the bank pay the bonus of $1,500,000? He answered in the words of the law, for the exclusive privileges and benefits conferred upon it by the law for its incorporation. Its corporate existence for twenty years, with the right to establish branches in the States, exempt from their authority; to have a capital of thirty-five millions; to hold property, including its capital, to the amount of fifty-five millions; to discount notes, with the faith of the government pledged that no other bank should be chartered during its existence; and that its notes should be received in payment of all public dues, until otherwise directed by law. The price paid for these privileges was exceedingly cheap. The government could now obtain for the same grant, five times the price paid by the bank.

It would have been a violation of the trust delegated to Congress to have sold to the bank the possession of the public money; if the bank was made the depository of the money of the United States, for public purposes, and not for the benefit of the bank; if the bonus paid by the bank was a very small consideration for the exclusive privileges and benefits conferred upon it, then the conclusion was irresistible, that the bank was not entitled by contract to be the depository of the money of the United States.

But, said Mr. G., what kind of contract was that, the benefits of which could be taken away from the party paying for it, by the party receiving the pay, at any time, without conditions, and without the consent of the other party? These charges of violated rights, and plighted faith, and broken contracts, brought against the government by the bank, and sustained by its advocates, could not be used, and would not have been listened to for a moment, but that all the elements of party strife contending for power had been mingled with private interests to conceal the truth from the public eye.

Arguments had been used for the purpose of enlarging the rights of the banks, which, Mr. G. said, he had been surprised to hear addressed to the American Congress. Public feeling had been attempted to be excited, by dwelling on the sacredness of chartered rights. The House had been solemnly warned against trifling with what was so dear to the people of this country. It had been said that, in interpreting the grant by which chartered rights were secured, the law was to receive the most liberal construction. Mr. G. said that no portion of the history of human society was more replete with interesting and instructive matter than the origin, progress, and general effect of chartered institutions. They had their origin in Europe, when the feudal system had rendered the people abject slaves to the crown, the nobility, and the church. They were the means by which the people reacquired some portion of their natural rights, by which society was improved, and many of the abuses of government reformed. The friends of liberty had therefore, in every part of Europe, endeavored to enlarge the sphere of chartered privileges. Emigrants from Europe, and especially the colonists of this country, who were generally the ardent lovers of freedom, brought with them the most sacred regard for those privileges, and, in most of the colonies, obtained some security for their enjoyment by grants from the crown. The revolution effected an entire change in the whole order of things in this country. By that great event the people were restored to all their natural rights. The government which they established was founded upon the principle that all its citizens were equally free, and entitled to equal privileges. Under such a government, exclusive privileges ceased to be objects of popular regard. Grants of corporate powers became monopolies. They were stricti juris, because they derogated from common right. The construction of such grants, instead of being, as formerly, exceedingly liberal in favor of natural right, and against the absolute powers of government, had become strict, because they detracted from common right in a government where it was intended that the same advantages should be enjoyed by all. Chartered rights, derived through banking corporations, so far therefore from being considered peculiarly sacred, and entitled to an enlarged construction, ought to be strictly limited to the privileges expressly granted.

Mr. G. said, there was one view of the subject which appeared to him to extend over the whole ground, and to be decisive against the power of the United States to charter a bank. Whence, he asked, came the power of banking, of issuing notes, or bills It was the natural right of every citizen, unless restricted by law. Extended as banking by corporations was, the amount of notes and bills of exchange depending for payment upon individual capital and credit, was probably greater, in this country, than the amount of bank notes. The power to pass laws for the regulation of the right of individuals to issue notes and bills, belonged exclusively to the States. What individuals had the right to do, artificial beings could be constituted with authority to do. Credit was an important means of acquiring wealth. It gave more employment and activity to industry and intelligence, than any other agent whatever, except capital itself. Like all other means of acquiring, diffusing, and transferring wealth, it was a subject to be regulated by the laws of the State in which the citizen or corporate body using them resided. The power to create banks by a State, was not the exercise of the power of emitting bills of credit. It was the creation of an artificial being, by law invested with authority to do what belonged by right to individuals to do; but which the State supposed could be done more advantageously, for the interest of the community, by corporate bodies. That right the States had not granted to the United States. The United States could not, therefore, assume it, without an act of usurpation. The constitutional prohibition against the States issuing bills of credit, it was said, had taken from the States the authority to create banks; that what they could not do themselves, they could not do by others. The argument, so far as it had any application, was true; but could only apply to such banks as were authorized to issue bills of credit upon the faith of the government, and depending for payment upon its funds. The prohibitory clause alluded to, most assuredly did not take from the States the right to regulate the employment of credit or capital by its citizens, or to create corporate institutions, with the authority to issue notes and bills, founded upon the capital or credit of those institutions. It had been also said, that, if the States had the power of creating banks, it was impossible for the United States to regulate the currency. And whence, he asked, did' the United States get the right of regulating the currency? Certainly, said Mr. G., the constitution conferred upon it no such authority. Its power was the regulation of the coin.

Mr. G. remarked that before he proceeded to discuss the last question which he had proposed for examination, viz., the inexpediency of rechartering the bank, he thought it proper to make a brief reply to what had been said of State governments and State banks. The losses from broken State banks, and the depreciation of State bank paper, had been described in strong terms, for the purpose of proving the folly of the State governments to be so great as to render them inadequate to exercise the power of chartering and governing banking institutions, and the unfitness of those institutions to supply a beneficial currency.

Mr. G. said, that in the legislation of newly formed communities, like most of our States, there would always be great errors committed. It was, however, the peculiar genius of our State governments to profit by experience. They were founded upon the capacity of the people to govern themselves. That capacity was often most strikingly exhibited in the recuperative energy with which the State governments recovered from great mistakes. This very quality of our free representative governments was never more clearly exhibited than in the history of banking. In the new States, whilst capital was scarce, the demand for it was necessarily very active and urgent. Many banks had under such circumstances been created without capital, to supply the place of capital by bank credit. Such banks had, of course, failed to pay when specie was demanded. What was the situation of those States where the evil of broken banks had been most felt? Look, said Mr. G., at the rapidly increasing wealth and rising importance of Kentucky, Ohio and Tennessee. Mistakes in banking, and all other errors, would correct themselves without difficulty in governments, which were practically the agents of a free, active, and intelligent people. Such were not, he said, the operations of governments whose powers were not directly responsible to the people. In our General Government, he said, vast and complicated evils existed, which would not be tolerated for a moment in the State governments. Abuses of power often strengthened the power to abuse.

Mr. G. then proceeded to consider the inexpediency of rechartering the bank. It has been said, that whilst the currency furnished by the United States Bank was the best in the world, better than gold and silver, the State banks were wholly unable to redeem their notes in specie. He said, that the statement was partly true, but that the inability of the State banks to redeem their notes was the consequence of the operations of the United States Bank. The receivability of the United States Bank bills in the payment of all government dues, the possession of the public money, and the establishment of its branches in every part of the United States, had given such an extended and universal credit to the bills of the United States Bank, as to drive specie from circulation. That effect was increased by the use which the United States Bank had made of the notes of the State banks. He knew it had been said that one of the great benefits of the United States Bank had been to control over-issues by the State banks, so as to make their bills convertible into specie. The reverse was true, both of the present and first bank. The disproportion between the paper of the State banks in circulation, and the specie in their vaults, was never so great as at present, and at the time of the expiration of the charter of the first bank. The expiration of the charter of the United States Bank would be the destruction of that extended credit by which the notes of the State banks had ceased to be converted into specie, especially, if accompanied by judicious legislation on the part of the General and State Governments. The want of confidence in the banks would be the people's security against their over-issues.

But it had been asked, how were exchanges to be regulated between different parts of the country? He replied, as they were then between New York and Liverpool. The productions which each section furnished the other, was the principal medium through which commerce would be carried on. The payment of balances would be made, he said, in bills of commercial houses of established credit, in bills furnished by the State banks, or in gold coin. Mr. G. said, that it was exceedingly important for keeping the rate of exchange uniform, and at a fair price, that Congress should regulate the value of the gold coin, by increasing its nominal value, so as to retain it within the country, and so to direct the collection of the public revenue, as to force the State banks to make their bills convertible into coin at the will of the holders.

Mr. G. said, that the opinions which he then expressed were not those of yesterday. They were the settled convictions of his mind. They had been formed with his first examination into the structure of the government, and his mature observation and experience had but added confirmation to the truth of his first judgment. He avowed his entire unconsciousness of the operation of the slightest influence upon him, except his conviction that the public good forbade the restoration of the deposits to the Bank of the United States. He had never owned one dollar of bank stock, either in the State or the United States Bank, or any other stock whatever. He had never borrowed a dollar of any bank. His rule was, not to be indebted at all. He had never committed an act of speculation. He held his personal independence of higher value than any consideration connected with the acquisition of property. He had never asked from the United States office for himself nor for any relation of his. He would never receive any office from the hands of any President. He discharged but the obligation he owed to those he represented, when he urged them not to be carried off from the maintenance of the rights of the States and the people, by the contests for power among the ambitious aspirants for the first office of the country.

Chapter XIII

Whilst I was attending the session of Congress, 1833-34, a large imposthume rose upon my breast-bone. For many years before, there had been occasionally schirrous tumors at the same place. I had some apprehension that the inflamed part would become cancerous.

The imposthume was very large and deeply inflamed. I attended the House, doubled up with the swelling and pain, until I had finally to take to bed. When my wife decided that it was ready for the lancet, I sent for a physician. He opened, letting out only blood, and giving me great pain. After the physician went away, my wife, taking up the lancet which he had used, discovered a speck of pus on its point. She insisted that I should send for him again. I told her that the place was so sore that I could not bear the touch of any one about it but herself, and urged her to use the lancet if she thought it was ncessary. She accordingly applied it so strongly that the discharged pus flew over her. I had been without sound sleep for a week. After thanking and kissing her, I took a good nap, and rose up almost well.

For forty-five years I suffered very much from toothache. Extraction was tried several times, after my last set of teeth were formed, but without success. The tooth always broke, producing the most violent pains in my head. The danger from tooth-drawers was so great that I would no longer permit their application. When a tooth became so decayed as to break, my wife cut out the pieces. She would shake each fragment, and cut round it so softly with her little fingers, that what would have been insufferable from the hard hands of a doctor, scarcely occasioned any pain when done by her. The suffering was usually forgotten in the pleasure which I felt from observing the great effort she made to avoid hurting me.

Immediately after the termination of the session of 1834, we went to Philadelphia to consult Dr. Physic. My health, always bad, had become much worse. When I called upon the doctor, he told me that his own health was so infirm, that I must put myself under the care of his son-in-law, Dr. Randolph. When I returned to the carriage where my wife was, and informed her what Dr. Physic said, she replied that she must see him herself. We accordingly went to his house. When he came into the room, my wife was in tears. She immediately went to him, told him that she had no child; that her husband was every thing to her; that her reliance was upon him, under Providence, for his life; and that she could not trust him in the hands of any body else. Dr. Physic's marble features began to relax as he looked at her earnest face. He replied, Well, madam, if your husband is so precious, go to the mountains for the present. The weather is too hot to operate upon him safely. Return when the weather becomes cold, and I will do what I can for you.

Whilst I was in Philadelphia, I saw some of the demonstrations of the political parties of the city, which were very novel to me, who had been but little accustomed to the action of the people in great masses. It was a time of excitement, on account of Gen. Jackson's removal of the public deposits from the Bank of the United States. That strong measure was resisted by all the means which the moneyed men of the country could make bear against the President. Wealth and numbers were striving for the ascendency. The 4th of July passed during my stay. The greatest preparations had been made for the celebration of the day. Each party invited to its own feast its own distinguished members (the members of Congress, among others). Col. Benton had been long the most thoroughgoing opponent of the bank. The democratic committees and leading men, with the whole tagrag and bobtail of Philadelphia, met him upon his landing from the boat, on the morning of the 4th, and escorted him to his lodgings, with the most uproarious demonstrations of political devotion. I declined attending the democratic dinner, to which I had been invited, but accepted an invitation from the committee of arrangements to accompany them to the place of public speaking. An elevated stand was occupied by Gilpin, the orator of the day, the committee of arrangements, and the invited members of Congress. Each one, except myself, was carried to the front of the stand, introduced to the mob, and saluted with thundering halloos. I declined being made a show of. The stand was just within one of the most beautiful public gardens of the city. The audience occupied the open space outside. The dinner table was inside. As soon as Gilpin concluded his speech, I descended from the stand, and attempted to get out of the garden. The press of the crowd to get to the dinner inside was too great. I amused myself for a while walking around the garden, and examining its beautiful plants and flowers. A fight took place outside. The press took that direction. I went along with it until I found an opportunity of escaping to my lodgings. The aristocratic dinner was to be in a theatre close by. My wife and several other ladies went into the room to look at the arrangements of the table, which, in accordance with the quality of those who were to partake of the dinner, was not to be occupied until a late hour. When we left the room, I was required to pay the price of the feast for each of the ladies and myself. Mr. Biddle, the president of the bank, came into the public room of the house where I was. He filled, at the time, a station so elevated in his own opinion, and those of his party, that he declined being introduced to any anti-bank member of Congress.

We went to the valley of Virginia, and remained with our friends until the time arrived for attending Congress.

During the short intermission from labor, during the Christmas holidays, my wife and myself went to Philadelphia. Dr. Physic had forgotten me. But when I mentioned his promise to my wife, "Ah," said he, "I recollect the lady whose husband was so precious to her." He said that he had not waited on a patient at night for years, but that he would come to her husband, at her request, whenever she thought it necessary.

After a minute and thorough examination of my diseased body, he declared that evils numerous as those in Pandora's box had been fastened upon me. I supposed that the matter which required the most immediate attention was a carbuncle upon my breast. He said that the operation for its cure would be very painful, and doubtful of success, and advised that it should be let alone, predicting that it would pass away. He was right. The carbuncle is gone. He destroyed several internal tumors by strangulation. I was put to bed, and fed on a spoonful of dry rice, and a cup of hot water tea, without cream, three times a day for near three weeks. During that time my wife was my only nurse, not leaving me day nor night.

Whilst we were in Philadelphia, I made the acquaintance of a kinswoman whose kindness I can never forget. She was the sister of Gen. Cadwalader Irvine, and widow of Dr. Charles Lewis of the Sweet Springs, Virginia, a first cousin of my mother's. Whilst I was under the hands of Dr. Physic, and confined to my room, she called every day at the house where we were, to see my wife, inquire how I was, and offer her services for our assistance and comfort.

Eliza Grantland, the daughter of Mr. Fleming Grantland of Georgia, a great favorite, was at school in Philadelphia at the time. We recommended her to Mrs. Lewis. During all the time she was in Philadelphia, Mrs. Lewis took her to Gen. Irvine's, with whom she lived every Saturday and Sunday, and treated her in every way as her own near kinswoman.

I heard from Mrs. Lewis, whilst in Philadelphia, that her youngest son, a lad, had been so excited by the desire to see Gen. Jackson, as he passed through Pennsylvania the year before, that he ran away from his school, and joined the President's escort. The extreme admiration of the youth for the military chieftain, indicated so decidedly the pursuit in which he would probably excel, that I advised Mrs. Lewis to get him into the navy if possible, as the service best suited for calling into useful action his love for distinction.

When I returned to Washington City, I wrote to Gen.

Jackson, asking from him a midshipman's warrant for young Lewis, in which I mentioned the military services which had been rendered the country by his ancestors, particularly in defending the State of Virginia against the Indians and the British, alluded to his like services to the United States, and referred to the great regard which I understood he had for John Lewis, the uncle of young Lewis. I applied to John Robertson (now Judge Robertson), then a member of Congress from Virginia, whose wife was the niece of Dr. Charles Lewis, to aid me in my efforts. When he read what I had written to Gen. Jackson, he swore that he would sign no paper which flattered the old rascal as my letter did.

I went to the office of the Secretary of the Navy, and applied to Mr. Dickerson, then Secretary, to favor my application to the President. He answered that he would do what he could with the greatest pleasure; that he knew Mrs. Lewis and her family very well; but that General Jackson had spoken for the first midshipmen's warrants for two of his, or his wife's kin, and therefore doubted any immediate success.

When Dr. Physic came to see me, to determine whether I was sufficiently cured to travel, we conversed very freely upon the political state of the country, and particularly about the probability of a war with France, which General Jackson's strong temper and energetic measures were rendering probable just then. My opinions happened to coincide so entirely with his, that, upon ending the conversation, he said, "Sir, you can go to Washington City; you cannot be spared from your post there." The next morning I went in a carriage through a snow-storm to the river. The Delaware had been frozen up: a thaw had followed. The river was covered with broken ice. The wind blew violently, so that the water was rough and the boat very unsteady. From Newcastle to Frenchtown the track of the railroad was covered with snow. The car got along very badly. When we arrived at Frenchtown, the boat from Baltimore had not come. There were no accommodations at the depot. We had to seek shelter at a farm-house, about a quarter of a mile off. Some one was kind enough to procure a cart for the transportation of my infirm body. The Russian minister and his secretary, Krofmer, were of the party. Krofmer was a particular acquaintance of ours. He set off full speed for the house, and succeeded in procuring a room and a bed for me—great luxuries in a house which had to hold seventy travellers. I do not know how many beds were found for others. The whole party had eleven knives and forks and three spoons to eat with. I could not very well describe the inconveniences and suffering from such accommodations to me, who had been confined to bed in a close room for three weeks, with food scarcely sufficient to sustain a mouse, and was then not well. The next day, when the smoke of the steamboat was seen rising in the air over the waters of the Chesapeake Bay, we had a most joyous shout from all the company at the farm-house. We passed the night in Baltimore. The earth was covered with snow the next morning. It was determined that I should go to Washington City at once, in a stage with slides, as easier than the road would be after the snow melted. We had not proceeded more than a third of the way, before the snow began to disappear in places, so that the slides occasionally dragged on the ground and stones. Before we got to Washington City, the slided stage broke down. Two gentlemen gave us their places in a stage, whilst they followed on in an open wagon. I arrived in Washington City with many additional reasons for thinking well of the world. I suffered very little from the cold to which I had been exposed; the slight feverish action which still remained after the operation which had been performed upon me, most probably saving me from what might otherwise have been very injurious.

General Jackson went into office by the force of his own individual popularity, and independent of party divisions. The supporters of his administration were therefore Jackson men, and not democratic nor federal republicans. The opinions of sensible and honest men about forms of government and matters of public policy, are necessarily different. Great latitude of action is therefore permitted to their members, by parties formed upon principle. Not so with men united for the advancement and support of individuals and their followers. Such adherents must toe the track, or be driven off it.

As the discordant materials which had been united for the time to bring General Jackson into office, began to manifest their true character, by their pursuing the course of public conduct which seemed to them right, efforts were made by the party leaders to tighten the cords of party discipline.

In the session of 1833-4, the Jackson party determined to change the officers of the House, as not being sufficiently supple instruments for their purposes. They were excellent agents for doing the public business. The leaders, apprehending that some of the members who had supported General Jackson would not be willing to turn out public officers who did their duty, determined to force them, by subjecting them to the proscription of the party at home by making their votes public. A resolution was introduced, proposing to change the mode of voting by the House for its officers, from ballot, to viva voce. I was among the number on whom this measure was intended to operate. I was feeble from disease, and very easily excited. I addressed the House in opposition to the passage of the resolution. I repelled, in very indignant terms, the imputation that I was to be thus controlled, and poured forth the expression of my feelings in a manner which produced a very sensible impression upon the House. When I concluded, and retired to a recess back of the Speaker's chair, very much exhausted, I was surrounded by a crowd of members, expressing their strong sympathy with me and for me. When I went home, my wife had retired to her room, to avoid meeting me in the presence of others. She gave me a salutation, worth more than all the shaking of hands and plaudits which I had received from the listeners and lookers-on.

I could not have written out for publication what I said if I had desired to do so. The debate was unexpected. I had made no preparation for speaking. I was too unwell even to correct the very imperfect report made for the newspapers by the reporters. The resolution was introduced by a member from Illinois, whom I knew to be utterly worthless for investigating any subject.

On the 3d of March, the last night of the session, when twelve o'clock arrived, I rose in the House, amidst the struggle for the floor by speakers, and the turmoil and confusion which attends the press of business during the last moments, when hope still continued the desire to do what each member wished to have done, and, addressing the Speaker, I took from its fob an old gold watch, which had descended to me from my great-grandfather, and holding up its broad face and large figures, announced that the time had arrived when my right of representing the people of Georgia terminated, bowed, and left the hall. Soon after, Mr. Adams made this disappearance the occasion of speaking of me in the most flattering terms. My colleague and friend, Colonel Tom Foster, who was present, said that the old watch, not satisfied with living for ever itself, had used its time to confer immortality upon its owner.

Chapter XIV.

IN 1836, I left home for Alabama. During my absence, I was nominated by the State-rights party a candidate for elector of President and Vice-President. I accepted the nomination. In my letter of acceptance I said:—

> I am decidedly in favor of the election of Judge White, because I believe him to be an honest, sensible, practical man, who has never sought office by vile means—whose firmness and patriotism will secure to the people, if he shall be elected, an impartial and faithful administration of the Government. I am in favor of the election of Judge White, from the hope that the great body of the intelligent and upright citizens of all classes and all parties may be induced to unite in his support, upon such principles as will avert the evils which at present endanger our political system.
>
> The continued prosperity of the country for the last twenty years, and the extinguishment of party divisions, which, when existing, kept public attention alive to the public interest, have gradually withdrawn the people from politics to private pursuits, so that the honors and rewards of office have become greatly more accessible than formerly to those who seek them for selfish rather than noble and patriotic purposes. From this state of things is forming a party, who, without holding any political principles in common, or agreeing upon any of the great questions of policy which divide public

opinion, is united only in the attempt to appropriate to itself the exclusive possession of all the offices of Government.

Between Mr. Van Buren and Judge White, the contest ought to be considered a struggle between the patronage of the Government and the independent action of the people—the love of office and the love of country.

The opinions expressed in this letter show distinctly enough why I was opposed to Mr. Van Buren. The political course which I then took caused me afterwards some embarrassment. In opposing Mr. Van Buren and the agents through whom he worked, I was led into connection with those whose political principles were very different from my own. Mr. Van Buren's conduct justified my opposition to him. But the evidence upon which I acted could only have its proper weight with those who were famaliar with the facts, from their public service. Although every citizen of Georgia probably concurs with me now in the justness of the judgment which I then passed upon Mr. Van Buren and his special friends, they thought very differently then.

The party which has since become the democratic, were then the advocates of the most questionable measures of Gen. Jackson's administration; whilst the nullifiers, who are now advocating the most doubtful powers, were formerly the supporters of popular rights and the sovereignty of the States. These changes have proceeded from the direction given to parties by the leading men whose elevation to power they advocated, who were themselves governed by their ambitious looking ahead rather than by the principles which they professed.

On our way to Alabama we stopped at Columbus, and passed a day or two visiting our acquaintances, and examining the location of the town destined to be one of the largest inland cities of the South. We went from Columbus to Montgomery, through the Creek Indians, then in the greatest excitement on account of the near approach of the time for their removal from the country they occupied, to the territory provided for them beyond the Mississippi, and by the great frauds practised by the whites, in purchasing the reservations secured to them by the terms of the treaty between the Government and the tribe.

They were ready for murder, and preparing for war. Without being fully aware of their irritated state, we entered their country. We found them drinking and carousing at every station on the road. A few miles beyond the village of Tuskegee we passed, late in the evening, three Indian men standing by the side of the road in a deep hollow, and near a swamp, with rifles in their hands. I saw from their looks that the devil was in them. I requested my wife not to look back, or show any concern. I kept a bold face upon them myself, directing my driver to go along unconcernedly until out of sight, and then to drive as fast as possible. That night, a family of white people living close by, were murdered by the Indians. The next day we got to Montgomery. The day after, eighteen travelers left there for Columbus. In passing through the Creek country, they were fired upon by the Indians. They cut the horses from the stages, and fled on their bare backs. The Indiant burnt the stages, and the baggage which they did not want. The travellers fled into the woods and wandered about, and on towards Georgia, where they all finally arrived in a state of starvation, and nearly dead from the continued apprehension of death.

After remaining in Montgomery for a few weeks, my wife's health, then very bad, became so injuriously affected by the water, that it was necessary that we should get away.

Whilst we were in Montgomery, the murders and robberies committed by the Indians induced the Government to order out large bodies of militia from Alabama and Georgia, to protect the inhabitants exposed to their attacks. All travelling through the Creek country from Montgomery to Columbus was stopped. We set off for home; crossed Montgomery to the southern side of the Alabama River and proceeded up it. We met the Alabama army the morning after. The people along the road were in the greatest alarm, and flying from their houses to escape the apprehended danger from the Indians. On the second day we stopped at twelve o'clock, at a house where the road enters a gorge between two ranges of high hills or low pine mountains. The road was almost impassable, and the country very sparsely inhabited. The people of the house were four men. One red-headed, thick-set, barefooted rascal, had the scar of a large cut entirely across his face, as if his head had been laid open by a sword. The house was two pens, united by an open passage. My wife laid down to rest in one of the rooms, where she heard all that was said by these four scamps, then talking in the passage of how they had killed people, and how they intended to kill more. The troops had passed there the day before, and in various ways roused all their ferocity. The next day we crossed the waters of the Alabama River, there called the Coosa. We found many persons on the bank of the river looking over into the Indian country as if to see what mischief was doing. The Indians cabins were in view. No one was to be seen. Those who were on the bank looking over, imagined that the Indians of the town might be in concealment, ready to pounce upon any one who should venture to cross over. We had in our company a lawyer, who was going to Talladega Court, and who acknowledged that he would not have ventured to pass through the Indian country, but that he was ashamed to avoid what a lady ventured to do. We found the Indian cabins on the Talladega side of the river deserted. At the house where we stopped to feed our horses and get dinner, the dwellers had fled, leaving the overseer and the negroes to take care of their property. We arrived in the evening at Talladega County town. In the morning I met on the road, a few miles from the courthouse, my old friend, Alexander Bowie. It is one of the most delightful pleasures of my life, to look upon the countenance, shake hands with, and hear the voice of a friend whom we have loved from youth to old age, have not seen but a few moments at long intervals, and just time enough to keep his identity fresh in memory.

Alexander Bowie and myself were of the same age, had commenced our classical eduction with the same teacher, had continued together gathering knowledge for several years, eating at the same table, often occupying the same bed, and sympathizing with each other in our compositions, speaking, and all the other employments of school.

Soon after I went to Milledgeville as Governor, we were

visited by Miss Sarah Ann Wiley, a young lady of the neighborhood. I observed her eyes fixed upon me with great intentness. She at last asked me something about her uncle Bowie. I had never seen her before, and could not therefore take her in my arms, hug and kiss her, as I wanted to do, but we talked and talked of that uncle Bowie. She told me how he had directed her education, what very pleasant visits she had made him, and how often she had heard him talk of the friend of his youth. When Sarah Ann was courted her uncle Bowie was not near by to consult; so she advised with me. Her husband, Richard Hays, was ready during his life, to do me any favor. Mrs. Wiley, the sister of Mrs. Bowie, her daughter Mrs. Baxter, her son-in-law Mr. Baxter, and Mr. Leroy Wiley, who have been long my excellent friends, were drawn to me at first by their knowledge of the attachment between Alexander Bowie and myself. Mrs. Baxter's two charming daughters, Mary and Sally, have been since they were children, like my own children. They are now married. When their husbands look at me, and talk to me, I can observe the effect of the repeated expressions of regard for me which they have heard from their wives. Mrs. Baxter's cleverest son is named after me, and all the children akin to Alexander Bowie, call me by some title of affection. Alexander Bowie and I did not talk over all these matters whilst we were standing in the road, shaking hands and looking at each other. He had to go to Talladega, where court was to be in session, and he had cases to attend to professionally. He urged me to go to his house, which was not very far from the road which we had to travel. But my wife was not well enough to enjoy delay.

We went on our way through a wilderness country, occasionally passing by plantations where the great fertility of the land had attracted some hasty improvements. As the evening began to close, we became anxious about our resting-place for the night. We saw but few Indians; but we knew that they were scattered over the country, in a highly irritated state. Traveling with my wife, without a guard, through a wilderness occupied by Indians anxious to revenge what they felt to be injuries, upon any one who might be thrown in their way, was no pleasurable pastime.

After going for some distance between pine hills, without inhabitants, we found ourselves approaching two young ladies, dressed in white, walking along the same road in the course which we were going. It was a strange sight for such a place. We were soon at the house where we intended stopping for the night. Our landlady was the daughter of old Mat Clay, long a member of Congress from Virginia. Her husband was an industrious wealthy man by the name of McGehee. I had been familiarly acquainted with his family from infancy. The young ladies were very pretty and agreeable. I found a young man visiting the family and courting one of them. I knew him to be a base fellow, who was married to a woman from whom he was separated, without a divorce. He pretended not to know me, and evidently hoped that I would not recognize him. I discovered his rascality, and felt it to be due to the young ladies to let them know who he was.

We left Mr. McGehee's in the morning, and stopped to get dinner at the house of a son-in-law of old Jim Blair of Franklin, Georgia. The old fellow was there. When we were about leaving, he insisted that we should go direct to Georgia by the McIntosh trail, through the Creeks, instead of the road by Benton court-house through the Cherokees. The road forked about half a mile from the house. When we got to the place, my wife declared that if we went the road advised by Blair, she would imagine that she saw him behind every tree with his gun directed at me.

The mail rider had been murdered on the road which Blair advised us to take a short time before, with the expectation by the perpetrators that the deed would be charged upon the Indians. Blair had spent his life on the frontiers, had traded much with the Cherokee Indians, and was very unscrupulous. When I was first a member of the Legislature, McKinnie and Shultz, extensive private bankers, endeavored to strengthen the credit of their issue by obtaining a charter for their bank. They gave notice of their scheme, and a portion of stock to several leading members of the Legislature, to

Blair among others. He went to Milledgeville, opposed to the proposed bank. He became a clamorous advocate for it. I charged him before the House with corruption, and dared him to have an inquiry into his conduct. He answered my remarks by saying, that he did not fight with pistols, but that he would wait for time and opportunity to take his revenge.

These circumstances were known to my wife. She would not therefore trust to him for directions about the road. We did him and ourselves great injustice by our suspicions, for which we suffered much, by taking the wrong road, turning over our carriage, being delayed, and undergoing other losses and crosses.

When we arrived at Benton court-house, we found the people collecting there, and talking of fortifying themselves against the Cherokees, who it was said were assembling to commence hostilities. I had to determine whether I would venture among the enraged Cherokees, or cross over to Carrol County, through the Creeks. I took the latter course. We left Benton court-house to go so far on the road that evening, that we might perform the journey to the Georgia frontier the next day. We soon ascended a very steep mountain. In passing along side of the ridge, the carriage was overturned. After struggling for a long time to right it, and having nearly given it up as a bad job, two men came by, who had followed the carriage track from curiosity, to know what people could be after, who were going among the Indians when every one else was running away from them. They kindly afforded us the necessary assistance to put the carriage on its wheels. We arrived a little before night at the house of a man who had sixteen children, and who seemed to have so much to do, that he had heard but little of the preparations for war. He, his wife, and house full of children, lived in a cabin of one room, and that without a loft. There were three beds in the room. We occupied the middle one, between the old people's and the three eldest girls. The younger children lay on the floor, between the beds and the fireplace. It was a sight to see their heads in the morning raised up and looking at me as I got up. We had insisted on sleeping in the wagon under a shelter, but the very proposition hurt our hostess so much, that we could not urge it. In the morning I rose early, and went to a most beautiful spring of water at the foot of the hill, to wash my face and hands. Not having a towel to carry with me, I used my handkerchief for wiping; I carried our travelling pitcher filled with water to the house; and asked for a towel, so that I might have it ready for my wife when she got from bed. Our hostess was greatly bothered. She had no towel. She went to a heap of clothes on a plank in a corner of the room, which reached to the joist, took from it a shirt of one of the boys, tore off the tail, and gave it to me for my wife to wipe her face and hands on. She was sleeping whilst this preparation was making for her comfort. When she got up, she washed and wiped on the rag, without suspecting its previous use. It was the best the kind old woman could do. It was indeed very kind of her thus to demolish a boy's shirt, for a lady's momentary convenience. After breakfast we set off for Carrol County in Georgia. We passed two cabins. At one of them we stopped, and had our horses fed. The man told us that the night before his wife heard the colt kick in the stable, and imagining the noise to be made by Indians getting into the house, ran out at the door opposite, and remained in the *woods* all night. Travelling on, we met a youth in a carryall, looking very earnest, and driving as fast as he well could. Fortunately we said nothing to him. He was going after the people with whom we had stopped, to remove them into the settlement. A report had reached the frontiers that the Indians would attack the whites that night. How we should have been able to travel fifteen miles under the constant apprehension of massacre, it is difficult to imagine. When we left Montgomery, one of my nephews supplied my wife with a loaded pistol. She carried it in her basket, to save, as she said, my scalp from the Indians. During the day that we passed through the Creek wilderness, we stopped at a small creek to water the horses. The road was causewayed for some distance along the creek. My wife was so unwell, that she could not bear the jolting of such a road. She got out, and walked forward until she was out of sight. She observed that a cane thicket was on each side of the road, so as to form just such concealment as would suit the Indians if they intended attacking travellers. I was delayed longer than usual for watering horses, by some accident which had happened to the carriage, which the driver and myself were repairing. My wife became restless, and walked back until she saw me. This was the only evidence she gave of alarm during our travel through the country of the hostile Indian savages. When we got within two miles of the Tallapoosa River, we found cabins. The doors were open; spinning wheels were in the yard; nobody was to be seen. It was evident that the inhabitants had fled upon some sudden apprehension of danger. Upon crossing the river, we went to the house where we had been directed to apply for lodging. The mistress had been carried away in a fainting fit. We had to travel six miles before we found a cabin occupied. We stayed at one located in a potato patch, had for our supper sobbed Irish potatoes, and coffee, with a grain to the gallon of water, without milk or sugar. The woman said that so many had fled to her house the night before, that she had used all her meat and her sweetening.

We arrived at Carrollton the next day, and found every body looking out for Indians, and news of Indians. A few miles from Newton court-house, we stopped to get water from a house near the road. My carriage driver told the owner of the place who we were. He was an old acquaintance, by the name of Smith, to whom I had rendered some very acceptable services. He came to the carriage to see me, with the greatest demonstrations of regard. He was an officer in a volunteer company in the army then operating against the Creek Indians under Gen. Scott. He gave us the first news from the Georgia army; who of our friends belonged to it; some of the incidents of their operations against the Creeks, particularly of our friend Captain Dawson's going down the Chattahoocha River in a boat with his company; the fight which he had had with the Indians; his dangerous position and his gallantry. Smith so magnified the danger, and marvellousness of what had occurred, that we were greatly excited by what we heard. The account brought so forcibly to my wife's imagination the dangers which we had escaped, and made her realize so forcibly those which had been encountered by our friends, that she cried heartily. Smith, who was a kind, sympathizing fellow, cried in company with her. The tears proved a great relief to her pent-up feelings. It was still greater relief to her when we got home, and knew that our travel was over, that we were surrounded by a great many comforts which she had been deprived of for some time, and which she could not do well without, and could rest until rest was not wanted.

The electoral ticket for President and Vice-President which had been nominated by the States-rights party, was elected. The Legislature was in session when the electors assembled in Milledgeville to give their votes. I was chosen president of the college. The votes of the electors were given, counted out, and the result announced in the House of Representatives, in the presence of the senators and representatives. The ups and downs of public life give relish to the enjoyment of particular instances of elevation, far beyond the pleasure derived from the even tenor of unvaried success. The defeat which I had met with when last a candidate for Congress, made the display attendant upon the doings of this most important act which a citizen of the United States is ever called upon to perform, agreeable to me, to whom display of any kind is not usually very acceptable.

About the first of July, 1837, my wife and myself left home in company with Mr. and Mrs. Prince, they for Boston and New York, and we for Western Virginia. We four had passed the time of the session of the Legislature of 1824, in the same public house, where we had a private table, and our own drawing-room. Mr. Prince and myself had served in Congress together in 1834-35. We had acted together as trustees of Franklin College, and belonged for many years to the same bar in the practice of the law. Mrs. Prince was a very pretty and exceedingly amiable woman. Mr. Prince was a man of wit and social habits. We went by the way of Charleston to Norfolk. A voyage on the ocean was new to Mrs. Prince, my wife and myself. The ladies were sick as soon as they got on board the vessel. I buttoned up my coat, put down my feet firmly, and determined that I would not be sick. I was not sick. We do not know what manner of men we are. How much my freedom from sickness, so universally incident to a first sea voyage, proceeded from the control of my will, I do not know. I had looked upon the ocean once before, but had never been out of sight of land. Its vast expanse of ever moving waters is always a great sight. It kept me so excited that I scarcely left the deck of the vessel until we got to Norfolk. Mr. Prince went to the north to have printed a new edition of his Digest of the Public Laws of Georgia. When the work was completed, he and Mrs. Prince left New York for their home in the steam vessel, the "Home." The dreadful catastrophe which brought destruction upon that vessel, Mr. and Mrs. Prince, and almost all the passengers, made such an impression upon the whole country, that the event is yet freshly remembered by every one when the bursting of boilers, the burning of steamers, and the wreck of vessels are heard of. Soon after the steamer left New York a violent storm came on, which drove the vessel to the North Carolina coast in a leaking, sinking condition. All were stimulated to do whatever could be done to save the vessel and themselves. Mr. Prince took command of the hands at the pump, where his self-possession and strong strokes showed that he worked for a nobler purpose than fear for his own life. When exhausted by his efforts, he joined his wife to devote himself to her safety. Her self-sacrificing nature would not yield to the temptation of clinging to her husband, when his exertions might be necessary for the safety of all. She urged him to return to his efforts at the pump. Immediately afterwards she attempted to obey the advice of the captain, to remove from one part of the vessel to another less exposed to danger. As she stepped out of the cabin into an open space, a wave passed over and through the vessel, and carried her into the ocean. When the storm subsided, her body was found deposited on the shore. Mr. Prince, resuming his labors at the pump, was spared the pangs of knowing the fate of his wife. To a young man who lived to report the expression, Mr. Prince said, "Remember me to my child, Virginia," what else the uproar of the ocean prevented being heard. No account was ever given of the last struggle for life by those who worked at the pump. In a great heave of the ocean, the vessel parted asunder and went to the bottom.

We left Norfolk in a steamboat bound up James River for Richmond. Judge May, of the General Court of Virginia, was a passenger. Hearing my name he introduced himself, and asked if I was a relation of Mr. Peachy Gilmer. I answered that I was, knew him well, and liked him very much. He told me that they had been college class-mates and intimate friends. I had the full benefit of his regard for my kinsman during our trip up the river. He knew very familiarly all the places in sight from the boat. The day was clear and pleasant. We remained most of the time on the top of the boat. The houses and plantations of many of the old aristocratic families of Virginia were within view. My time passed delightfully in listening to his accounts of the antique buildings, their builders, and various occupants. I have a great taste for the subject, and was feasted to my heart's content. As we went by the island of Jamestown, on which the first effective settlement was made in Virginia, we took on board a curiosity hunter, who had just been on the island searching for relics of the first settlers. He showed his broken pipe-stems, rusty buttons, and other odd matters to attach value to. All that remained of the old town was part of the wall of a church, and a chimney. The only house on the island was occupied by Dr. Peachy, a distant relation through my great-grandmother, Mary Peachy Walker.

My ancestors of every stock had been for the preceding century Virginians. The difficulties which the first settlers had encountered, the massacre by the Indians, the marvellous adventures of Captain Smith, the love of Pocahontas, had been conned over in childhood like Sandford and Merton, Robinson Crusoe, and the Pilgrims' Progress.

We spent a few days in Richmond with my wife's brother, P. R. Grattan; went to Goochland, where we stayed a short time with our brother-in-law, Dr. Harris, and then made our way to the valley. The time was enjoyed so sweetly, and stole on so imperceptibly, that our allotted time was gone long before we were prepared to leave our friends. I found on my return to Georgia the election for Governor waxing warm. It was very uncertain who would be elected. I had been defeated three years before, when a candidate for Congress, although circumstances had given me unusual popularity at the time. I was opposing the Governor then in office, who had some special means in his power to aid his re-election. The state of the polls as heard from, kept the result very doubtful for two or three weeks. Each mail added to the interest by continuing uncertainty. Most civilized nations have games or shows of some sort, for keeping alive the spirit of the people. Our popular elections answer that purpose most admirably. Every body, men, women, and children, from the most learned to the most ignorant, are stirred into action or thought when elections are going on. All talk, all feel, and all know something more than they did before. Some time after the election was over, but before the state of the polls was known, my wife and myself whiled away a rainy day which restlessness would not let us devote to regular business, in the reading of letters which had passed between us before we were married. We found one which had been written soon after I was first chosen a member of the Legislature twenty years before. It described the drinking and fighting, the bravado and palavering, the speaking and cheering, on the day of the election, and concluded by declaring, that I would never again enter the arena where such disgraceful scenes were exhibited. We forgot for a while the election, in a hearty laugh at my expressions of disgust at the ways of electioneering, my observation that I would never offer again for any office, and my continued offering from that time to then, when I was listening on the tiptoe of excitement to hear whether or not the majority of the votes of the State had been given to make me Governor.

Chapter XV.

I WENT to Milledgeville a few days before the time for my inauguration. Mr. Dawson was there. He and my wife being sticklers for the punctilious observance of etiquette, insisted that I should pay my respects to Gov. Schley in the Executive office. Knowing but little about forms, I felt that my success over Gov. Schley required that I should be very courteous to him. So I did as I was advised, made my bow to the Governor, and attempted to enter into familiar conversation with him. Taking my call for a display of arrogance, he treated it accordingly. I tried to conciliate his wounded feelings, by drawing off his thoughts from ourselves, and directing them to some subject upon which we could talk freely. I ventured to speak of the loss of "the Home," then fresh in the minds of every body, our friends Mr. and Mrs. Prince, our travelling together, &c., &c. It would not do. The Governor spoke in reply so harshly of Mr. Prince, that I could be in no doubt but that the etiquette was out of fashion or did not suit the case, bowed again, and took my leave. *Nil disputandtum, &c., &c., &c.*

The following is an extract from my inaugural address.

Fellow Citizens,—Before I enter upon the duties of the office to which I have been called by your favorable opinion, I must avail myself of the present opportunity to express to you the deep sense of gratitude which I feel for this proof which you have given of your renewed confidence.

Whilst I am very sensible of the high honor conferred upon me, I cannot but feel the weight of responsibility which it brings with it, and my inability to serve the State to the extent of its wants, and my own wishes. It is some relief, however from the consciousness of my deficiencies, that the office has been conferred, not assumed, nor sought for; that in the canvass I left the election to the free and unbiased suffrages of the people; that I excited no expectancies, alarmed no fears, made no promises, and shall enter office, without incurring any obligations but in accordance with the public will, and the solemn oath I am about to take.

In making appointments, I shall select from those whose services I can command, the best qualified to do what the law requires. Placing the greatest value upon the freedom of political opinions myself, I shall endeavor to do justice to others who may differ from me. Those who have sought the aid of party power to procure office, by ejecting faithful incumbents, can scarcely expect to escape the application of the same rule of conduct to themselves.

I believe it to be important to perfect our State institutions by reforming the Constitution, simplifying and rendering certain the laws, improving the mode of their administration, making their execution efficient, and correcting the defects of our system of public education.

The rapid settlement of the Cherokee country, the abundance of its iron, lime and marble, the fertility of its soil in producing grain and tobacco, and its distance from navigation, have created new and strong inducements to the State, for availing itself of the improvements which are constantly making in the construction of railroads, to develope the great resources of that portion of it, by increasing the facilities for carrying its heavy productions to market.

I believe it to be our highest political duty to retain the organization of the Government in the form which our forefathers gave it; limiting the United States to legislation upon the general subjects specified in the Constitution, and preserving unimpaired the rights of the States and the people. Our peculiar domestic relations, slave labor, and its productions, render this duty imperative upon the Southern people. Those interests are in constant danger of being sacrificed to selfish cupidity, or the zeal of fanaticism; and being represented in the General Government by a minority, as they always will be, can only be protected by unceasing vigilance.

Knowing from experience the difficulties to be encountered by your Chief Magistrate in times of high party strife, I am sure I shall stand in need of your kindest indulgence and most liberal support. Unconscious of any selfish object in accepting office, I confidently trust my conduct will be directed exclusively to the public good.

A short time after I went into office, fifteen hundred mounted men, headed by Gen. Nelson, came down from the Cherokee counties, and marched into the suburbs of Milledgeville, with the military display of an army going to war. They said that they were on their way to Florida. But the United States had made no call upon Georgia for such an army; and it was obvious to any one who knew any thing of the public service, that so many troops would encumber instead of promoting it. They encamped, and asked the Legislature for money. Resolutions were immediately passed by both Houses, appropriating thirty thousand dollars for their use, directing that the General Government should be charged with the amount, and requesting the Governor to use means to have it repaid to the State by the United States. As soon as the resolutions received the sanction of both Houses, two distinguished members, and very intimate friends, came into the Executive Office and urged me to sign them. They apprehended gross insult or great personal violence to me if I should refuse. They reported to those who deputed them, my answer, that I would veto the resolutions if I died for it. When the resolutions were presented to me for signature, I declined, and returned them with the following message:

Executive Department, Milledgeville, 21st Dec., 1837.

I return to the House of Representatives the resolutions which originated in that body, passed both Houses, and were presented to me on the 21st inst., upon the subject of an appropriation of money for the use of the large body of mounted men, stated to be now on their march to Florida, with my reasons for disapproving them.

From the account already laid before the House, it is evident that the men for whose benefit the appropriation is intended, have been raised without the authority of this State, or the United States; that the requisition which had been made upon Georgia for volunteers to serve in the Florida campaign, had been withdrawn; and that Gen. Nelson, by whom they have been raised, had no orders, and held no commission from either Government justifying such a measure. I cannot, therefore, perceive how the public money can, with propriety, be applied to their use. They can only be considered as so many individuals directing themselves according to their own wishes, to whatsoever course or purpose they may please; that although they allege that they are on their way to Florida, they are under no legal obligation to serve against the Seminoles; and that if they should receive the money and use it, they would still be at liberty to go to Florida or not.

If they should go to Florida, the probability is that they will not be received into the public service. The Secretary of War and Gen. Jesup, who have been directing the operations for carrying on the campaign in Florida, and know best the materials which they want, and what force can be maintained, show by their letters that it will be difficult to support mounted men there; that even when they required twelve hundred volunteers from the State, few, if any, mounted men were desired by them. The unexpected accession of this large force under Gen. Nelson, consisting of fourteen or fifteen hundred men, and near seventeen hundred horses, must necessarily embarrass, instead of advance the objects of the campaign. The expenses of the Seminole war have been so great for what has been effected, that the officers directing it must be very unwilling to incur the additional cost which the acceptance of this force must incur, especially as it is not the kind wanted for the service. If they should not be received, they must sustain losses and undergo suffering in making their way home through a country already scarce in provisions, and which must necessarily be rendered greatly more so by their march to Florida, which it would be difficult to describe. I do not, therefore, think the Legislature ought to do any thing to aid them in continuing their march. The part of the country through which they must pass whether accepted into service or not, will have its quiet and rights of property disturbed by their necessities. The very assembling together of so many men without discipline, and marching through the country without authority of law, the orders of the State or General Government, or being under the command of officers having the right to control them, is an evil itself of great magnitude, and ought to be repressed if possible. They have been drawn exclusively from the Cherokee counties and those adjoining them. It is matter worthy of consideration, whether the Government, bound, as it is, to look to the defence and protection of its own people, should encourage them to leave their homes for other service, surrounded as they are by Cherokee Indians, now about to be removed.

For the purpose of showing the necessity which exists for retaining in the Cherokee and adjoining counties all the men capable of bearing arms, I submit to the House of Representatives copies of communications from Gov. Schley, Col. Nelson and other persons, upon that subject, to the President of the United States. From these communications it appears, that Gov. Schley considered the danger to the Cherokee country so great and immediate as to justify him in assuming an authority not given by the laws, in organizing a large military force for its defence, notwithstanding that the United States had at the time eleven companies stationed in it; that by a military order, issued the 3d of August, from Athens, addressed to Col. Nelson, he directed him to raise and organize and report a regiment as ready for duty. Early in September, Col. Nelson advised Gov. Schley that the time had already arrived when this regiment should take the field to protect the people from the Indians. Gov. Schley and Gov. Lumpkin (the Commissioner of the United States, then residing at New Echota, and having the best means of correct information) concurred in the opinion that the raising and organizing of the regiment under Col. Nelson was producing the happiest effect, in removing the Indians from the country. Gov. Schley, during the month of September, expressed his determination to arm and call it into active service. If there was any justification whatever for raising this regiment by Gov. Schley, and Col. Nelson, at the time they did, or any reliance to be placed upon the opinions of Gov. Schley, Col. Nelson and the United States Commissioner as to the danger to be apprehended by our citizens from the Cherokee Indians, and the happy effect which it had in inducing the Indians to emigrate, I submit to the Legislature, whether it is proper now, when the time for the removal of the Indians comes nearer, to withdraw from the Cherokee and adjoining counties the large force now marching to Florida. Admitting that Col. Nelson's raising the regiment, and stationing one company in each of the Cherokee counties had another purpose than the defence of the people, still fears must have been created among them by these warlike preparations. It is indeed highly necessary that every one capable of bearing arms in the Cherokee counties should, if possible, be at home, to keep down any disposition which the Indians may have to do mischief.

Strong as I consider these objections to the adoption of the resolutions, they would probably have been overcome by my disposition to acquiesce in the will of the Legislature, but for others of a higher and more imperative character.

If the appropriation be made for the benefit of the men described in the resolution, it cannot be for any services which they have rendered to the State; or in consideration of any services which they are bound by law or contract to render hereafter. By the Constitution, the General Assembly cannot, by resolution, grant any donation or gratuity, in favor of any person whatever, but by the concurrence of two-thirds. If the money attempted to be appriated by the resolution is not for services already rendered to the State, nor hereafter to be rendered, I do not perceive clearly how the appropriation can be considered any thing but a gratuity. This conclusion has probably been intended to be avoided by the second resolution, which orders that the money expended in pursuance of the first resolution, shall be charged to the Federal Government, and that the Governor shall take the means to have the State reimbursed. I cannot perceive by what rule of right or law the State can expend money for its own citizens, and charge the amount to the United States, when their services have neither been required by, nor rendered to the General Government. I should feel at a great loss to know what means could properly be taken to reimburse the State for such an expenditure.

The resolution appears to recognize the authority of Gen. Nelson to command the men as Brigadier General. The States reserved the right in the Constitution to appoint the officers of the militia which may be called into the service of the United States. The law of Congress which authorizes the President to raise volunteers for the Florida service, directs that the officers shall be appointed according to the law of the State to which they may belong. The Constitution of this State directs that all general officers of the militia shall be directed by the General Assembly. If, therefore, these men had been raised under the authority of the President of the United States, still they must be commanded by a Brigadier General chosen by the Legislature, and called into service through the orders of the Governor of the State.

I am not satisfied that the Legislature has the constitutional power to appropriate, by resolution, thirty thousand dollars for the purposes stated, by directing that the money shall be paid out of the contingent fund by the Governor. The Constitution provides, that no money shall be drawn out of the treasury, or from the public fund of the State, except by appropriation made by law. The object of this provision is, to secure the people from inconsiderate and improper dispositions of the public money, by subjecting each appropriation made by the Legislature to the investigation produced by reading the bill containing it three times, on three separate days, in each House, as must be done before a law can be passed. A contingent fund is created during each session of the Legislature, for the Executive Department, because the Legislature cannot foresee, and, therefore, cannot provide specially for all the objects requiring an advancement of money by the Governor from one session of the Legislature to the succeeding.

If these men now marching to Florida had passed by the seat of Government when the Legislature was not in session, the Governor could not have advanced to them thirty thousand dollars to defray their expenses, out of the contingent fund, because they are not in the service of the State, and the Legislature could not have intended to provide for such a contingency. The last contingent fund was appropriated for the political year 1837, which, according to the practice of making up acounts at the treasury office, expired the last day of October; so that the unexpended balance of that fund has become a part of the unappropriated funds of the State, to be appropriated by law, as other public money, except for such expenditures as were made during the political year 1837, and properly charged upon that fund.

For these reasons, it appears to me inconsistent with the spirit of the Constitution for the Legislature, at its present session, to appropriate thirty thousand dollars by resolution, charging it upon the contingent fund of the last political year; and for an object which has presented itself to the Legislature during the present session, is understood, and therefore not contingent. For these several reasons, I cannot approve the resolution.

GEORGE R. GILMER.

This matter will not be fully understood, unless it is known that General Nelson, the leader of this military band, was a man of lawless violence. He had some years before, when a sub-officer of the guard of forty men, then stationed in the

Cherokee country, under the command of General Sanford, chained the ministers of the Gospel who had been found residing among the Chrokees, and been greatly offended at the inquiry which I ordered to be made into his conduct on that account.

He and his fifteen hundred followers went to Florida, where they killed one Indian squaw; for which service the General Government, then under the sway of President Van Buren, paid them more than half a million of dollars.

A company had been organized in each of the Cherokee counties, immediately before the election for Governor, and the members promised the very desirable pay given by the United States to mounted infantry, with the evident expectation that all of them would vote *esprit de corps* for candidates of the Van Buren party.

A citizen, who had held the highest office in Georgia, and was then very popular, and always very conciliatory, had been sent into the Cherokee country by Mr. Van Buren (where political connections were less fixed at the time than elsewhere), previous to the election, with some little commission which kept him there whilst the canvass was going on.

The following veto of the resolution of the Legislature, authorizing the borrowing of $150,000 by the Directors of the Central Bank, for distribution among the people of a portion of the State, requires a word of explanation. The Central Bank was a State institution, created for managing profitably the money which belonged to the State, which had been derived from the sales of public lands, fees for grants, &c. It was, however, made so subservient to party purposes, that it was discontinued, and its funds ordered to be distributed among the people.

This distribution was carried on so much more in accordance with the demands of the people for money than the ability of the bank to pay; that the people of many counties got none. The Legislature authorized the Directors to borrow $150,000, to make up the deficiency, and stop the clamor of those who said that they were equally entitled with those who had received a share to a portion of the public money.

Executive Department, Georgia, 2d Dec. 1837.

The resolution which originated in the Senate, and has passed both Houses, authorizing the Directors of the Central Bank to borrow one hundred and fifty thousand dollars, to enable the bank to meet the dividends to the counties declared by the Directors, and yet unpaid, was on the 1st of December presented to me for approval.

The law by which the Central Bank was created, determines the extent of the authority of its Directors. Tnat law cannot be altered, nor the powers conferred by it upon the Directors lessened by a resolution of the Legislature.

The law, in pointing out the duties of the Directors of the Central Bank, as special agents of the State, grants them no power to borrow money. It appears to me, therefore, to be inconsistent with the principles of legislation to attempt, by resolution, to give them that authority.

By the Constitution, all bills fcr raising revenue, or appropriating money, must originate in the House of Representatives, and be read three times, on three several days, in each branch of the General Assembly. This resolution originated in the Senate, passed through none of the forms required by the Constitution for money or appropriation bills, and yet authorizes the raising by loan of one hundred and fifty thousand dollars by the Central Bank, and appropriates the money thus to be raised to meet the dividend which has been declared by the Directors of the bank. With due respect for the two Houses, it appears to me that the Legislature cannot, in this form, raise and appropriate money; and, not having the power, it cannot confer it upon the bank.

The possession and management of three millions of money by the Directors of the Central Bank is a vast power, and capable of being made, in a popular government, where the practical administration is constantly dependent upon the expression of the people's will, through frequent elections, an instrument of fatal mischief. The guards thrown around the bank by the vigilance of those who administer the Government, can neither be too numerous nor too watchful to prevent its influence from being directed to improper purposes.

If the Government desires to continue to the people the advantages they derive from the bank, it should prevent, by the most decided means, any departure of the Directors from the special authority intrusted to them. I do not perceive very clearly the force of the position assumed by the Legislature, that because the Directors of the Central Bank have borrowed money at seven per cent., to distribute at six among the people of some of the counties, that therefore the Legislature ought to do the same thing for the people of the remaining counties.

It is indeed no novelty for Governments to dispense favors to individuals and portions of the people, at the expense of the whole community; but it is scarcely in accordance with the fundamental principle of our legislative authority, that every measure must be conducive to the good of the State.

For these reasons, I cannot approve of the resolution, and return it to the Senate, where it originated.

GEORGE R. GILMER.

Those who had opposed my election, endeavored to excite the ill-will of the inhabitants of the Cherokee territory against me, by trying to make it appear that I was not inclined to secure them against Indian violence, nor to gratify the militia, who desired to be called into the public service to get good pay from the United States.

They succeeded in passing a resolution through the Senate, calling upon the Governor for such information as might be in his possession relative to the necessity of providing for the defence of the Cherokee counties of the State, and what amount of forces, mounted or infantry, was necessary for said service; as well as the best method of raising and organizing the same; and what force, if any, had been organized for that section of the country, and, if any, what force is considered in readiness to act for that purpose. I answered—

I have received no official communication upon the several subjects submitted to me for information since I have been in this department. Those received by my predecessor, have already been laid before the Legislature. I am not able to give to the Senate the information asked for, as to the amount of force organized for the Cherokee country, and ready to act. I have understood, unofficially, that it consists of eleven companies, amounting together to six or seven hundred men.

It is proper to state, from its connection with the call made upon me by the resolution, that, by the fourth section of the fourth article of the Constitution, the United States are bound to protect the State against domestic violence, upon the application of the Legislature of the State, or, if the Legislature is not in session, of the Executive. I have no doubt that the authorities of the Genral Government, if they have not already provided troops sufficient to protect the people of the Cherokee country from Indian violence, will do so, upon proper representations being made to them, either by the Legislature or Executive.

There is a difficflulty of another kind, in relation to the raising of such troops for the service of the State as seems to be contemplated by the resolution of the Senate, which I would respectfully suggest as worthy of some consideration. By the tenth section of the first article of the Constitution of the United States, every State is prohibited from keeping troops in time of peace, unless actually invaded, or in such imminent danger as not to admit of delay.

In addition to the security to be derived from the presence of the United States troops, I would recommend that danger shall be guarded against, by requiring every captain of every militia company in the Cherokee country to hold his command in readiness, to aid the civil officers in arresting Indians charged with the commission of crimes, and for suppressing combinations among them for violent purposes.

To render militia companies more officient than they can be made under our present laws, I would respectfully recommend to the Legislature to pass a temporary law, applicable to the Cherokee counties, authorizing the sheriff and other civil officers to require the captains, and those under their command, to aid them in the execution of their duties, whenever the number of Indians charged with the violation of the laws, or intended mischief, shall be so great as to require such assistance.

For the purpose of avoiding any violence on the part of the Indians, I consider it highly necessary that they should be protected in the enjoyment of all their legal rights.

The volunteer companies, which had been organized in the frontier counties adjoining the Cherokee territory, for the purpose of overawing the Indians, and suppressing any risings for doing violence, became very eager to be called into the public service, to enjoy the pleasures of the camp and to get pay for doing nothing. In answer to their demands, I addressed to them the following communication:—

Head-Quarters, Milledgeville, 3d March, 1838.

Sir,—The peace and safety, the property and lives of the people of the Cherokee country, are deeply concerned in the conduct of your command. A mistake in your duties, or a departure from them, may involve the country in an Indian war—the greatest possible evil to those who are exposed to its destructive effects and exterminating cruelties. The principal object of the formation of your companies is, to give security to our citizens; to overawe the revengeful spirit of the lawless portion of the Indians; to prevent the people flying from their homes and the country upon every rumor of danger; to protect your families, neighborhoods, and the people of each county, upon sudden emergenices, when the United States troops may not be present, or in sufficient force to obviate danger.

The United States Government and the State authorities intend to preserve peace, and remove the Cherokees from the State without violence if possible. All their efforts are directed to the accomplishment of this object. You will, therefore, not only make no attacks whatever upon the Indians, but endeavor to prevent all others from molesting them whilst they remain peaceable. Until the 25th of May, the Indians have the right to retain their possessions, and to remain undisturbed in the country. You have nothing to do with disarming them, or removing them from their fields until that time; and then only in co-operation with, and upon the request of the United States officer, to whom the duty of removing them is intrusted by the President of the United States.

I have been asked by some of you, whether the captain of a company is not authorized by the third section of the law, to call his company to the field? Certainly not. The colonel of the regiment is the commander spoken of who has that power, and he can only do so when the Indians assemble together for hostile purposes, and under circumstances which do not admit of the delay of sending for orders to the commander-in-chief, and when the United States troops cannot prevent the danger.

I have received a great many applications to call the companies into the field at once. Mixed up together as the Indians are with our people throughout the the whole Cherokee country, it is believed to be impolitic to call you into service, except in cases of actual danger, and for self-defence. The men of the country could not consent, nor ought the Government to require them, to leave their families and property exposed to the attacks of neighboring Indians when hostilities commence. The whole country might be depopulated by such policy. Until there is a probable prospect of the Indians rising in arms, I have no right to call you to the field.

I have understood that some of those who will be the owners of the lands now occupied by the Indians, are very desirous of using the companies as the means of getting rid of their occupants in time to put the lands into profitable cultivation. The lives of unoffending women and children, and the whole property of the citizens of the Cherokee country, are not to be endangered for such an object. Indeed, I hope that the number of those who, for their own selfish and lawless purposes, would thus trifle with the rights and interest of the whole community, are too few to have any influence whatever upon the conduct of the companies.

I have also been warned, that there are many persons who have desired to connect themselves with the companies, for the purpose of getting the pay of mounted men, by directing the companies from the purpose of preserving the peace of the country, and effecting the quiet removal of the Indians to such course as would require the companies to be called to the field. I know that there are such persons; but it would appear to be impossible that they can be sufficiently numerous to be able to control the conduct of any one company, composed as they all are of citizens, whose families, friends and property belong to the Cherokee country. If any person should be detected in such conduct, his punishment will be made a warning example to those who would sacrifice the public safety to their own private ends. Some of you have complained that troops have been drawn from other parts of the State, for the defence of the Cherokee country, instead of calling your companies into service. The duty of protecting the people of the State from Indian violence, and executing Indian treaties, belong to the President of the United States. It is only when the President fails to discharge that duty within Georgia, that the Governor of the State is authorized to call the militia into the field. The President is of the opinion, that the lives and property of the people of the Cherokee country will be most certainly guarded by drawing the troops necessary for that purpose from parts of the country where there are no Indians; leaving the volunteer companies and militia of the Cherokee country to strengthen the defence of their own homes, neighborhoods, and counties. He has promised that an ample force shall be provided for the protection of those who are exposed to attack of the Indians. He is accordingly ordering companies into those positions where the people are most exposed to numerous bodies of Indians, as rapidly as the extent of the danger appears to require. So long as the President continues to do this, it is not proper to order out any of your companies. It is surely no serious cause of complaint, that you are permitted to remain at home, attending to your own affairs, ready to protect your families and property—that you have arms put into your hands, and companies organized to give protection to your homes and neighborhoods—and that troops are sent from other parts of the State to give you additional security.

Whenever I am convinced that the protection of the Cherokee people requires any of your companies to be ordered into service, I will not fail to order them. I will do whatever I can to add to the security of the country, give peace and quiet to the people, and remove the Indians in each county. You are, therefore, requested to write to this office as often as may be necessary for that purpose. Take care to have your arms and ammunition constantly in good order, and ready for immediate action.

Give your orders to your non-commissioned officers in such manner, that the company may be assembled in the shortest possible time. Muster them frequently, so as to improve their discipline and render them efficient when called to the field. If the Indians in your county should commence hostilities, you will not wait for orders from the colonel of the regiment, or the commander-in-chief, but put yourselves under the command of the militia officers of the county, or otherwise defend the people in the best manner you can. The laws of self-defence will justify you in this course.

GEORGE R. GILMER.

In giving an account of Mr. Wirt's proposal to submit to the Supreme Court for its decision, the question whether the State of Georgia had the rightful power to govern its Indian population, I mentioned that I was made more angry than I ever was but once. The course of my narrative has brought me to the occasion referred to.

As the time for the removal of the Cherokees approached, they became more and more restless, and the Georgians among them, and on the frontiers, more and more fearful lest they should suffer from some murderous outbreak. I requested the Secretary of War to guard against the danger by stationing additional troops among the Indians, and to appoint an agent whom I named, who was known to be related to some of the influential chiefs; was a man of character and intelligence; was confided in by them, and admirably qualified to do what was wanted to be done; who should be directed to go among them, ascertain whether their designs tended to massacres, and if they did, to notify the General and State Governments; and that their true interest required them to remove to the west of the Mississippi. The Secretary of War, and some of his special party friends among the members of Congress from Georgia, concurred in appointing an agent who was unknown to the Indians, and had no useful qualifications whatever for his agency. This they did lest some popular good might be done by one to whom they were politically opposed. When I knew that the safety of the women and children under my official care, was thus trifled with by those whose duty it was to aid me in protecting them, and that the use of the best means for removing the Indians peacebly and willingly to their home in the West was neglected from selfish party motives, my anger was such as I desire never to feel again.

The following correspondence with the Secretary of War,

John Ross, and the members of Congress from Georgia, is considered of sufficient historical value to be inserted entire.

Executive Department, Milledgeville, 9th March, 1838.
To Mr. John Ross:

Sir,—The President having declined receiving any further propositions from the Cherokee delegation for setting aside or altering the treaty, and your memorial to Congress having been rejected by the House of Representatives, all hope of success in your efforts to effect that object must be at an end. The policy which you may adopt, under these circumstances, is of great importance, not only to your own people, but the numerous white population residing among them.

The law of necessity, or, if you please, the harsh and unyielding will of superior power, has determined that the portion of the Cherokees remaining in this State, must remove to the country provided for them in the West. How will you meet this necessity, against which you can no longer contend? Will you bend to the blast to rise with renewed energies when it passes away, or by resisting it sink beneath its force? If these were questions which concerned yourself alone, the dictates of pride, or determined self-will, might disregard consequences. But the peace and happiness of thousands may be involved in your course. Your unwearied and unwavering exertions in behalf of your people, have been unavailing, except to secure to you their highest confidence. The time has arrived when that confidence enables you to render them the most important service. You must be aware that the Cherokees are not preparing to emigrate; that they are yet hoping that you and their other chiefs will obtain a modification of the treaty, so as to permit them to remain where they are; that when the time arrives for removing them, force must be applied—and that great suffering, the loss of many lives, and destruction of much property, will probably be the consequence, unless, in the mean time, they can be convinced, that all expectations of retaining their present possessions are delusory, and do voluntarily what must otherwise be effected by compulsion.

It requires no strong invention to imagine the suffering and distress which must be inflicted upon your people, if hunted up by an undisciplined soldiery, and forced from their homes. You, at least, stand in no need of the description. Your people are looking to you to direct them in this their greatest difficulty. You can save them from the evils that threaten them, by persuading them to unite with their friends in the west, before the time arrives when, by the terms of the treaty, force can be used.

I know how easily the motives for the best actions may be misrepresented. The Cherokees have been rendered so suspicious of all contracts with the Government, that I believe it to be important even to your success in removing them, that you should return home and convince them that all hopes of retaining their present possessions are vain; that your efforts for that purpose have proved fruitless, and that a proper regard for their interest and safety require that they should no longer resist the views of the Government. If, upon doing so, you find an acquiescence (as I am satisfied you will) upon the part of your people, the Government will unquestionably furnish ample means to remove them, and a liberal compensation, in addition, if they go without the aid of contractors and agents.

Sir, I could not write you upon this subject, but with the fullest consciousness that what I say is in good faith, and my motives such as your own people would approve. It is my anxious desire that the Cherokees should be treated with humanity. I am using every exertion to prevent violations of their rights of possession and property. It is true, that I have long been thoroughly convinced that their present situation is not the best suited for their continued improvement and preservation as a distinct people, but I believe I have at all times adopted the kindest policy towards them which my official station would permit.

I once saved the lives of two of our Indian people. It has ever remained a green, sunny spot on the field of my life. What a deep and abiding source of happiness it will be to you, if you shall save many lives, by leading your people peacably to their homes in the West?   Very respectfully, yours, &c.,
GEORGE R. GILMER.

Executive Department, Milledgeville, 14th April, 1838.
To the Hon. Joel R. Poinsett:

Sir,—I hope that your severe illness, about which every one having business to transact with the War Department, must, like myself, feel great concern, will have passed away before this time.

I send you an extract of a letter just received from Ross, in answer to a communication which I addressed him at the same time I wrote you. I am convinced that I was mistaken in my endeavor to make him an instrument for doing good.

The loss of all hope of obtaining the co-operation of Ross in removing the Cherokees, has added to my anxiety that the most ample means should be used to secure our citizens from the effects of his machinations. The troops which are ordered into the Cherokee country, from this and the adjoining States, being raw and undisciplined, and scattered over the country in small detachments, will stand very much in need of a regular force, to give confidence and success to their movements.

Permit me to urge the importance of concentrating in the Cherokee country, in as short a time as possible, the whole of the United States army, which can with propriety be drawn from other service.

The Indians are as yet entirely quiet, but they are not enrolling for emigration. Those who have enrolled are refusing to leave the country, and they are generally continuing their preparations for another crop. Ross's refusal to return home after the conclusive action of both Houses of Congress upon his memorial, renders it certain that force must be used in removing his people. The more controlling that force may be, the less will be the mischievous effects of the opposition of Ross and his friends.

Very respectfully, yours, &c.,
GEORGE R. GILMER.

(Copy of a letter from the Hon. Joel R. Poinsett to Governor Gilmer.)

Department of War, December 16th, 1837.

Sir,—In my letter of the 9th instant, I had the honor to inform your Excellency, that you should be timely advised of the termination of the correspondence with John Ross. That correspondence I now consider at an end, and transmit you copies of it for your information.

Very respectfully, your most obedient servant,
J. R. POINSETT.

His Excellency George R. Gilmer,
Governor of Georgia, Milledgeville, Ga.

(Extract of a letter from John Ross to the Governor.)

Washington City, April 6th, 1838.

To his Excellency George R. Gilmer:

Sir,—Your Excellency, I hope, will long ere now have been aware of the reasons why I have not sooner personally acknowledged the receipt of your letter of the 9th of March. To the honorable Mr. Dawson, who called upon me to say that he had received a copy by the same post, I explained myself fully. I presume he has mentioned my conversation. I need, therefore, only repeat in general terms, that I can see no necessity whatever for any collision between your citizens and the Cherokees, as I am making every effort in my power to accomplish such arrangements as may relieve Georgia, in obtaining the utmost extent of her desire among us, from the remotest pretext for employing force. It is my wish to settle all difficulties by amicable treaty, and on perfectly reasonable terms. I sincerely hope that my earnest efforts for that end may ultimately prosper, as one word of the Executive is now enough to save the expense and inevitable danger which must result from the employment of an uncalled-for army. Should blood be spilt, therefore, which I trust can never be the case, the blame can never rest on us.

With regard to my immediate return into the Cherokee nation, I differ with your Excellency, and am sustained in my dissent by many who have better opportunities than either of us, to understand any thing which bears upon the case. If I were to desert a post assigned me by the Cherokees, and a line of duty prescribed by their expectations, they would be lost in wonder and distrust. They expect me to superintend their interests here at the seat of the United States Government, as the source from which their weal or woe must emanate, and as the only source to which they can look for protection, in case of need. They would be sorry to see me among them while our affairs remain thus unsettled. Indeed my appearance among them, on the mission you suggest, would at this moment produce inextricable confusion, of which the consequences might be awful.

Department of War, May 23, 1836.

Sir,—I have the honor to transmit herewith to your Excellency, a copy of a proposed arrangement with John Ross and other chiefs, and head men of the Cherokee nation, now in this city. Your Excellency will perceive in these proposals, that the Government, while it seeks to procure the co-operation of the delegation, in the peaceable removal of the Cherokees, has carefully abstained from compromising the rights of the States concerned in the execution of the treaty. It is not supposed that it will require so long a period as two years to remove the remaining Cherokees to their new homes west of the Mississippi; but whatever term of time may be necessary to their comfortable emigration, the Department relies upon the generosity of the States interested not to press their claims, so long as they are satisfied that due diligence is used by the agents of the nation to effect this desirable object as speedily as practicable.

Very respectfully, your most obedient servant.
J. R. POINSETT.

To the Governors of Georgia, Tennessee,
Alabama and North Carolina.

Executive Department, Milledgeville, May 28, 1838.
To the Hon. Joel R. Poinsett:

Sir,—I have had the honor of receiving from you the proposals of the Government to John Ross, and instructions to General Scott.

The surprise and regret excited in myself at these proceedings of the Government, I am sure will be felt by every citizen of the State. I can give to them no sanction whatever. The proposals to Ross could not be carried into execution but in violation of the rights of the State. The very making of them must prove exceedingly injurious to the interests of its people.

The lands which are in the occupancy of the Indians are the private property of its citizens, and the owners are now entitled by the law to possession. For the purpose of preventing all unnecessary suffering and hardships on the part of the Cherokees, the proprietors have been earnestly entreated not to enforce their rights at once, but to wait until the Indians should be removed by the army. They have been assured that this will be done by the President as soon as possible, and in perfect good faith. Sincere regret is felt that the success of these efforts in the cause of humanity has been defeated by the Government. As soon as the proposals to Ross and the instructions to General Scott are known to the proprietors, they will no longer be restrained from taking possession of their property. It becomes necessary, therefore, that I should know whether the President intends, in the instructions to Gen. Scott, to require that the Indians shall be maintained in their occupancy by an armed force, in opposition to the rights of the owners of the soil. If such is the intention of the President, a direct collision between the authorities of the State and the General Government must ensue. My duty will require that I shall prevent any interference whatever by the troops with the rights of the State and its citizens. I shall not fail to perform it. To avoid misunderstanding, permit me to request that you will communicate to me, and as early as you can conveniently, the President's views upon this subject.

I have no doubt but the Indians can be removed from the State, in the execution of the treaty and by the troops now organized and stationed in the country with that avowed purpose, with more ease and expedition, and a readier acquiescence on the part of the Indians, than by any means in the power of this State. If, however, the Government consents that Ross and his friends shall remain two years longer, the State will be obliged to get rid of the evils which must necessarily arise from such policy, by exercising its own right of jurisdiction, and remove them by the most efficient means which it can command. Very respectfully, yours, &c.,

GEORGE R. GILMER.

I wrote to Mr. Dawson, and expressed to him fully what I was doing, and intended to do. We were natives of the same part of the country, had known each other for a long time, been intimately associated together in various ways, and were in constant familiar correspondence.

Milledgeville, 30th May, 1838.
To the Hon. William C. Dawson:
Dear Sir,—I send you a letter addressed to the owners of the lands occupied by the Indians in the Cherokee country, immediately before they acquired by law the right to take possession. I confi-

dently believe that most of them were disposed to pursue the course recommended. The very best feeling prevailed every where. The alarms and distrust which had existed some time ago were subsiding. This proceeded in a great degree, from the incessant exertions which had been used, to prevent any violation of the rights of the Indians, and the assurances given to the people, that the Government would remove the Indians as soon as possible, and afford every one protection against violence. In Gilmer and Union Counties, where Indians are twice as numerous as the whites, the people were two weeks ago perfectly quiet, and travelling was as safe there as any where. But for a lingering expectation, that Ross would be able to retain their country for them, a great proportion of the Cherokees would have been now preparing to remove. So satisfied were the people, that no difficulty or violence would occur in their removal, that they were indicating a disposition to complain against the Government, for sending so many troops among them. No one ever felt more satisfaction than I have done, at the result of my labors for the last six months. No violence of any kind had occurred between the whites and Indians, when General Scott took the command. I had suffered great anxiety whilst the troops were in preparation. Difficulties seemed to be over. No one who had not striven as I have done to save the lives and prevent the suffering of a whole community, can understand the deep mortification I felt in knowing that the happy result of all my exertions may be destroyed by the late proceedings of the President.

Our people have been so harassed for a long time by the Indian disturbances, alarms, and wars, that they will not bear the presence of the Indians longer than the treaty requires. To ask them to suffer Ross and his friends to remain for two years longer, with the knowledge that every citizen of the Cherokee country has, that the Indians would have been contented at their home in the West long before this, but for the exertions of Ross, and his friends the white men, is utterly idle. When I proposed to the Secretary of War and John Ross, two months ago, that Ross should remove his people voluntarily before the time agreed upon, for a large compensation to be allowed him by the Government, I received a direct refusal from Ross, and my letter to the Secretary of War was not honored with an answer. That the Secretary now, when the Government has no power over the treaty, except to enforce it, should propose to reward Ross for denouncing the Government as dishonest and faithless, by possession of the lands of the people granted them by the State, is indeed an act of dishonesty and faithlessness. The President will not be permitted to sell the rights of the people of Georgia, to buy votes elsewhere. The people will prevent, if the public authorities do not.

If my health permits, and the President determines that he will maintain the Indians in their occupancy of the territory of this State, I will proceed to the Cherokee country, and try whether the rights of the State are to be trampled upon, or violated by military force. We have two thousand men in the field under General Floyd, not one of whom will obey any order to set at defiance the sovereignty of the State. If the United States troops shall attempt to resist our laws, they will be required to leave the State, and our volunteers withdrawn from the service. The requisition through which they went into service was to remove the Cherokees, not to maintain them upon our soil. The Government may yet stop in its work of unmixed mischief. The Indians can be removed by the United States Government and the troops now assembled, with more ease and less suffering, than by the State, and I shall continue to insist upon its proceeding to remove them at once. If the President refuses, the consequences must be upon his head.

For the purpose of giving you as much information as I readily can, as to the course taken by the State and General Governments, in removing the Cherokees, I forward to you the inclosed copies of papers.

The requisition of General Scott for troops from this State, my orders for raising them, and the special commission given to the officers, show that these troops are only authorized to remove the Indians and protect the people.

The letters to the owners of the lands occupied by the Indians, to Generals Scott, and Floyd, show the rights of the people, and at the same time the exertions which have been made to prevent any collision between them and the Indians, the general state of peace, and my confidence that the Indians would, with prudence, be removed without difficulty.

The proclamation of the 13th of March, shows the anxiety with which I have protected the rights of the Indians.

The address of General Scott to the Cherokees shows what his original instructions were. He says he has no right to grant them further delay, and that within one month, every man, woman and child must be moving from the country.

My letter to the Secretary of War and Ross, shows that more than two months before the arrival of the time for the removal of the Indians, by force, I proposed that Ross should remove them voluntarily. Ross's answer shows for itself. None was received from Mr. Poinsett.

I send you the late instructions to General Scott, which show that the President is proceeding, without the consent of the State or Congress, to stop the removal of the Indians by the troops, and to rely upon contracts with Ross's friends, and the intention of the President to make the owners of the lands in this State dependent upon General Scott for possession.

In my letter of the 30th of November, I requested Mr. Poinsett to put an end to his correspondence with Ross. In his reply of the 9th of December, he says it was continued with the hope of inducing Ross to aid in the peaceable removal of the Indians; but when he was satisfied that this could not be done, he would inform me of it. In his letter of the 10th December he writes, that in conformity with that promise, his correspondence with Ross was at an end.

Several communications have been received this morning from the Cherokee country.

A state of quiet prevails every where. I send you an extract from Dr. Hamilton's letter. I cannot but hope that the friends of humanity will induce the Government to retrace its steps.

Yours, &c.,
GEORGE R. GILMER.

Executive Department, Milledgeville, 30th May, 1838.

Sir,—I inclose to you my answer to the letter of the Secretary of War, upon the subject of his proposals to John Ross, and late instructions to Gen. Scott.

All here concur in the opinion that these proceedings of the Government are in violation of the rights of the State, and calculated to produce the most extensive evils to the Cherokee country.

Permit me to request that the delegation in Congress from this State, will unite in ascertaining from the President whether it is his intention to continue the present delay in removing the Cherokees by the troops under Gen. Scott, for the purpose of effecting that object by contracts to be made with the agents of Ross and his friends, or for any other purpose? and whether it is his intention to maintain the Indians by force upon the soil of Georgia in opposition to the will of the State and the rights of its citizens, to whom the lands have been granted? And that you communicate to me his determination. Very respectfully, yours, &c.,
GEORGE R. GILMER.
To the Georgia Delegation.

After I had written to Mr. Dawson, it occurred to me that the communication of the Secretary of War was sufficiently important to call the attention of the whole delegation to it. The foregoing letter was accordingly written. The members who were special friends of Mr. Van Buren, seized upon the fact that the letter to Mr. Dawson was received by him before they received the communication addressed to them, to write me the following singular epistle. Its matter indicates how much the public service was then obstructed by selfish party politics, and the many difficulties which I had to overcome for securing success in such times when operating together with such men.

Washington, 15th June, 1838.

Sir,—We have the honor to acknowledge the receipt of your letter dated the 30th of May ultimo, inclosing a copy of yours to the Secretary of War, of the 28th of the same month, requesting the delegation to call on the President of the United States, and ascertain his intentions in relation to the execution of the Cherokee treaty.

Some short time before your letter was received, we had heard as a report, that a communication, having reference to the Cherokee treaty had been transmitted by you to one of the delegation. What the real character or object of that communication was, we had no means of ascertaining, not having had an opportunity of reading, or hearing it read.

When your letter of the 30th of May was received, and which reached us two days after that addressed by you to the delegate before alluded to, you may readily suppose it created some surprise, if not astonishment. If a combined effort of the delegation was desirable, it was to have been presumed the communications would have been simultaneous. That the views of the Executive of Georgia, upon a most delicate and exciting subject, should have been made known to one alone of the delegation, whilst the others were kept in ignorance, and to remain so until it suited him who was informed to make them known, or await the tardy communication afterwards received, was a subject not only of regret, but of mortification. Why your Excellency adopted this mode of procedure, unless in conformity with the practice pursued in relation to the agent you wished some months back to send into the Cherokee country, and in reference to whose appointment you corresponded with the Secretary of War and a few selected individuals of the delegation, leaving the greater portion of the members totally unapprised of the intentions of the Executive, in regard to a measure in the opinion of the majority, if not all of the delegation, of more than questionable expediency.

These acts, to say the least of them, are not very courteous; this distinction made among members of the same delegation, and on a subject of vital importance to the State, and in which all are equally interested, would nevertheless not have prevented us from complying with your request. But on the subject of the Cherokee treaty, and the policy to be pursued, we never entertained but one opinion; to be quiescent; to do nothing; to consider the treaty as a settled question; as the supreme law of the land, that must be executed according to its spirit and letter.

Our action, both in our legislative and private capacity, has squared with this our deliberate opinion. We have always moved, and generally succeeded in laying on the table, every memorial presented having for its object the abrogation or modification of the treaty; and in all our private interviews with the members of the administration, we have uniformly made known as our deliberate conviction, that the only true policy to be exercised towards John Ross and his friends, in or out of the House, was to inform them distinctly and sternly, that now the Executive of the United States had no discretion on the subject; that the treaty must be executed; that it was required not only in reference to the welfare and true interest of the Indians themselves, but to the people of Georgia, to prevent delusion on the one side, and to allay the excitement of the passions on the other, on a subject which for more than 20 years has been used as a weapon for party warfare, regardless both of the interest of the State and the stability and permanency of the Union itself.

Under the operation of these feelings, and entertaining the sentiments herein expressed, it was with no little surprise and regret we heard the late message of the President of the United States read in the House of Representatives. No previous communication or intimation was given to us that such a document was to be sent. If others were in on the secret, we were not of the number. As soon as the document was received, one of the undersigned called for its reading. It produced great excitement in the House. The contents of it were of so extraordinary a character, and so well calculated, in our opinion, to do great mischief, and without the slightest probability of producing beneficial results, that we instantly determined to pursue a bold and decisive but perhaps unparliamentary course, and moved to lay the message of the President on the table, and by that means prevent any action of the House upon it; the result of which motion your Excellency has no doubt seen in the public prints.

The undersigned having no agency, either in word or deed, by private verbal consultation or written communication, with the President, or Heads of Department, or John Ross, or any of his friends, on the subject of the message, and having upon all occasions refused to enter upon a subject having reference to a modification of the treaty, so far as delay in the removal of the Indians was involved, though at all times disposed to give every facility to such removal, have, since the presentation of the message, deemed it the most prudent and politic course, and one calculated to serve the best interest of the State, to abstain from all communication with the Executive of the United States or the War Department on the subject; looking with a steady eye to the terms of the treaty, and insisting with a stern determination on its faithful execution. Leaving to those to call for explanations who were here or elsewhere, as rumor says, were playing the part of diplomatists on this "untoward" affair. To him who, more particularly it is said, made a proposition to John Ross to have a supplemental article incorporated in the treaty, extending the time for removal, provided the Indians went beyond the limits of Georgia, thereby leaving the inhabitants of our border exposed to their predatory incursions of savage warfare, and at a time when their passions were most inflamed; or, to him also, who, it is said, was consulted by the Department, and assisted in concocting the propositions submitted to John Ross, and presented to the House with the message of the President of the United States; and who, if he did not approve, certainly did not oppose them, or give notice to any of his colleagues that such a subject of negotiation was going on.

As these gentlemen seem to have been desirous of claiming all of the merit of these diplomatic arrangements, justice requires they should not assume all the responsibility, and if their political bed be a bed of torture, they have made it for themselves; we shall not interrupt their repose. This little incident will be of service to them hereafter; experience purchased, provided it is not at too high a price, is said to be most valuable. The gentlemen will now see and feel the force of the poet's observation, "that to be too busy there is some danger."

In the foregoing reasons, combined with the belief that your letter was uncalled for, the views of the Government, since the message, as well as before, having been distinctly stated in their instructions to the commanding general, as well as the proclamation of the same officer, that the removal of the Indians was not to be delayed one hour, but with the assent of the States interested; together with the opinion of every reflecting man, in or out of Congress, of the imperious political necessity of the full and speedy execution of the treaty, which opinion has been confirmed by the almost unanimous action of both Houses of Congress, in the appropriation bill to carry it into effect; your Excellency, we are induced to believe, will see not only a propriety, but justification, in our not joining in the communication to the Secretary of War, according to your request.   We remain your obedient servants,
    (Signed) GEORGE W. OWENS.
         JESSE F. CLEVELAND.
         GEORGE W. TOWNS.

His Excellency George R. Gilmer,
  Governor of Georgia.

When I received information of the measure adopted by Mr. Van Buren, for avoiding the unpopularity of removing the Cherokees, I immediately addressed the following letter to the citizens of the State who resided among the Cherokees. The strong desire of the owners of the land occupied by the

Indians, to get possession, each one of his own tract (the Indian land having been already distributed among the people by lottery), and the unrestrained temper of the frontier people, excited fears lest there should be an outbreak among them when they were informed of the conduct of Mr. Van Buren. How far this letter contributed to quiet their restlessness I had no means of knowing.

To the Citizens of the Cherokee Counties:

Before this reaches you, the newspapers will have conveyed to you the information that the President of the United States has instructed Gen. Scott to stop his preparations for removing the Indians from among you, by the army, on account of the proposals which he has made to John Ross, that the Indians shall be permitted to remain upon your lands, for two years longer, and remove themselves.

The President, in thus changing the measures which had been previously adopted, and which, it is confidently believed, would have effected the immediate and peacable removal of the Cherokees, against the will of the people, and without consulting the authorities of the State, has forgotten what was due to Georgia, your rights, and peculiar and important interests. Do not be alarmed. The President cannot alter the treaty with the Cherokees, without the consent of the State. He has already been informed, that his proposals to Ross will not be sanctioned, and that the instructions to Gen. Scott are inconsistent with the sovereignty of the State.

Means have been taken to induce the President to withdraw the proposals to Ross, and to give instructions to Gen. Scott, to proceed under his original orders, to remove the Indians, by the troops under his command. If, contrary to our expectations, the President shall persist in his present course, be not alarmed. Your Chief Magistrate, aided by the power of a united people, will not fail to defend your rights.

Whether the conduct of the President shall bring upon us most disastrous consequences, or pass away as harmless as it has been faithless, will depend much upon yourselves. Let me, therefore, entreat you, to make no movement which may bring you in collision with your Indian neighbors. Let no alarm for your rights, or feelings of indignation at the conduct of the President lead you to acts of violence. Wait until the authorities of your State can secure your disregarded interests. Do not, in the spirit of resentment, for the violated pledge of the President, do wrong to an ignorant, dependent and savage people. Treat them with kindness, and you disarm the power of the Government which threatens you.

Be not alarmed lest the federal troops shall trample upon your rights. The commanding general of the Cherokee army is a gallant soldier, whose fame is identified with the honor of his country, and the advancement of the people's prosperity. He will aid your cause, in giving a patriot's advice to the councils of the President, and if he shall be ordered to do you injustice, his arm will be rendered nerveless.

Be not alarmed. You have as true a soldier as ever defended his country, in the command of our own spirited Georgia troops, not one of whom but will stand by you and your country in the time of need. Be but true to yourselves, in being just and humane to your Indian neighbors, and you have nothing to fear. The friends of humanity, who know the true state of the Cherokees—the ruin and degradation which has been brought upon the unmixed Indians by their present situation—do not doubt but that it is their interest to remove to the country provided for them in the West. Do not strengthen the calumnies against your country and its statesmen, by acts of oppression to the Indians.

They are ignorant and revengeful; pity them. Do not make them, in their blindness, responsible for the acts of those who are using them for their ambitious and mercenary causes.

The abandonment of your cause by the President,. to purchase the good opinions of those who are weeping over imaginary Indian wrongs, has made you the objects of attention to the whole country.

Your character, the character of your State, and the united wishes of your friends, urge upon you not to interfere with the Indians, in the spirit of unkindness. Leave their removal from the State to the United States Government, if it will, or to you own Government, if it must.

(Signed)   GEORGE R. GILMER.

A requisition for four thousand men was made by the Secretary of War, upon the Governors of Georgia, Tennessee, Alabama, and North Carolina. Twenty companies were called for from Georgia. No call was made upon me for an officer of the proper grade to command them—Mr. Van Buren intending that they should be under one of his own selection. Indeed, that this was his design, was not denied, when I wrote to General Scott (who was to command the whole), and asserted the right to place the troops of the State under a Georgia general, selected by myself. I gave the command to General Charles Floyd.

Immediately after, I was notified of the demand for troops by the War Department. Orders were sent by express to the militia officers of the counties nearest to the Cherokee country, urging the immediate raising of the required number, and that they should march without delay to New Echota—the appointed place of rendezvous—to be organized into appropriate corps. The spirit of the orders, and the directions given to the persons who carried them, induced the readiest compliance on the part of the officers to whom they were directed. The twenty companies were all at New Echota before the day arrived when the Cherokees were, according to the treaty, to leave Georgia, and before a beginning had been made in the other States to comply with the requisition. General Floyd showed his fitness for command by his prompt obedience. He was at the place of rendezvous at the appointed time, though the distance was so great, and the time so short, that it seemed impossible. A very trivial incident had the most fortunate influence in effecting the desired result. Col. Augustus Kennan, of Milledgeville, whose daring, fearless temper made him ever ready for any active enterprise, was favorably known to General Scott. Colonel Kennan applied to me for a military aidship, to assist him in an application, which he wished to make to General Scott, for the same rank in his military family. His request was complied with. He joined General Scott by the time the troops were organized; and by the manner in which he urged the matter upon General Scott, contributed essentially in inducing that officer to disregard the unofficial information which he had received, that Mr. Van Buren was scheming to delay the removal of the Cherokees.

General Floyd, his officers and men, collected the Indians together at once from their towns, and placed them in the fortified positions, which had been previously provided for the emergency by Colonel Lindsay, at my request. The Indians went into the forts without resistance, from the assurance given them by their chiefs at Washington City, that the treaty which required them to leave the country would be set aside, or so modified that they would be at liberty to continue where they were.

As soon as the Indians were under the control of the troops, Colonel Kennan came express to Milledgeville, to let me know it. I communicated the information to the President by express. The news reached Washington City whilst Congress was discussing the proposals of the Cherokee Chiefs, and the President and the Chiefs were negotiating the terms of a new treaty. Mr. Van Buren's schemes were blown sky-high. Nothing could be said about further delay. The dreaded difficulty in controlling the Cherokees had been met and overcome. All concurred at once in the propriety of carrying on what had been begun so successfully. I had the very great pleasure of saying to the Legislature when assembled:—

Fellow-citizens of the Senate and House of Representatives,
I congratulate you upon the successful removal of the Cherokees from the State;—that you will no longer be harassed in your legislative proceedings, by the perplexing relations which have hitherto existed between them, the United States, and Georgia;—that our citizens are at last in the quiet possesson of all ther lands, and the State the undisputed sovereign over all her territory.

I felt that it was something to have overcome, by directness of purpose, and the means at my command, the power and subtility of Mr. Van Buren and John Ross, and to have secured to the State and the people the great good which has followed what was done.

No one out of Georgia seemed to know how much the people had suffered from the plunderings and barbarities of the Indians; that the State had been obliged to sell to the United States more than half of its territory, to procure the extinguishment of the Indian title to the remainder; that the United States had made no effort to execute that contract, except at the earnest entreaties of the Representatives of Georgia; that the first movement of Cherokees to the west of the Mississippi had been of their own accord; that, when General Jackson and General Meriwether, a Georgian and Tennessean, made a treaty with the Cherokees, by which the whole tribe would have removed beyond the Mississippi, the Secretary of War had altered its terms by another, by which he attempted to fix the Indians upon the territory of Georgia, by ceding to the chiefs the fee-simple title to the soil.

Nobody now doubts that the immediate contact and constant intercourse with the vicious white population among them, and around them, made it absolutely necessary, for the preservation of all the unmixed Indians, that their location should be changed, and that their removal from Georgia to the west of the Mississippi has been for their advantage.

The Cherokee country, instead of being wandered over by listless, objectless, ignorant savages, whose only satisfying employments were destroying the beasts of the forest and their fellow-men, and being the receptacle of the lawless from every where, is now cultivated by a population rapidly advancing in all the arts of civilized life. Fine houses, valuable farms, beautiful meadows, schools, colleges, churches, and railroads have taken the places of wigwams and scalp-poles. And yet every public man who was employed in bringing about this admirable change for-the better, was for a time a target for shooting defamation at, by every intermeddling politician, from the lowest scribbler, to the Supreme Court of the United States.

Those who are disposed to yield to authority and the opinions of the wise and experienced, may be induced to acknowledge the completeness of this justification of Georgia and its Governor for removing the Cherokees from the State, which I have presented to them, by what Gen. Jackson and President Adams have said upon the subject.

Mr. Adams says:

"We have been far more successful in the acquisition of their lands than imparting to them the principles, or inspiring them with the spirit of civilization. But in appropriating to ourselves their hunting grounds, we have brought upon ourselves the obligation of providing them with subsistence, and when we have had the rare good fortune of teaching them the arts of civilization and the doctrines of Christianity, we have unexpectedly found them forming, in the midst of ourselves, communities claiming to be independent of ours, and rivals of sovereignty within the territories of the members of our Union. This state of things requires that a remedy should be provided. A remedy which, while it shall do justice to those unfortunate children of nature, may secure to the members of our confederation their rights of sovereignty and soil. As the outline of a project to that effect, the views presented in the Report of the Secretary of War are recommended to the consideration of Congress.'

Extract from the project recommended by Mr. Adams in his message:—

Nothing can be more clear to one who has marked the progress of population and improvement, and is conversant with the principles of human action, than that these Indians will not be permitted to hold the reservations on which they live within the States, by their present tenure, for any considerable period. If, indeed, they were not disturbed in their possessions by us, it would be impossible for them long to subsist, as they have heretofore done, by the chase, as their game is already so much diminished, as to render it frequently necessary to furnish them with provisions, in order to save them from starvation. In their present destitute and deplorable condition, and which is constantly growing more helpless, it would seem to be not only the right, but the duty of the government to take them under its paternal care; and to exercise over their persons and property, the salutary rights and duties of guardianship.

General Jackson says:—

Towards this race of people, I entertain the kindest feelings; and am not insensible that the views which I have taken of their true interests are less favorable to them, than those which oppose their emigration to the West. Years since, I stated to them my belief, that if the States chose to extend their laws over them, it would not be in the power of the Federal Government to prevent it. My opinion remains the same; and I can see no alternative for them, but that of their removal to the West, or a quiet submission to the State laws. If they prefer to remove, the United States agrees to defray their expenses, to supply them the means of transportation, and a year's support after they reach their new homes—a provision too liberal and kind to deserve the stamp of injustice. Either course promises them peace and happiness, whilst an obstinate perseverance in the effort to maintain their possessions independent of the State authority, cannot fail to render their condition still more helpless and miserable. Such an effort ought, therefore, to be discountenanced by all who sincerely sympathize in the fortunes of this peculiar people, and especially by the political bodies of the Union, as calculated to disturb the harmony of the two Governments, and to endanger the safety of the many blessings which they enable us to enjoy.

As connected with the subject of this inquiry, I beg leave to refer to the accompanying letter from the Secretary of War, inclosing the order which proceeded from that Department, and a letter from the Governor of Georgia.   ANDREW JACKSON.

The Cherokees were but just removed from Georgia, when the people of the south-eastern frontier of the State were put into the greatest alarm by the presence of hostile Indians. Some of the Creeks had united with their kinsfolk in Florida, when the mass of the tribe removed to the west of the Mississippi in 1836. A band of warriors made a lodgment in the Okefinokee swamp, with the intention it was supposed of harassing the inhabitants of the neighborhood, by forays from that fastness, then supposed to be inaccessible to our troops.

The militia companies called into the public service, for the defence of the people, when marching in search of the enemy, came upon a few Indians around their camp-fire, and seeing them start up and cry woo-ah, took to their heels, and increased the terror of those whom they were sent to protect.

Gen. Taylor, since then President of the United States, and Gen. Floyd, then lately returned from his successful removal of the Cherokees, marched to the defence of the alarmed inhabitants. They found many difficulties in the way of operating against the Indians successfully.

I wrote to Gen. Taylor,—"The distance of the Okefinokee swamp from the seat of Government,—the difficulty of obtaining correct information as to the number of Indians,—the extent of the danger to be apprehended from them,—the want of knowledge of the force which may be necessary, and how to employ it, to protect the people, &c., &c., have occasioned much embarrassment to this Department," and requested him to direct what his experience might find to be necessary.

Gen. Floyd passed through the Okefinokee swamp with a detachment from his command. He found about the centre of the Island, so long celebrated among the Indians for its romantic scenery, and the beauty of its inhabitants, Indian huts, but the occupants, the beautiful beings of romance, were gone.

The following correspondence will show the success which attended the means used for driving away hostile Indians from the southern frontiers of the State.

HEAD-QUARTERS, ARMY OF THE SOUTH.
Camp Gilmer, Suwanee, River.
(Near the Mouth of the Suwanouchee, Ware County, Georgia.)
April 13, 1838.

To his Excellency the Governor of Georgia:

Sir,—I have received from the Secretary of War, under date of 16th of June, a copy of a letter, inclosing documents transmitted by your Excellency to that Department, concerning disturbances around the Okefinokee swamp.

In relation thereto, I have the honor to inform you that I reached this on the 9th inst., and am now here with two companies of infantry and one of dragoons, the latter of which, with one of the infantry companies, will continue to occupy this position. One company of infantry will be located at some suitable point intermediate between this and Trader's Hill, on the St. Mary's River. A company of dragoons is now on the march for the vicinity of Waresborough, where it will take a position to protect that neighborhood. A company of militia is also employed to act as guides and spies for the troops in this quarter.

I flatter myself that this force will be sufficient for the defence of the region around the swamp, by confining the Indians to it, or cutting them up, should they attempt to leave it, as there will be reconnoitering and scouting parties constantly in motion. But should it prove otherwise, Maj. Dearborn, who locates the company of dragoons near Waresborough, is empowered to muster into the service such an additional militia force as may at any time be required.

From the best information I can obtain, I am induced to believe that there are not exceeding fifty warriors in the Okefinokee, which are believed to be refugee Creeks, of the tribes, migrated from Georgia and Alabama.

Col. Twiggs, who was commanding at Black Creek, and on this side of the peninsula, previous to my crossing from Tampa Bay, ordered a company of dragoons, a short time since, to the swamp, in the vicinity of this place, but as neither forage nor provisions could be obtained there, it was compelled to fall back.

An officer of the Quartermaster's Department is now ordered to Trader's Hill, to make such arrangements as will insure supplies to the posts now or about to be established, as well as to any other troops that may be called into the service.

The dispositions above having been completed, I shall return through East Florida to Tampa Bay, where I shall be happy to receive any communications you may think proper to address to me.

With the highest respect, I am
Your Excellency's most obedient servant,
Z. TAYLOR,
Bt. Br. Gen. U. S. Army commanding.
To his Excellency Geo. R. Gilmer,
Governor of Georgia.

Executive Department, Ga.
Milledgeville, 7th August, 1838.

To Major E. Hopkins:

Sir,—I have received your letter of the 1st inst., giving an account of the great alarm of the people of Camden, on account of the murders lately committed by the Indians in Ware County, and asking my advice what you are to do.

It is a great misfortune to the people to be exposed to the attacks of these merciless savages. It is difficult to perceive, however, in what manner this Government can secure each family from the possibility of injury. Those who were murdered in Ware County, were under the almost immediate protection of a company of the United States troops. The arrangements made for the protection of the people of Ware and Camden, are from Gen. Taylor, a most excellent officer, and upon his own personal examination of the country, and approved by Gen. Clinch, both of whom from their military experience and knowledge cf the country and the Indians, understand this subject better than myself. If the troops now in service are not sufficient, the United States officer in command in Ware and Camden, is authorized to receive any additional numbers which he may think necessary.

I know of no better arrangement which can be made than this for the protection of the people. I have already sent you two copies of Gen. Taylor's letter. I now forward to you a copy of Major Dearborn's. Very respectfully, yours, &c.,

GEORGE R. GILMER.

Extract of a letter from Gov. Gilmer to Gen. Taylor, dated August 7th, 1838.

I send you the copies of two letters from Maj. Hopkins, commanding officer of the militia of Camden County, and the copy of a letter from Col. Hilliard, of Ware County. You will perceive that both of these officers are of the opinion that you will take into the service of the United States such an additional force of the militia from Ware and Camden, as may give security to the inhabitants.

Executive Department, Milledgeville, 11th August, 1838.
To the Hon. Joel R. Poinsett, Secretary of War:

Sir,—I inclose to you for the information of the President, a communication just received from a committee appointed by a public meeting of the citizens of the counties of Camden, Wayne, and Glynn, to address this Department upon the subject of the incursions of the Indians into this State.

This communication is from gentlemen of high respectability. The great alarm and distress which exist among the inhabitants of all the counties near the Okefinokee swamp, and the general abandonment of their homes and property, on account of the inefficiency of the troops, or their want of sufficient force to restrain the murderous and destructive inroads of the Indians, would seem to demand some further interposition on the part of the Government for their relief.

I was very well satisfied with arrangements made by Gen. Taylor for the protection of that part of the country, from my confidence in him as an officer, his knowledge of the country and the Indians, and because I supposed that it would be dangerous to the health of the troops, if, previous to cold weather, a sufficient force should be collected and remain long enough in service to drive the Indians from the Okefinokee swamp. It appears, however, that the country exposed to the attacks of the Indians is too extensive to be defended by the companies now in service, and that quiet and security can only be afforded to the people by subduing the enemy.

I would therefore, respectfully suggest to the President, that an attempt be made at once to effect that object. I suppose that a competent number of mounted volunteer companies could be assembled immediately from the counties around the swamp, if such a requisition were made upon me as to authorize my offering the command to Gen. Charles Floyd. The want of funds, and a regular organized Quartermaster's Department, form an almost insuperable obstacle to the successful operation of a large body of troops, on the part of the State. I, therefore, propose that the Government will authorize this Department to call out two regiments of militia, to act against the Indians, that they be mustered ino the service of the United States, and the necessary provisions and supplies be provided for them as soon as they are organized.

This proposition is only made upon the supposition that Gen. Taylor may not be able to undertake this service. If he can, and the Government will order him upon it, I am well satisfied that it will be executed faithfully.

The suffering of the people from alarm, and the abandonment of their property, appears to be so great, that whatever is to be done for their relief, should be done quickly.

Very respectfully, yours, &c.
GEORGE R. GILMER.

Head-Quarters, Okefinokee District,
Camp Hope, Jan. 4th, 1839.

Sir,—Since my last communication to your Excellency, of December 7th, every exertion has been made to bring the enemy to battle, without success. They have fled before my detachments, leaving their clothing, cooking utensils, &c., without firing a gun; and have either gone to Florida, or are so securely hid, that they have escaped the most active movements from various points, both inside and outside the swamp.

I cannot yet report positively to your Excellency, that no Indians remain on the soil of Georgia, although it is my belief, (from the late discovery of trails leading to Florida near the Suwannee), and other circumstances, that they have gone there.

I send herewith a map of the Okefinokee, roughly drawn on the field by Lieut. McLane, topographical engineer of the United States Army. The mean diameter of the swamp is between 35 and 40 miles.

I am, with high respect,
Your Excellency's obedient servant,
CHARLES FLOYD,
Bri. Gen. Commanding (as Col.) Okefinokee Dist.
His Excellency, Geo. R. Gilmer.
Governor of Georgia.

All in Georgia were Jackson men whilst Gen. Jackson was in office, the Clark party from choice, the Crawford party from necessity, so that the old factions began to lose their lines of demarcation, and new parties to be formed upon the general principles which divided the people of the United States.

In May, 1838, a call was made by some of the leaders of the superadhesive Jackson men, for the assembling of a Convention to select candidates for the high offices of the State, and for putting forth to the public their notions upon government. The call met with a ready response.

On the morning of the day when the Convention was to meet, I told my wife as I went to the Executive office, that I would invite some of the members to dinner. Not one of them, however, called at the Executive office, to offer the usual civilities to the Governor on such occasions, though their assembling place was in the State House.

My messenger was a raw youth, the son of a poor widow. His elevation to office so magnified the importance of the incumbent in his own eyes, that he considered himself but little below the Governor in official dignity. After the Convention met, and not a member had made his bow, I wrote the following words upon a slip of paper:—"None of the members of the Convention will be invited to dinner today," gave it to the messenger, and directed him to carry it up to the house, the Governor's residence being on the top of the hill in Milledgeville. Mr. Lewis, one of my secretaries, was standing near the entrance into the Representative Hall, where the Convention was in session, in conversation with some one, when he observed the messenger approach. His attention was attracted particularly to him by noticing his unusually eager, intent looks. He asked him what he was going to do. The messenger answered that he was directed by the Governor to carry a communication up to the House. Lewis asked him what it was. He showed the note which I had sent to my wife, containing the words, "None of the members of the Convention will be invited to dinner to-day," which he was preparing to address to the President, as he had seen the secretaries do when they delivered messages to the Senate and House of Representatives. The President of the Convention was Mr. Spalding, a very proud, aristocratic Scotch gentleman of the McIntosh clan, who had travelled over Europe, attended the British Parliament, heard Erskine, Fox and Pitt speak, was as consequential as a lord, and as irascible as a Highlander. It is difficult to conceive what would have been the effect of the address of my official, after the formal announcement of the Secretary of the Convention to the body,—"A message from the Governor,"—the words, "None of the members of the Convention will be invited to dinner to-day."

When Lewis read the note, and comprehended what the messenger was about to do, he was so overcome by convulsions of laughter, that the message was near being delivered before he could sufficiently recover himself to explain to him that the note was for my wife, and must be carried up to the Governor's house.

The people of every free, wealthy, prosperous community are subject to occasional fits of excess, in their haste to grow rich. The Georgians have had their gold mania, land mania, cotton mania, and bankmania.

In 1838, the active speculating class became eager to acquire wealth rapidly, by issuing notes to pass for money. They proposed to do this upon the pledge of their land and negroes, for the repayment of the notes which they might put into circulation. They beset the Legislature, to give the force of law to their schemes. Whilst the bill for the purpose was on its passage, apprehensions were so generally felt and expressed, that I would veto the bill if it passed, that considerable agitation was excited in the country on that account. The advocates of the measure were induced thereby to use so many precautions to secure the payment of the notes which might be put into circulation by the banks which might be formed in pursuance of the law, that I signed the bill, when it passed, without hesitation.

The intentness of the many, to pocket what they considered money, to the amount of the value of their land and negroes, without parting with their property, thereby doubling their estates, would most probably have produced the ruinous effects of excessive bank issues, but for the difficulties thus thrown in the way. One or two banks went into operation, and closed their business to the great discomfiture of all concerned.

The constant and excessive labor which I had to perform, and the responsibility and anxious care which attended my exertions to remove the Cherokees from the State without bloodshed; the sympathy which I felt for the population of the South-Eastern Counties, when exposed to the massacreing attacks of the Creeks; and the earnest attention which I gave to the assembling and organizing of troops for their defence, added to the necessary performance of the ordinary duties of the Executive office, proved too burdensome for my feeble system. My health failed. I became so dangerously ill in the spring of 1839, that my family, physicians and friends, despaired of my recovery. Dr. White and Dr. Fort found it necessary to be with me every day, for months, and three times a day for many weeks. I received from them not only the benefit of their great professional skill but the kind treatment of the best of friends. They watched with great intentness the effect of their medicines, and every change of the disease, so as to avail themselves of each incident in their endeavors to effect my cure. There were many starts of the disease so immediately tending to death, that I am convinced that my life could not have been saved, but by their presence and skill. Whatever could be done for my relief and cure was done by them. I never see them, nor think of them, but with the strongest feelings of gratitude for their services, and the kind manner in which they were rendered. Mrs. White and Mrs. Fort were with my wife whenever they could be of any service to her.

Two of my friends, Col. Lumpkin and Mr. Dawson, came to me when I was thought to be in the last extremity. I remember well their distress when they parted from me, with the evident belief, that when we met next, it would not be in this life.

My wife was ever at my side through all the danger of the disease, administering all the medicines, and doing with her own hands whatever could be done for my relief. Her natural feebleness seemed to become enduring strength. Her eyes were never off me, except to take the snatches of sleep necessary for sustaining her own life. Her hands were constantly employed in smoothing my pillow, applying cold cloths to my hot head, directing my attention from the pain by rubbing the diseased parts, or soothing away irritation by some gentle emollient. Her aptitude for understanding diseases and their proper cure, derived from her sympathy with the sick, her keen observation of each minute particular of cases and their successful remedies, enabled her to aid the physicians in all that they did for me. To her unwearied, never ceasing watchfulness, skilful nursing, affectionate tenderness, and loving kindness, I owe my life.

Whilst I was in the greatest peril she sent for Dr. Henry Branham. We had some peculiar claims upon his friendship, as he had upon ours. He had attended me once before, when I was expected to die, and had been singularly successful in the application of remedies. He came. But believing that no treatment could prevent the disease proving fatal, and finding that he would only add to the distress of my wife from his inability to bear with fortitude the sight of my dying, he returned home and sent to us my brother-in-law Dr. Grattan, who then resided in Madison. It was fortunate that he did so. Dr. Grattan found my wife exhausted, and almost hopeless. Her confidence in his affectionate and watchful care, induced her to take some rest, without which she would have been unable to continue her nursing, so indispensably necessary to my recovery. Indeed, it was wonderful how my feeble body endured for so long time constant scorching fever. I owed my cure, under Providence, to nursing which had never been equalled, and professional skill and attention which had never been surpassed. Months went by in the struggle between life and death, until the energy which belonged so surprisingly to my frail system, carried me beyond the apprehended danger.

During my sickness, the business of the Executive office so accumulated, that the first day after my physicians permitted me to think of what had to be done, I signed sixty grants, and examined the record of the trial of a criminal condemned to be hung, and granted his reprieve.

The necessity for laboring rendered it impossible for me to gain strength. When the time at last arrived for quitting office, and the great seal of the State was transferred to my successor, I felt that a weight beyond endurance was taken off me. I could not be kept in Milledgeville. I left it a few hours after, and set off for my home, with the eagerness of an untamed bird escaping from its cage.

When I went into the Executive office preparatory to my inauguration in 1829, I found Mr. Forsyth surrounded by his political friends. He received me with as much self-possession and courtesy, as if he had aided my election, instead of using against me, as he had done, all the means which his supercilious temper and indolent habits permitted. I was very much embarrassed by the strange situation and company in which I found myself, and my entire ignorance of the forms to be observed.

When Mr. Lumpkin, my successful opponent in 1831, came into the Executive office on the morning when he was to be inaugurated, where I was still in possession officially, I forgot the mortifying circumstances of my own situation, upon witnessing his own confusion. Previous to his becoming a candidate, he assured me that he approved my recommendations to the Legislature, that the gold mines should be reserved for the use of the State, and the Indians protected against injustice; telling me he would not avail himself of the unpopularity which had followed what I had done to become Governor, though he had been greatly urged to do so. But the temptation to office increased with the increasing probabilities of success, until the assurance which had been given to me unnecessarily, was necessarily forgotten.

When I was elected over Governor Schley in 1837, the excitement which usually attends success was unfelt. I had the disposition to relieve as far as I could the wounded feelings of my defeated opponent. But he belonged too decidedly to the stiff-necked class to be pacified by courtesy.

I had not been a candidate for re-election in 1838, when I was succeeded in office by Judge McDonald. Though of opposite parties, we had always been civil to each other. He was too much embarrassed, to indulge in any exhibition of party triumph; and I was so feeble and emaciated by disease, as to be looked upon with kindness by every one who saw me deliver up the insignia of office.

Before I arrived at my home, a report reached me that my friends in Lexington being dissatisfied with the shapeless appearance of my old house, had purchased a residence for me, more suitable to an ex-Governor. The report was not exactly true. One or two of them believing that I would like a house and lot which was offered for sale at the time, better than my own, made a conditional bargain for it, which I complied with upon reaching Lexington.

I left the place where I had passed many years as happily as belongs to our condition in this world, for another dwelling nearer a perfect paralellogram, and covered with boards fresher painted than the old one. It was a sore trial to leave the trees which I had planted, the garden which I had cultivated, and the office where I had attended to professional business. My wife liked the new fixations. But when she found the change distressed me, and that the attachment which I had for the old house was derived from the pleasure we had enjoyed there together, she proposed that we should stay where we were. We came to the conclusion however, after talking over the matter, that we ought not to let others know that circumstances could make children of us. So we thanked our friends with a satisfied air for their consideration about our comfort, moved every thing away from the old to the new house, and were soon as happy in it as we had ever been elsewhere. Indeed, the change was greatly for the better, as my wife's taste had perceived at first. We set to work industriously, to make every thing accord with my wife's fancy. We have found an ample field for labor; I in building barns, clearing and fencing land, making meadows, planting fruit trees, and adding to the house; my wife, in fitting up a conservatory with rare and beautiful flowers, ornamenting the garden, walks, and grounds, selecting and arranging furniture, and providing every thing else necessary for pleasure and comfort.

I had endeavored, years before, to purchase from the then owner of the new place, a very romantic spot, which had been a favorite haunt of mine when young. Now that it belonged to me, I endeavored to make it inviting to others. Woods cover the side of two precipitious hills, which are separated by a clear rapidly running stream. Masses of granite rocks, which have been divided by some great convulsion, are scattered about, the parts usually lying so near, and being so shaped for fitting into each other, that the most casual observer discovers that they were at one time united. There is a large bowlder, twenty or thirty feet long, and twelve or fifteen thick, which rests upon several other granite rocks at the height of about ten feet. Its form, as it lies out to the sight, shows by the rounding of its exterior, that it has been fashioned into its present shape, by being rolled over and over among other rocks by some vast power. The rocks on which it rests evince in the most obvious way the truth of what geologists say of the antiquity of the world. Passing by this bowlder, a shower of rain compelled me to take shelter under its projecting end. My attention was drawn to the pouring of the water from its sides upon the rock which supported it. I saw that the surface of the lower rock was worn into holes along its whole face, large at the exterior and less and less as the rocks approach nearer and nearer to each other. A little below, on the descent of the hill from the bowlder, is a large mass of granite rocks, one side of which forms a high precipice. Two trees have grown up from below, since my first knowledge of the place. Their bodies have continued to press upon the edge of the projecting mass, until enlargementes have been formed which have taken hold of the rocks, so that the trees are now pillars, upholding what seems ready to fall and crush persons standing beneath.

On the top of the mass of rocks are two other trees, showing by their decayed tops that the supply of matter for their growth cannot be increased. Near by their roots, is a rock which weighs ten or fifteen tons, which rests upon two small points at its transverse ends so equally, that it is easily moved. A level space of several feet extends from this movable rock to the precipice. The young people of the village assemble here to try the state of their hearts, by trying to set the rock in motion. As this is easily done, every one over fifteen is found to be in love. Along the side of the rocks are fissures in which grape-vines and honeysuckles grow. From the top is a near view of a beautiful meadow, through which meanders a creek in circuits so graceful, as to appear the work of design. Beyond rises a high hill, the side of which is covered with a forest of unsurpassed beauty. Through its trees may be seen many large granite rocks. A schoolmistress, just arrived South. accompanied a party on a visit to the Lover's Leap. She saw, whilst she stood by the movable rock an opening under one of these granite rocks, and asked for a description of the place. One of the company who knew it well, answered, to the young lady's terror, that it was a cavern where some wild men had concealed themselves to escape the observation of the world.

Soon after our return from Milledgeville, I laid out a walk from the house to the Lover's Leap, and ornamented it with a great number and variety of flowers, fruit trees and grape-vines. The flowers found the soil ungenial for their growth, and have perished. The fruit trees and grape-vines now shade the walk, and supply to visitors at the proper season, an abundance of delicious fruit.

I have always been a lover of little girls, and young ladies. I invited them all to visit the Lover's Leap along this walk, to take with them their beaux, and to eat of the fruit without restraint. My plan to please has had its embarrassments. When it was discovered that the walk to the Lovers Leap was free to some, others would go; so that my friends often found fruit scarce. I have had to confess myself mistaken. To correct the error, I have given notice that my fruit is my own, and must not be taken without my permission.

In 1840 I was a candidate for elector of President and Vice-President of the United States. My opposition to Mr. Van Buren had become very determined, as the developments of his conduct and character made it more and more evident that his rare adroitness and great tact for managing party materials disqualified him for using power for noble purposes. I had been an elector in 1836 and voted for Judge White. The same reasons which induced me then to oppose Mr. Van Buren continued to operate with additional force in 1840. I again disregarded party ties from the strong conviction that Mr. Van Buren and those associated with him in office were destroying confidence in the Democracy by the manner in which they conducted themselves in office. A democrat myself, I considered it better for the country to have honest men to administer the Government without clearly defined political principles, than those who professed well, but acted badly. I was elected, made President of the Electoral College, and proclaimed the result of the election, that all the votes of Georgia were given for William Henry Harrison to be President and John Tyler to be Vice-President.

Although I made several public speeches during the canvass for General Harrison, and attended in the usual way to my private business, I continued for several years to suffer from the effects of the disease which prostrated me so long immediately before I left Milledgeville. I had almost at all times a slight fever, and was in consequence so excitable as to be constantly carried away with the hurry of my thoughts, when speaking or conversing upon political or other subjects of interest. Not agreeing in the party course pursued by many of my intimate friends, I often belabored them for what they were doing in the most impassiond way. They suffered, without anger or retort, my apparently rude treatment, in a manner which, though it only irritated me then, I remember very gratefully now. The conduct of Colonel Hardeman, Mr. Dawson, Mr. Hall and Mr. Stevens, I especially treasure up in memory. My wife's hand was often placed upon me in the gentlest way, to remind me how loud and rudely I was talking. Occasionally the top of my head became blood-red, and at the highest fever heat. My health grew worse, until I was confined to bed. For many months my wife watched over me with unceasing care, applying day and night, without ever leaving me, the remedies prescribed for my relief. At my lowest state, when life hung upon the slenderest thread, she was ever at my side, watching every indication for hope. Once, late at night, she noticed the usual symptoms which immediately precede death. Brandy was poured down my throat in a moment, in larger quantities than I had ever drank in my strongest days, and until the weakening, fluttering pulsation acquired strength to overcome the obstruction which was stopping its movement. Perpetual watching and anxiety reduced her to the feeblest condition. Her own life could not have lasted much longer with such pressure upon it. Her sister, Mrs. Harris, was informed of our dangerous state. She received the letter as she was going from her home to church. She and Dr. Harris returned to their home in the greatest haste, threw a few clothes into a trunk, set off for Richmond, got on the railroad, and were with us in the shortest possible time. My wife, confiding in her sister's love and care, as she would have confided in nobody else, slept for the first time for a long while a sleep of restoration. My wife, aided by Dr. Harris and my sister Lucy, rubbed my hands and feet, soothed every irritation, administered medicines, applied palliatives, until some signs of recovery began to appear. My negroes waited upon me as few persons have been waited on by their nearest kindred.

Indispensable business obliged Dr. Harris to return home; I could not part with his wife. I felt that my wife's life might depend upon her sister's staying. The doctor consented that she should remain with us for a while longer, if means could be provided for her safe return to Virginia. My wife sent for my neighbor, Lewis J. Deupree, and asked him if he would take charge of Mrs. Harris as far as Richmond, as he went to New York. He answered, "My dear madam, it is immaterial whether I go to New York or not. I will go home with your sister whenever she desires to return, if she will remain with you." I recovered, with an abiding spirit of thankfulness for my preservation; increased love, if possible, for my wife; the warmest, most grateful affection for our sister and her husband; and enhanced regard for my friends, neighbors and negroes.

In the beginning of January of the year of the sickness which

I have been describing, I was seated one morning before a table, with my back to the windows of my dressing-room shaving, when I heard a noise, and turning, saw a mocking-bird, apparently endeavoring to get in. After watching its movements for some time, I finished what I was about. The bird still continued to fly against the window. Supposing that it might be tame, and had lost its way home, I raised the sash, so that it might enter; but it would not. I imagined that it might be hungry, as the cold had been very severe. I put bread crumbs on the sill and other places near by. The bird took no notice of the bread, in its eager flying against the window. Its perch was on a tall largestreamia bush, which grew near, to which it would return after exhausting its strength by flapping its wings against the glass. It would then droop its feathers, look wearied and mournful, sit for a few moments, perfectly still, and again fly against the glass. The alternate flying against the glass, and sitting motionless on the largestreamia bush, continued for several hours. The next morning the mocking-bird was again on the largestreamia bush, and flying against the glass of the window. Each morning, for several months, it renewed the work of the day before. My health continued declining from about the time of the appearance of the mocking-bird at the window, until I was confined to bed. Each succeeding day for months increased the probability that I would never quit it, but to be carried to the grave. Whilst thus confined and sick, I often noticed the startling effect upon visitors at my bedside, from the noise made by the flapping of the wings of the mocking-bird against the window of my room, saying, as they interpreted the sign more forcibly than words could have done, "Hear the warning of approaching death!"

The mocking-bird was the female of a pair which nested and raised their young in a rose-bush near the house, the male of which had been caught by a cat. The window against which the female continued to fly so long, was shaded by a blind of slats on the inside, and then let down half-way, so that when the bird was perched on the largestreamia bush, it saw its reflected image, moving when it moved, and meeting it on the glass when it flew against it. This reflected image the faithful female bird took for its lost mate.

When my grandfather Lewis was dying, a white bird was observed upon the house-top. It was, according to Irish belief, the family Benshee, who had crossed the ocean to be present at the death of the head of the Lewises, and attend his spirit to the land of his ancestors, before it passed away forever.

My grandfather lived on the Shenandoah River—a favorite resort of the white heron—one of whom, in going up and down, had passed by the house, to avoid going round a great bend, and stopped on the house-top to take its direction. The vivid imagination of any unaccountable incident, genii, fairies, hobgoblins, and spirits suited to the occasion. The habit of minute and accurate observation, which characterizes the people of this country, is teaching the people of the Old World among us, that these creations of superstition are not fitting existences for the New World.

Negro slavery has been, since the formation of the Federal Government, a subject of controversy between the North and the South. Public attention has been directed to it, for some years past, with increased excitement, by its forced connection with party politics. Petitions to Congress, the Wilmot proviso, the law for the arrest of fugitive slaves, the admission of California into the Union, the formation of new territories, the proceedings of the State Legislature, and Conventions of the people in reference thereto, and the debates in Congress, have created so much agitation throughout the entire country, as to cause many to fear for the integrity of the Union.

In consequence of resolutions passed by the Legislature of Georgia, in 1849, and the subsequent proclamation of the Governor, a Convention of the people of the State met in Milledgeville, in November, 1850. It passed various resolutions, and adjourned. Before their separation, a portion of the members met, and agreed to convert the Convention, to save the Union, into a meeting to form a political party. The following extracts from a letter written to a friend, and from a speech made in the Convention, are given here because of the great and continuing importance of the subject discussed:—

        Lexington, January 8th, 1851.
Dear Sir,—The pleasure you feel at the result of the action of the

late Convention, is participated in by almost every one. You ask my opinion of what was done. I will give you my experience as my answer.

My wife and myself were in Virginia during August and September. When we returned home, we were attending to flowers, collecting minerals, reading and talking cheek by jowl, scarcely observing that the face of society was ruffled by any unusual excitement. A fire-eating meeting was held one day in our town. I was not invited to it. I nevertheless took my cane and stalked in. I listened to the reading of a most extraordinary report to the meeting, and speech in support of it. Calls were made for speakers. Some one in the crowd called for me. I stepped forward—attacked the report and resolutions so furiously, that, like the raw militiaman, who, striking with might and main hither and yon, succeeded in driving the whole host before him. There was a unanimous vote against the report, and all the resolutions except one, and that was altered so as to make it inoffensive. The election for members of the Convention came on. I was elected by nearly every vote. I went to Milledgeville, shook hands heartily with my old friends, kissed the younger ones, and was very much pleased to be where I had passed a long time very pleasantly. Judge Sayre and Dr. Terrell, old friends, just from Europe, were at Mr. Orme's, our host. They kept us amused and excited, by their accounts of the novelties of Europe. I never saw, except by accident, any of the leaders of the Convention. My enthusiasm was for the preservation of the Union of the States, and not for the union of party aspirants, for party purposes. I soon found myself out of place. I give you an extract from my speech, made in the Convention, which will show you what were my opinions and position.

"The condition upon which the committee would make the continuance of the Union depend, and the causes set forth in its report as sufficient for its disruption, are alarming propositions to those who consider the Union the greatest political blessing which any form of government ever secured to me.

The people have been, and yet are, congratulating themselves upon the removal of some of the dangers which threatened the country, when the Legislature called this Convention. The passage of the compromise bill, the admission of California into the Union, providing territorial governments for Utah and New Mexico, settling the disputed boundary line of Texas, and the passage of the fugitive slave act, though not approved by every one, are such measures as most are disposed, and all ought, to acquiesce in. The cry for disunion and secession which was at one time heard from every part of the Southern country, have been hushed up by the sober second thoughts of the people. Investigation is leading to the conviction, that no people ever prospered before, as the people of the United States, and that no determination can be too strong to preserve unimpaired the institutions which have been so successful in their operations.

Causes for the dissolution of the Union are set forth by the committee, which show that we are either not in earnest in what we say, or that we value but lightly the vast advantages which we enjoy. And yet the agitation at the North on account of slavery at the South, and the excitement occasioned thereby, are fearful indications of dangers impending over us. Cannot this Convention do something which will be better suited to further the purposes of its meeting, than exciting the ill-will of the Northern people by threats, and stirring up strife at the South, by alarming the people for the safety of their negro property? Let us endeavor to convince the Northern people, that their agitation about slavery is doing wrong to their Southern brethren, and cannot possibly do any good to themselves. Let us intimate to them whilst they, a thousand miles off, are prying after motes in our eyes, they may have neglected to examine the beam which is protruding from their own.

Would disrupting the Union relieve the people of the slave-holding States from interference with their slaves by the Northern people? Disruption would but increase the evil. We would then be forced to raise an impassable barrier between us and them.

The dealings of God with the Israelites of old were given to us for our instruction. Let us profit by them. The twelve tribes separated each other. The ten were lost, utterly extinguished from the face of the earth, so that not even a remnant can be found. The other two have been scattered over the whole world, to be a byword and a reproach. We, too, have been the favored people of God; have been preserved, and have prospered beyond any other people. Will the Convention obstruct the glorious onward course of the Union, and weaken its strength, by setting forth light and trivial causes for its dismemberment? The tables of the law written by the finger of God, did not keep the descendants of Jacob together. Will we also disregard the hand which has guided and guarded us as obviously as the cloud by day and the pillar of fire by night? Will we shut our eyes to the lights of experience, and turn into new and untried paths in search of what we already possess? Ought we not rather to hold on to what has been found so good? Now is the time for patriots to come up to the help of their country. The ark of our Covenant is in danger. Let us remember our obligations to protect it. We have all at some time, and as we ought to have done in becoming members of this Convention, taken an oath to support the Constitution which has for sixty years held the States together. Will we observe the solemn requirements of that oath by striving to weaken or destroy the Union, instead of supporting and giving it strength.

The Northern people, by their opposition to negro slavery, and resisting the law for the arrest of fugitive slaves, are distracting the North and annoying the South. Why should they insist upon taking care of the consciences of the people of the South for owning slaves? They have no slaves, and do not understand the relation between master and slave at the South. Let us remind them that negroes were held as property by the laws of each of the Northern States, when their people claimed the distinction of being the purest of the pure. Ought they not, out of respect for their ancestors, to let us enjoy our slave property unmolested? Because the climate is too cold and the population of the Northern States too dense to admit of the profitable employment of negro slaves, they have set theirs free, and left them to support themselves as they can. Does it follow that the South, with its sparse population and sunny climate must follow the example? The settlement of the Southern colonies progressed but slowly, for a long time, because the heat of the climate, the swamps of the coasts, and the rich, alluvial lands on the rivers, proved too unhealthy for laborers from Europe. The commercial people of Old England and New England, in their search after profit, purchased slaves in Africa and transferred them to the Southern colonies. Have the negroes been injured by this change? They were slaves in Africa, and subject there to capricious despotism, which the laws of the Southern States have relieved them from by well-defined enactments.

The strong animal appetites of the negroes so control them that they are incapable of self-government and self-improvement. They were but little superior to the beasts of the forest, when brought to the Southern colonies and States. They are yet so in Africa. Under the control of masters, they have been made the best of laborers. They are now the producers of the great staples of cotton, rice, tobacco, and sugar, which are rendering this country the richest in the world, and creating more efficient means for its advancement in the arts of cultivated life than all other causes together. The transportation of these products gives the principal and surest employment to Northern shipping, as their manufacture does to Northern laborers. Negro slaves thus profitably employed for the benefit of both North and South, and for the advantage of other countries, afford the most indisputable proof of their happy condition, by their unexampled increase. The three millions of slaves now in the Southern States, are better fed, better clothed, less burdened with work and care, and more joyous than the lowest class of the same number of people in any country in the world: better than the same number of the lowest class in England or France, in China or Hindostan: better far than the same number of negroes in Africa; and are more comfortable in every respect than the Indians who once hunted where they now work.

The negroes of the South have, by their transfer from Africa, been enabled to know something about the true end of their being. They have the Gospel preached to them. There is, too, a current of improved, liberated negro people passing back to Africa from the United States, who are doing more to enlighten and Christianize their countrymen, than all which has been done for that purpose, by all the white race together. These evident truths entitle us to ask our Northern brethren, why endanger the Union, and distract the peace of the country on account of negro slavery?

The happy results to the African slaves who have been transferred to this country, and to their descendants, who have been born here, have only been equalled by the improved, prosperous condition of their masters. Our Northern brethren err in their imaginings about the hardships imposed upon the negroes of the South. When infants, they are our fond nurses; in childhood, our playmates; and in after life, our obedient and willing servants. It does not enter into the hearts of our Yankee brethren to conceive of the kindly relations which exist between us and our negroes.

If the Northern people believe it to be wrong for the Southern people to retain their negroes in servitude, why do they not point out some possible way, by which the millions of slaves at the South may enjoy liberty consistently with their own and the well-being of the whites? If liberated and permitted to remain where they are, they know that the social state would become intolerable to both whites and blacks; that destruction to one race or the other would inevitably follow. They owe it to themselves to examine well into their purposes in continuing to disturb the quiet of the whole country about our negroes. Is it that the stirrers up of strife intend only to gratify their selfish ambition, by inducing the firm, strong-willed laborers of the North to imagine themselves in the place of the slaves of the South, and serving masters, so that they may ride them into office? And shall the Union be endangered, the peace of our country disturbed, the confident security with which we have hitherto enjoyed life, liberty, and prosperity, be taken away, to satisfy lustings after power? The Northern people should see to it, that they do not part with their noble birthright, for a mess of pottage. The Southern people should understand the price of liberty and good government too well, to intrust their interests long, to those who would lessen their value by taking away their peaceful enjoyments."

When my health became sufficiently improved to devote some of my time to active pursuits, I commenced raising grass, and hay. Having found a wife among the clover fields of the Valley of Virginia, sweet milk and well-flavored butter were indispensables for her eating enjoyments. The cotton seed, which keeps the cows of the Southern people alive during the winter, gives such a vile taste to the milk and butter, that I was obliged to look out for something better than the market supplied.

The low, damp, marshy bottoms of the small streams and creeks of the Southern country, were considered in past times of little value. They were with difficulty cleared of their heavy timber, and when they were, and cultivated in corn and cotton, the hasty flooding rains of our climate carried off most of the alluvial soil, and soon left them sterile. Nobody would be at the exepnse of twenty and thirty dollars an acre, for draining by ditching, when the fertile lands of Alabama and Mississippi could be had for the fourth of that price.

I cleared the low lands upon a small creek near my house, and sowed it in herds grass and clover, and thus obviated what reduced such lands to poverty in the hands of others. Flooding the land when in grass, made it richer by the deposit of top soil. washed from the bottoms above. I succeeded in creating a beautiful landscape, of what had been previously an eyesore, and making a productive meadow of what had generated nothing but musquetoes and miasma. I provided plenty of nutritious grass in summer and hay in winter, for my cows, so that my wife has better milk and butter than are supplied by the largest cotton plantation, and more uniformly plenty of these good things than most are accustomed to in her native country I have been often amused at the looks of distrust and derision, with which some of my cotton-producing neighbors listen to my directions of how to make grass grow—their most pressing occupation being to kill it. Every one who makes cotton seems to think, that it is better to have white frothy butter, and thin milk, rather than lessen the sum of money from the sale of their crops, by substituting a good deal of grass for a little less cotton.

Until of late years, I never saw a meadow in Georgia. Fodder had been the sole accompaniment of corn in feeding horses on the plantations, though the most unhealthy of all food for them. My horses eat hay. One of them is now twenty-three years old, and looks as if he might do good work for many years more. My barn is large, and three stories high, is usually filled with hay once a year, and has never been empty since it was built. My garden and lots, are made rich through my hay and cattle. My corn, peas, potatoes, and vegetables are so succulent, that it does one good to eat them. I have cabbage-heads all the year, in consequence of manuring well where each plant is grown, and so can eat them in the way which never gives the colic. The long collards are given to the cows. The fame of my hay-making has extended to the North, where it has been published, that I was the model farmer of the South. It seems to be loud-sounding praise, but lessons to nothing when it is known that I am the only farmer there, all others being planters. During the last year, the Agricultural Association of the slaveholding States constituted me a member, and made me its President. The following short address upon a matter of never-failing interest, will, I hope, be considered appropriately inserted here.

ADDRESS
BY GEORGE R. GILMER, OF GA.
President of the Association.

Gentlemen,—The great number of planters, who have assembled together here from the surrounding States, give the most certain assurance of the good which we may expect to follow from what we may do. Improvement in agriculture, which has so lagged behind advancement in other arts, is beginning now to be considered an imperative necessity. Formerly, whatever was done in improving, was effected by the genius and exertion of individuals. Now entire communities are uniting, to give force to the power which impels society forward to better its condition by making the earth bring forth increased quantities of what is necessary for man's well-being. Throughout civilized Europe, the foot of the reading clodhopper is upon the neck of the crowned head; triumph begins to be awarded to him who makes two blades of grass grow where only one grew before, rather than to the skilled in the art of war. In this country the surest passport to honor and to office, is success in adding to the numbers of living, increasing the means for their support, and enlarging the sources of their enjoyment. We are the most obedient of all people to the divine command, "be fruitful, multiply, replenish the earth, and subdue it": and are receiving our appropriate reward, by being the most prosperous. One of the great difficulties which the country is seeking to overcome, through the consultation of this Convention, is how to make the replenishing the earth and subduing it, equal to our success in multiplying the numbers who are to feed upon it. If our agricultural improvements shall not correspond with the increasing demands which increasing numbers are making for increased production, we must soon suffer the sorest evils from our neglect. The world will not be enlarged for our sakes.

The Indians are nearly gone. New lands and new territories will soon cease to draw off our surplus population. We have reached the Pacific Ocean, and can go no further. We have been skimming the top of the soil and living upon its cream until we are beginning to taste the blue bottom. We must not only discover some way of renewing the primitive richness of our exhausted lands, but force them to produce more than they did in their virgin freshness. Our country is the most favored of lands, in its peculiar fitness for the production of cotton, corn, wheat, rice, tobacco and sugar.

Our cotton is the most wonderful talisman of the world. By its power we are transmuting whatever we have into whatever we want. It is adding to the industry, trade and commerce of the world, as nothing else does, or ever did before. It is making its cultivators more independent than princes, and richer than nabobs. Those who take short-sighted views of God's providence and His creatures' good, sometimes urge planters to make less, so as to sell it for higher prices: to fill their pockets by lessening the extent of its usefulness. We should be too sensible of the value of the gift bestowed upon us, thus to abuse it. Cheapness is extending demand and extinguishing rival produce, and will go on increasing these effects until all civilized nations will become united together by such strong ties of interest, that none will be able to war against us, without bringing ruin upon themselves. It is pulling the helmet from the soldier's head, until he may soon find his occupation gone. It is hastening the time when the trumpeter shall proclaim peace on earth and good will to men. The important question now is, how shall we do our duty so as to make the future perform what the present is promising? Let us improve the manner of cultivating the earth, and increase its productive capacity so as to make our homes so profitable and cheering that we cannot but stay at them, and go on improving them.

Gentlemen, we who have been instruments for assembling this Convention, have brought together a great mass of agricultural knowledge, science, and experience. It is for you to make from your materials, a light so bright that every one, however ignorant, may know how to work aright.

One of the most difficult things to do, is to find out what to do, when one is too old and feeble to do any thing well. Law and politics are too exciting: Money-making too engrossing; and keeping up the spirits by pouring spirits down too overpowering, to be suitable employments for advanced life. When I got up from the bed of sickness to which I was confined so long, in 1844, I was unable to do any thing which required much exertion of body or mind. I commenced daily exercise on horseback, or in a carriage. Acting without object, produced ennui and fatigue. After a while, by some accidence or providence, my attention was directed to the minerals and quartz crystallizations which cover the surface of the earth around my residence. The ridings which in the beginning were continued with tiresomeness from the want of some immediate and tangible object in view, improved my health after I had acquired a taste for hunting rocks. Treasuries of matter for thought are often unknown or unobserved, because observation is too listless to look at them. I found abundance of the wonderful, where nothing had been seen before. In addition to the pleasure which I have derived from increasing good health through my daily excursions, I have found many incidental accompaniments, which have added to its benefits. I discovered about a mile from Lexington, in a little cove formed by the surrounding hills through which a stream of water flows, the remains of an altar, where the people who preceded the Indians made sacrifices. I found a great many places where the people have secretly dug into the earth among the crystallized quartz, in search of gold. I have gone on carrying home from each day's excursion a basket full of rocks, until my collection of crystallized quartz about my house and yard has become very large, and my cabinet of minerals very beautiful and valuable. Friends and strangers have continued to add to it curious things, of various sorts, until it is now the means of giving pleasure to the old, and instruction to the young. Among the things which attract attention are some large and highly colored amethysts, whose angles are so perfect, as to show that they are not the work of human hands. Emeralds from Bogota and other precious stones from elsewhere; marbles from Hindostan, Italy and Alabama; gold from California and Upper Georgia; silver from Peru; mercury from Mexico; copper from the bowels of the earth in Mississippi and the shores of the Northern Lakes; spar from England; agate from Germany; a piece of the rock of Gibraltar; coal from Pennsylvania; jasper from Connecticut; porphyry, vinc, mica, asbestus, gypsum, from the Blue Ridge and Alleghany Mountains; lead from Illinois; lava from Etna and Vesuvius; basalt from the Giants' Causeway; lime crystallizations from the caves of Virginia, and ocean deposits of the alluvial region of Middle Georgia; petrifactions of dead animals and trees; two ammonites in the form of snakes, petrified in their coil, from Rockingham, the place which gave me my middle name; matrix of the diamond from Upper Georgia; two chrystals, each of which contains a drop of water inclosed when matter assumed its appropriate shape upon the formation of the planet, Earth; sand from the desert of Sahara; a witch's bill as big as a child's fist; the half hour glass, by which Santa Anna marked the time for shooting American prisoners; a dirk handle of one of the Spaniards who accompanied DeSoto as he passed from the seaboard to the Cherokee gold mines; a chip from the tree under which Gen. Oglethorpe made the first treaty with the Creek Indians; a vase made of the Georgia live oak which formed a part of the timbers of the frigate Constitution; half of the bombshell which fell through the roof upon the floor of the Cathedral Church in Vera Cruz when the city was besieged by the American army, and killed and wounded eighteen or twenty nuns on their knees; the first gold watch owned by a *native* Virginian; a snuff-box made of the wood of the outer coffin which inclosed the body of Gen. Washington when it was deposited in the family vault; Indian pipes, idols, armulets, lances, and arrowheads; coral and shells from the Indian and Atlantic Oceans; a marble image of Rebekah at the well from the London fair, with a great many engravings, some original paintings, and a library of books formed by continual additions from childhood to old age.

THE END.